NEGOTIATED INTERACTION IN
TARGET LANGUAGE CLASSROOM DISCOURSE

Pragmatics & Beyond
New Series

Editor:
Andreas H. Jucker
(Justus Liebig University, Giessen)

Associate Editors:
Jacob L. Mey
(Odense University)

Herman Parret
(Belgian National Science Foundation, Universities of Louvain and Antwerp)

Jef Verschueren
(Belgian National Science Foundation, University of Antwerp)

Editorial Address:
Justus Liebig University Giessen, English Department
Otto-Behaghel-Strasse 10, D-35394 Giessen, Germany
e-mail: andreas.jucker@anglistik.uni-giessen.de

51

Jamila Boulima

Negotiated Interaction in Target Language Classroom Discourse

NEGOTIATED INTERACTION IN TARGET LANGUAGE CLASSROOM DISCOURSE

JAMILA BOULIMA

Ecole Normale Supérieure, Rabat, Morocco

JOHN BENJAMINS PUBLISHING COMPANY
AMSTERDAM/PHILADELPHIA

The paper used in this publication meets the minimum requirements of American National Standard for Information Sciences — Permanence of Paper for Printed Library Materials, ANSI Z39.48-1984.

Library of Congress Cataloging-in-Publication Data

Boulima, Jamila.
    Negotiated interaction in target language classroom discourse / Jamila Boulima.
        p.   cm. -- (Pragmatics & beyond, ISSN 0922-842X ; new ser. 51)
    Includes bibliographical references (p.   ) and index.
    1. Language and languages--Study and teaching. 2. Interaction analysis in education. 3. Scond language acquisition. I. Title. II. Series.
P53.447.B68   1999
418'.007--dc21   99-27156
ISBN 90 272 5064 2 (Eur.) / 1 55619 813 2 (US) (alk. paper)   CIP

John Benjamins Publishing Co. • P.O.Box 75577 • 1070 AN Amsterdam • The Netherlands
John Benjamins North America • P.O.Box 27519 • Philadelphia PA 19118-0519 • USA

For my mother and father
with love

Contents

Acknowledgements

I am greatly indebted to Piet van de Craen for his invaluable support and encouragement since the first day I met him and throughout the years I have been working on this book. His unfailing support and boundless enthusiasm have lent me the energy and instilled a great deal of self confidence to set out and pursue this work through to its conclusion. I also gratefully acknowledge my indebtedness to Sera de Vriendt for his critical acumen in reading through the drafts of several chapters of this book. Thanks to his insightful comments and stimulating discussion, I have been able to improve the quality of the final version of the work. I would like to express my thanks to Hugo Baetens Beardsmore, Marc Spoelders, and Jeff Verschueren for having accepted to read and comment on the present work in its dissertation form. Their valuable feedback and insightful criticism and suggestions have been most helpful.

I would, particularly, like to express my gratitude to Mohammed Dahbi who introduced me to the field of discourse analysis. He ever since has been a source of insights and ideas. It is to him that I owe my passion for empirical research, in general, and for the study of spoken discourse, in particular. I am also grateful to the secondary school teachers whose lessons constitute the data on which this study is based for having accepted to have their lessons observed and recorded for the sake of this research. I must confess that without their and their pupils' cooperation, the study would not have been possible.

I especially thank Alex Housen for having provided me with important material and Gino Verleye for his unflagging willingness to discuss issues related to the statistical analyses undertaken. Last, I would like to express my ample gratefulness to my sister Fatima for the moral support she provided throughout the years I have been working on this book and to Aziz for being Aziz.

Transcription Conventions

The conventions the present study has used in the transcription of classroom talk are presented below:

1) Extracts from the data are transcribed line by line indicating the exchange type in the left margin, followed by the type of move (Initiation (I), Response (R), or Feedback (F)), followed by the number of the turn and then by the speaker, as illustrated in the following example:

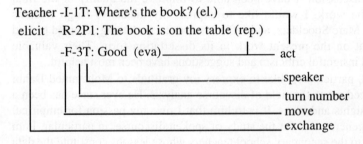

As illustrated in the above example, the name of the act (i.e., the function of the utterance) is given in abbreviation in brackets after the utterance. The abbreviations of the acts used are presented below:

m.	: 'marker'
s.	: 'starter'
ms.	: 'metastatement'
el.	: 'elicitation'
p.	: 'prompt'
rep.	: 'reply'
d.	: 'directive'
rea.	: 'react'
i.	: 'informative'
ack.	: 'acknowledge'
cu.	: 'cue'

nom.   : 'nomination'
b.   : 'bid'
acc.   : 'accept'
eva.   : 'evaluate'
com.   : 'comment'
ch.   : 'check'
cl.   : 'clue'
re.   : 'repair'
re. ini.:   'repair-initiation'
com. ch. : 'comprehension check'
con. ch. : 'confirmation check'
cla. req. : 'clarification request'
cha.   : 'challenge'
con.   : 'conclusion'
z.   : 'aside'

2) If an act is cancelled as soon as it has been uttered this is represented by a horizontal line, as in -el-.

3) An utterance that has a double function is followed by the appropriate acts separated by a diagonal line, as in (eva./re.).

4) Following Sinclair and Coulthard (1975), in feedback moves, intonation is indicated where necessary using the symbols below:
[3]: a low rising tone which signals that something more is required.
[2]: a rising tone which negatively evaluates a pupil answer.
[4]: a rising falling rising tone which implies reservation.
[1+]: a high falling tone which shows strong agreement.
[1-]: a low falling tone which accepts but does not evaluate the response.

5) The study has also made use of the following symbols for discourse transcription (cf. Jefferson 1979; Schiffrin 1987, van Lier 1988; Tannen 1989; DuBois 1991).
T: teacher.
P1: identified pupil.
P: unidentified pupil.
PP: several or all pupils simultaneously.
=: the turn continues below, at the subsequent identical symbol.
., .., ..., etc.: short pauses. Three periods stand for approximately one-second pause.
[...]: omission of elements not necessary for current analysis.

He   witnessed: onset and end of speech overlap. The space in the turn above
[   ]   does not indicate a pause unless marked by periods.
  saw
<unint>: unintelligible item.
he-: a hyphen indicates an abrupt cut-off, with level pitch, usually due to self-
interruption.
READ: capitals denote articulatory emphasis, with falling intonation.
[wær]: square brackets indicate phonetic transcription.
< >: angle brackets indicate information provided by the investigator.
->: arrow indicates the placement of the element under discussion.
Sh::: : one or more colons indicate lengthening of the preceding sound.

List of Tables

List of Figures

CHAPTER 1
Introduction

L2 classroom-oriented research has primarily been concerned with establishing a link between the observable behaviours of the learners and the teacher and the extent of learner language development. It is argued that "the meaningfulness for learners of classroom events [...] will depend on the extent to which communication has been jointly constructed between the teacher and learners" (Chaudron 1988: 10), and that interaction in which learners struggle to make output comprehensible is important for language development (Swain 1985). Negotiated interaction, "which includes routines or exchanges that involve indications of nonunderstandings and subsequent negotiations of meaning" (Gass & Varonis 1991: 127), in L2 classroom and nonnative speaker discourse is a process which has received much attention recently, for it is believed to be a key variable in L2 development. Gass & Varonis (1991: 138) contend that "[t]he negotiation routines [...] give learners an opportunity to test their hypotheses about the second language in their follow-up turn" and that "negative evidence [information indicating to the L2 learner that his utterance has been deviant in some way] and negotiation play a significant role in the internalization of linguistic information."

This introductory chapter describes the research area, attempts to clarify the term 'negotiated interaction', presents the three research questions which the study sets out to address as well as the hypotheses designed to predict answers for these questions, and sheds light on the rationale for this type of research. The chapter closes with a preview of the contents of the following chapters.

Research Area

Until the late sixties, target language (TL) researchers were concerned primarily with such issues as the comparison of syntactic development between first language and TL learners, the universal nature of language acquisition, the impact that the mother tongue (or other languages known) can have on TL acquisition, the role of language universals in TL development, and social and affective factors that affect the acquisition of a TL. Since the early seventies, however, the field of TL acquisition research has widened its scope of inquiry to encompass the effect of the learning environment on learners' 'interlanguage' (Selinker 1972) development. Accordingly, two main aspects have been focused on, namely the input that is provided to the learners and the interactions in which they become involved.

Among the pioneering works which have contributed to broaden the scope of inquiry of TL acquisition research is Corder's (1967). This seminal work has paved the ground for the crucial distinction which has been made between *input* and *intake*. Another important work in this direction has been by Wagner-Gough & Hatch (1975) in which they highlight the importance of going beyond the acquisition of sentence-level syntax and taking into consideration the conversational interactions in which learners engage. They argue that it is impossible to understand the acquisition process if research is confined to a consideration of acquisition as a syntactic process happening inside the learner, because acquisition is a process which depends on conversational interactions.

Hatch (1978b) further suggests that it is out of conversational interaction that syntax develops. In concert with Stevick (1976, 1980), she claims that being involved in conversation is part of the learning process. The following pioneering insightful contention sums up her position: "one learns how to do conversation, one learns how to interact verbally and out of this interaction syntactic structures are developed" (Hatch 1978b: 404). Hatch (1978b, 1983a) does not deny that TL acquisition takes place through rule formation. The idea revealed in the above quotation is that nonlinguistic processes may be crucial to the learner's discovery and internalization of linguistic elements because such processes provide a setting that is more favourable for the learner to form and test hypotheses about the target language. Yet, as Larsen-Freeman & Long (1991) note, Hatch would readily admit that the link between conversational interaction and interlanguage development towards TL norms is, unquestionably, a complex one.

Conversational interaction in the TL classroom has come to be viewed as significant, for at least three reasons: 1) interaction enables learners to analyze the TL structure, to make and test hypotheses about it and to negotiate meaning in order to make sense of classroom events (Swain 1985, Schachter 1984, 1986, Gass & Varonis 1991); 2) interaction provides learners with opportunities to make use of 'scaffolding' (Hatch 1978b), and in this way, incorporate TL structures and vocabulary items into their own speech; 3) the degree to which classroom talk has been jointly constructed between the teacher and learners will determine learners' understanding of classroom events (Allwright 1984a, Breen 1985).

As Chaudron (1988: 10) argues "[w]hile the overall meaningfulness of instruction is a difficult construct to observe and evaluate, each characteristic of interaction that is considered to promote L2 development needs to be individually investigated for its contribution to communication and learning." Since negotiation, a feature of interaction, is claimed to be a key factor in the acquisition process (Long 1980), it is important to investigate the process whereby teachers and learners in TL classrooms confer with each other, and go about negotiating interaction so as to construct a piece of discourse that is comprehensible and acceptable. This will probably give insights into how learners in the TL classroom make use of interaction in acquiring the target language.

Given the fact that interlocutors take turns in conversations, each participant must understand the other participant's contribution in order to maintain the flow of the discourse. When learners engage in interaction, it is this discourse flow which provides them not only with the opportunity to formulate short-term hypotheses about the meaning of their interlocutors' utterances, but also with appropriate data to formulate long-term hypotheses about the linguistic, semantic and pragmatic rules of the target language (Gass & Varonis 1984). Furthermore, when learners are negotiating for meaning, the linguistic, semantic, and pragmatic rules of their interlanguage are presumably put to test, with regard to their communicative outcome (Chaudron 1988).

Breakdowns of understanding occur frequently in conversations between native speakers since anything said may constitute a potential 'trouble source' (Schegloff et al. 1977). Conversations between native speakers and nonnative speakers and between nonnative speakers and other nonnative speakers have been shown to involve even more misunderstanding because TL learners are faced with an additional burden to interaction, namely the limited proficiency in the language of communication (cf. Long 1980, Gaskill 1980, Schwartz 1980, Scarcella & Higa 1981, Porter 1983, Varonis & Gass 1985a,b,c, Gass & Varonis 1985a,b). Accordingly, Gass & Varonis (1985a and elsewhere) suggest that negotiation of meaning almost inevitably arises in conversations involving nonnative speakers. Interestingly, they further argue that "negotiation of meaning [...] may be an important aspect of the acquisition process because it allows nonnatives the opportunity to make input comprehensible" (Gass & Varonis 1985a: 38).

Several theories of TL acquisition (Hatch 1978b, 1983a,b, Long 1983a,b,c, 1985, Swain 1985, Schachter 1984, 1986) together with supportive empirical research (Gass & Varonis 1984, 1985a,b, Pica, Doughty & Young 1986, Varonis & Gass 1982) have emphasized the importance of negotiated interaction in the process of TL acquisition. The role attributed to negotiated interaction, undoubtedly, stems from the fact that it is a fertile soil for the provision of both 'comprehensible input' (Krashen 1980a,b, 1982a) and 'comprehensible output' (Swain 1985) which have been claimed to be major factors in TL development.

'Negotiated Interaction': Operational Definition

Longman Dictionary of Applied Linguistics defines the term *negotiation* as follows:

> (in conversation) what speakers do in order to achieve successful communication. For conversation to progress naturally and for speakers to be able to understand each other it may be necessary for them to:
> (a) indicate that they understand or do not understand, or that they want the conversation to continue [...]
> (b) help each other to express ideas [...]
> (c) make corrections when necessary to what is said or how it is said [...].
> These aspects of the work which speakers do in order to make successful conversation is known as negotiation, in CONVERSATIONAL ANALYSIS (Richards et al. 1985: 190).

Scarcella & Higa (1981) also offer an insightful definition of 'negotiated interaction'. They write:

> when participating in face-to-face interaction, conversationalists cooperate to sustain the conversation and establish understanding (Goffman 1974). As Garfinkel (1967) points out, this is an ongoing negotiation process. Here we describe it in terms of the "work" involved in helping one another to communicate, for example, by jointly expressing messages, filling in lapses in the conversation, indicating gaps in understanding, and repairing communication breakdowns (Scarcella & Higa 1981: 410).

The above definitions have been useful in locating 'negotiated interaction', in the data. However, to operationalize 'negotiated interaction', we shall further account for it in terms of both structure and function. Given that we have used an adapted version of Sinclair & Coulthard's (1975) system of analysis for coding and analyzing the data (cf. Chapter 4), in terms of structure and function, it is worth noting that 'negotiated interaction' is that interaction which violates - by making the structure of the exchange more complex - the basic functional structure of teaching exchanges, namely Initiation-Response-Feedback (IRF), as proposed by Sinclair & Coulthard (1975). Similar proposals to those of Sinclair

& Coulthard (1975) have been made by Mishler (1972) and Mehan (1979, 1985) in their works on classroom interaction. Mishler (1972) proposes a discourse pattern consisting of a 'question', a 'response', and a 'confirmation'. Likewise, Mehan (1979, 1985) suggests the discourse sequence: 'initiation', 'reply' and 'evaluation'.

In non-negotiated interaction, the moves 'initiation', 'response', and 'feedback' usually succeed one another, and have a clearcut function. 'Initiation' opens the exchange, 'response' constitutes a reply to the preceding 'initiation', and 'feedback' evaluates the preceding 'response', and closes the exchange. In 'negotiated interaction', however, these moves do not necessarily succeed one another, and their functions seem to overlap. It is noteworthy that the location of the violation of the basic functional structure IRF depends on the aim of the negotiation as well as on who initiates it (teacher or pupil). Negotiated interaction may be initiated for two main purposes: to resolve an interactional problem or to sustain the conversation.

In the first case (i.e., when negotiation aims at resolving an interactional problem), the violation of the basic functional structure IRF mainly occurs at the feedback slot. Accordingly, when the negotiation is teacher-initiated, the third move of the previous teaching exchange, i.e., 'feedback', becomes overtly missing. Thus, instead of the occurrence of a feedback move which evaluates the 'response' and closes the exchange, another 'initiation' move occurs; it simultaneously but covertly performs the evaluation function of the missing 'feedback' move, but, of course, does not close the exchange. This type of negotiated interaction results in a sequence with the following structure: I R [I R (F)]^n (F) - the parentheses indicate an optional element. Consider the following extract from the data:

(1)

Teacher	-I-	1 T :	What did the old man do? (el.)
Elicit	-R-	2 P1:	He cry (rep.)
Teacher	-I-	3 T :	He- ? (re. ini.)
Initiated	-R-	4 P1:	He cried (rep.)
Negotiate	-F-	5 T :	Yes (eva.)
			(3rd grade - Lesson 3)

In the above extract, 3 T simultaneously functions as the initiation move of the 'negotiate' exchange and as the feedback move of the preceding 'elicit' exchange. 3 T implicitly lets the pupil know that there is something wrong with his reply; therefore, it may be considered 'covert feedback'. At the same time, it explicitly urges the pupil to provide a 'repaired' (Schegloff et al. 1977) reply;

therefore, it is an 'overt initiation'. This analysis is in accordance with Griffin & Mehan's (1981) and Van Lier's (1988). Griffin & Mehan (1981: 198) contend that

> [w]hat looks at first glance like irregularities in classroom discourse (especially after incorrect replies) - irregularities occasioned by missing third parts to sequences like (T: 'elicitation', C: 'response', T: 'evaluation') - turn out instead to be grounded in those regularities by way of mechanisms involving simultaneous functions.

On the same wavelength, Van Lier (1988: 206) argues that

> [s]ince the learner's turn [...] can be extended indefinitely, the notion of third-place evaluation in not always relevant, since evaluation can and does occur at various places during the construction of the learner's allocated turn. [...] the teacher's repair initiation and error-replacements clearly fulfil an evaluatory as well as a (re)-initiating function. Repairing, correcting, evaluating and (re)-initiating overlap and are conflated (see also Chaudron 1977), and their sequential purposes and implications are in many cases identical.

On the other hand, when the negotiation (aiming at resolving an interactional problem) is pupil-initiated, the feedback move of the preceding exchange is not necessarily missing. When 'feedback' is present, the mere occurrence of 'pupil-initiated negotiation' interferes with the main function of the feedback move, namely that of closing teaching exchanges, and accordingly affects the basic structure of a teaching exchange, as it results in the following structure I R F [I (R) (F)]^n. Consider the following extract from the data:

(2)

Teacher Elicit	-I- 1 T	: Now (m.). The second one (s.) ... The cottage was damp because- ? (el.) The cottage was damp because-? (el.) Oubaydi (nom.)
	-R- 2 P1	: The cottage was damp because the roof leaked (rep.)
	-F- 3 T	: Because the roof leaked [1+] (eva.)
Pupil Initiated Negotiate	-I- 4 P2	: IS LEAKING. WAS LEAKING (cha.)
	-F- 5 T	: Yes, it's correct (com.)
Re-initiate	-I- 6 T	: Or because the roof- ? (p.) <addressed to P2>
	-R- 7 P2	: was leaking (rep.)

-F- 8 T   : was leaking (acc.). Yes (eva.)
(3rd grade - Lesson 1)

In the above extract, the pupils are doing a language and comprehension exercise after reading a text. They are supposed to complete a sentence, taking into consideration the structure used in the first clause and the ideas conveyed in the text. P1 gives a correct reply which is positively evaluated by the teacher who, in so doing, closes the exchange (3 T). Nevertheless, P2 is daring enough to re-open the exchange (4 P2) after the teacher has closed it, in order to repair P1's reply, thereby challenging the teacher's positive evaluation offered in 3 T. The teacher provides a 'comment' (5 T) which informs P2 that the reply offered by P1 is correct. Then she performs a re-initiation (6 T) whereby she prompts P2 to repeat his reply since it is also correct. In 8 T the teacher explicitly accepts and evaluates P2's reply, and thereby closes the exchange.

In the case of a pupil-initiated negotiation aiming at resolving an interactional problem and occurring before the teacher has provided 'feedback', the basic functional structure IRF is also violated, as the exchange structure results in: I R [I R (F)]^n (F). This usually occurs when a pupil provides a 'repair' to another pupil's utterance. Consider the following extract from the data:

(3)
Re-   -I- 1 T   : <T. had asked pupils to repeat the model sentence:
initiate   "There are three floors in our school"> mhm (nom.)
          -R- 2 P1 : There is three= (rep.)
                     [
Pupil   -I- 3 P2 :   There are (re.)
Initiated   -R- 4 P1 : =There are three floors in our school (rep.)
Negotiate -F- 5 T   : mhm (eva.)
(1st grade - Lesson 1)

In the above extract, P1 offers a 'repairable' (Schegloff et al. 1977) reply in terms of form. This incites another pupil to initiate a negotiation exchange by providing a 'repair' (3 P2) which helps P1 to correctly reformulate her reply (4 P1). The teacher does not interfere, but waits until the correct reply has been given; then, she positively evaluates the reply, and, in so doing, closes the exchange.

As has been pointed out above, 'negotiated interaction' may be initiated for two main purposes: 1) to resolve an interactional problem, and 2) to sustain the conversation. In the second case, the violation of the basic functional structure IRF mainly occurs at the 'initiation' and/or 'feedback' slot when the negotiation is pupil-initiated, or at the 'response' slot when the negotiation is teacher-initiated. Thus, the exchange structure results in: I [R (F)]^n (I) (R) (F) or I R F [R (F)]^n when the negotiation is pupil-initiated and I R [I R (F)]^n (F) when the negotiation is teacher-initiated. Consider the following examples:

(4)

Teacher -I- 1 T	:	Now (m.). If a house leaks uh.. OK (m.) the ceiling of a
Inform		house leaks and all the walls are damp like that one <T.
		points to a damp wall in the classroom> ... all the walls
		are damp .. may be one day the house will= (i.)
		[
-R- 2 P1	:	fall down (ack.)
-I- 3 T	:	=collapse or fall down (i./eva.). Collapse means to
		fall down (i.)
		[
-R- 4 P1	:	fall down (ack.)
-F- 5 T	:	Yes (eva.)
		(3rd grade - Lesson 1)

In the above extract, the teacher explains the verb 'to collapse' by making use of a previously explained word (*viz.* 'damp'). P1 seems to understand the teacher's 'informative' in 1 T; therefore, he tries to display his understanding and sustain the interaction by attempting to complete the teacher's utterance via the act 'acknowledge' (2 P1) (cf. Chapter 4). This pupil intervention, occurring at the 'initiation' slot, brings about a teacher move (3 T), whereby she proceeds with her previous utterance, but simultaneously and covertly evaluates positively the pupil's 'acknowledge'. The same pupil repeats the same 'acknowledge' once again to display his understanding of the verb 'to collapse' (4 P1). So, the teacher provides a positive evaluation which closes the exchange.

(5)

Teacher -I- 1 T	:	Now (m.). Number two (s.). Did the writer's uncle
Elicit		continue to live in his cottage? (el.)
-R- 2 PP	:	No (rep.)
-F- 3 T	:	No, he didn't (eva./re.). Okay? (com. ch.). No, he didn't
		(eva./re.). In the text, it is said he = (com.)
		[
-R- 4 PP	:	gave up (ack.)
-F- 5 T	:	=gave up (acc.) mhm (eva.).. He gave up his cottage
		(com.)
		(3rd grade - Lesson 1)

The above extract occurs while the pupils are doing a comprehension exercise after reading a text. The teacher asks a question (1 T) which is correctly answered by the pupils (2 PP). Yet, because the pupils' reply is a one-word answer, the teacher evaluates it providing a feedback move which simultaneously evaluates and repairs the reply. Then, she starts a 'comment' (3 T) which is interrupted by an 'acknowledge' - a 'supportive move' (Zuengler 1989b) by means of which the pupils aim to display their understanding and sustain the interaction (4 PP). This is followed by another feedback move (5 T), whereby the teacher accepts and positively evaluates the pupils' 'acknowledge', and then proceeds with her previous 'comment' started in 3 T.

```
(6)
Re-        -I- 1 T    : <T. had asked pupils to answer the question:
initiate                 "What are the things which you shouldn't do in the
                         classroom?">
           -R- 2 P1   : We shouldn't uh we shouldn't smoke= (rep.)
                                                        [
           -I- 3 T    :                                 mhm (eva./p.)
           -R- 4 P1   : =in the classroom (rep.)
           -F- 5 T    : Yes (eva.)
                         (2nd grade - Lesson 2)
```

The above extract starts with a re-initiation of a previous teacher 'elicitation' in which she asks the pupils to tell her what things they shouldn't do in the classroom. P1 starts a reply which seems to be potentially good, but since she hesitates, the teacher provides a 'supportive move' (Zuengler 1989b) (3 T) to encourage the pupil to go on, and to prematurely inform her that the reply is a good one. The pupil proceeds with her reply (4 P1) which is positively evaluated by the teacher in 5 T.

In the context of TL classroom discourse, IRF is an idealized structure for at least three reasons. The first one is that the learner is not yet proficient in the target language, which calls for numerous interruptions from the teacher, or from other learners, in order to help her/him overcome speaking problems (see 'helping' in Van Lier 1988). This results in missing third turn overt feedback moves, and hence breaks the basic structure IRF. In this connection, Sinclair and Brazil (1982: 23) argue that in classes where a foreign language is used all or most of the time, "a two level structure appears. The 'outer' structure is a mechanism for controlling and stimulating utterances in the 'inner' structure, which gives formal practice in the foreign language" (Sinclair & Brazil 1982: 23). The second reason is related to the fact that in TL classroom discourse, as in all kinds of face-to-face interaction, meaning is negotiated in the process of interaction. Stubbs (1983: 134) notes that Sinclair & Coulthard's (1975) descriptive system "has the effect of playing down the way in which meanings are negotiated in the course of interaction." Interaction involving the negotiation of meaning is that sort of interaction in which "the speakers are explicitly oriented to getting things clear" (Stubbs 1983: 171). The third reason concerns the occurrence of what we call 'conversational continuants' (see also Varonis & Gass 1985b), the primary function of which is to display understanding, encourage the speaker to go on with her/his contribution, and thereby sustain the interaction. These conversational continuants also result in a breakdown of the ideal structure IRF.

Hence a negotiated exchange, as revealed by the data, has a more complex structure than IRF, and usually results in a sequence - a discourse unit larger than the exchange (cf. Chapter 4; see also Coulthard & Brazil 1981, Sinclair & Brazil 1982, Van Lier 1988). Accordingly, in TL classroom context, 'negotiated interaction' may have a structure as complex as the following structures, where the parentheses indicate an optional element:

- $I [R (F)]^n (I) (R) (F)$
- $I R [I R (F)]^n (F)$
- $I R F [R (F)]^n$
- $I R F [I (R) (F)]^n$

The rationale behind attempting to capture the structure of 'negotiated interaction' is primarily to show how complex and unpredictable this structure is and how much it can divert from the basic but idealized structure IRF.

From this standpoint, it might be argued that 'negotiated interaction' is that sort of interaction which displays a 'vertical' structure instead of a horizontal one (see also Scollon 1974, 1979, Hatch 1983a, Hawkins 1988). To quote Varonis & Gass (1985b: 73), in such interaction "the conversational flow is marred by numerous interruptions. These may be seen as vertical sequences in a horizontal progression." Interestingly, it is through the negotiation occurring in such vertical constructions that learners not only acquire the 'horizontal' word order of the TL (Larsen-Freeman & Long 1991: 70) but develop their TL 'communicative competence' (Canale 1983) as a whole.

In such vertical constructions, the teacher and learners collaborate to produce a meaningful and acceptable piece of discourse, with the learner relying on the strategy of 'scaffolding' (Hatch 1978b, Slobin 1982, Chaudron 1988, Larsen-Freeman & Long 1991), that is to say, building her/his utterances on those of the teacher or another learner. To define and direct attention to the importance of the concept of 'scaffolding' in language acquisition research, Chaudron (1988: 10) writes:

> scaffolding refers to the provision through conversation of
> linguistic structures that promote a learner's recognition or

production of those structures or associated forms. The import of this concept is that in various conversational [...] interaction, the "vertical discourse" [...] aids learners in gradually incorporating portions of sentences, lexical items, reproducing sounds, etc., in meaningful ways rather than in mechanical repetition or lengthy monologues.

This state of affairs implies that in the TL classroom context, 'negotiated interaction' is not necessarily disruptive, nor is it a 'side sequence' (Jefferson 1972) constituting a break from the main flow of the interaction. Most instances of 'negotiated interaction' are sequences that specifically involve the interlocutors in the negotiation of TL classroom events, namely T-events, P-events, TP-events, Text events, and Disputable events (cf. Chapter 3). Therefore, they are crucial to make classroom participants speak on the same wavelength, and hence crucial to the success of the discourse.

Negotiated exchanges are initiated by what the present study refers to as 'interactional negotiation devices' (cf. Chapter 3) which are employed "to locate and deal with both troubles of *accessibility* and *acceptability,* and, moreover, can be used when trouble is neither present nor imminent" (Aston 1986: 138), as in cases where the negotiation rather aims to sustain the conversation, lower the 'affective filter' (Krashen 1982a) and maintain social rapport than to negotiate for accessibility or acceptability.

'Negotiated interaction' reveals the complex and dialectical processes through which troubles, dissatisfactions and even satisfactions are sequenced and come to be recognized in interaction. In the case of trouble or dissatisfaction, 'negotiated interaction' is manifested as a retrospective action on on-going discourse; trouble is acted upon with the view of repairing it, before the interaction can proceed. In the case of satisfaction, 'negotiated interaction' is revealed as a prospective action on on-going discourse, aiming at sustaining the conversation, and encouraging the speaker to go on, and hence maintaining social rapport, displaying the convergence of the participants' worlds, and, probably lowering the *affective filter* in the TL classroom.

Research Questions

Our purpose is to investigate negotiated interaction in Moroccan secondary school classrooms, a context where English is taught as a foreign language. Investigating that interaction where "the speakers are explicitly oriented to getting things clear" (Stubbs 1983: 171) and acceptable at least to the participants involved in the interaction will certainly contribute to illuminating the understanding of how negotiated interaction - such a crucial process of TL classroom talk - contributes to communication and learning in the TL classroom.

Starting from the theory that "more negotiated interaction would enhance L2 acquisition" (Chaudron 1988: 130), and the theory that the classroom is a setting of 'unequal-power discourse' (Hatch & Long 1980), we aim to provide answers to the questions below.

1. What are the main discourse functions of 'negotiated interaction' in EFL classroom discourse, in Moroccan secondary schools?
2. How frequent is 'negotiated interaction' in EFL classroom discourse, in Moroccan secondary schools, and does this frequency vary by proficiency level?
3. In what way could the initiation of 'negotiated interaction' be interpreted in view of the fact that the EFL classroom is a setting of unequal-power discourse?

Hypotheses

Five hypotheses have been formulated on the basis of an examination of previous works on 'negotiated interaction'.

The body of literature on 'negotiated interaction' (cf. Long 1980, Scarcella & Higa 1981, Long 1983b, Varonis & Gass 1985a,b,c, Gass & Varonis 1985a,b, 1986, 1989, 1991, etc.) has particularly been concerned with a specific type of negotiation, namely the negotiation of meaning. However, on the basis of Aston's (1986: 135) claim that "not all conversational trouble concerns issues of comprehensibility," and on the basis of our EFL teaching experience, the following hypothesis has been formulated:

H1: 'Negotiated interaction' in EFL classroom discourse is not restricted to resolving problems of comprehensibility.

Concerning the second research question, several researchers (Long & Sato 1983, Pica & Doughty 1985, Doughty & Pica 1986, Pica & Long 1986, and Pica 1987) claim that there is a relative lack of negotiated interaction in the ESL classroom. Yet, on the basis of our experience, first, as an EFL learner, and then, as an EFL teacher, the subsequent hypothesis has been elaborated:

H2: A considerable amount of 'negotiated interaction' does occur in EFL classroom discourse.

On the other hand, other researchers (Brock 1986, Rulon & McCreary 1986, and Bremer et al. 1988) suggest that the more proficient L2 learners are, the less likely they are to involve in negotiated interaction. However, Deen & Van Hout (1991) argue that interaction with more proficient learners probably involves more attempts to negotiate comprehensibility since the likelihood of successful negotiation is greater. They further maintain that "in the interaction between a native speaker and a real beginner in a target language many factual or potential non-understandings may remain implicit" (Deen & Van Hout 1991: 124). In accordance with this argument, the following hypothesis has been generated:

H3: The higher the proficiency level of the class, the more likely it is for negotiated interaction to occur in the EFL classroom.

Concerning the third research question, Scarcella & Higa (1981: 410) suggest that

> [o]ne of the most salient features of negotiation work is that it is not always evenly distributed among conversational partners. Specifically, the more competent speaker (socially, cognitively, or linguistically) generally assumes a greater responsibility for sustaining the conversation and establishing understanding.

On the same wavelength, Van Lier (1988: 178) maintains that "[t]he teacher controls classroom interaction, undoubtedly, almost all the time." In agreement with these observations, the following hypothesis has been generated:

H4: The teacher is the initiator par excellence of negotiated interaction in EFL classroom discourse.

However, on the basis of findings in Richards & Skelton (1989) and Boulima (1990), giving evidence of the occurrence of pupil-initiated negotiation, and pupil 'challenge' of teacher contributions, and on the basis of findings that standards of correctness (Mehan 1974a) and the acquisition of speaking turns (Allwright 1980) "are the result of a continuing process of negotiation among teachers and students" (Long 1983d: 11), the following hypothesis has been elaborated:

H5: Power in EFL classroom discourse is not a property of the teacher. Rather the exercise of power through discourse is a negotiated process between the teacher and the pupils.

Rationale

Since TL communicative competence can be acquired only through doing conversation - one does conversation, one interacts verbally and out of this interaction, the four components of 'communicative competence' (Canale 1983) are developed - and since much of what TL teaching processes involve is interaction, comprehending how language operates in TL classroom discourse is critical for understanding the teaching process, and might even give insights into the learning process.

Our interest in 'negotiated interaction' stems from our belief that the process of negotiation allows TL learners to obtain 'comprehensible input' (Krashen 1980a,b, 1982a, Long 1980) and to produce 'comprehensible output' (Swain 1985). If, as Krashen (1980a,b, 1982a) and Swain (1985) respectively contend, these are key variables in the acquisition process, researching the negotiation work occurring in TL classroom discourse, in general, and across proficiency levels, can but be important in finding clues to explain the acquisition process. As Van Lier (1988: 182) argues "[t]here is no doubt that it is important to find out how trouble is repaired in L2 classrooms, as a precursor to finding out how repairing may assist in L2 development."

To shed light on the teaching and learning processes, researchers, from the early seventies onwards, have attributed a greater role to interactive features of classroom behaviours such as questioning, answering, feedback, turn-taking, repair, and negotiation of meaning. This reflects a perspective that is out of tune with "a more traditional view of teaching and learning which conceptualizes classroom instruction as the conveyance of information from the knowledgeable teacher to the "empty" and passive learner" (Chaudron 1988: 10). Being concerned with 'negotiated interaction', the present work is a contribution to the study of interactive features of classroom behaviors. With such a discourse analysis stance, the study has insightful implications for classroom discourse analysis, in general, and TL classroom discourse analysis, in particular, as it contributes to enlighten the understanding of a process which, as shown in Chapter 5, constitutes a considerable part of TL classroom interaction. Moreover, attempting to confirm or disconfirm claims made in previous works on 'negotiated interaction' (e.g., Aston 1986, Pica 1987, Rulon & McCreary 1986, Deen & Van Hout 1991, Scarcella & Higa 1981), this research may possibly lend further empirical support to those works.

Furthermore, given that 'negotiated interaction' has been held to be a key variable in TL acquisition (Hatch 1978b,c, 1983a,b, Long 1980, 1983a,b,c, 1985, Gass & Varonis 1984, 1986, 1989, 1991, Varonis & Gass 1985a,b,c, Pica, Doughty & Young 1986), the present study has insightful implications for TL teaching and teacher training. It reveals the characteristics of classroom interaction that is most favourable for promoting learners' TL development. For, as many classroom-oriented researchers have pointed out, it is only through a better understanding of classroom interaction processes that teachers can render their teaching more profitable for learners. In this connection, Fanselow (1977a: 17) suggests that "we can learn a great deal about how to teach by analyzing descriptions that show how practicing teachers and their students communicate." Likewise, Bailey (1985: 118) contends that

> the findings of classroom-centered research may be more directly applicable to teachers' needs than other types of second language research. Ultimately, these findings will help teachers and researchers alike to better understand the teaching and learning process, thereby facilitating that process in all its complexities.

Also, since 'negotiated interaction' is mainly concerned with problematic talk, discovering what type of behaviours trigger 'trouble' in the flow of interaction will give us important insights into the nature of those tacit rules operating in the TL classroom which the teacher and learners draw upon in order to construct meaningful and acceptable discourse. To echo Garnica (1981: 230),

> Just as the study of ungrammatical sentences gives the syntactician information concerning the form of syntactic rules and constraints on their application, so the study of communicative behavior patterns which disrupt the ongoing flow of social interactions can provide information on the appropriate rules for such interactions. Since the rules that group members know and use to make sense of behaviors and situations are tacit and often quite subtle, the technique of studying violations of such rules can potentially contribute information as to the nature of these rules.

Furthermore, by studying 'negotiated interaction' in terms of the power factor, the study contributes to shed light on the role and power relationships in the TL classroom which is one of the most outstanding institutionalized settings characterized by 'unequal-power discourse' (Hatch & Long 1980).

Last but not least, by virtue of revealing how teachers and pupils go about accomplishing EFL classroom lessons in the Moroccan context, the study may be of considerable use for researchers who are interested in investigating how EFL classroom discourse differs across cultural contexts.

Organization of the Work

The next chapter reviews relevant literature on negotiated interaction in SL acquisition. Chapter three explains the methodology used in analyzing 'negotiated interaction' in EFL classroom discourse. Chapter four presents the descriptive system used in coding the data, i.e., in structurally and functionally analyzing EFL classroom talk. Chapter five, six and seven provide answers to the research questions, and simultaneously discuss the results in terms of opportunities for TL acquisition, and compare them with the findings of other studies. Finally, Chapter eight summarizes the findings, draws conclusions, directs attention to some of the limitations of the study, points out some of its implications, and makes suggestions for future research.

CHAPTER 2
Negotiated Interaction in Second Language Acquisition

Introduction

A century ago, Henry Sweet (1899/1964: 219) noted that

> conversation in a foreign language may be regarded from two very
> different points of view: (1) as an end in itself, and (2) as a means
> of learning the language and testing the pupil's knowledge of it.
> But there is, of course, no reason why the second process should
> not be regarded as being at the same time a preparation for the
> first (cited in Gass & Varonis 1989: 71).

Although the importance of conversation to second language acquisition
(SLA) has long been acknowledged, it is only lately that it has become the major
focus of study. The current view of the role of conversation in L2 learning is
noticeably different from an earlier view of learning which claimed that learners
first learned grammatical rules and structures; and "in some as yet unknown
fashion, the learner then puts these structures to use to carry on conversation"
(Day 1986: vi). According to this earlier view, classroom drills, classroom
interactions and everyday conversations with native speakers (NSs) are
important only insofar as they reinforce the grammatical rules already acquired
by the learner.

However, a different role for conversation in second language acquisition
has been suggested by Wagner-Gough & Hatch (1975) who contend that instead
of being just talk designed to practice grammatical structures, conversational
interaction constitutes the *basis* for the development of syntax. Syntax, they
claim, develops out of conversation rather than the reverse; as Hatch (1978b:
404) puts it: "one learns how to do conversation, one learns how to interact
verbally, and out of this interaction syntactic structures are developed". In the
same train of thought, Hatch et al. (1986: 5-6) argue that

> language clarifies and organizes experience and, conversely, that
> language grows out of experience. That is, the development of

language is not completely preordained and internally driven. Thus, language is developed as a way of structuring experience as that experience takes place.

In a similar vein, Ellis (1984: 95) observes that

interaction contributes to development because it is the means by which the learner is able to crack the code. This takes place when the learner can infer what is said even though the message contains linguistic items that are not yet part of his competence and when the learner can use the discourse to help him modify or supplement the linguistic knowledge he has already used in production.

This process which is known as 'scaffolding' has its origins in cognitive psychology and L1 research, and was first applied to L2 acquisition by Hatch (1978b).

From this standpoint, namely that language development results from doing conversation, emanates a body of research primarily concerned with second language conversational interactions. At the centre of this research is Krashen's (1980) notion of 'comprehensible input' which relates to the modified input addressed to nonnative speakers (NNSs), a phenomenon also referred to as 'foreigner talk'.

Though the importance of the role of comprehensible input has been recognized, the extent to which second language development can be solely attributed to comprehensible input is a matter of continuing debate. Shifting the focus from the speaker (usually a NS), Gass (1988) maintains that crucial importance should be given to the concept of *comprehended* input rather than comprehensible input. On the other hand, Swain (1985) argues that second language development does not depend only on comprehensible input, as Krashen (1982) claims, but also, and more importantly, on comprehensible *output*. In other words, the learner's opportunity for language production, especially through interaction, is a necessary condition for successful language learning, because as Schachter (1984) contends using the second language in interaction provides an opportunity for the learner to confirm or reject hypotheses s/he may have made about the language and to experiment means of expression in order to see if they work.

In 1980, Long makes an important distinction between modified input (foreigner talk) and modified interaction; in other words, he distinguishes between the modified talk (foreigner talk) directed to the learner and the modified structure of the conversation itself. The findings of Long's (1980) study gave evidence that there are greater modifications in features of NS-NNS interaction than in input, and that interaction features are more sensitive to the communicative demands of a conversation. According to Long (1980), modified interaction is related to conversational trouble, in the sense that it occurs either to avoid conversational trouble or to repair it when trouble does occur. In this process, Hatch (1978) has drawn attention to the way in which questions are recoded in alternative interrogative forms; this recoding often involves the substitution of yes-no for wh-questions. Long (1980, 1981b, 1983a, 1983d) makes use of interactional features such as comprehension checks, topic shifts, and clarification requests to locate modified interaction. Interactive modifications, he claims, are more important for L2 acquisition than modifications of NS speech.

Long's work (1980) has been furthered by other works which have emphasized the importance of modified interaction. Scarcella & Higa (1981) and Varonis & Gass (1985b), for example, accord paramount importance to the interactional feature of negotiation of meaning in the process of L2 acquisition. In fact, in many other researches, negotiated interaction between a native speaker (NS) and a nonnative speaker (NNS), or between an NNS and an NNS has been held to play an important role in the development of a second language (Brock et al. 1986, Bruton & Samuda 1980, Chun et al. 1982, Day et al. 1984, Ellis 1985a, Long 1983b, Long & Porter 1985, Pica 1988, Scarcella & Higa 1981, Varonis & Gass 1985a, 1985b, 1985c).

Much of the emphasis in current second language literature is predicated on the notions of input (Krashen 1980), interaction (Long 1980) and output (Swain 1985). Accordingly, the present chapter focuses on three related issues:

First, it considers the role of comprehensibility in SLA by giving an account of prominent and conflicting hypotheses concerning what variable of comprehensibility is most crucial for SLA. Furthermore, various means designed to attempt or negotiate comprehensibility, such as comprehensible input, interactional modification devices, repair, L2 communication strategies are analyzed.

Second, the chapter reviews some empirical studies of negotiated interaction in NS-NNS and NNS-NNS conversation on the one hand, and in the ESL classroom on the other hand. These studies have addressed issues such as 'the organization of negotiated interaction', 'negotiated interaction in NS-NNS vs. NNS-NNS interaction', 'negotiated interaction in one-way and two-way tasks', 'comprehensible output in negotiated interaction', 'the one-way flow of information in the ESL classroom as a barrier to negotiation of meaning', 'negotiated interaction in teacher-fronted vs. group-work organization', and 'learner feedback as a device for negotiating comprehensible input'.

Third, the chapter focuses on the relationship between negotiated interaction and SLA. More precisely, it examines how certain researchers have endeavoured to answer the question of whether and how negotiated interaction is a necessary condition in SLA or at least whether and how it contributes to SL development. The idea we aim to convey in this chapter is that

> [i]f one accepts that there is already substantial evidence of a [...] causal relationship between comprehensible input and SLA, then one can deduce the existence of *an indirect causal relationship between linguistic and conversational adjustments and SLA* (Long 1985: 388).

On the Role of Comprehensibility in SLA

Introduction

Comprehensibility is, no doubt, of critical importance in second language acquisition. It is a widely held claim that linguistic input which is understood by the learner, in Corder's (1967, 1978) terms 'intake', constitutes primary data for SLA (cf. Hatch 1983b, Larsen-Freeman 1979, Krashen 1980a, 1980b, Long 1983a). Yet, current research is moving beyond the hypothesis that comprehensible input "delivered in a low (affective) filter situation is the only 'causative variable' in second language acquisition" (Krashen 1981b: 57). In their attempt to find out what is most effective for L2 development, researchers have tackled comprehensibility from different angles. Hence, conflicting arguments have been advanced concerning what sort of comprehensibility is most efficient, namely Krashen's (1980b) 'comprehensible input' hypothesis, Long's (1983a) 'negotiation of comprehensible input' hypothesis, Swain's (1985) 'comprehensible output' hypothesis, and Gass'(1988) 'comprehended input hypothesis'.

The Comprehensible Input Hypothesis

"'Input' refers to the language which the learners hear or read - that is, the language samples to which they are exposed" (Allwright & Bailey 1991: 120). 'Comprehensible input' is a term popularized by Krashen (e.g., 1977, 1980b, 1982a) and refers to the target language samples which make sense, i.e., are understandable, to the L2 learner. Krashen (1977, 1980b, 1982a) believes that in order for input to become *intake* (Corder 1967, 1978) (i.e., data taken in and used by the L2 learner to promote L2 acquisition), it has to be comprehensible. He argues that L2 learners "acquire structure by understanding messages and not focusing on the form of input, by 'going for meaning'" (Krashen 1981b: 54). Comprehensible input, he claims, is one of the key elements in second or foreign language development.

By comprehensible input Krashen specifically means to imply language addressed to the learner that contains some new element in it but that is nonetheless understood by the learner thanks to linguistic, paralinguistic, situational cues, or world knowledge backup. Krashen (1980b) claims that in order for acquisition to occur, the input the learner receives has to be comprehensible at the $i+1$ level, where i stands for the learner's current linguistic competence and $i+1$, the stage just beyond. Hence, according to Krashen, acquisition takes place "when we understand language that contains structure that is a 'little beyond' where we are now" (Krashen 1982a: 21), when we understand input that is challenging but not overwhelming.

To support the comprehensible input hypothesis, Krashen (1982a, 1982b) cites literature on four issues: (1) caretaker speech, (2) foreigner talk, (3) the 'silent period' in child L1 and SL acquisition, (4) comparative methods studies of language teaching. He argues that caretaker speech and foreigner talk respectively play a facilitating role in first and second language acquisition, since they accompany all successful cases of language development. As for the period of silence witnessed in L1 acquisition and advocated by several L2 teaching methods, Krashen (1982a) claims that it implies that the child or the L2 learner is listening to and trying to comprehend the language before starting to produce. The comparative methods studies, as reviewed in Krashen (1982b), indicate that 'input-based' methods are, generally, more beneficial to the learner than 'production-oriented' methods. Hence, according to Krashen (1982b), methods such as Total Physical Response, Suggestopedia, and the Natural Approach (which advocate that learners should, at the beginning, be provided with large amounts of simple and comprehensible language before they are asked to produce the language) do better than methods such as Audiolingual, Silent Way, Audiovisual or Community Language Learning (which advocate early production, often through repetition, and after minimal exposure).

Larsen-Freeman & Long (1991: 140-1) capture the problem with the above arguments:

> While these arguments are initially appealing, some qualifications are in order. To begin with [...], the fact that caretaker speech and FT [foreigner talk] co-occur with successful acquisition does not necessarily mean that they cause it. Next, a 'silent period' is by no means observed in all learners. Gibbons (1985) argues that the evidence for silent periods is in fact very weak, and that there is great individual variation among children as to their duration, where they occur at all. He suggests that they initially signify incomprehension not intake processing [Gattegno (1985) claims that what the baby is doing during the pre-verbal period is learning to control its own articulatory system and is learning to listen to

itself], that prolonged silent periods seen in some children probably indicate psychological withdrawal rather than the acquisition process at work, and that pedagogic recommendations for delayed production are not justified (on the basis of this evidence, at least). Finally, the comparative methods studies, often with problematic designs (see Long 1980b), did not systematically manipulate the +/- comprehensible input characteristic Krashen now claims was the crucial variable in interpreting their findings.

Nevertheless, further evidence has been put forward to support the comprehensible input hypothesis (cf. Long 1983b). This encompasses the superiority of immersion over foreign or second language programmes, the lack of an effect for additional out-of-school second language exposure for children in immersion programmes, and non-acquisition without comprehensible input. Immersion programmes, of which comprehensible input is an outstanding feature, have consistently given such good results in Canada (for a review, see Swain 1981, Genesee 1983) that are impossible to obtain in foreign and second language programmes. However, as Larsen-Freeman & Long (1991: 141) point out,

> this is evidence derived from co-occurring phenomena, and may be due to the greater amount of exposure to SL that immersion children receive (time on task), and to the fact that the children are self-selected, as much as to the type of input they receive.

The lack of effect for additional out-of-school exposure for children in immersion programmes, used as evidence to support the comprehensible input hypothesis, is based on a reinterpretation of the findings of Swain (1981). Long (1983b) suggests that such lack of effect is due to the fact that the language samples available to these children (on the street, on the radio, on TV, at the movies or in newspapers) were not beneficial for them since they were not adjusted to their proficiency level; in other words, they formed incomprehensible input. This interpretation, however, is, to quote Larsen-Freeman & Long (1991: 142) "admittedly a *post hoc* interpretation, and only one of those available." According to Larsen-Freeman & Long (1991: 142),

> the best evidence for Krashen's viewpoint has to be the fact that children or adults who are not provided with comprehensible input, but only NS-NS models, either do not acquire at all or acquire only a very limited stock of lexical items and formulaic utterances, such as greetings, leave-taking and advertising jingles.

This theory is supported by several studies of first and second language acquisition (for a review, see Long 1981a, 1981b, 1983b). Snow et al. (1981), for example, show that Dutch children do not acquire German by watching large amounts of German TV; and Sachs et al. (1981) indicate that Hearing children of deaf parents do not learn how to speak via watching TV; however, once they get normal input for children, they surmount their impediment and catch up with age-peers. As Larsen-Freeman & Long (1991: 142) note, "the *amount* of input in these and other cases is unlimited. It is the quality of input - unadjusted, so incomprehensible - which distinguishes them."

In nonnative discourse, it is widely assumed that comprehensible input is attained through the speech modifications made by native speakers (NSs) when addressing nonnative speakers (NNSs) of the target language. The notion of comprehensible input has been closely related to that of foreigner talk and teacher talk, in the sense that these provide for comprehensible input. (For a review of the research findings on foreigner talk, see Hatch 1983b, Chapter 9; for a review of similar findings on teacher talk in SL classrooms, see Gaies 1983a and Chaudron 1988).

Foreigner Talk
The term foreigner talk was first introduced by Ferguson (1971) to refer to the speech variety used by native speakers (NSs) when addressing nonnative speakers (NNSs). Comparing foreigner talk to baby talk, Ferguson (1971) suggests that native speakers (NSs) make use of this variety because they believe it is the way nonnative speakers speak, in the same way as baby talk stands for the way adults believe babies speak. Foreigner talk has been viewed differently by different scholars; according to Bloomfield (1933), it is an NS's contemptuous imitation of an NNS's endeavour to communicate in the target language, designed to make her/himself understood to an NNS. Conversely, Whinnom (1971) conceptualizes foreigner talk as a stereotyped version of an NNS's use of the target language induced by the desire to achieve a comic effect rather than actual imitation of the NNS. Meisel (1980) criticizes the view which explains foreigner talk on the basis of imitation and claims that the type of simplification witnessed in foreigner talk results from the same cognitive processes employed by NNSs when acquiring a second language.

Studies of L2 acquisition have come up with a bulk of research concerned with speech by NSs addressing NNSs of the language of interaction. A common finding of such research is that the NSs use a reduced or 'simplified' variety of their language (i.e., foreigner talk), characterized with shorter utterances, lower syntactic complexity, and avoidance of low frequency lexical items and idiomatic expressions (see for example, Arthur et al. 1980, Freed 1978, Gaies 1977a, Henzl 1979). The following Table, quoted from Hatch (1983a: 183-4), summarizes foreigner talk and points to its benefit for the SL learner.

Table 1: Summary of foreigner talk

Slow Rate = clearer articulation (less "sandhi variation")
- Final stops are released, voiced final stops are voiced.
- Some glottal stops used before words beginning with Vs.
  (Benefit: Learner should be able to identify word boundaries more easily.)
- Fewer reduced vowels and fewer contractions.
  (Benefit: Learner receives the full word form.)
- Longer pauses.
  (Benefit: Learner gets more processing time and the major constituent boundaries are more clearly marked.)

Vocabulary
- High frequency vocabulary, less slang, fewer idioms.
  (Benefit: Learner is more likely to know and/or recognize topic.)
- Fewer pronoun forms of all types.
  (Benefit: Reference should be clearer.)
- Definitions will be marked:
  Explicitly by formulas (This means X, it's a kinda X).
  Implicitly by intonation (a nickel? a 5-cent piece?).
  (Benefit: Marking should make definitions salient.)
- Derivational morphology frames (miracle - anything that is miraculous? Sum up - summarize?).
  (Benefit: Gives learner information on morphology class membership.)
- Form class information (funds or money, industrious and busy).
- Semantic feature information (a cathedral usually means a church that's a very high ceiling).
- Context information (If you go for a *job in a factory* they talk about a wage scale).
- Gestures and pictures.
  (Benefit: Learner gets information on lexical form class, features and vocabulary sets.)
- Endearment terms.
  (Benefit: May give an affective boost to learning.)

Syntax
- Short MLU, simple propositional syntax.
  (Benefit: Should be easier to process and analyze.)
- Left dislocation of topics (Friday, Saturday, you have a nice weekend?).
  (Benefit: Should help learner identify topic.)
- Repetition and restatement.
  (Benefit: More processing time and relationship of syntactic forms may be clearer.)
- Less pre-verb modification.
  (Benefit: New information should be at the end of the utterance where it is more salient.)
- Native speaker summarizes learner's nonsyntactic utterances.
  (Benefit: Provides a model of syntax.)
- Native speaker "fills in the blank" for learner's incomplete utterance.
  (Benefit: Provides a model of syntax.)

Table 1 (continued)

Discourse
- Native speaker gives reply within his question (WH-questions restated as yes/no or or-choice questions.)
  (Benefit: Learner is able to stay in the conversation by using the model supplied.)
- Native speaker uses tag questions.
  (Benefit: Identifies ends of utterances and supplies learner with model for response.)
- Native speaker offers correction.
  (Benefit: Identifies trouble source the learner should work on.)

Speech Setting Interaction
- Child-child language play.
  (Benefits: Practice on the possible sounds, their range of articulation, and combinations with other sounds. Practice with syntax via buildups, breakdowns, and transformations.)
- Language during play.
  (Benefit: Many chunk utterances to stockpile for later analysis.)
- Adult-child interactions.
  (Benefit: Vocabulary negotiation and question-answering helps build sentence syntax via interactions).

From *Psycholinguistics: A Second Language Perspective*, by E. Hatch. 1983. Copyright ©
1983 by Newbury House Publishers, Inc. Excerpt from pp. 183-4. Reprinted by permission of
Heinle & Heinle Publishers

Ferguson (1975), Meisel (1977) and Hatch et al. (1978) found out that
foreigner talk may at times be ungrammatical, as when native speakers delete
articles, copula, or other inflectional morphology for the sake of simplification.
According to Long (1983a: 126),

> use of this 'broken' form of a language is restricted, seeming to
> occur only when two or more of the following conditions are met:
> 1/ the nonnative speaker has very low or no proficiency in the
> language of communication; 2/ the native speaker is, or thinks s/he
> is, of higher status than the nonnative speaker; 3/ the native speaker
> has considerable prior foreigner talk experience, but of a very
> limited kind; and 4/ the conversation occurs spontaneously, i.e., not
> as part of a laboratory study.

Teacher Talk
Teacher talk, or "teachers' foreigner talk discourse" (Chaudron 1983: 141) in L2
classrooms is itself a special register of language. It has many characteristics in
common with foreigner talk since teachers find themselves confronted to the
problem of conveying information with a code that is explicit, lucid, and
accessible to the learners. This frequently requires simplifications and

restructurings of the information. Chaudron (1988) argues that the adjustments L2 teachers make in their speech serve a short-term purpose, namely that of maintaining communication by clarifying information and eliciting learners' responses; and unlike foreigner talk, which constitutes a special sociolinguistic register, teacher talk does not identify classroom interaction as a completely different social situation. As Chaudron (1988: 58) notes,

> [t]his is an important finding, which indicates that if teachers' efforts to modify their classroom speech have any effect on L2 learners, it is more likely that the effects contribute to comprehension and learning than that they mark the classroom events as unusual or stigmatized.

Several studies of teacher modifications have been undertaken in the areas of phonology, lexis, syntax and discourse, focusing on different linguistic features of teachers' speech. (For a review of these studies, see Chaudron 1988: 54-89). These studies show that a wide range of phenomena in teacher speech seem to adjust, to a certain degree, to the needs of L2 learners. Subsequent are examples of the findings concerning speech to lower-level L2 learners:

1. Rate of speech appears to be slower.
2. Pauses, which may be evidence of the speaker planning more, are possibly more frequent and longer.
3. Pronunciation tends to be exaggerated and simplified.
4. Vocabulary use is more basic.
5. Degree of subordination is lower.
6. More declaratives and statements are used than questions.
7. Teachers may self-repeat more frequently.
   (Chaudron 1988: 85).

Teacher modifications have been of great interest to current researchers in L2 classrooms due to the assumption that these aid learners' comprehension; in other words, they provide comprehensible input. Such research has presented evidence of teachers' awareness of their learners' immediate but changing needs for comprehension and participation. A few relevant studies with regard to this issue have investigated the extent to which teachers' modifications might influence learners' comprehension and, subsequently, acquisition. To our knowledge, two types of teacher speech modifications have been investigated with regard to comprehensibility, namely rate of speech and syntactic complexity. Studies related to these issues are considered below.

Rate of Speech. Several benefits of slower speech to L2 learners have been put forward by Hatch (1983a: 183-4) (see Table 1), for instance that it should allow more processing time and clearer segmentation of the structures in the input. Although several of the studies, which have investigated teacher modifications with respect to rate of speech, revealed that there is a tendency for teachers' speech to be slower when addressed to less proficient learners, the relationship between rate of speech and comprehensibility was not further investigated except by very few researchers such as Dahl (1981) and Kelch (1985). Dahl (1981) found that despite the fact that L2 learners estimated the more comprehensible messages to be spoken more slowly, there was no correlation, in reality, between these estimations and the measured speech rate. To explain this finding, Dahl (1981) argues that some unmeasured characteristics regarding clarity of articulation or conciseness of information possibly affect perceived rate of speech. Kelch's (1985) study, on the other hand, reveals that slow rate of speech has a positive effect on comprehensibility. It shows that university L2 students did significantly better in dictation when the speech rate of lecture listening passages was slowed down from 200 to 130 word per minute. Hence, the study provides some support for the theory that slower speech enhances comprehension. However, further research is needed to determine whether comprehension in the classroom context is attributable to the slower speech rather than the other prosodic features in teacher talk, and whether and how it affects target language development.

Syntactic Complexity. Current research on L2 acquisition assumes that "less syntactically complex speech could contribute to comprehensibility by aiding the perception of segmentation and the clarity of form/meaning relationships" (Chaudron 1988: 155). Although studies of the degree of syntactic complexity reveal that syntax tends to be simplified in speech to lower-proficiency L2 learners; it is surprising that very little research has been done on the comprehensibility of such syntactically simplified speech.

In a study involving lecture comprehension, Long (1985) addressed the question 'What is the effect of modified input on the learner's ability to comprehend?' He constructed two versions of a lecture, one displaying foreigner talk features and the other lacking these features. The former was a modified version of the latter, in the sense that both syntactic complexity and rate of speech were reduced and rephrasings and restatements were added. The findings reveal that in the foreigner talk version, actual and perceived comprehension were higher than in the other version. In other words, when the lecture displayed foreigner talk features, L2 learners were significantly better at answering comprehension questions about the lecture, and rated their perceived comprehension significantly higher than the learners who heard the unadjusted version. However, as Chaudron (1988: 155) points out,

[s]ince several factors were modified simultaneously in the foreigner talk lecture, it is difficult to ascertain the source of this advantage. For example, the repetition of information had been shown to aid its immediate recall in an L2 listening comprehension experiment with simulated lectures (Chaudron 1983b), and similarly in a dictation experiment by Cervantes (1983). So, since Long's subjects were allowed to answer their comprehension questions *during* the lectures, one might suppose that the repetition modification alone could have led to the improved comprehension for the foreigner-talk version.

Speidel et al. (1985) conducted a similar study to that of Long (1985), but they, unexpectedly, found out that simple syntax did not lead to higher comprehension. Fugimoto et al.'s (1986) study is a modification of Long's (1985). The study elaborated three versions of a lecture: (1) a 'native speaker' version with no modifications, (2) a 'modified input' version where difficult lexical items and complex sentences were simplified, and (3) a 'modified interaction' version marked with greater redundancy of information. The results show that L2 learners' comprehension was significantly higher in the modified versions. Thus, it seems that the modifications, whether lexical and syntactic simplifications, or the addition of redundancy, do enhance comprehensibility.

To conclude, the hypothesis claiming a causal link between simplification modifications and learning outcomes has received some supporting evidence for the first step in the argument, namely that speech simplification of a certain sort enhances comprehensibility. The second step, the impact of comprehensibility on learners' grammar, is still untested. Indeed, it is not easy to see how exposure to comprehensible input actually enhances language development. One possibility is that "it is the effort made by the learner to comprehend the input that fosters development. Where this effort is made in face-to-face interaction, we may suggest that it is the interaction itself which is productive" (Allwright & Bailey 1991: 121). The next section focuses on the importance of interaction in second language development, and more precisely on what Long (1983a) refers to as "the negotiation of comprehensible input."

The Negotiation of Comprehensible Input Hypothesis

As has been noted above, it is widely believed that input becomes comprehensible through the speech modifications NSs make when talking to foreigners, in other words through modifications of the input itself. Long (1983b) captures several problems with this position. First, many of the input modifications often attributed to foreigner talk lack an empirical basis. Second, there seems to be no evidence that the input modifications made by NSs are actually beneficial for NNSs. In this regard, Chaudron's (1983) study comes to the conclusion that many speech modifications may actually hinder rather than facilitate comprehension. Third, according to Long (1983b: 211),

> there is a logical problem with the idea that changing the input will aid *acquisition*. If removal from the input of structures and lexical items the learner does not understand is what is involved in making speech comprehensible, how does the learner ever advance? Where is the input at i+1 that is to appear in the learner's competence at the next stage of development?

Hence, this kind of modification of the input itself may "serve only the immediate needs of communication, not the future interlanguage development of the learner, for by definition it denies him or her access to new linguistic material" (Long 1983b: 212). Clearly, besides modifying the input itself, there must be other ways in which input might be made comprehensible. One way, as Krashen (1982a) and others have argued, is by use of the linguistic and extralinguistic context. Another way, is through use of the "here and now" principle (see Gaies 1982a, Long 1980, 1981a). A third method "is modifying not the input itself, but the interactional structure of the conversation" (Long 1983b: 211). Long (1983b) points out that while all three methods may aid communication, the second and the third methods are those likely to aid second language development "for each allows communication to proceed while exposing the learner to linguistic material which he or she cannot yet handle without their help" (Long 1983b: 212). Accordingly, the "here and now" orientation in conversation, and modifications of the interactional structure of the conversation "serve to make that *unfamiliar* linguistic input comprehensible" (Long 1983b: 212).

Recent research on NS-NNS conversation suggests that while speech modifications may actually facilitate comprehension, these are in no way sufficient. Native speakers also make many *interactional* modifications when talking to nonnatives; that is adjustments to the interactional structure of conversation, exemplified by self- and other-repetitions, clarification requests, comprehension and confirmation checks, expansions, and so on (cf. Long 1980, 1983a, 1983b). According to Long (1983a: 127), it is modifications of this sort "that are greater, more consistently observed, and probably more important for providing comprehensible input."

Long's (1980) distinction between input and interaction, and accordingly between modified input and modified interaction, is quite revealing for research on L2 acquisition. Therefore, a brief clarification of the terms 'input' and 'interaction' is in order. While linguistic input refers to the forms the learner hears, interaction refers to the functions of those forms in (conversational) discourse. Hence, while the analysis of input involves a consideration of the native speaker's speech in isolation,

> [a]nalysis of interaction necessitates taking the non-native speaker's participation into account, for identification of turns in conversation, as e.g. other repetitions, confirmation checks, comprehension checks, expansions and clarification requests, is only possible by considering the relationship which utterances enter into with those preceding and/or following them, including those by the non-native interlocutor (Long 1983a: 127).

Despite Long's (1980) distinction between input to and interaction with a language acquirer (two phenomena which have often been conflated in the literature on both L1 and L2 acquisition), he points out that distinguishing between these phenomena, at one stage of the analysis of NS-NNS conversation, by no means suggests that these should permanently be separated. "It seems, after all, that several features of each are often related" (Long 1983a: 127). An illustration of this may be Long's (1981a) finding that there is a statistically significant preference for the NS's use of questions as topic-initiating moves when addressing NNSs than when addressing NSs. Though input-interaction relationships do exist, modifications in input and in interaction, at times take place independently. Long (1983a: 128) illustrates this by the following examples:

(a) NS : What time you finish?
    NNS: Ten o'clock

(b) NS : When did you finish?
    NNS: Um?
    NS : When did you finish?
    NNS: Ten clock
    NS : Ten o'clock?
    NNS: Yeah

The first example is an instance of input modification (with no modification in the interactional structure of the conversation). The native speaker modifies input by making use of an inverted question lacking do-support. The second example, on the other hand, is exactly the opposite: an instance of interactional modification with no modification in the input. In the second example, the NS's initial question fails to elicit an appropriate response; therefore s/he makes use of an exact self-repetition. However, the NNS's response is ambiguous enough to incite the NS to perform a confirmation check (Ten o'clock?) to ascertain that s/he has, indeed, correctly heard the NNS's reply. The following Table quoted from Larsen-Freeman and Long (1991: 125-6) is a taxonomy of linguistic and conversational adjustments to NNSs:

Table 2: Linguistic and conversational adjustments to NNSs in grammatical foreigner talk discourse

---

Linguistic adjustments

Phonology
    slower rate of delivery
    more use of stress and pauses
    more careful articulation
    wider pitch range/exaggerated intonation
    more use of full forms/avoidance of contractions
Morphology and syntax
    more well-formed utterances/fewer disfluencies
    shorter utterances (fewer words per utterance)
    less complex utterances (fewer S-nodes per T-unit, fewer clauses per T-unit,
        fewer adjectival, adverbial and noun clauses per T-unit, fewer relative clauses
        and appositives per T-unit)
    more regularity/use of canonical word order
    more retention of optional constituents
    more overt marking of grammatical relations
    more verbs marked for present/fewer for non-present temporal reference
    more questions
    more yes-no and intonation questions/fewer WH-questions
Semantics
    more overt marking of semantic relations
    lower type-token ratio
    fewer idiomatic expressions
    higher average lexical frequency of nouns and verbs
    higher proportion of copulas to total verbs
    marked use of lexical items
    fewer opaque forms (greater preference for full NPs over pronouns, concrete
        verbs over dummy verbs, like do)

Table 2 (continued)

Conversational adjustments

Content
　　more predictable/narrower range of topics
　　more here-and-now orientation
　　briefer treatment of topics (fewer information bits per topic/lower ratio of
　　　　topic-initiating to topic-continuing moves)
Interactional structure
　　more abrupt topic-shifts
　　more willing relinquishment of topic-choice to interlocutor
　　more acceptance of unintentional topic-switches
　　more use of questions for topic-initiating moves
　　more repetition (self- and other-, exact and semantic, complete and partial)
　　more comprehension checks
　　more confirmation checks
　　more clarification requests
　　more expansions
　　more question-and-answer strings
　　more decomposition

From *An Introduction to Second Language Acquisition Research.* by D. Larsen-Freeman and M. H. Long. 1991. Copyright © 1991 by Longman Group UK Limited. Excerpt from pp. 125-6. Reprinted by permission of Addison Wesley Longman Ltd.

It is evident that when speakers make the above linguistic and conversational adjustments, they are "concentrating on communicating with the NNS; that is, their focus is on what they are saying not on how they are saying it" (Long & Porter 1985: 213). Long (1980; for a report see Long 1983a) compared NS-NS conversation with NS-NNS conversation with respect to eight measures of the modification of the interactional structure of conversation. He found out that with non-native interlocutors, native speakers used a non-significantly lower number of *conversational frames* (e.g., Now, Well, So, etc.), but significantly more *confirmation checks*, more *comprehension checks*, more *clarification requests*, more *self-repetitions*, more *other-repetitions*, and more *expansions*.

Having evidenced the occurrence of modifications in the interactional structure of NS-NNS conversation, Long (1983a) attempted to investigate the role these play in providing comprehensible input. He found out that native speakers seem to modify interaction for two purposes: "(1) to avoid conversational trouble, and (2) to repair the discourse when trouble occurs" (Long 1983a: 131). Modifications designed to achieve the first purpose are referred to as conversational *strategies;* while those aiming at achieving the second purpose are called *tactics* for discourse repair. Further, a subset of the modifications of each type (strategies and tactics) is employed both to avoid and repair trouble.

Interactional Modification Devices
The following Table gives examples of devices employed by native speakers to modify the interactional structure of their conversation with NNSs. As the Table shows, these devices are used as strategies and/or tactics:

Table 3: Devices used by NSs to modify the interactional structure of NS-NNS conversation

Strategies (S) (for avoiding trouble)	Tactics (T) (for repairing trouble)
S1 Relinquish topic-control	T1 Accept unintentional topic-switch
S2 Select Salient topics	T2 Request clarification
S3 Treat topics briefly	T3 Confirm own comprehension
S4 Make new topics salient	T4 Tolerate ambiguity
S5 Check NNS's comprehension	

Strategies and Tactics (ST) (for avoiding and repairing trouble)	
ST1 Use low space	ST4 Decompose topic-comment constructions
ST2 Stress key words	ST5 Repeat own utterances
ST3 Pause before key words	ST6 Repeat other's utterances

From "Native Speaker/nonnative speaker conversation and the negotiation of comprehensible input," by M. H. Long. 1983. *Applied Linguistics* Vol. 4, N° 2 (pp. 126-141) Copyright © 1983 by Oxford University Press. Excerpt from p. 132. Reprinted by permission of Oxford University Press

Strategies. S1: Relinquish topic-control. According to Long (1983a: 132), "native speakers will often attempt to pass control of current and subsequent conversational topics to the nonnative speaker." This suggests that the NS is willing to talk about whatever topic the NNS feels comfortable with, which apparently may explain the occurrence of the so-called 'or-choice' questions (cf. Hatch 1978). Hatch observes that 'or-choice' questions provide the NNS with a series of potential topics to talk about; furthermore, they often function to suggest possible answers to the questions s/he asked. As Long (1983a: 132-3) notes, "[o]f course, native speakers use or-choice questions, too (and, at times, all the devices discussed here), when talking to other native speakers. Their use in NS-NNS conversation seems to be much more frequent, however."

S2: Select salient topics. Despite native speakers' use of S1 when interacting with a nonnative speaker, there is a tendency for them to select most topics, because the nonnative speaker's linguistic proficiency is often so limited that s/he cannot initiate topics. By S2, Long (1983a: 133) means to imply that "[n]ative speakers try to avoid introducing difficult topics by talking about the nonnative speaker him- or herself, or about whatever seems to interest him or her whenever possible." Such topics encourage the NNS's participation, as they suggest that s/he has interesting information to communicate. Via S2, NSs also tend to be more oriented to the 'now' of the 'here and now' principle, as in caretaker-child interaction (Cross 1977). Long (1980, 1981a) found out that the 'now' orientation (measured through the frequency of verbs marked temporally for present and non-present) was higher in the NS-NNS conversation than in NS-NS conversation.

S3: Treat topics briefly. Arthur et al. (1980) and Long (1981a) found out that brief treatment of topics is a common characteristic of NS-NNS talk. Likewise, Long (1983a) maintains that NS-NNS conversations tend to treat briefly a large number of topics rather than a small number in more detail. "The idea seems to be to lighten the non-native speaker's conversational burden by eliciting a simple confirmation or denial of a proposition" (Long 1983a: 133). This results in discourse where question/answer sequences prevail rather than statements functioning as reacting moves which are more characteristic of NS-NS conversation.

S4: Make new topics salient. To render new topics salient for the NNS, NSs make use of several devices. For example, to indicate closure of one topic and introduction of a new one, the NS makes use of conversational frames, such as OK, So, Well, Now, etc. Saliency in introducing new topics is also achieved by moving topics to the front or end of utterances, using a slow pace, and stressing key words. Yet, according to Long (1983a: 135), "[p]erhaps the most noticeable effort to make topics salient is the use of questions to encode topic-nominating moves." One final device for achieving saliency is what Long (1983a) calls 'decomposition' which serves as strategy and tactic. Consider the following examples quoted from Long (1983a: 136):

(a) NS   : Uh what does uh what does your father do in uh you're
             from Kyoto, right?
     NNS : Yeah
     NS   : Yeah. What does your father do in Kyoto?

(b) NS   : When do you go to the uh Santa Monica? . . . You say
             you go fishing in Santa Monica, right?
     NNS : Yeah
     NS   : When?

In (a) and (b), the NS's aim is to make the NNS comment on a new topic. When this task proves or as in (b) is believed likely to prove too difficult, the task is broken down (decomposed) into two parts. First, the topic is established by its repetition in isolation from the request for commentary, often with a rising intonation and a tag (right?) asking for confirmation that the topic has been established. Then, if the requested confirmation follows, the request for commentary is restated. In (a), decomposition is functioning as a strategy, in other words, to avoid a conversational trouble. In (b) decomposition serves as a tactic, in other words, to repair a conversational trouble, since the NS's first question did not get any response. Long (1983a: 136) argues that

> [d]ecomposition is clearly a more complex device, whether used as
> a strategy or as a tactic, than others we have discussed. It has not
> occurred as frequently as others in data analyzed so far, and seems
> to be confined to non-native speakers with considerable prior
> foreigner talk experience when it does occur.

S5: Check nonnative speaker's comprehension. Comprehension checks, such as Right? OK? and Do you understand? saliently indicate the NNS's attempt to avoid conversational trouble. "They are used significantly more frequently with nonnative speakers than in NS-NS conversation" (Long 1983a: 136).

Tactics. T1: Accept unintentional topic switch. When a communication breakdown arises because the NS does not succeed in establishing a new topic, the NS may abandon the topic altogether. The following example (quoted from Long 1983a: 136) illustrates such a tactic

    NS   : Are you going to visit San Francisco? Or Las Vegas?
    NNS: Yes I went to Disneyland and Knottsberry Farm
    NS   : Oh yeah?

In the above example, the NNS misunderstands the question as one concerning her previous sightseeing visits. The NS repairs the discourse by treating the inappropriate response as a topic nomination. According to Long (1983a), NSs do not seem to use this tactic very frequently. Apparently it is used by NSs with great previous foreigner talk experience. Further, as can be clearly seen, T1 is linked with S1 (relinquish topic control) and T4 (tolerate ambiguity).

T2: Request clarification. Clarification requests refer to any NS utterance which aims at eliciting clarification of the interlocutor's foregoing utterance(s); "they require that the interlocutor either furnish new information or recode information previously given" (Long 1983a: 137). Clarification requests, Long (1980) found, were significantly more frequent in NS-NNS than in NS-NS conversation.

T3: Confirm own comprehension. Confirmation checks refer to any NS utterance, occurring immediately after an utterance by the interlocutor, and aiming at eliciting "confirmation that the utterance has been correctly heard or understood by the speaker" (Long 1983a: 137). They always involve repetition of all or part of the interlocutor's preceding utterance; they are answerable by a simple confirmation (e.g., Yes, Mmhm) and require no new information from the interlocutor. Like clarification requests, confirmation checks were found (Long 1980) to be more frequent in NS-NNS than in NS-NS conversation.

T4: Tolerate ambiguity. Due to their limited proficiency in the target language, NNSs may produce ambiguous utterances. Via T4, the NSs tolerate ambiguity in order to sustain conversation. Accepting an unintentional topic-switch, Long (1983a) holds, is an extreme example of this tactic. It is noteworthy that

> [w]hile impressionistically pervasive in NS-NNS conversation, T4 is difficult, if not impossible to qualify, for ambiguity clearly exists in all conversation, and varies in degree according, among other factors, to the amount of common knowledge shared by speakers (Long 1983a: 137).

Strategies and Tactics. ST1-ST4. These have already been considered with respect to their function as strategies. As tactics, they function in the same way except that they occur after a communication breakdown.

ST5: Repeat own utterances. As defined in Long (1980), self repetitions "include partial or complete, and exact or semantic repetition (i.e., paraphrase) of any of the speaker's utterances which occurred within five conversational turns (by both speakers) of the turn containing the repetition" (Long 1983a: 138). Self repetitions, as illustrated in Long (1980, 1983a), are pervasive in NS-NNS conversation; they occur in NS speech significantly more often in NS-NNS interaction than in NS-NS interaction.

ST6: Repeat other's utterances. Long (1980) defined other repetitions in the same way as self-repetitions, except for the obvious difference as to which speaker's utterances were involved. Again other repetitions were found to occur significantly more often in NS-NNS than in NS-NS interaction.

The fifteen interactional modification devices depicted above are some of the interactional resources available to NSs in their interaction with NNSs. They aim at negotiating comprehensibility, since "without them communication, conversation breaks down; with their use conversation is possible and is sustained. Nonnative speakers understand and so can take part appropriately" (Long 1983a: 138). These negotiation routines enable the SL acquirer to receive comprehensible input which is, no doubt, an essential factor in promoting SL acquisition.

Historically, the opportunities for learners to engage in negotiated interaction with their interlocutors, bringing about modifications and adjustments of the interaction by both interlocutors was only available to NNSs interacting with NSs outside instructional contexts. However, these opportunities have become also available in the L2 classroom context through interactive pedagogical techniques such as conversation games, role plays and simulations (cf. Brumfit & Johnson 1979, Johnson & Morrow 1981, Brumfit 1984).

The strategies and tactics reviewed above show only what NSs do to avoid or repair trouble in their interaction with NNSs. Another area of relevance for the present study is the analysis of what NNSs, themselves, do to avoid or repair trouble when they attempt to use their second language for conversation, that is to say, the analysis of what has been called 'communication strategies' (Tarone 1980, Faerch & Kasper 1980, 1984, Bialystok 1990). Research on 'communication strategies' attempts to shed light on how L2 learners are able to use their interlanguage in such a way as to transcend its limitations. Actually, as Tarone (1980: 427) points out, "the research on communication strategies, foreigner talk, and repair in interlanguage has, in many cases, focused on the same phenomenon in communication."

L2 Learner Communication Strategies
"Communicating is a problem-solving activity and one which requires skilful planning and choice on the part of the speaker" (Bialystok 1990: 12). How do L2 learners manage to communicate when they have limited command of the target language? Systematic study of this problem has started in the 70s (e.g.,

Varadi 1973, Tarone 1977, Faerch & Kasper 1983, 1984, Bialystok 1990) and includes research on *communication strategies* which is a sub-area of research on second language acquisition. As Bialystok (1990: 1) notes,

> [t]he familiar ease and fluency with which we sail from one idea to the next in our first language is constantly shattered by some gap in our knowledge of a second language. The gap can take many forms - a word, a structure, a phrase, a tense marker, an idiom. Our attempts to overcome these gaps have been called *communication strategies*.

Understanding these communication strategies adds in part to our knowledge of linguistic structure and L2 learners' psychological processing; it also contributes significantly to the practical business of L2 language teaching. Thus, a clear definition of what constitutes a communication strategy is in order. The following definitions (cited in Bialystok 1990: 3) have been proposed:

> a systematic technique employed by a speaker to express his meaning when faced with some difficulty (Corder 1977);

> a mutual attempt of two interlocutors to agree on a meaning in situations where requisite meaning structures are not shared (Tarone 1980);

> Potentially conscious plans for solving what to an individual presents itself as a problem in reaching a particular communicative goal (Faerch & Kasper 1983a);

> techniques for coping with difficulties in communicating in an imperfectly known second language (Stern 1983).

As pointed out by Bialystok (1990), although the above definitions diverge on certain features, they converge on three features, namely *problemacity, consciousness*, and *intentionality*. As the above definitions suggest, problemacity is perhaps the most basic feature of a communication strategy. The idea behind problemacity is that communication strategies are used when a speaker perceives that there is a problem which may cause a breakdown in communication. However, as Bialystok (1990: 4) argues

> it is not clear that problemacity accurately delineates the domain of second language communication strategies. [...]. To claim that problemacity is not criterial to a definition is to assert that this feature is not *defining* of communication strategies. Communication strategies can occur in the absence of problemacity.

Consciousness, which is implicit in most of the definitions proposed for communication strategies, suggests that these strategies are conscious events of language use. However, as Bialystok (1990: 4) contends,

> it is not self-evident that speakers are indeed aware that their utterances constitute strategic uses of language. Communication always involves choice, and the choices evident when a strategy has been used may have been made no more or less consciously than any other choice.[...]. In communicative contexts, these choices serve strategic purposes and perhaps avoid potential misunderstanding by the listener. The choices, however, may be made entirely without the conscious consideration of the speaker.

Intentionality implies that the learner has control over a repertoire of strategies from which he may select particular ones and deliberately make use of them. Such intentionality presumes consciousness which as has been argued above presents certain limitations. According to Bialystok (1990: 5), "the intentionality of communication strategies is questionable."

In short, the above definitions of a communication strategy are unprecise because of the ambiguities inherent in the three identifying features implicated in these definitions. Actually,

> the concept of second language communication strategy, as traditionally used in the field, cannot be defined exclusively by reference to its unique features.[...], communication strategies are continuous with 'ordinary' language processing and cannot be severed from it by virtue of distinctive features (Bialystok 1990: 5).

It has been argued that use of communication strategies is profitable for second language learners. Wong-Fillmore (1979) directly advises L2 learners to use communication strategies: 'Make the most of what you've got' (Wong-Fillmore 1979: Chapter 4). The assumption implied in such a recommendation is that communication can proceed from an incomplete linguistic system, and that learners' efforts at using communication strategies are beneficial to them in their acquisition process. Similarly, Stern (1983: 411) argues that it is good language learners who "will tend to develop and use communication strategies." By utilizing communication strategies, L2 learners overcome obstacles to communication thanks to their use of an alternative form of expression to convey the intended meaning. However, it is important to note that

> [i]n the process of creating these strategies, considerable compromise to the meaning initially intended may occur. Most descriptions of the changes inflicted on meaning document the

extent to which portions of the ideal message have had to be avoided, deleted, or altered (Bialystok 1990: 35).

Tarone (1981: 288) suggests that the following criteria characterize a communication strategy:

1. a speaker desires to communicate meaning x to listener;
2. the speaker believes the linguistic or sociolinguistic structure desired to communicate meaning x is unavailable or is not shared with the listener; thus
3. the speaker chooses to
   (a) avoid - not attempt to communicate meaning x - or
   (b) attempt alternate means to communicate meaning x. The speaker stops trying alternatives when it seems clear that there is shared meaning.

Most attempts to describe communication strategies have been presented as taxonomies. One of the earliest taxonomies of communication strategies and which is typical of later taxonomies (such as Varadi 1980, Bialystok & Frohlich 1980, Bialystok 1983, Corder 1983, Faerch & Kasper 1983a, Paribakht 1985) is that of Tarone (1977). This taxonomy is reported below.

---

1. *Avoidance*
   a. Topic avoidance
   b. Message abandonment
2. *Paraphrase*
   a. Approximation
   b. Word coinage
   c. Circumlocution
3. *Conscious transfer*
   a. Literal translation
   b. language switch
4. *Appeal for assistance*
5. *Mime*

Figure 1: Taxonomy of Tarone's conscious communication strategies.
From "Conscious communication strategies in interlanguage," by E. Tarone. 1977. In H. D. Brown, C. A. Yorio, and R. C. Crymes (eds), *On TESOL '77, Teaching and Learning English as a Second Language: Trends in Research and Practice* (pp. 194-203) Copyright © 1977 by Teachers of English to Speakers of Other Languages, Inc. Excerpt from p. 197 used with permission.

Each of the five major categories of Tarone's (1977) taxonomy reflects, as explained below, a different way of how an L2 learner may attempt to solve the communication problem. The fourth and fifth strategies (i.e., appeal for assistance and mime) are rare in the data reported in literature on communication strategies (cf. Tarone 1977, Varadi 1980, Bialystok & Frohlich 1980, Bialystok 1983, Faerch & Kasper 1983a, Bialystok 1990).

Avoidance. Learners sometimes refrain from speaking because they expect communication problems to arise. "This avoidance is a common strategy for second language learners, causing them to remain silent when they would otherwise contribute to a conversation simply because some aspect of vocabulary or grammar is not known" (Bialystok 1990: 40). Tarone (1977) distinguishes between two subcategories of avoidance: *topic avoidance* and *message abandonment*. For the former, learners manage to prevent the occurrence of topics which they believe will present difficulties. For the latter, the learner stumbles into a topic that is too difficult for her/him, starts to talk but is unable to continue; so s/he gives up stopping in mid-utterance. As Bialystok (1990) observes, though avoidance is one way through which learners assure that communication continues, "restricting conversation to those topics that are well controlled linguistically is an ineffective way to communicate or to improve competence with the language" (Bialystok 1990: 40).

Paraphrase. Tarone (1977: 198) defines paraphrase as "the rewording of the message in an alternate, acceptable target language construction, in situations where the appropriate form or construction is not known or not yet stable." Within this category, she distinguishes between three types of paraphrase strategies: *approximation, word coinage* and *circumlocution.* Approximation is "the use of a single target language vocabulary item or structure, which the learner knows is not correct, but which shares enough semantic features in common with the desired item to satisfy the learner" (Tarone 1977: 198). By word coinage, "the learner makes up a new word in order to communicate a desired concept" (Tarone 1977: 198), as when a learner creates the word airball to refer to balloon. The final paraphrase strategy, circumlocution "is a wordly extended process in which the learner describes the characteristics or elements of the object or action instead of using the appropriate target language structure" (Tarone 1977: 198). To illustrate this, Tarone gives the example of a learner attempting to refer to waterpipe: "She is, uh, smoking something. I don't know what its name. That's uh, Persian, and we use in Turkey, a lot of" (Tarone 1977: 198).

Conscious transfer. This strategy can be manifested either as *literal translation* or as *language switch.* In literal translation, the learner translates word for word from the native language. For example, a Mandarin speaker produced: "He invites him to drink" when he intended to say "They toast one another" (Tarone 1977: 198). Language switch, on the other hand, is the straightforward insertion of words from the learner's native language. In her work of 1981, which is an extension of her work of 1977, Tarone changes the name of this strategy from *conscious transfer* to *borrowing.*

Appeal for assistance. This is a strategy whereby the learner consults a source of authority (a native speaker, a dictionary, etc.) to get the correct term.

Mime. When the learner lacks a target language word, s/he may use nonverbal strategies in place of a lexical item. Tarone (1977) gives the example of clapping one's hands to indicate applause.

Tarone's (1977) taxonomy "has proven robust and complete - subsequent taxonomies can invariably be traced to her original categories, and data collected by different researchers for different purposes has confirmed the logic and utility of her distinctions" (Bialystok 1990: 57). However, as Bialystok's (1990) study has revealed, the exercise of classifying utterances into Tarone's (1977) taxonomic categories presents some problems, such as the problem of embeddedness, due to "the conflation of different strategies into a single strategic utterance" (Bialystok 1990: 70), and the problem caused by the ambiguity inherent in each of Tarone's (1977) definitions (For further discussion of these issues, see Bialystok 1990: 69-75).

> [T]he criteria for assigning an utterance to a specific strategic category are sometimes vague, sometimes arbitrary, and sometimes irrelevant. [...]. These vagaries of classification directly challenge the reliability of the taxonomies and limit their potential for forming the basis for explanations of communication strategies (Bialystok 1990: 75).

Furthermore, as Bialystok (1990) argues, classifying an utterance into a taxonomic category depends in part upon the listener's response and in part upon the speaker's willingness or desire to communicate more information. This is a point to which Tarone (1980: 420) was very sensitive, as she regards communication strategies as "tools used in a joint negotiation of meaning, in situations where both interlocutors are attempting to agree as to a communicative goal." This negotiation, however, is not formalized in the definitions of the strategies. Tarone (1981) herself acknowledges this limitation. She notes that it is unfortunate that the *interactional function* of communication strategies has been overlooked both in her own research (Tarone 1977) and in that of others. The function of communication strategies, she contends, "seems to be primarily to negotiate an agreement on meaning between two interlocutors" (Tarone 1981: 288) (see Tarone 1980 for a discussion of the relationship among communication strategies, repair, and foreigner talk).

To conclude, it appears that target language learners using a limited linguistic system have at their disposal a finite number of communication strategies which they may resort to to solve communication problems. Various studies have shown that certain L2 learners succeed more efficiently than others in solving such problems. The ability to solve problems of this type may be an aspect of a person's strategic competence which, according to Canale & Swain (1980), is part of communicative competence. Strategic competence, to quote Swain (1984: 189) is "the mastery of communication strategies that may be called into action either to enhance the effectiveness of communication or to compensate for breakdowns in communication."

Repair: A Process of Negotiation

In this section, we take a brief look at an area of NNS discourse (NS-NNS, NNS-NNS, and L2 classroom discourse), namely 'dealing with problems of language use', or in Schegloff et al.'s (1977) terms, 'repair'. Two studies are reviewed: Van Lier (1988) which focuses on the organization of repair in second language classrooms, and Gass & Varonis (1989) which deals with incorporated repair in NNS speech.

As maintained by Schegloff et al. (1977), Day et al. (1984), and Van Lier (1988), repair is much broader than the mere correction of errors. Repair is the generic term and correction is one type of repair. In this sense, repair can be defined as the treatment of trouble occurring in interactive language use. Repair is probably a crucial variable in language learning; although it is not a sufficient condition, it may safely be assumed that it is a necessary condition (Van Lier 1988). Accordingly, it is important to find out how trouble is repaired in NNS discourse, because, to quote Van Lier (1988: 182), it is "a precursor to finding out how repairing may assist L2 development."

As Van Lier (1988) points out, an ethnographic approach to the issue of repair indicates that it is not simply a matter of learners committing errors and NSs or teachers correcting them. It is rather a matter of continuous adjustment between interlocutors who have to use a code which gives them problems. "This adjustment-in-interaction may be crucial to language development, for it leads to noticing discrepancies between what is said and what is heard, and to a resolution of these discrepancies" (Van Lier 1988: 180). To capture the relationship between adjustment and repair, Van Lier (1988: 186) presents an interesting argument:

> Given that adjustment in general is essential for communication to occur (it can be regarded as the nerve system of talk), repair is in a sense a mechanism to correct for imperfect adjustment. In other words, the better we are at adjusting, the less we are likely to have to rely on repair. In this sense, repair, in the context of not-yet-competent interactants, is a stop-gap procedure to compensate for lack of ability to adjust appropriately.

It is a fact that inside the classroom, the teacher has the automatic right to repair students' repairable contributions whereas in NS-NS conversation outside the classroom, no participant has got such a right (except in caretaker-child communication). Repair does occur outside the classroom; but it is done tactfully and with deference because as Schegloff et al. (1977) have found there is a preference for self-repair; that is to say, before being corrected, speakers are given a chance to self-correct. Comparing repair in natural conversation and in L2 classrooms, Van Lier (1988) observes that repair in the first setting is a 'face-threatening act' (Brown & Levinson 1978); thus, it is usually mitigated by implying that it results from mishearing or misunderstanding; moreover, it is usually postponed till the speaker has completed her/his turn, to give her/him a chance to self-repair (see Schegloff et al. 1977). However, in the L2 classroom the situation is different: more problems needing repair occur; the pedagogical orientation of talk justifies overt correction; and the learners are not ordinary people communicating but members of the classroom community which has its own rules as to what is appropriate and what constitutes face-threat. Therefore, it would be unrealistic to expect the same rules and procedures that apply in natural conversation. Nevertheless, this creates a paradox in the classroom.

> This paradox is that, in order to become a competent member of a speech community, one must participate in the affairs of that community. Also, in order to develop communicative competence one must learn to use the language code [...] in the way that people making everyday conversation use it. This crucially involves letting speakers do their own monitoring and repairing, rather than doing it for them (Van Lier 1988: 184).

Van Lier (1988) found that self-repair does occur in L2 classrooms but that other-repair is particularly frequent. This leads him to inquire about whether other-repair replaces or interferes with self-repair in the L2 classroom and whether this is detrimental to the learners' interlanguage development. However, he confesses that his research could not achieve a conclusive answer.

In Van Lier's (1988) data other-repair can occur while the trouble-source turn is in progress or in the next turn. Thus, a distinction has been made between 'same-turn other-repair' and 'next-turn other-repair'. Van Lier (1988) regards the former category as didactic, or classroom specific, on the basis of Schegloff et al.'s (1977) assertion that this category does not occur in conversation. Furthermore, on the basis of Mchoul's (1990) finding that this category is also absent in L1 classrooms, Van Lier (1988) concludes that it may be an L2 specific way of repairing.

Interestingly, Van Lier (1988) claims that certain types of other-repair need to be done in the next turn following the trouble source, while others need to be done within the same turn as the trouble source. 'Next-turn other-repair' is generally related to content and is due to problems of hearing or understanding the talk; whereas, 'same-turn other-repair' aims at 'helping out' the student with speaking problems; therefore, it does not wait the turn to end but occurs immediately after the trouble spot. This type of repair, as Van Lier (1988: 211) argues, "may deny the speaker the opportunity to do self-repair, probably an important learning activity." Therefore, in accordance with the notion of *wait time* which implies delayed evaluation, and which was proposed by Holley & King (1971) and Fanselow (1977b), Van Lier (1988: 211) suggests that

> [s]ome delay of other-repair (both initiation and error-replacement) may be beneficial, since it would promote the development of self-monitoring and pragmatic adjustment which is essential to competence in the target language (and to socialization in general, as Schegloff et al. point out).

Another recent study of repair in NNS discourse is that of Gass & Varonis (1989) who explore NNS-NNS interaction, focusing precisely on incorporated repair in NNS speech. Data from 10 NNS-NNS dyads were examined. Each dyad took part in two tasks: free conversation and a picture description task. The findings reveal that not only do learners repair deviant forms in the speech of their interlocutors (other learners) but that "as a result of these repairs, the "repaired" learners incorporate standard language forms into their own speech. The corrected forms may appear immediately or after considerable delay" (Gass & Varonis 1989: 75). As the examples below illustrate, after a significant amount of negotiation, repaired learners were able to make phonetic, syntactic and lexical modifications in their output. Another source of modification in Gass & Varonis' (1989) data stems from 'incorrections'.

Phonetic modification. In the example below, Chinatsu attempts to say 'dog' but comes up with something like the English word 'duck'. After some negotiation, Yoko understands what Chinatsu means and provides an implicit repair "what kind of dog?" Interestingly, eight turns later Chinatsu uses the word again, but this time pronouncing it correctly: "the dog wear s- some clothe."

>   Chinatsu : ...woman has a [dək]
>   Yoko   : duck? (surprised)
>   Chinatsu : [dɔk]
>   Yoko   : [dɔk] ah, I see-
>   Chinatsu : a [dək]
>   Yoko   : What kind of dog?
>   (eight turns)
>   Chinatsu : The dog wear s- some clothe ...
>   (Gass & Varonis 1989: 78).

Syntactic modification. In the datum below, syntactic incorporation results from negotiation. Tomoko self-corrects, thereby providing an appropriate model for Toshi who incorporates the repaired form in his next turn.

>   Toshi   : He stands up? He stands, you mean? He stands up?
>   Tomoko   : He stand. He is standing and-
>   Toshi   : He's standing
>   (Gass & Varonis 1989: 79).

Lexical modification. In the example below, Hiroko incorrectly uses the preposition 'to' after the verb 'bark'. Izumi interrupts and provides a repair: "at", correcting the preposition. Hiroko incorporates this repair in her turn as she proceeds her utterance: 'at the woman'.

>   Hiroko   : Ah, the dog is barking to-
>   Izumi   : at
>   Hiroko   : at the woman
>   (Gass & Varonis 1989: 80).

Incorrections. Another source of modification in Gass & Varonis' (1989) data comes from 'incorrections', in which one of the NNSs provided an incorrect repair. Though there were only four instances of incorrections, it is important to note that in all these cases, the NNSs did not incorporate the incorrect repair into their own speech but on the contrary maintained the form they had originally used. Consider the example below:

>   Hiroko : A man is drinking c- coffee or tea uh with uh the saucer
>   of uh uh coffee set is uh in his uh knee.

Izumi   : in *him* knee
Hiroko : uh on *his* knee
Izumi   : yeah
Hiroko : on *his* knee
Izumi   : so sorry. On *his* knee
        (Gass & Varonis 1989: 81).

Izumi provides an incorrect repair "in him knee." Interestingly, in the next turn, Hiroko maintains the original form, but changes the preposition from the incorrect form 'in' to the correct one 'on'. As Gass & Varonis (1989: 81) point out "it may be that Izumi's first response forced Hiroko to focus on the form of the utterance, thus triggering the resulting modification." The negotiation comes to an end with both NNSs agreeing on the correct form: 'on his knee'.

Gass & Varonis (1989) found that the large majority of the repairs that occur and the incorporations that are made in learners' speech are in the direction of the target language. These findings, they argue,

> are important for at least two reasons. First, they provide evidence for the direct positive effect of conversational interaction on second language acquisition, even between two NNSs of a language. Second, they provide evidence for the way learners internalize second language knowledge (Gass & Varonis 1989: 81-82).

Gass & Varonis' (1989) findings concerning the first issue (i.e., the direct positive effect of conversational interaction on SLA) sustain those of Long (1980) and Varonis & Gass (1985a, 1985b) that tasks requiring the negotiation of meaning optimize the opportunities for target language acquisition. As for the second issue (i.e., that of learner's internalization of knowledge), the study offers some evidence that "different parts of learners' grammars are more or less susceptible to external influence" (Gass & Varonis 1989: 82). Susceptibility, Gass & Varonis (1989: 82) suggest, "is determined by the strength of knowledge which learners have over given forms." Swain (1985) reports an immersion student saying "I can hear it in my head how I should sound when I talk; but it never comes out that way." In a similar vein, many L2 learners report dreams where their L2 mastery is far better than it is when they are awake. These examples are in line with a position which purports that

> strength of knowledge representation may in part determine what output will result, the means by which output takes place, and what changes in a learner's grammar will take place. In other words, there are limitations on the translation of knowledge into output, since it is possible to have a target in mind, but not necessarily have a plan available to implement it (Gass & Varonis 1989: 83).

A methodological limitation of Gass & Varonis' (1989) study, as they themselves point out, concerns the lack of an adequate means of measuring interlanguage destabilization (as a result of repair) and of determining whether the modifications observed in such examples as those cited above are long term or only temporary. Gass & Varonis (1989) rightly argue that despite this limitation, it is premature to argue that repair (or corrective feedback) is of little value in acquisition.

The Comprehensible Output Hypothesis

On the basis of her years of research with French immersion programmes in Canada, Swain (1985) has offered an interesting hypothesis, namely the 'comprehensible output hypothesis' which claims that L2 development results from learners producing the target language more frequently, more accurately, and in a wider variety of circumstances. This hypothesis follows the rather traditional assumption that acquisition of a skill results from productive practice of the skill. Smith (1978, 1982) has asserted that one learns to read by reading, and to write by writing. Similarly, Swain (1985: 248) argues that "one learns to speak by speaking." It is noteworthy that Ellis (1980) has already argued in favour of this view. Yet, its most recent expression lies in Swain's (1985) 'comprehensible output hypothesis'.

Swain (1985) challenges the by then familiar notion of the importance of comprehensible input by suggesting that what is needed is comprehensible output rather than comprehensible input. She feels that while comprehensible input may be sufficient for acquiring semantic competence in the target language, comprehensible output is of crucial importance in order for learners to attain grammatical competence. In other words, if learners are to acquire grammatical competence in the target language, they must struggle with producing output that is comprehensible to their interlocutors.

Swain (1985) compared the proficiency of grade 6 French as a second language immersion students with 10 grade 6 native French speakers, in Ontario and Quebec, respectively. The L2 learners had had seven years of French immersion experience, that is to say, with their instruction being mostly in French from kinder-garten through grade 6. The theoretical framework within which the study was undertaken includes as traits several components of communicative competence put forward by Canale & Swain (1980b), namely grammatical, sociolinguistic, and discourse. Furthermore, it includes as methods oral- and literacy-based tasks.

The first trait measured, namely grammatical competence, was operationalized as "rules of morphology and syntax, with a major focus on verbs and prepositions" (Swain 1985: 237). The results revealed that "the native speakers score significantly higher (p<.01) than the immersion students, indicating clearly that, although the immersion students are doing quite well, they have not acquired nativelike abilities in the grammatical domain" (Swain 1985: 238).

The second trait measured, namely discourse competence, was defined as "the ability to produce and recognize coherent and cohesive text" (Swain 1985: 238). The results revealed, though nonsignificantly, that "native speakers generally perform better than the immersion students on the oral story retelling task but do not differ in their performance on the written production tasks" (Swain 1985: 241).

The third trait measured, namely sociolinguistic competence was defined as "the ability to produce and recognize socially appropriate language within a given sociocultural context" (Swain 1985: 242). The results suggest that on the whole, native speakers rate significantly higher than the immersion students on the sociolinguistic tasks. Interestingly the only discernible pattern in the results, besides the use of *vous* as a polite form of address,

> is that in those categories of sociolinguistic performance where formulaic politeness terms are possible, immersion students tend to perform as well as native speakers, whereas in those categories where grammatical knowledge inevitably plays a role in the production of the appropriate form, immersion students' performance is inferior to that of native speakers (Swain 1985: 244).

This result, Swain (1985) argues, is not particularly surprising in light of the grammatical results reviewed earlier, which provides evidence for the dependence of some aspects of sociolinguistic performance on grammatical knowledge .

In line with results of a previous study by Lapkin, Swain & Cummins (1983), the picture emerging from the results of Swain's (1985) study is one of a group of L2 learners who, despite having reached, in some respects, a high proficiency level, are still very far from nativelike proficiency with respect to some aspects of the language. "This appears to be particularly evident in those aspects of communicative performance which demand the use of grammatical knowledge" (Swain 1985: 245).

The results presented above seem to challenge the hypothesis that comprehensible input is the only causal variable in SLA, since the immersion students in Swain's (1985) study had actually been receiving comprehensible input in the target language for a period of almost 7 years. Studies such as Swain & Lapkin (1982) and Swain et al. (1981) reveal that the input immersion students in Canada receive is in fact comprehensible. Yet, as Swain's study evidences, "after 7 years of this comprehensible input, the target system has not been fully acquired" (Swain 1985: 245).

As has been pointed out previously, and as will further be elaborated on in following sections, many researchers (Long 1980, 1983a, 1983b, Varonis & Gass 1985b, and others) have put forward the hypothesis that it is not comprehensible input *per se* that is the key factor in second language acquisition but comprehensible input that results from interaction where meaning is negotiated. Swain (1985: 247) argues that "[i]f this is the case, then, we may have part of the explanation for the immersion students' less than nativelike linguistic performance."

In the context of an immersion class, as in any other type of classroom, the teachers talk and the students listen. Thus, relatively few exchanges are motivated by a two-way flow of information where both teacher and student enter the exchanges as conversational equals. In this connection, Swain (1985: 247) contends that

> [i]mmersion students, then, have - relative to "street learners" of the target language - little opportunity to engage in two-way, negotiated meaning exchanges in the classroom. Under these circumstances, the interaction input hypothesis would predict that second language acquisition would be limited. This prediction is consistent with the immersion students' performance if it is confined to grammatical acquisition. Confining this prediction to grammatical acquisition is compatible with what appears to be an assumption underlying the input interaction hypothesis - that second language acquisition is equivalent to grammatical acquisition [...], however, we consider second language acquisition to be more than grammatical acquisition, and to include at least the acquisition of discourse and sociolinguistic competence as well, in both oral and written modes. From this perspective, the relative paucity of two-way, meaning-negotiated exchanges does not appear to have impeded the acquisition of discourse competence.

On the basis of these considerations, Swain (1985) questions the adequacy of the interaction input hypothesis (Long 1980, 1983a, 1983b) particularly with respect to (1) the assumption that it is the exchanges, themselves, in which meaning is negotiated that are facilitative to grammatical acquisition as a result of comprehensible input, and (2) the assumption that the key facilitator is input rather than output. She argues that the first assumption implies that a learner can attend to meaning and form at the same time. According to her, this seems unlikely, since the learner cannot attend to the form of the message being conveyed unless its content is comprehended. In other words, it would seem that negotiating meaning [...] is a necessary first step to grammatical acquisition. It paves the way for future exchanges, where, because the message is understood, the learner is free to pay attention to form. Thus, comprehensible input is crucial to grammatical acquisition, *not* because the focus is on meaning, *or* because a two-way exchange is occurring, but because by being understood [...] it permits the learner to focus on form. But this would appear to be the sort of comprehensible input that immersion students do, in large part, receive (Swain 1985: 248).

What then is missing? Swain suggests that what is missing is output. According to Krashen (1981b), the only role of output is that of generating comprehensible input. Yet, for Swain, in second language acquisition, output has other roles that are independent of comprehensible input. For instance, one of its functions is that it provides the opportunity for meaningful use of one's linguistic resources. One learns to speak by speaking, and

one-to-one conversational exchanges provide an excellent opportunity for this to occur. Even better, though, are those interactions where there has been a communicative breakdown - where the learner has received some negative input - and the learner is pushed to use alternate means to get across his or her message (Swain 1985: 248).

Negative input (cf. Schachter 1984) is feedback provided to the learner to let her/him know that there is something wrong with her/his output. Negative input encompasses explicit corrections, confirmation checks, clarification requests, etc., and functions to incite the learner to revise her/his output in some way because the current message has not been comprehended. Yet, for learners to achieve nativelike competence, Swain (1985: 248) suggests that

the meaning of "negotiating meaning" needs to be extended beyond the usual sense of simply "getting the message across." Simply getting one's message across can and does occur with grammatically deviant forms and sociolinguistically inappropriate language. Negotiating meaning needs to incorporate the notion of being pushed towards the delivery of a message that is not only conveyed, but that is conveyed precisely, coherently, and appropriately. Being "pushed" in output, it seems to me, is a concept parallel to that of the i+1 of comprehensible input. Indeed, one might call this the "comprehensible output" hypothesis.

Besides "contextualized" and "pushed" language use, Swain (1985) reports two other additional functions of output in second language acquisition. The first one is that, as suggested by Schachter (1984), it provides learners the opportunity to test their hypotheses about the language, or as Swain (1985: 249) puts it, "to try out means of expression and see if they work." The second function is that actually using the language, as opposed to simply comprehending it, "may force the learner to move from semantic processing to syntactic processing" (Swain 1985: 249), since as Krashen (1982a: 66) has pointed out, "[i]n many cases, we do not utilize syntax in understanding - we often get the message with a combination of vocabulary, or lexical information plus extra-linguistic information." However, in production, the learner must impose some syntactic structure on her/his utterances. The idea that input may be comprehended without a syntactic analysis of that input could account for the phenomenon of understanding a language and yet not being able to produce it.

In short, the argument put forward by Swain (1985: 249) is that immersion students do not achieve nativelike productive competence "*not* because their comprehensible input is limited but because their comprehensible output is limited." On the one hand, the students are simply not provided with adequate opportunities to use the target language in the classroom. On the other hand, "they are not being "pushed" in their output" (Swain 1985: 249); put otherwise, in later grades, they no longer receive what Schachter (1984) calls 'negative input' though they actually continue to receive comprehensible input.

It is noteworthy that the written production, evaluated on the basis of discourse performance, is the only task in which the performance of immersion students was mostly similar to that of native speakers. Swain (1985) attributes such a finding to the fact that all students (natives and nonnatives) have had a great amount of practice in writing tasks, in school: "That immersion students do as well as native speakers may reflect, then, their comprehensible output in this domain of language use" (Swain 1985: 250).

Studies by Naiman et al. (1978), Strong (1983) and Peck (1985) provide evidence that more production and more correct production goes hand in hand with target language proficiency. This may give support to Swain's (1985) comprehensible output hypothesis; however, as pointed out by Chaudron (1988: 99), "these studies demonstrate a correlation rather than causation." A more direct causal relationship is examined in studies such as Johnson (1983), Saville-Troike (1984), Chesterfield et al. (1983) and Ramirez & Stromquist (1979). Nonetheless, as Chaudron (1988: 170) notes, these studies had "rather weak findings" which "probably do not indicate the true relationships but rather reflect inadequate research on the topic." On the same wavelength, Allwright & Bailey (1991: 149) note that research has not yet revealed

> how and to what extent learners' observable participation is related
> to their success in mastering the target language . [...], the research
> results so far are very mixed. There are theoretical and practical

reasons for expecting learner participation to be productive, but no really compelling evidence that it actually is.

Allwright & Bailey (1991) hypothesize along with VanPatten (1987) that, perhaps, it is the learners' level of L2 proficiency which should, partly, determine the extent to which they should be expected to contribute verbally to classroom discourse. They further point out that 'invisible' participation, or in Schumann's (1980) words 'eavesdropping' may be just as important, at least for some learners, as observable participation and production. Hence, Allwright & Bailey (1991: 149-50) conclude that

> we should not be too determined to make sure that all of our learners are equally and fully active contributors to our lessons, because there are likely to be some who think they will learn best by simply paying attention to what other people are saying, rather than by saying very much themselves.

It goes without saying that Swain's (1985) comprehensible output hypothesis contradicts the above position since the hypothesis entails that learners must try to make themselves understood if they are to achieve grammatical competence in the target language. Such competence would come about as a result of negotiations learners involve in, in the process of interacting. It seems clear that there are possibly important effects arising from the quality of learners' interaction with native speakers, peers, or teachers, in or outside the classroom context, namely the quality and the degree of interactive negotiations between interlocutors. Yet, different researchers have put emphasis on different aspects of the interactional process; thus, if Krashen (1980b) argues that comprehensible input is the key factor in SLA, Long (1980, 1983a, 1983b) has emphasized the importance of comprehensible input resulting from negotiated interaction; whereas Swain (1985) attributes crucial importance to comprehensible output. In contrast to these hypotheses, Gass (1988) rather stresses the role of comprehended input. This brings us to the topic of the next section, that is the comprehended input hypothesis.

The Comprehended Input Hypothesis

Criticizing Krashen's (1980b) 'comprehensible input' hypothesis, Gass (1988: 200-1) writes:

> the notion of *comprehensible* input is not a priori necessary for a theory of L2 acquisition, at least not in the way it is dealt with in his framework. Krashen's theory depends on the concept of a linguistic stage 'i'. I will not go into any detail about the lack of precision

relating to what the defining characteristics of a stage i are, nor about how we can determine what a learner's **i** level is, but suffice it to say that without such precision his theory is unfalsifiable and thus limited in explanatory power.

According to Gass (1988), the ultimate goal of research on second language acquisition is to grasp what is acquired (and what is not) and the mechanisms which bring about L2 knowledge. In an attempt to incorporate sociolinguistic, psycholinguistic, and linguistic aspects of acquisition, and to bring together the diverse perspectives constituting the field of L2 research, she proposes a framework (schematically represented in Figure 2) which encompasses five levels of a learner's conversion of ambient speech (input) to output.

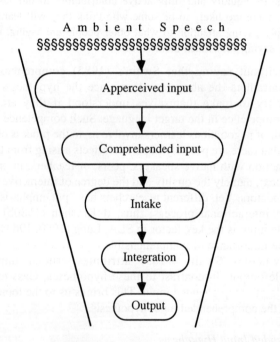

Figure 2: From input to output.
From "Integrating research areas: a framework for second language studies," by S. Gass. 1988. *Applied Linguistics* Vol. 9, N° 2 (pp. 198-217) Copyright © 1988 by Oxford University Press. Excerpt from p. 200. Reprinted by permission of Oxford University Press.

Ambient speech stands for the second language input surrounding the L2 learner or at least that input to which s/he is exposed. Of course not all of 'ambient speech' is employed by the learner since some does pass through to the learner and some does not.

Apperceived input is input that does pass through. It is "that bit of language which is noticed in some way by the learner because of some particular features" (Gass 1988: 202), such as frequency, affect (social distance, status, motivation, attitude) prior knowledge, and attention. Gass (1988) acknowledges that certain conversational interaction factors may also account for how the input may be adjusted so that it can be comprehended, namely speech modifications in the sense of foreigner talk (cf. Hatch 1983b), and interactional modifications in the sense of negotiation of meaning (cf. Long 1980). However, according to her, negotiation and modification are by no means necessary conditions in the acquisition process; they "rather serve to increase the possibility of a greater amount of data becoming available for further use" (Gass 1988: 204).

Comprehended input is different from comprehensible input in that the latter is controlled by the person providing input, usually (but not necessarily) a native speaker of the second language, while the former is controlled by the L2 learner. Comprehended input implies that "it is the learner who is doing the 'work' to understand as opposed to the person providing the language data. It is this distinction which is crucial in the eventual relationship to intake, since it is the learner who ultimately controls that intake" (Gass 1988: 204). A further difference is that comprehensible input, in Krashen's (1980b) sense, is considered as a dichotomous variable: input is either comprehensible or it is not; whereas, comprehended input, in Gass' (1988) sense, implies that there are different levels of comprehension that can occur. "Comprehension represents a continuum of possibilities ranging from semantics to detailed structural analyses. In other words, comprehended input is potentially multi-staged" (Gass 1988: 204).

Gass (1988) argues for the separation of apperceived and comprehended input, because there is an important difference between the two levels which warrants the maintenance of two separate components. For example, in learning a second language, one could apperceive that tone is a relevant parameter, but he would not have comprehended the precise nature of tones only if s/he is able to do detailed analyses about it. "It is thus plausible that a learner can apperceive a relevant parameter without comprehending its nature" (Gass 1988: 205).

Gass (1988) also separates comprehended input from intake because "not all input which is comprehended becomes intake" (Gass 1988: 205). For example, the L2 learner may comprehend input for the immediate purpose of a conversational interaction, or he may use it for purposes of learning. It is in the latter case that one can speak of intake; "intake refers to the process of attempted integration of linguistic information. Thus, input that is only used in a conversation and for the sake of conversation is not regarded as intake" (Gass

1988: 205). Gass' (1988) distinction between the levels of 'comprehended input' and 'intake' is comparable to Faerch & Kasper's (1980) distinction between 'intake as communication' and 'intake as learning'. According to Gass (1988), one factor which may determine whether or not comprehended input becomes intake

> is the level of analysis of the input which a learner achieves. For example, it is possible that an analysis at the level of meaning is not as useful for intake as an analysis at the level of syntax. [...]. A related factor is the time factor. Pressures of conversational interaction may preclude sufficient analysis for the purposes of processing intake (Gass 1988: 206).

Anyway, Gass (1988) claims that the crucial variable in determining intake is not 'comprehensible input' but rather 'comprehended input'.

Intake is a term which was first introduced by Corder (1967) and defined as "what goes in and not what is *available* to go in" (Corder 1967: 165). By this definition, Corder (1967) aimed at stressing the non-equivalence of input and intake. Following Chaudron (1985), Gass (1988) defines intake as "a process of mental activity which mediates between target language input and the learner's internalized set of rules." "It is thus differentiated from apperception and comprehension since the latter two do not necessarily lead to grammar formation" (Gass 1988: 206).

Integration, according to Gass (1988), results from the process of intake. A factor which motivates the L2 learner to alter her interlanguage grammar is the recognition (not necessarily at a conscious level) of a mismatch between what is present in the ambient speech and her/his own grammar.

With regard to the fifth level in Gass' (1988) framework, namely *'output'*, Gass (1988) agrees with Swain (1985) that "[u]sing the language forces the learners to make sophisticated analyses of the grammar, a factor which is important in moving the learner from comprehended input to intake" (Gass 1988: 210). But she emphasizes that learners' output should not be equated with their grammatical system, because output is a matter of performance not competence, and therefore may reflect "limitations of control or access that one has over one's knowledge base" (Gass 1988: 211). In this connection, Swain (1985: 248) reports on a student who said "I can hear in my head how I should sound when I talk, but it never comes out that way."

In sum, Gass (1988) shifts the focus from the speaker (usually a NS) to the L2 learner by maintaining that crucial importance should be accorded to the notion of *comprehended* input rather than comprehensible input. She claims that the important variable in determining intake, and hence L2 acquisition, "is not comprehensible input since, in a sense, it says little about what the learner is doing" (Gass 1988: 206). This important variable is rather *comprehended* input, because among the five levels proposed in Gass' (1988) framework (cf. Figure 2), "it is the level of comprehended input which feeds into intake" (Gass 1988: 205).

Conclusion

Comprehensibility is primordial in SLA. The linguistic input which is understood by the learner, in Corder's (1967, 1978) terms 'intake', constitutes primary data for SLA (cf. Hatch 1983b, Krashen 1980b, Larsen-Freeman 1979, Long 1983a). Yet, current research is moving beyond the hypothesis that comprehensible input "is the only 'causative variable' in second language acquisition" (Krashen 1981b: 57). Attempting to find out what is most effective for L2 acquisition, researchers have investigated and stressed different aspects of comprehensibility. As a result, prominent and conflicting arguments concerning what facet of comprehensibility is most efficient for SLA have been put forward, namely Krashen's (1980b) 'comprehensible input' hypothesis, Long's (1983a) 'negotiation of comprehensible input' hypothesis, Swain's (1985) 'comprehensible output' hypothesis, and Gass' (1988) 'comprehended input hypothesis'.

Empirical Studies of Negotiated Interaction in SLA

Introduction

In the field of target language acquisition, the term 'negotiated interaction' refers to the modifications occurring in conversations between NSs and NNSs, target language teachers and learners, or between advanced NNSs and less proficient NNSs. These interactional adjustments include a whole range of attempts to understand and be understood. Comprehension checks, confirmation checks, and clarification requests (cf. Long 1983b) are three of the most important processes. 'Negotiated interaction' is meant to imply modified interaction as illustrated in the following example quoted from Long (1981b: 269):

NS	: Do you wanna hamburger?
NNS	: Uh?
NS	: What do you wanna eat?
NNS	: Oh! Yeah, hamburger

As Long (1981b) points out, this example which is typical of NS-NNS conversation illustrates a breakdown in communication followed by a repair. "After the initial failure to communicate, the NS repairs with a semantic repetition, thereby modifying the interaction" (Long 1981b: 269). This section reviews some empirical studies of negotiated interaction, first in NS-NNS and NNS-NNS conversation, and then in SL classroom discourse.

Negotiated Interaction in NS-NNS and NNS-NNS Conversation

Negotiated interaction witnessed in NS-NNS conversations has been considered the *sine qua non* of second language acquisition (Long 1983b, 1983c). Therefore, many investigations of NNS discourse have focused primarily on NS-NNS conversation (see Long 1983c for a review). However, both departing from and building upon this research, several studies have investigated the nature of conversational interactions in NNS-NNS discourse. Studies of both NS-NNS and NNS-NNS negotiated interaction are reviewed below, under the following five headings: 'the organization of negotiated interaction', 'negotiated interaction in 'NS-NS/NS-NNS vs. NNS-NNS interaction', 'negotiated interaction in one-way vs. two-way tasks', 'learner- vs. NS-initiated negotiations', and finally 'comprehensible output in negotiated interaction'.

The Organization of Negotiated Interaction

In a paper dealing with an extended misunderstanding between a NS and a NNS, Varonis & Gass (1985a) point out that in real conversations there are often instances of a lack of understanding of the message conveyed. In such cases one of the participants may behave in one of the possibilities presented below and graphed in Figure 3:

1. Immediate recognition of problem but no comment.
2. Immediate recognition of problem and makes comment.
3. Later recognition of problem but no comment.
4. Later recognition of problem and makes comment.
5. Recognition after conversation but no comment.
6. Recognition after conversation and makes comment.
7. No recognition.
(Varonis & Gass 1985a: 328).

As Figure 3 illustrates, the participants may or may not realize that there has been a breakdown in communication. If there is realisation of the misunderstanding, it may occur immediately, sometimes later in the conversation or even after the conversation has come to an end. In any of these cases, one of

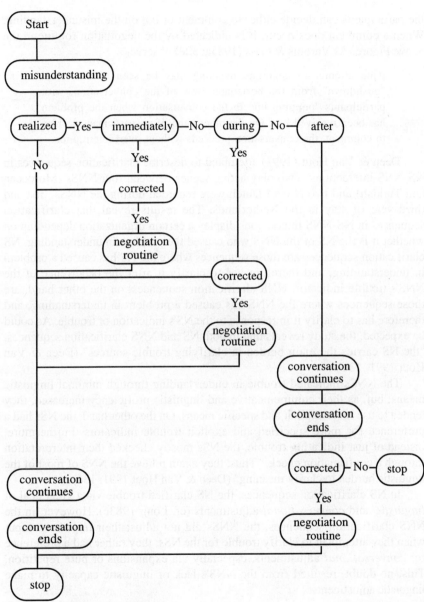

Figure 3: Misunderstandings.

the participants can decide either to comment or not on the misunderstanding. When a comment does occur, it is indicated by the negotiation routine in the above Figure. As Varonis & Gass (1985a: 328) observe,

> [t]he attempt to negotiate meaning may be seen as a vertical "pushdown" from the horizontal flow of the conversation, with participants "popping up" to the conversation when the problem has been resolved [...]. On the other hand, if no participant decides to comment, the conversation proceeds without overt interruption.

Deen & Van Hout (1991) attempted to describe clarification sequences in NS-NNS interactions. Two play-acting scenes between four NNSs (Moroccan and Turkish) and two NSs of Dutch were recorded during the NNSs' first and third year of stay in the Netherlands. The results reveal that clarification sequences in NS-NNS interactions display a certain organization depending on whether it is the NS or the NNS who caused the problem in understanding. NS clarification sequences are those sequences where the NS has caused a problem in understanding, and therefore has to clarify it after the occurrence of the NNS's trouble indicator. NNS clarification sequences, on the other hand, are those sequences where the NNS has caused a problem in understanding, and therefore has to clarify it in response to the NS's indication of trouble. As could be expected, the study reveals that in both NS and NNS clarification sequences, "the NS carries the main burden in clarifying trouble sources" (Deen & Van Hout 1991: 136).

The NNSs indicated trouble in understanding through minimal linguistic means; but, as their communicative and linguistic proficiency increased, they tended to use more explicit and specific means. On the other hand, the NSs had a preference for more specified and explicit trouble indicators. Furthermore, instead of just indicating trouble, the NSs mostly checked their interpretation through a confirmation check. "Thus, they again relieve the NNS of most of the linguistic burden to clarify meaning" (Deen & Van Hout 1991: 136).

In NS clarification sequences, the NS clarified trouble via a great deal of *linguistic* and *conversational* adjustments (cf. Long 1983c). However, in the NNS clarification sequences, the NNSs did not adjust their *linguistic* input when they attempted to clarify trouble for the NSs; they rather had a preference for *conversational* adjustments, especially via expansions or pure repetition. This, no doubt, resulted from the NNS's lack of linguistic capacity to make linguistic adjustments.

Negotiated Interaction in NS-NS/NS-NNS vs. NNS-NNS Interaction
Varonis & Gass (1985b) compared interlanguage talk in NNS-NNS conversational dyads with NS-NNS dyads and NS-NS dyads. The learners were from two native language backgrounds and were students from two levels of an intensive English program. Varonis & Gass (1985b) computed the frequency of 'nonunderstanding routines' leading to negotiation for meaning via repair sequences. The major finding was that the frequency of negotiation sequences was greater in NNS dyads than in Dyads involving NSs. Varonis & Gass (1985b) following Stevick (1976, 1980, 1981) argue that attention and involvement in the discourse by all participants are indispensable for successful communication. They found that "the more involved non-native speakers are in a dyad, the more time interlocutors will spend moving down, or in other words, in the negotiation of meaning, rather than moving forward, in other words, in the progression of the discourse" (Varonis & Gass 1985b: 83).

Actually, the data indicated that in NNS-NNS conversation interlocutors not only spend more time negotiating than in conversation involving NSs, but that more work is involved in the resolution of the miscommunication before the conversation continues. Another finding was that the most negotiation occurred when the NNSs were of different language backgrounds and different proficiency levels. The next highest incidence of negotiation occurred in pairs sharing a language background or a proficiency level; and the lowest frequency was in pairs with the same language background and proficiency level. These results support Varonis & Gass' (1985b: 84) hypothesis that "the greater the degree of difference which exists in the backgrounds of the conversational participants, the greater the amount of negotiation in the conversation between two nonnative speakers." These results are revealing for teachers, since they reflect the optimal makeup of small groups in target language classrooms.

Varonis & Gass' (1985b) results have been sustained by Takahashi (1989) who considered NS-NNS interethnic (Spanish and Japanese) talk. The study revealed that in interethnic dyads there is a greater amount of meaning negotiation than in dyads in which the participants share a native language. Takahashi (1989) found that in dyads composed of participants of the same native language, there was less need to negotiate meaning because of the greater shared background knowledge.

On the basis of their findings, Varonis & Gass (1985b) underline the importance of NNS-NNS conversations as a beneficial and non-threatening context which enables L2 learners to practice language and make input comprehensible through negotiation. They observe that

> nonnative speakers, in conversations with other nonnative speakers,
> may feel that as learners they have little to lose by indicating a
> nonunderstanding, because they recognize their 'shared

incompetence'. In fact, in the NNS-NNS dyads, participants
frequently commented on how bad their English was. [...] it is the
shared incompetence in the domain of English which allows them
to 'put the conversation on hold' while they negotiate meaning. As
seen, this type of deviation occurs much less frequently in NS-NNS
discourse, where the nonnative speaker recognizes the inequality of
the conversational situation (Varonis & Gass 1985b: 84-5).

In other words, by negotiating meaning in NNS-NNS conversations,
NNSs do not lose face in the same way they might with NSs. In NS-NNS
conversations "the inequality in the status of the participants (with regard to the
language medium) actually discourages negotiation, because it amplifies rather
than marks the differences between them" (Varonis & Gass 1985b: 86).

However, Schumann's (1975) data does indeed give an example of NS-
NNS conversation which approaches the levels of complexity witnessed in the
negotiation work in NNS-NNS conversation in Varonis & Gass (1985b).
Consider the example below:

      NS   : What's the movie tonight? (referring to TV)
      NNS : I don't know.
      NS   : What was it last week?
      NNS : Yesterday?
      NS   : Yeah.
      NNS : Em, ah, no me no, no looked, no?
      NS   : You didn't look at it ?
      NNS : No, eh, eh, I look play.
      NS   : You play?
      NNS : No, I look play hockey. The game.
      NS   : You play hockey? You play the game?
      NNS : No! In the television.
      NS   : Uh huh?
      NNS : I'm looking one game.
      NS   : At a game, you looked at a game on television. What kind of
              game?
      NNS : Hockey.

(Data from Schumann 1975 transcripts - cited in Varonis & Gass 1985b: 85).

The above extract took place between two friends, a NS and a NNS;
accordingly, Varonis & Gass (1985b: 85) contend that "it may be the fact that the
participants are friends which allows them the toleration of the suspended
conversation." On the same wavelength, Day et al.(1984) argue that in

conversations between NS-NNS friends, NSs make more use of *on-record* than *off-record* corrections, probably because NSs feel secure to provide *on-record* corrections to their NNS friends.

To conclude, agreeing with Schwartz (1980: 152) that "second language learners of English can learn more from one another than they think they can," Varonis & Gass (1985b) contend that negotiated interactions occurring in NNS-NNS conversation facilitate the second language acquisition process.

Negotiated Interaction in One-way vs. Two-way Tasks
In both first and second language research, feedback from the language learner has been held to partly enable the caretaker or NS to adapt her/his speech to the learner (Berko-Gleason 1977, Gaies 1983b). Long (1983b) refers to the tasks which do not incite the competent speaker (caretaker or native speaker) to make significant changes in her/his speech as *one-way* tasks; for example, vicarious narrative, giving instructions, and expressing an opinion, in which participants communicate information to others who lack it. *Two-way* tasks, on the other hand, are those in which each interlocutor starts with information which the other participant lacks but needs for the completion of the task. Conversation games are examples of these tasks (cf. Long 1980). Such tasks are claimed (cf. Long 1980, 1983b, 1983c) to induce interactional modifications.

The results of Long's (1980) study show that performance by the NS-NNS dyads was significantly different, in terms of interactional modifications, from that by NS-NS dyads on two-way tasks, but not so, on one-way tasks. Long (1983b: 214) argues that the need to not simply transmit information to but also obtain information from the less competent speaker indicates that "the competent speaker cannot press ahead (in largely unmodified speech) without attending to the feedback (verbal and non-verbal) he or she is receiving." Not surprisingly,

> [t]he option to provide feedback allows the less competent speaker to negotiate the conversation, to force the competent speaker to adjust his or her performance, via *[interactional]* modifications [...], until what he or she is saying is comprehensible. Comprehensible input, it has already been argued, feeds acquisition (Long 1983b: 214).

Gass & Varonis (1985b) investigated negotiation in NNS-NNS conversation in communication contexts involving what Long (1981, 1983b) calls *one-way* and *two-way* tasks. They were concerned with the effect of these tasks on learners' indication of nonunderstanding, in other words, on their initiation of negotiation. According to Gass & Varonis (1985b), one-way task interaction involves "the giving of information from only one participant to the other"; whereas two-way task interaction involves "exchanges of information -

that is, exchanges in which both participants have information which must be shared in order to complete a given task" (Gass & Varonis 1985b: 149). It is noteworthy that one-way task as conceived by Gass & Varonis (1985b) differs slightly from Long's (1980, 1981, 1983b) use of the term, "in that there is some exchange between participants. That is, it is not exclusively one-way, as a lecture would be, but information flows *primarily* in one direction" (Gass & Varonis 1985b: 153).

The subjects of the study were nine intermediate students from four different language backgrounds (Spanish, Arabic, Korean, Japanese) in an intensive ESL program. In the one-way task, one participant had to describe a picture which the hearer had to draw to the satisfaction of the speaker. In the two-way task, each member heard different information about a robbery, and the group was supposed to identify the robber; in other words, each member of a group had information which the other member(s) lacked but needed to determine the identity of the robber.

The study revealed that there were no significant differences in the frequency of negotiation sequences between the one-way and the two-way task, although on the one-way task, the participant who lacked the primary information, not surprisingly, produced significantly more indicators of nonunderstanding. Accordingly, Gass & Varonis (1985b) argue that the control of information is an important variable to consider in the study of negotiated interaction; participants who are in need of a particular information are more likely to initiate negotiation than those holding the information.

Hence, the study does not support Long's (1983c) prediction concerning the differences in the frequency of negotiation sequences across the two task types, since Long (1983c) predicts that two-way tasks constitute a more favourable context for negotiated interaction to occur. According to Gass & Varonis (1985b), a possible explanation for the discrepancy between the results of the two studies is that in their study there may have been more need for negotiation on the one-way task due to the lack of shared background information. There is a shared set of assumptions in the crime task but not in the picture task; and of course the greater the shared set of assumptions, the less need for negotiation. Thus, Gass & Varonis (1985b: 159) conclude that "the kind of information exchange is *not* the only determining factor of modified interaction. The kind of task interacts with the amount of shared background that the participants bring to the task." On the other hand, following Stevick (1976, 1980, 1981) and Scarcella & Higa (1981), they also conclude that negotiation in NNS-NNS conversation is a useful activity in that it enables the learners to manipulate input. Negotiation of input, they observe, is desirable for two reasons: (1) it allows conversation to proceed with a minimum of confusion, (2) it renders input more comprehensible to the learners because of their involvement in the negotiation process.

The import of Gass & Varonis' (1985b) study is that it has extended Long's (1983a, 1983b) idea that input becomes comprehensible through the speech modifications of NSs addressing NNSs. Gass & Varonis (1985b) place more responsibility on the NNS:

> a nonnative, whether in interaction with a native or nonnative speaker, may *make* input comprehensible by signalling that it has not been accepted, thus initiating a nonunderstanding routine. Such routines, while interrupting the main flow of discourse, are a very important part of conversations involving nonnatives because they make previously unaccepted input comprehensible, thus facilitating acquisition (Gass & Varonis 1985b: 161).

Learner- vs. NS-initiated Negotiations

It is a widely held claim that input which is not comprehensible to the learner is of no useful purpose for acquisition. The question that arises then is what can the learner do if the input s/he receives is not comprehensible? Put otherwise, how can the learner make it comprehensible?

Scarcella & Higa (1981) were interested in studying conversations between adult NSs and NNS children on the one hand, and NNS adolescents on the other hand. The main hypothesis the study set out to test is that

> older second language learners do more negotiation work than younger learners (of the same low proficiency level) when participating in conversations with native English speakers. That is, they use more conversational management devices which ensure understanding and sustain the conversation (Scarcella & Higa 1981: 411).

Scarcella & Higa (1981) examined another hypothesis, namely that younger learners receive more simplified input than older learners. The data were collected from fourteen conversational dyads. Fourteen ESL learners (seven children and seven adolescents) were paired with fourteen adult native English speakers. Each dyad was asked to take part in a block-building task. The conversations which occurred in the course of this activity were audiotaped, transcribed and analyzed.

The results revealed that there was a greater amount of simplified input to NNS children but that the NNS adolescents "worked" harder than the children in order to make input more comprehensible and also to maintain the conversation going. With regard to NNS "work" to make the input comprehensible, Scarcella & Higa (1981) found that just as NSs work to provide their NNS conversational partners with comprehensible input, NNSs work to obtain it. For example, when a NNS does not understand what the NS is saying, s/he may bring this to the attention of the NS by either a verbal or nonverbal nonunderstanding routine. "This feedback may be all that is necessary for the native speaker to identify the source of communicative difficulty and repair his or her utterance in such a way as to make it understood by the second language learner" (Scarcella & Higa 1981: 423). The NNS adolescents indicated their nonunderstanding by making use of such devices as Wh-questions, yes/no questions, expressions such as 'huh?', and repetition with a rising intonation. These techniques as Scarcella & Higa (1981: 423) note, "were virtually absent from the child L2 data."

Besides discussing the negotiation of understanding, Scarcella & Higa (1981) tackle another component of negotiated interaction, namely sustaining a conversation. They suggest that it is perhaps this aspect of negotiation which enables the learner to "maintain a conversation with native speakers long enough to obtain sufficient input for language development" (Scarcella & Higa 1981: 424). Accordingly, to cope with the difficulties of early conversation performance, older learners resort to a variety of "conversational strategies which allow them to stretch their linguistic competence" (Scarcella & Higa 1981: 425). Examples of these conversational strategies are:

Stepping in sideways. It is one of the primary strategies utilized by the L2 learner to share in the conversation work with native speakers. This strategy can be phrased as follows: "allow the native speaker to introduce a topic. Then, subsequently, comment on the topic, adding new and relevant information" (Scarcella & Higa 1981: 426). This strategy encompasses expansions and completions.

Repetition. It includes partial and complete repetition of the speaker's previous utterances; its function is twofold: "(1) to check on the comprehensibility of the message, and (2) to fill in one's turn at talk" (Scarcella & Higa 1981: 427).

Conversational fillers. They include fillers like 'you know', 'let's see', and 'uhm' used by the L2 learner "to hold and take their turn at talk while simultaneously keeping the conversation going (and frequently buying time to think of just the right word or phrase to use next)" (Scarcella & Higa 1981: 428).

Stevick (1976, 1980, 1981) claimed that involvement in the discourse is the *sine qua non* of successful communication. This active involvement in the conversation facilitates language acquisition, "charging" the input and allowing it to "penetrate" deeply. In Stevick's framework, it is the hearer who charges the input. The adolescents in Scarcella & Higa's (1981) study received more "charged" input than the children, because they were more involved in sustaining the conversation. On the basis of these considerations, Scarcella & Higa (1981) argue that the "optimal" input (cf. Krashen 1978, 1980b, 1981a) is that input resulting from negotiation work as opposed to that input which is only simplified.

Porter (1983) (for a review, see Long & Porter 1985 and Porter 1986) investigated the language produced by adult learners in task-centred conversations carried out in pairs. The study involved 18 subjects (12 NNSs and 6 NSs) which represented three proficiency levels: intermediate, advanced, and native speaker. The NNSs were all NSs of Spanish. Each subject took part in separate conversations with a subject from each of the three levels; thus, a comparison between NNS/NNS and NS/NNS conversations as well as an investigation of differences across learner proficiency level were possible.

With regard to negotiation of meaning (termed 'repair', and including comprehension checks, confirmation checks, clarification requests and three communication strategies (verification of meaning, definition request, and indication of lexical uncertainty), Porter (1983) found that it was practised equally frequently between the NNSs and the NSs in the study. Porter (1983) stresses the importance of this finding, suggesting that it indicates that L2 learners are capable of negotiating repair in a way similar to NSs. The finding concerning communication strategies, which Porter (1983) considers a subset of repair features, reveals very low frequencies of 'appeals for assistance' (Tarone 1977, 1981) which Porter (1983) redefines to encompass 'verification of meaning', 'definition request', and 'indication of lexical uncertainty'. Furthermore, the frequency of learner 'appeals for assistance' was the same whether learners were talking to NSs or to other learners.

So, the study refutes the idea that other learners are not good conversational partners on account of being unable to provide accurate input when requested. Learners seldom ask for help no matter who their interlocutor may be. Porter (1983) argues that similar social constraints as those operating to minimize the occurrence of foreigner talk repair (cf. McCurdy 1980) are at work in NNS/NNS conversations. The low frequency of other-correction by both learners and NSs is further evidence of these social constraints.

Porter (1983) investigated another interactive feature which she labelled *prompt*, that is "a word, phrase, or sentence added in the middle of the other speaker's utterance to continue or complete the utterance" (Porter 1986: 206). The results showed that NNSs and NSs provided similar numbers of prompts. Nevertheless, one significant difference was that NNSs prompted each other five times more than they prompted NSs; accordingly, Porter (1983) argues that with regard to prompts, learners make better partners to other learners since they enable each other to get more practice employing this conversational resource. Porter (1983, 1986) concludes that

> though learners cannot provide each other with the accurate grammatical and sociolinguistic input that native speakers can provide them, learners can offer each other genuine communicative practice including the negotiations of meaning that may aid second language acquisition [...]. If we are truly committed to communicative language teaching, we need to determine the optimum balance of learner input and teacher-controlled input so that our students can get sufficient practice in genuine communication in addition to sufficient exposure to accurate models (Porter 1986: 220).

In another study of negotiation of meaning in NS-NNS conversation, Gass & Varonis (1985a) undertook a quantitative as well as a qualitative analysis of negotiation of meaning. The subjects of this study were eight female NNSs (four of a high and four of a low proficiency level) and two NSs. Each NNS subject made 10 telephone calls to NSs to interview them on nutrition. The findings revealed that there were more NS-initiated negotiations than NNS-initiated negotiations, and that there were differences between NS-initiated negotiations with NNSs of a high proficiency level and with NNSs of a low proficiency level. The NS-initiated more negotiation routines per conversation to the low-level NNSs than to the high-level NNSs. Gass & Varonis (1985a: 41) explain this by arguing that "[t]he amount of NS-initiated negotiations is in a sense an independent measure of comprehensibility since the more difficult it is to understand someone the more clarifications are needed in order for the conversation to proceed."

The NNS-initiated negotiations were rare, but low-level NNSs initiated more negotiations than high level NNSs. According to Gass & Varonis (1985a), the design of the study may have partially contributed to the low frequency of NNS-initiated negotiation routines. The NNSs, as pointed out above, had to act as interviewers in a telephone conversation with NSs, but

> [s]ince the questions were *read* and did not involve spontaneous production, and since the responses were being tape recorded, there was little need for the NNS actually to understand what was being said. She only had to know when someone had finished speaking so as to ask the next question. This may partially account for the low number of NNS-initiated negotiation routines (Gass & Varonis 1985a: 41-2).

On the other hand, Gass & Varonis (1985a) focused on the scope of repair. They were particularly interested in how much of the initial response was repaired after the NNS initiated a negotiation. They predicted that the scope of repair would be greater to the low-level NNSs than to the high-level NNSs. However, these predictions were only partially sustained because of the interference of the 'question' variable . The results differed on the basis of the question asked by the NNS.

In addition to the quantity of speech repaired, Gass & Varonis (1985a) investigated the quality of the repair; that is the sort of information used in the response. Two measures were used in this analysis: *elaboration* and *transparency* . By *elaboration* is meant information that was not part of the original response but which the NS added after the NNS indicated nonunderstanding. *Transparency*, on the other hand, "involves giving information in a less compact, and thus potentially more easily interpretable manner" (Gass & Varonis 1985a: 50). Hence, increasing the transparency of the repaired response may involve, among other things, reducing the information load per clause, rendering implicit information explicit, and making information more specified (cf. Gass & Varonis (1985a: 50-1) for examples).

Gass & Varonis (1985a) hypothesized that there would be a greater amount of elaboration and transparency in response to the low-level NNSs than to the high-level NNSs. This hypothesis was made on the basis of the consideration that NSs would attribute the nonunderstanding of two groups of NNSs to different reasons. NSs would assume that high-level NNSs may have had problems of hearing rather than of understanding; whereas, they would assume that low-level NNSs had had problems of understanding because they simply lacked sufficient skills in English. Neither the results concerning elaboration nor those concerning transparency were significant.

Comprehensible Output in Negotiated Interaction
Pica (1988) was interested in analyzing negotiated interaction in NNS discourse in order to investigate Swain's (1985) 'comprehensible output' hypothesis. The study was directly motivated by Swain's (1985) claim that opportunities to produce the second language are as crucial to SLA as opportunities to comprehend it. Negotiated interactions between an NS of English and 10 NNSs were examined to find out ways in which NNSs made their output comprehensible when the NS indicated difficulty in understanding them. On the basis of anecdotal evidence from previously collected data (cf. Pica 1987) and also from the theoretical work of Hatch (1978, 1983a), Schachter (1986) and Swain (1985), and in the light of the assumption that mutual understanding is promoted when interlocutors share background experiences, world views, and a

linguistic code, Pica (1988: 52) hypothesized that "in making their production more comprehensible, the NNSs would also make it more target-like."

However, the data from Pica's (1988) study offered somewhat limited confirmation for this hypothesis. The study revealed that NNSs were, in fact capable of adjusting their speech and producing comprehensible output after NS's signals of nonunderstanding: in one-signal negotiated interactions, 91% of the NNS's own adjustments "showed some indication of movement towards target-like use of English" (Pica 1988: 58). Nonetheless, such NNS adjustments were relatively infrequent. This may be explained by the fact that they were indeed unnecessary because while the NNSs were attempting to modify their interlanguage to provide comprehensible output, "the NS [...] modeled target, (modified) versions of NNS interlanguage utterances for them" (Pica 1988: 45). The NS, at times, even incorporated the modifications into the signal, thereby leaving no opportunity to the NNS to adjust her/his interlanguage utterances towards target-like use but only inviting her/him to confirm the modification by repeating it or by acknowledging it with 'yes', yeah', 'right', etc. The study shows that 77% of the NS signals of noncomprehension contained the NS's interpreted L2 version of the NNS's interlanguage utterance "modified morphosyntactically, phonologically, or semantically according to native speaker norms" (Pica 1988: 65), as in the following examples quoted from Pica (1988: 54):

(a) NNS : Me the book the baby
     NS   : Did you say the baby's book?

(b) NNS : At Christmas we have cena
     NS   : Cena? does that mean supper?

The NS involved in this study was a teacher, experienced in talking to NNSs; therefore, she had mush skill in finding out what the NNSs were attempting to convey. Yet, "had data been collected during classroom interaction", Pica (1988: 69) speculates, "perhaps results would have shown more of the NNS's own modification of output and less NS modelling of the L2 target."

While the studies reviewed above do not bear directly on the issue of negotiation work in TL classroom discourse, it is felt that such research provides background for teachers and researchers who are interested in the phenomenon of negotiated interaction, since these studies are concerned with various variables affecting in one way or another the organization and the impact of negotiated interaction on the process of second language acquisition. This brings us to the next section which attempts to review some studies of negotiated interaction in the second language classroom.

Studies of Negotiated Interaction in the ESL Classroom

Studies of negotiated interaction in ESL classroom discourse are reviewed below under the following three headings: 'One-way flow of information: a barrier to negotiation of meaning', 'negotiated interaction in teacher-fronted vs. group-work organization', and 'learner feedback: a device for negotiating comprehensible input'.

One-way flow of information: A Barrier to Negotiation

Many traditional analyses of classroom discourse (e.g., Barnes 1969, Flanders 1970, Bellack et al. 1966, Sinclair & Coulthard 1975, Moskowitz 1976, Fanselow 1977a) have emphasized its instructional purpose. The aim of study has been the language of participants in the roles of 'teacher' and 'student' rather than the conversation of native and nonnative speakers or proficient NNSs and non/less proficient NNSs. Accordingly, these analyses came with descriptive categories such as 'lecturing', 'praising', 'correction', 'drill', 'teacher question' and 'student response', 'presentation', and 'practice'. These categories reveal that "the pedagogic function of classroom language is clearly uppermost in the researcher's mind" (Long 1983b: 214-5). Long (1983b) observes that such research has also put more emphasis on *use* in the classroom rather than language *acquisition*. Furthermore, "[i]f non-instructional language is introduced as baseline data, it tends to be NS-NS conversation" (Long 1983b: 215). In short, such research has attempted to make classroom discourse approximate target language *use* in NS-NS conversations.

However, Long (1983b) suggests that when the focus is SL *acquisition* in a classroom context, it is necessary to change both the categories and the baseline data. He writes:

> Assuming that some version of the input hypothesis is correct, [...], NS-NNS (not NS-NS) conversation will also become a source of baseline data. NS-NNS conversation, after all, is the context known to be capable of producing fluent sequential bilinguals. Witness its success in this regard in many multilingual societies where indigenous languages, in which no instruction is available, are routinely acquired with near native proficiency by large groups of people, often illiterate or poorly educated (Long 1983b: 215).

These considerations motivated Long & Sato (1983) to study interaction in ESL classrooms and to compare it with NS-NNS conversation in an informal, non-instructional setting. The findings suggest, according to Long (1983b: 218) that "the SL classroom offers very little opportunity to the learner to communicate in the target language or to hear it used for communicative purposes by others." Most of the teachers' questions were 'display' rather than 'referential', in other words what Mehan (1979) calls "known information questions." Through display questions, the teacher asks students to display knowledge s/he already possesses. The predominance of such questions in SL classroom discourse entails that there is little two-way exchange of information. It reflects the one-way flow of information from teachers to students (cf. Long & Sato 1983, Brock 1986).

Long & Sato's (1983) data on negotiated interaction tell the same story. Three of the most important processes involved in the speaker and interlocutor's attempts to understand and be understood are *comprehension checks*, *confirmation checks* and *clarification requests*. In the definitions and examples that follow, the "speaker" denotes the teacher, native speaker or the proficient NNS, and the "interlocutor" denotes the second language learner. These definitions and examples are paraphrased from Long & Sato (1983: 276), Long (1983b: 218-9), Chaudron (1988: 45) and Allwright & Bailey (1991: 123-4).

Comprehension check is used by the speaker to find out if the interlocutor(s) understand(s) what was said; for example: "Do you understand?" or "Do you get what I'm saying?"

Confirmation check is the speaker's query as to whether or not the speaker's (expressed) understanding of the interlocutor's meaning is correct; for example:

> Learner : I wan one job
> Teacher : You're looking for a job?

Clarification request is a request for further information or help in understanding something the interlocutor has previously said; for example: "What do you mean?"

As Allwright & Bailey (1991: 124) note, "[t]hese conversational signals provide moments of concentrated focus on contextualized input tuned to the learner's level of understanding." Long (1983b) argues that comprehension checks will occur more frequently when the major flow of information is from teacher to student, whereas confirmation checks and clarification requests will occur more frequently when there is a two-way flow of information, in Long's (1983b: 219) terms "when information is also passing in the other direction," that is from students to teacher.

The study by Long & Sato (1983) shows that ESL teachers use significantly more comprehension checks and significantly fewer confirmation checks than the NSs in NS-NNS conversations. The frequency of clarification requests was also found to be lower in classroom discourse than in NS-NNS conversation outside the classroom, though this result was not statistically significant. The lack of a statistically significant difference may be explained, according to Long & Sato (1983), by the preference for confirmation checks to remove ambiguity from the NNS speech, both inside and outside the classroom. This finding is quite expected since ESL students, as has been shown by Long & Sato's (1983) study, rarely come up with an information unknown to the teacher. In short, the findings of Long & Sato's (1983) study reveal that the emphasis in ESL classroom discourse is on *usage* rather than *use* (cf. Widdowson 1972, 1978), that the norm is that most of what is said is, in Paulston's (1974) terms, *meaningful* (i.e., contextually relevant), but not *communicative* (i.e., bearing information unknown to the hearer), and that the focus is on the accuracy of the students' speech rather than its truth value.

As discussed earlier, Long (1983b: 220) stresses "the importance for SLA of target language input made comprehensible to the learner chiefly through the negotiation for meaning involved in its use for communicative purposes." However, according to him, the data from SL classroom discourse suggests that "at least at the elementary level, instruction in the SL *per se* is proceeding at the expense of SL communication and the provision of comprehensible input" (Long 1983b: 220). This is due to the fact that contrary to NS-NNS conversation outside the classroom, classroom discourse is seldom motivated by a two-way exchange of information.

> An easy way to remedy this is by ensuring that students enter classroom exchanges as *informational equals*. This can be achieved by use of tasks whose solution requires that students convey information that only they possess when the conversation begins (Long 1983b: 221).

Long (1983b) suggests that materials designed to improve the reader's Intelligence Quotient (IQ), problem solving skills and entertainment games are a particularly rich source. No doubt, the introduction of such two-way tasks in SL classroom activities will provide for more opportunities for negotiation of meaning, and accordingly for more comprehensible input and comprehensible output. "Principally, the need to convey and obtain unknown information will result in the negotiation for meaning characterized by modifications in the interactional structure of conversation as participants seek to make incoming speech comprehensible" (Long 1983b: 222).

Long (1983b) recommends that these tasks be carried out by students in small groups, since the students' active participation in the small group conversation will increase her/his amount of talk, as well as the amount of interaction negotiated to the appropriate level of her/his current interlanguage. This, according to Long, cannot be achieved "in lockstep classroom conversation between teacher and whole class, where what the teacher says may be too easy for some, right for some, and too difficult for others" (Long 1983b: 222). To conclude, Long (1983b: 223) argues that the use of two-way tasks in small group work is

> one way of introducing more communicative language use in the SL classroom, and in this way, more comprehensible input. While preserving the benefits to be obtained from a focus on formal accuracy in some phases of teaching, these changes are designed to make other phases approximate NS-NNS conversation outside the classroom, and thereby, if the input hypothesis is correct, to facilitate SLA in a classroom setting.

Brock (1986) undertook a study the main purpose of which was to determine whether higher frequencies of referential questions have an effect on adult ESL classroom discourse. She assumed that *display questions*, asking for factual recall or recognition are at low cognitive levels; whereas *referential questions*, requiring evaluation or judgement are at the highest cognitive level. She hypothesized that if the number of referential questions asked by teachers could be increased, this would have the following effects on classroom discourse:

1. NNSs' responses to display questions would be shorter and syntactically less complex than their responses to referential questions.
2. A greater number of referential questions would be accompanied by a greater number of confirmation checks and clarification requests by the teacher.
3. Confirmation checks and clarification requests by the teacher would occur more frequently following referential questions than following display questions.
   (Brock 1986: 50).

The subjects of this study included 24 NNSs and 4 ESL teachers, all with at least five years of ESL teaching experience. Two of the teachers were provided with training in incorporating referential questions into classroom activity; the other two were not provided with training. Each of the four teachers taught the same reading and vocabulary lesson to a group of 6 NNSs. Brock (1986) found out that the treatment group teachers asked significantly more referential questions than did the control-group teachers, and that the students' responses to referential questions in the treatment group classes were longer, syntactically more complex, and contained more connectives. Furthermore, students took significantly a greater number of turns in the treatment group.

As for the effect of an increase in referential questions on the occurrence of confirmation checks and clarification requests, the findings did not support the hypotheses, in that the control group made a slightly higher number of confirmation checks and clarification requests than the number made by the treatment-group teachers, but the difference was not statistically significant. Similarly, the difference between the number of confirmation checks following the two types of questions was not statistically significant. As for the frequencies of clarification requests following students' responses to display and referential questions, they were too small for a statistical analysis. Brock (1986) attributes this low frequency of confirmation checks and clarification requests to the learners' high proficiency level. She writes:

> The predicted alterations in the interaction between the teacher and the learners may not have occurred because of the generally high level of proficiency of the learners involved: There might have been more instances of unintelligible speech necessitating confirmation and clarification with students of lower proficiency (Brock 1986: 56).

Though Brock's (1986) study does not have revealing findings as far as negotiation work is concerned, it has inspired the present study to consider the correlation between teacher elicitation type (display or referential) and the occurrence of 'conversational negotiation', and to find out whether the frequency of negotiation work differs from one class proficiency level to another.

Another study concerned with display and referential questions is that of Young (1984) who examined teacher-fronted classroom discourse in an elementary school ESL classroom. He focused on questions asked by the same teacher, namely display questions to which the teacher knew the answer and was simply checking the students' understanding of a reading passage, and open-ended (referential) questions by means of which the teacher was seeking genuine information as a follow-up to the reading activity. Young (1984) found that there were significantly more negotiation routines (e.g., clarification requests) in the context of an open-ended question than in the context of a display question. (For a review of this study, see Young & Doughty 1987).

Pica & Long (1986) investigated the characteristics of teacher talk and teacher-student conversation in order to find an answer to the following questions:

1. What are the characteristics of teacher speech as modified linguistic input to the classroom learner, and of teacher-student conversation in classroom discourse as samples of modified conversation?

2. Is the ability to modify input and conversation appropriately part of any teacher's competence, or must it be developed through experience over time?
(Pica & Long 1986: 85).

The data for this study were collected in an ESL classroom setting with 10 ESL teachers and their students. Some of the teachers were expert teachers with several years of teaching experience; whereas others had little or no experience. Teachers were asked to record at least 10 minutes of a lesson. The lessons recorded were predominantly oral-aural and teacher-fronted, ranging from discussion of reading assignment to vocabulary review, conversation games, and other communication activities. The study also made use of baseline data on NS-NNS conversation coming from two former studies of foreigner talk discourse, namely Long (1980, 1981a).

Pica & Long (1986) report finding that the complexity of linguistic input to learners in the non-instructional NS-NNS conversations and in ESL classroom conversations is similar. To address the issue of conversational adjustments in teacher-students interaction and in NS-NNS conversation, Pica & Long (1986) put forward the following three hypotheses: 1) Teacher talk would contain fewer *confirmation checks* and *clarification requests* than NS speech in the informal conversations since 2) SL teachers are rarely in any doubt about what a student is trying to say because of the predominance of both display questions (to which the teacher already knows the answer) and the one-way flow of information. 3) In lessons of this type, new information generally comes from the teacher, who then needs to ensure that students have understood; hence, teacher talk would contain a higher frequency of *comprehension checks* than NS speech outside the classroom.

The three hypotheses were sustained. Accordingly, the study revealed differences between the two contexts in the amount of negotiation of meaning which was found to be much smaller in the classroom setting. Negotiation of meaning was measured by the significantly lower number of conversational adjustments by teachers, via confirmation checks and clarification requests. The reason for the low frequency of negotiation of meaning in the ESL classroom setting lies "in the other confirmed finding, namely the far higher frequency of display questions in the instructional talk, and the lack of two-way information exchange this indicates" (Pica & Long 1986: 89). This implies that teachers "structure discourse such that information flows in one direction only, from teacher to students" (Pica & Long 1986: 97). The study has shown that this state of affairs is true for both experienced and inexperienced teachers which suggests according to Pica & Long (1986: 97) that "the dominant role is 'natural' for teachers, and perhaps inevitable unless something is done about it."

Pica & Long (1986) conclude that the difference between the two contexts in the amount of negotiation of meaning presumably indicates that there is less comprehension of input by learners in the ESL classroom. The lessons examined "were found to provide less opportunity for the negotiation for meaning that is necessary if learners are to obtain comprehensible input than did informal NS-NNS conversation outside classrooms" (Pica & Long 1986: 96). Therefore, Pica & Long (1986) observe that their findings along with those of Long & Sato (1983) are less motivating for learners whose primary acquisition environment is the SL classroom, and less satisfactory for those who consider the SL classroom as the major source of comprehensible input, and hence of subsequent interlanguage development.

Negotiation in Teacher-fronted vs. Group-work Organization
The viability of peer and group organization for classroom instruction has already been evidenced at least in L1 research (cf. Peterson, Wilkinson & Hallinan 1983). As many L1 and L2 researchers argue, learner-learner interaction in peer or group organization may be more favourable than teacher-learner interaction in teacher-fronted classrooms. In L2 classroom contexts, although the teacher-fronted classroom continues to be the norm, there is a growing emphasis on group and pair work, which increases the learner's opportunities to use the target language. This growing emphasis on and increasing use of group and pair work activities is sustained by the findings of a number of empirical studies revealing that small group activities involve a greater amount and variety of negotiated interaction than teacher-fronted activities. In this connection, Rulon & McCreary (1986: 182-3) write:

> One of the advantages of the small-group setting appears to stem from the fact that the more intimate setting provides students with the opportunity to negotiate the language they hear, free from the stress and rapid pace of the teacher-fronted classroom (For a detailed review of the pedagogical rationale for small-group work, see Long & Porter 1985).

Some of the studies which have investigated how group work organization affects interactive behaviours in ESL classrooms, usually by comparing teacher-fronted and peer/small group classroom organization, are reviewed below.

To analyze verbal interaction in 'lockstep' (teacher-fronted) and small group classroom situations, Long et al. (1976) devise the Embryonic Category System which includes the following categories:

1. *Pedagogical moves*
   P 1. Student initiates discussion.
   P 2. Student focuses discussion.
   P 3. Student summarizes and completes a sequence/ends discussion or section of discussion.
   P 4. Student moves conversation on to a new topic.
   P 5. Student qualifies another person's contribution.
   P 6. Student implicitly accepts a qualification.
   P 7. Student extends a previous contribution of his own or of others.
   P 8. Student reformulates own or other's previous assertion.
   P 9. Student expresses understanding.
   P10. Students provides an example.
   P11. Student uses evidence to challenge an assertion.
   P12. Student asks for information.
   P13. Student asks for information about the target language.
   P14. Student gives information on request.
   P15. Student gives information about the target language.
   P16. Student asks for clarification.
   P17. Student clarifies.

2. *Social skills*
   S 1. Student competes for the floor.
   S 2. Student interrupts.
   S 3. Student completes other's unfinished utterance.
   S 4. Student contradicts.
   S 5. Student invites participation by other students.
   S 6. Student explicitly expresses agreement.
   S 7. Student makes explicit reference to other's contribution.
   S 8. Student encourages other.
   S 9. Student explicitly supports other's assertion with evidence.
   S10. Student jokes.
   S11. Student avoids discussion.
   S12. Student repeats.
   S13. Student confirms.

3. *Rhetorical Acts*
   R 1. Student predicts.
   R 2. Student hypothesizes.
   R 3. Student makes an observation.
   R 4. Student deduces.
   R 5. Student induces.

R 6. Student states generalization.
R 7. Student defines.
R 8. Student negates.
R 9. Student expresses cause and effect relationship.
R10. Student exemplifies.
R11. Student identifies.
R12. Student categorizes.
R13. Student classifies.
R14. Student concludes.
.
.
.
X Confusion/inaudible tape.
From "Doing things with words: verbal interaction in lockstep and small group classroom situations," by M. Long, L. Adams, M. Mclean, and F. Castaños. 1976. In J. F. Fanselow and R. Crymes (eds), *On TESOL '76* (pp. 137-153) Copyright © 1976 by Teachers of English to Speakers of Other Languages, Inc. Excerpt from pp. 144-145 used with permission

NB. The dots under 'Rhetorical Acts' imply that this list is far from complete.

As can be seen from the list of categories above, pedagogical moves and social skills behaviours include interactional acts. Long et al. (1976) found a significantly greater number of students' pedagogical moves, social skills behaviours, and rhetorical acts in group work than in 'lockstep' (teacher-fronted) classrooms. Dyads also revealed a significantly greater variety of pedagogical moves and social skills.

Pica & Doughty (1985) compared the interactional behaviours in teacher-fronted and group-work interaction on the 'one-way' decision-making tasks. The decision making tasks used in this study, while communicative in orientation, were nonetheless not 'two-way' information tasks, since completion of the task did not require participants to pool information known only to their interlocutor(s). Pica & Doughty's (1985) data were taken from three classroom discussions and three small-group discussions involving low-intermediate ESL students.

The data revealed a very low incidence of interactional negotiation devices such as comprehension checks, confirmation checks, clarification requests, and self-and other repetitions in both contexts. The teachers made relatively few conversational adjustments compared with native speakers in studies of NS-NNS interaction outside classrooms, as in Long (1980) for example. This finding is consonant with the findings of other studies such as Long & Sato (1983) and Pica & Long (1986). Furthermore, contrary to Pica & Doughty's

(1985) predictions, negotiation features were more available in teacher-fronted activities than in group work activities. Therefore, Pica & Doughty (1985) conclude that one-way communication tasks, as used in their data, do not appear to facilitate negotiation in either classroom organization. They suspect that they found relatively little negotiation in their teacher-fronted and group data because the decision-making tasks did not guarantee a two-way information exchange among participants in the study. Hence, they hypothesize that "communication activities which are two-way in design will foster a great deal of negotiated modification in the classroom" (Pica & Doughty 1985: 132).

In a follow-up study, Doughty & Pica (1986) compared the interactional behaviours in teacher-fronted and group work interaction on a two-way problem solving task. While Pica & Doughty (1985) employed an *optional* information exchange task, Doughty & Pica (1986) used a *required* information exchange. The interactive behaviours investigated as dependent variables were *conversational adjustments*, namely comprehension checks, confirmation checks, and clarification requests. The frequency of these conversational adjustments were significantly higher in the group activities than in the teacher-fronted classroom. This finding contrasted that of Pica & Doughty (1985), where the frequency of conversational adjustments was slightly higher in teacher-fronted activities than in group-work activities.

With regard to the comparison for task effects, Doughty & Pica (1986) found that the two-way task generated more negotiation sequences than the one-way task in the small-group setting; yet, task type had no effect in the teacher-fronted setting. Doughty & Pica (1986) also found out that negotiation work as a percentage of total talk was lower in teacher-fronted activities on both one-way and two-way tasks. This finding, they argued, may reveal that students are reluctant to indicate their non-understanding and to negotiate comprehensible input in the teacher-fronted classroom because of the 'audience effect' (Barnes 1973).

To conclude, Doughty & Pica (1986) observe that although the potential for modified interaction among students is present at all times in a *required* information exchange, some students may not participate in the interaction because their limited linguistic proficiency may prevent them from processing linguistic input. Others may understand everything and hence may not need to engage in modification of the interaction. Hence, as Doughty & Pica (1986: 322) observe, "[s]uch aspects of the interaction must be investigated further."

Rulon & McCreary (1986) also examine the difference between teacher-fronted and group-work activities in the ESL classroom, focusing on two aspects of negotiated interaction, namely the negotiation of both meaning and content. According to Young (1984: 1), the negotiation of meaning refers to "the process of spoken interaction between a native speaker (NS) and a nonnative speaker (NNS) whereby the meaning of an unclear or misunderstood word or phrase is clarified to the satisfaction of both parties." Rulon & McCreary (1986) expand this definition to also include the interaction between two NNSs. The negotiation of content, on the other hand, "is the process of spoken interaction, whereby the content of a previously encountered passage (aural or written) is clarified to the satisfaction of both parties" (Rulon & McCreary 1986: 182). Rulon & McCreary (1986) introduce the measure of 'negotiation of content' because they feel that previous studies of negotiation in group work and teacher-fronted classrooms considered the task more in isolation than as part of the lesson as a whole, hence focusing on the negotiation of meaning while ignoring the negotiation of content.

In Rulon & McCreary's (1986) study, students viewed a 14-minute videotape of a lecture on the American revolution. Immediately after the lecture, students triads, which were selected at random, were separated from the remaining class groups and their teachers in order to discuss the videotaped lecture. Both the teacher-fronted classes and the small groups followed the same outline of questions for discussions. The target language produced in the small groups was equal in quantity and complexity to the one produced in the teacher-fronted classes, and had equal frequencies of confirmation and clarification requests. Yet the small groups produced significantly more confirmation and clarification requests in regard to the lesson content; in other words, they produced more negotiation of content than the students in the teacher-fronted classes. To conclude, Rulon & McCreary (1986: 195) argue that enhancing the negotiation of content as well as the negotiation of meaning in small group discussions "may be essential to the promotion of interaction necessary for successful second language acquisition."

Deen (1991) also confirms previous findings concerning the importance of group-work activities and the effects of such classroom organization on interaction and L2 acquisition. She found out that in the group-work settings, students asked many more questions, had more opportunities to negotiate meaning, and hence received more comprehensible input than in the teacher-centred classroom. Following Scarcella & Higa (1981), Deen (1991: 168) holds that "[q]uestion asking is very important for learning and understanding [...]. Through questions, students can influence the language and content of the lesson. It helps them to break down the input to their comprehension level and check their understanding". However, as Deen (1991: 169) argues "in front of the whole class it is much harder for students to ask questions and thereby admit ignorance."

The studies reviewed above stress the importance of group-work activities in freeing the students from the stress resulting from the 'audience effect'

(Barnes 1973) of teacher-fronted classrooms. Such stress prevents students from 'manipulating input' (Gass & Varonis 1985b), and 'controlling their intake' (Gaies 1983), a behaviour that has recently been considered essential to L2 acquisition.

Learner Feedback: A Device for Negotiating Comprehensible Input
Stressing the importance of learners' ability to adjust input by providing feedback on its comprehensibility, Gaies (1983b) studied learner feedback which he defines as "information provided by a learner to a teacher about the comprehensibility and usefulness of some prior teacher utterance(s)" (Gaies 1983b: 192). Gaies (1983b) also refers to learner feedback as "learner intake-control" because he assumes that by the feedback learners provide, they negotiate the nature of input and hence control their intake. The data were collected in a total of twelve different ESL dyads (teacher-student) and triads (teacher, two-students) with six different teachers. The students were of various ages and proficiency levels. The major categories which Gaies (1983b) made use of were established on the basis of the four pedagogical moves developed by Bellack et al. (1966), namely structuring, soliciting, responding, and reacting. Besides these categories, he also developed a number of subcategories to account for the data.

Gaies (1983b) investigated learner feedback to teachers on referential communication one-way tasks which involved students in identifying and sequencing six different designs described by the teacher. The students were encouraged to request clarification or re-explanation wherever necessary. Of interest here are Gaies' (1983b) findings that (1) learners make use of the four major categories of feedback, (2) as in Fanselow's (1977) study, the most dominant type of feedback was *reacting moves* through subcategories such as 'confirmation by repetition', 'utterance completion', 'confirmation by paraphrase', 'request for definition' and 'halt signal', (3) the least frequent type of feedback was *structuring moves,* and (4) learners varied considerably with regard to the amount of feedback they provided.

Gaies (1983b) argues that *responding moves* reflect what teachers are doing to structure discourse; whereas the other categories reflect the way and the degree to which classroom discourse is influenced by learners. Thus, Gaies (1983b) was also interested in studying the effect that learner feedback produces on classroom discourse. For this purpose, he devised a five category system to analyze the teacher utterance following learner feedback. These categories are: (1) verbatim repetition, (2) reduced repetition, (3) expanded repetition, (4) restructuring, and (5) question. After a preliminary analysis of the data, Gaies (1983b) comes up with the conclusion that there is no considerable relationship between learner feedback and teacher post-feedback behaviour. In this regard, Van Lier (1988: 219) maintains that

> [t]he specific types of intake-control described by Gaies are all subservient to a teacher-controlled activity, i.e., they are *reactive* rather than *proactive*. They give evidence of some negotiation, but only in terms of surface aspects of an ongoing activity. They do not aim to shape that activity, merely influencing the rate and specific way in which it is conducted.

The study by Gaies (1983b) has given much insight into our data because it shows how learners' intake is the result of a continuing process of negotiation. His distinction between what teachers do to structure discourse and what students do to influence classroom discourse inspired us to investigate teacher-initiated negotiation and student-initiated negotiation. Furthermore, the present study has accounted for the student act 'acknowledge' (cf. Chapter 4) in the perspective of what Gaies (1983b) labels 'intake-control'; accordingly, some of Gaies' reacting subcategories have been borrowed and used as subcategories of the act 'acknowledge'.

Conclusion
The studies reviewed above reveal that there is a relative absence in SL classroom discourse of negotiation sequences through which learners and teachers check the understanding and seek clarification of each other's messages, by means of interactional moves such as comprehension checks, confirmation checks and clarification requests. The "absence of these interactional features in the classroom, [...] is a reflection of the unequal participant relationships which shape and are shaped by classroom activities" (Pica 1987: 3). According to Pica (1987), most classroom activities, in traditional language classrooms as well as in communicatively-oriented classrooms, necessitate that teachers and learners "engage in a social relationship which affords them unequal status as classroom participants, thereby inhibiting successful second-language comprehension, production, and ultimately acquisition" (Pica 1987: 4). The following section focuses on the relationship between negotiated interaction and SL acquisition.

The Relationship between Negotiation and SLA

It is a widely held claim that negotiated interaction is a crucial factor in second language acquisition (SLA), though a causal relationship is far from being established between these two variables. Actually, one of the strongest motivations for the study of negotiated interaction in NNS and SL classroom discourse is the possibility that it plays a role in SLA. In the present section, an attempt is made to shed light on how certain researchers have explicated the relationship between negotiated interaction and SLA.

Current literature suggests that interactional modifications are witnessed in all cases of successful SLA; however, as Long (1981b: 275) points out research is needed to test the current hypothesis that "participation in conversation with NS, made possible through the modification of interaction, is the necessary and sufficient condition for SLA." In other words, the question that arises is whether modified interaction is necessary for or facilitates SLA in a natural or classroom context. The answer, according to Long (1980, 1981b, 1983b, 1985), seems to be positive. He stresses the proposition that modified interaction is "the necessary and the sufficient characteristic of TL samples for SLA to occur" (Long 1981b: 273). Such a proposition is based on two assumptions: that negotiated interaction provides for comprehensible input, and that conversation is a consequential arena for successful SLA, for in their process of SLA, the great majority of uninstructed SL acquirers rely only on conversation/interaction. In accordance with these assumptions, Hatch (1983b: 81) argues that "when the language *is* negotiated, some trace of input must remain and works as "savings" for future learning even when that input is not fully processed."

Following Long (1985), Ellis (1990) maintains that it is not possible to investigate the relationship between interaction and acquisition by direct means; therefore, the alternative is to attempt to do so indirectly. Long (1985) suggests that this can be done in three stages:

Step 1: Show that (a) linguistic/conversational adjustments promote (b) comprehensible input.

Step 2: Show that (b) comprehensible input promotes (c) acquisition.

Step 3: Deduce that (a) linguistic/conversational adjustments promote (c) acquisition
(Long 1985: 378).

After reporting on two studies which provide evidence of a causal relationship between negotiated interaction and comprehensible input, Long (1985: 388) concludes that "[i]f one accepts that there is already substantial evidence of a second causal relationship between comprehensible input and SLA, then one can deduce the existence of an *indirect causal relationship between linguistic and conversational adjustments and SLA*.."

Gass & Varonis (1991: 138) also attempted to answer the question: "how can we determine that what is negotiated is retained? That is, how can we truly determine that negotiation is truly linguistically beneficial to a learner?" Following Schachter (1986), they contend that negative evidence or in Schachter's term 'negative input' (feedback indicating to the learner that her/his utterance is deviant in some way or cannot be properly decoded) "provides learners with metalinguistic information about the target language." Further, "[t]he negotiation routines that often follow give learners an opportunity to test their hypotheses about the second language in their follow-up turn" (Gass & Varonis 1991: 138). Gass & Varonis (1991) argue that their study of 1989 (for a review, see above) provides evidence that negotiated interaction has a direct positive effect on SLA. The study reveals several instances of self-corrections by a NNS after s/he has been involved in negotiated interaction. What is revealing is that many of these self-corrections occurred several turns after the negotiation, which according to Gass & Varonis (1991) reveals the internalization of the linguistic information provided during the negotiation sequence.

In another study (Gass & Varonis 1988), NS/NNS dyads were arranged and asked to perform two tasks. The NS had to describe to the NNS where to put objects on a picture board and the NNS had to follow the directives and place the objects in the proper place. In half of the dyads, negotiation was permitted, that is, the NNS participant was allowed to ask for clarifications; whereas in the other half no conversational interaction was allowed. After this task had been completed, the NNSs, in their turn, had to describe to their NS interlocutors where to place objects on a similar board. The study revealed that descriptions by those NNS participants who had been allowed to negotiate meaning on the first task were more appropriate than those of NNS participants who were not allowed to perform any negotiation in the first task.

On the basis of these two investigations (Gass & Varonis 1989, 1988), Gass & Varonis (1991:138) conclude that "negative evidence [cf. Schachter 1984, 1986] and negotiation play a significant role in the internalization of linguistic information." Similarly, Bremer et al. (1988: 260) suggest that

> [d]eveloping TL competence is about the quality of the interaction created which is about managing NUs [non-understandings] but also about keeping the conversation going. Learners who understand and acquire the fastest are those who combine negotiating on NUs with sensitivity to issues of face and with a weather-eye on the conversational climate.

In the same direction, Van Lier (1988: 180) argues that "adjustment-in-interaction may be crucial to language development, for it leads to noticing discrepancies between what is said and what is heard and to a resolution of these discrepancies." Further, he notes that repairing - the prime function of negotiated interaction - "is likely to be an important variable in language learning," and that "[a]lthough, it is not a sufficient condition, we may safely assume that it is a necessary condition" (Van Lier 1988: 182). In an attempt to account for the relationship between negotiated interaction, comprehensible input, and language acquisition, Long (1983b: 214) proposed the following model:

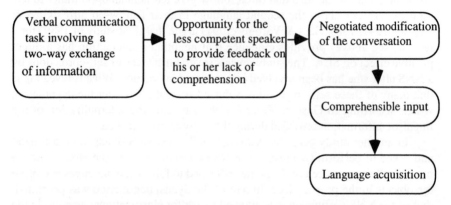

Figure 4: Long's model of the relationship between type of conversational task and language acquisition.
From "Native Speaker/nonnative speaker conversation in the second language classroom," by M. Long. 1983. In M. A. Clarke and J. Handscombe (eds), *On TESOL '82, Pacific Perspectives on Language Learning and Teaching* (pp. 207-225) Copyright © 1983 by Teachers of English to Speakers of Other Languages, Inc. Excerpt from p. 214 used with permission.

This model is out of tune with Krashen's (1982: 61) conception of the sequence of events involved in acquisition. According to him, "[c]omprehensible *input* is responsible for progress in language acquisition. *Output* is possible as a result of acquired competence. When performers *speak*, they encourage *input* (people speak to them). This is conversation." Conversely, Long's (1983b) model stresses the primacy of conversation (interaction/two-way communication) and the role it plays in enabling the learner to get comprehensible input. He writes:

> The model predicts, among other things, that communication involving a two-way exchange of information will provide more comprehensible input than communication which does not. Two-way communication tasks should also promote acquisition better than one-way tasks, for one-way tasks cannot guarantee the kinds of modifications needed to make input comprehensible (Long 1983b: 214).

Swain's (1985) 'comprehensible output hypothesis' claims that if language learners are to master the grammar of the target language, they are compelled to struggle with producing output which is comprehensible to their interlocutors.

This is meant to imply that acquisition of target language grammar would result, as depicted in the above Figure, from the negotiations occurring in the process of interacting. In a similar vein, Gass & Varonis (1991: 142-3) claim that

> [t]he more opportunity NNSs have to negotiate meaning and produce comprehensible output, the more they may advance their own language learning. Thus, the important issue is not whether NNSs have the opportunity to *converse*, but whether they receive the same message their interlocutors are sending and conversely send the same message their interlocutors receive.

However, as Allwright & Bailey (1991: 122) rightly argue, Long's model does not explicitly spell out the plausible interpretation noted in the above Figure: "that language acquisition can perhaps best be seen, not as the outcome of an encounter with comprehensible input *per se*, but as the direct outcome of the *work involved in* the negotiation process itself." Allwright & Bailey (1991: 123) diagrammatically represent this possibility, which is related to Stevick's (1976) notion of 'investment', in the subsequent figure:

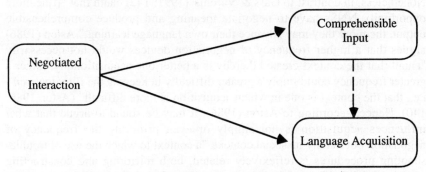

Figure 5: An alternative model of the relationship between negotiated interaction and language acquisition.
From *Focus on the Classroom: An Introduction to Classroom Research for Language Teachers*, by R. L. Allwright & K. M. Bailey 1991. Copyright © 1991 by Cambridge University Press. Excerpt from p. 123. Reprinted by permission of Cambridge University Press.

The important point suggested by Allwright & Bailey's (1991: 123) model is that "it is the work required to negotiate interaction that spurs language acquisition, rather than the intended outcome of the work - comprehensible input." The broken line between Comprehensible Input and Language Acquisition, in the above Figure, represents according to Allwright & Bailey (1991) the possibility that comprehensible input might still contribute directly to language acquisition. Further research should contribute to a better understanding of such possibilities.

In contrast to Long's (1980, 1981b, 1983b, 1985), Allwright & Bailey's (1991), and Gass & Varonis' (1991) propositions concerning the crucial importance of negotiated interaction in the process of SLA, Aston (1986) argues that the frequency of 'trouble-shooting procedures' (what the present study labels 'interactional negotiation devices') may reflect the perceived difficulty of the interaction, without revealing the quantity of input that is optimal to the learner's acquisitional mechanisms. According to him, "[t]rouble-shooting may therefore be at a maximum in 'difficult' interactions, but this does not seem to imply that the more negotiation takes place, the merrier from an acquisitional point of view" (Aston 1986: 140).

Aston (1986) recognizes that negotiation, in some cases, does enable the learner to receive comprehensible input by establishing utterance value. Furthermore, he contends that since negotiation devices may also be seen as concerned with maintaining social rapport, they contribute to create an optimal context for acquisition by lowering the 'affective filter' (Krashen 1982). Nonetheless, in contrast to Gass & Varonis' (1991: 142) claim that "[t]he more opportunity NNSs have to negotiate meaning and produce comprehensible output, the more they may advance their own language learning," Aston (1986) argues that a higher frequency of negotiation devices would not necessarily "entail that the context created thereby is a better one acquisitionally: rather a greater frequency could imply a greater difficulty in keeping the filter lowered - i.e., that the context is one in which acquisition is more difficult" (Aston 1986: 140). Hence, according to Aston (1986), it may be sound to argue that what influences acquisition is not simply or even primarily the frequency of negotiation but mainly its social context, "a context to which the use of trouble-shooting procedures is reflexively related, both mirroring and constructing participants' definitions of the situation" (Aston 1986: 140).

A question that is worth asking is: "to what extent it is valid pedagogical practice to place learners in particularly trying situations, in which negotiation will be maximized" (Aston 1986: 140). According to Aston (1986), interactions in which negotiation procedures are over-frequent may cause learners to become de-motivated since the over-frequency of these procedures contributes to raising the general level of the affective filter which, as Krashen (1982) claims, is an important variable in the acquisition process. Krashen (1982) suggests three categories to account for the affective variable, namely motivation, self-confidence, and anxiety. The affective filter hypothesis claims that acquirers are affected by their affective filters; thus, if the affective filter is high, input will not reach the language acquisition device, as illustrated in the following Figure:

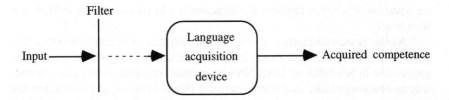

Figure 6: Operation of the "affective filter".
From *Principles and Practice in Second Language Acquisition*, by S. D. Krashen 1982. Copyright © 1982 by Stephen D. Krashen. Excerpt from p. 32. Reprinted by permission of Stephen D. Krashen.

As Aston (1986) observes, generally speaking, the sort of activities teachers ought to propose to learners should be such as to reduce their feeling that they are incompetent; and this scarcely appears to be the case in situations where negotiation is maximized. However, this is not meant to imply that learners should be engaged in activities which pose no difficulties whatsoever since these might lead to *fossilization* (Selinker's (1972) term for NNS structures that do not change to become more like the target language as time progresses). "A happy medium seems to be called for, whereby the learner can achieve an adequate sense of success in using the language, feeling neither too much of a social handicap nor of an informational moron" (Aston 1986: 141).

Though a causal link is far from being established between negotiated interaction and second language acquisition, it is sound to argue that the former is a facilitating factor in the process of the latter. As a matter of fact, most if not all of the studies undertaken within this research area have provided supporting evidence for the hypothesis that negotiated interaction is a key variable in the process of SLA.

Conclusion

This chapter has first reviewed four of the most prominent and conflicting hypotheses concerning the role of comprehensibility in SLA, namely Krashen's (1980b, 1982a) 'comprehensible input hypothesis', Long's (1983a, 1983b) 'negotiation of comprehensible input hypothesis', Swain's (1985) 'comprehensible output hypothesis', and finally Gass' (1988) 'comprehended input hypothesis'. Second, the chapter has focused on studies of negotiated interaction in nonnative speaker discourse and in SL classroom discourse. As shown above, these studies reveal different approaches to the study of negotiation work in SLA. Finally, the relationship between negotiated interaction and SLA has been addressed by reviewing some researchers' attempts to answer the question of whether negotiated interaction is a facilitating factor in SLA, and if so how?

As the reviewed studies reveal, various aspects of negotiated interaction have been investigated; for example, the organization of negotiated interaction, negotiation in NS-NNS vs. NNS-NNS interaction, negotiated interaction in one-way and two-way tasks, and comprehensible output in negotiated interaction. On the other hand, studies of negotiated interaction in the ESL classroom investigated issues like: the one-way flow of information in the ESL classroom as a barrier to negotiation of meaning, negotiated interaction in teacher-fronted vs. group-work organization, and learner feedback as a device for negotiating comprehensible input.

The studies related to negotiation work in the ESL classroom reveal a relative absence of negotiation sequences through which learners and teachers check the understanding and seek clarification of each other's messages. As Pica (1987: 3) suggests, the absence of negotiation of meaning in the classroom, "is a reflection of the unequal participant relationships which shape and are shaped by classroom activities." The present study intends to investigate further the issue of negotiated interaction in TL classroom discourse. Accordingly, it aims to provide answers to questions like 'how frequent is negotiated interaction in the TL classroom?, 'how does this frequency vary by proficiency level?', 'what are the main functions of negotiated interaction in TL classroom discourse?', 'who mostly initiates negotiated interaction, teacher or pupil?', and 'does the initiation of negotiated interaction affect the power asymmetry usually attributed to classroom settings, and if so how?'

It is hoped that the findings will contribute to enlightening the understanding of the process of negotiation in TL classroom discourse, and reveal interesting pedagogical implications, especially that negotiated interaction has been held to be a promoting factor in the process of SLA. The design of the study as well as the method of analysis are presented in the next chapter.

CHAPTER 3
Methodology

Introduction

This chapter presents the procedures followed in the collection and analysis of the data. It consists of two sections. The first one describes the design of the study; that is, the data collection and transcription procedures, the subjects, the type of lesson recorded, the classrooms where the data were collected, and the researcher's relation to the context investigated The second section describes the unit of analysis and outlines the method used in locating and analysing 'negotiated interaction'. The section also provides a description of teacher 'elicitation' types and of teacher-fronted TL classroom participants' events.

Design of the Study

Data Collection and Transcription

The data were collected in three Moroccan secondary schools situated in the centre of Rabat, Morocco. These are: 'Allaymoun School', 'Omar El-khayam School', and 'Lalla Nezha School'. The study is based on fifteen lessons, of about 45 to 50 minutes each, taught by eight Moroccan EFL teachers. Each five lessons were taught to different classes of the three grades of the secondary school; that is to say, five lessons were taught to beginning, five to intermediate, and five to advanced classes . In view of the fact that each lesson contains an average of 243 teaching exchanges (3653 teaching exchanges in all the data), it is sound to argue that the data recorded is a fairly representative corpus of EFL classroom interaction, in Moroccan secondary schools, on which some generalizations can be built. The data were collected in the beginning of the third term of the school year. Thus, when the data were collected, first grade pupils had studied English, as a foreign language, for 6 months, second grade for 15 months, and third grade for 24 months.

The data were audio-recorded. Admittedly, video-recording would have been more appropriate because much of the non-verbal behaviour (facial expressions, head and eye movements, gestures, etc.) occurring in classroom discourse may be relevant in the analysis of what in being said. We contented ourselves with audio-recording, however, because of the practical difficulties video-recording involves, and the impact it may have on increasing the effects of the observer's paradox, especially when the subjects whose interaction is being recorded are not used to being video-taped, as is the case with the subjects involved. Nonetheless, to make up for what might be considered a limitation in the data collection procedure, we were always present when the data were being collected, observing what was going on, and trying to take as many field notes as possible, including relevant non-verbal behaviour and other classroom events which may be helpful in the transcription and analysis of the recorded material.

As far as the transcription of the data is concerned, although our prime focus was on 'negotiated interaction', the whole lessons were transcribed because the occurrence of 'negotiated interaction' is, certainly, affected by what has preceded and affects, in turn, what follows. As Schwartz (1980: 138) argues, "[s]ince much of speech in communication involves negotiation, it is difficult to isolate one person's utterance for analysis without examining its relation to other utterances in the interaction." Each lesson took at least 24 hours to transcribe; furthermore, segments which were used for closer analysis were polished again and again, because we believe that there is much truth in Van Lier's (1988: 241) claim that "a transcription is never finished." Labov and Fanshel (1977: 355) noted that after 9 years of working on the same recording, they found they were still making non-trivial corrections in the transcription.

After the data were transcribed, they were coded in terms of structure and function using an adapted version of Sinclair & Coulthard's (1975) system of analysis (cf. Chapter 4). Then 'negotiated interaction' was located and analyzed with regard to the three research questions which the study set out to address.

Subjects

The teachers were mostly female; and the pupils were both male and female. The pupils were all Moroccan, aged from 15 to 20; they had French as a second language and were studying English as a foreign language. The average size of each class varied from 20 to 25 pupils. The teachers were, also, all Moroccan, that is to say non-native speakers of English. But, they had at least five years of EFL teaching experience, and most of them collaborating with teacher training schools, and having trainees attend their lessons and teach their classes under their supervision for two months each year. Thus, it may be argued that our presence, while the data were being collected, was not much of a disturbance nor a source of frustration either for the teachers or for the pupils, since they were accustomed to having visitors come and watch their lessons.

.   The teachers were informed that their lessons would be observed and recorded for a study on classroom discourse, and that the study was interested in examining classroom interaction in the normal class activities; and hence no changes should be made in their lessons. Of course, teachers were not informed about the specific aim of the study; thus, their interaction with their pupils was, possibly, more or less the same as in normal classroom discourse when no visitors are present. And, the lessons on which the study is based may be considered more or less natural, reflecting, to a great extent, what is going on in Moroccan secondary school EFL classes. Indeed, an omnipresent problem with data collection of the kind used in the present study is that of the observer's paradox. Therefore, as Watts (1991: 13) argues,

> [t]he degree to which the researcher's presence effects the behaviour of the [...] participants and the subsequent nature of the data is a factor which must be included in the interpretation of verbal interaction. Wilson [...] has shown that it is impossible to solve the problem entirely and that it may even be undesirable to go to great lengths in the attempt to exclude the effects of the observer and/or the equipment.

Lesson Type

In EFL classes in Moroccan secondary schools, lessons differ according to the type of activities involved: teaching a text, word study, functional practice, writing, guided composition, extensive reading and group work. EFL classroom discourse is, undoubtedly, affected by the type of activity going on. Therefore, to control the 'type of activity' variable, and to restrict the independent variable only to the pupils' level of English proficiency, the 'teaching of a text' was chosen as the type of lesson to be recorded with all three grades. The rationale behind such a choice rests upon the researcher's assumption that 'teaching a text' is the most frequent activity for teaching EFL in Moroccan secondary schools. In a 'teaching of a text' lesson, the teacher presents new structures and vocabulary items, a text is read, comprehension and then extended questions are asked by the teacher and answered by the pupils. It is a lesson type where much interaction - and, probably, much 'negotiated interaction' - takes place. However, in this type of lesson, interaction is mostly between teacher and pupils. Pupil-pupil interactions are practically non-occurring.

Classroom

The classrooms where the data were collected were all teacher-fronted. Long et al. (1976: 138), who refer to this type of classroom as 'lockstep', note that "lockstep work sets severe restraints on discourse potential." Similarly, comparing small-group with teacher-fronted classrooms, Rulon & McCreary (1986: 182) argue that

> [o]ne of the advantages of the small-group setting appears to stem from the fact that the more intimate setting provides students with the opportunity to negotiate the language they hear, free from the stress and rapid pace of the teacher-fronted classroom .

Conversely, Doughty & Pica's (1986) have a different view. Their study shows that, in group work activities, more proficient students tend to dominate the interaction and structure the discourse so as to limit the need for adjustments and negotiations. Hence, Doughty & Pica (1986) conclude that there is little difference between teacher-fronted and group-work settings.

Stubbs (1983) criticized Sinclair & Coulthard (1975) for deliberately focusing on traditional lessons where status and power relations are obvious. This same criticism might be voiced against the present research for choosing to study classroom interaction in teacher-fronted rather than group-work activities. In answer to such a criticism, it is noteworthy that our choice for teacher-fronted classrooms stems from the fact that in EFL classrooms, in Moroccan secondary schools, the time allocated for teacher-fronted activities far exceeds that allocated for group work activities. Thus, while pupils, generally, spend four hours a week in the former, they spend only one hour a week in the latter, which reveals that the most outstanding EFL classroom organization, in Moroccan secondary schools, is the teacher-fronted organization. The choice of the teacher-fronted classroom was also determined by the type of lesson we wanted to investigate, i.e., the teaching of a text. In Moroccan secondary schools, this type of lesson is taught in teacher-fronted and not in small-group classrooms.

Researcher

As a pupil, the present researcher studied EFL, herself, in a Moroccan secondary school. Later, she became a teacher of English in the same context. At the time of writing, she had seven year experience in teaching EFL in the three grades of secondary school in Morocco and four year experience as an EFL teacher-trainer, visiting classes with the trainees and observing how lessons are being accomplished both by experienced teachers and their pupils and by trainees and pupils. This suggests that the researcher is not an outsider to the EFL classroom community in Morocco nor to the TEFL profession. As a result the conclusions she draws reflect, to a great extent, an appropriate vision of what is really going on in the context investigated and are, no doubt, also revealing about target language classroom discourse in general.

Method of Analysis

Unit of Analysis

As claimed by many discourse analysts, "exchange is the primary unit of language interaction" (Sinclair and Brazil 1982: 49). In classroom discourse, the basic exchange structure is a three part structure, with *ideally* three consecutive moves, initiation-response-feedback (IRF for short), as in the following exchange quoted from Sinclair & Coulthard (1975: 72):

I : Does anyone know that special name? ('elicitation')
R : Is it Arabic ? (reply)
F : No, it isn't Arabic (evaluate)

As in the above example, 'exchange' - as conceived by Sinclair & Coulthard (1975) - includes three functionally and structurally linked moves (IRF). This notion of 'exchange' has been criticized by researchers such as Edmondson (1981) and Stubbs (1983), to name only these two. As has been demonstrated in Chapter 1, variables of the structure IRF do occur. The present data support Labov & Fanshel's (1977: 62) assertion that "ending [feedback] is a more complex act than beginning [initiation]." Accordingly, when we attempted to analyze the data using 'exchange', as a unit of analysis, we were confronted with the problem of 'Janus-faced' moves, which close one exchange and open the next (see Stubbs 1983: 132). On the basis of this evidence, we made appeal to another discourse unit, namely 'sequence' (cf. Chapter 4) which gave much insight into the understanding of the structure of 'negotiated interaction' and was helpful in distinguishing between negotiated and non-negotiated interaction.

Locating Negotiated Interaction

The first step in the analysis of the data was to identify negotiated exchanges. To locate 'negotiated interaction', we made use of the operational definition provided in Chapter 1. Furthermore, it was necessary to determine what 'acts' (cf. Chapter 4) are used to initiate 'negotiated interaction', in other words, what acts function as 'interactional negotiation devices'. By and large, an interactional negotiation device is "an utterance on the part of the hearer that essentially halts the horizontal progression of the conversation and begins the downward progression, having the effect of 'pushing down' the conversation rather than impelling it forward" (Varonis & Gass 1985b: 75).

Though we endeavoured to be objective in coding the data, the outcome might just reflect our own expectations and personal interpretation of what is going on in a given interaction. As Duranti (1985: 221) notes "interpretive procedures are inevitable and the only way of avoiding imposing the analyst's ideology upon the actor's doing is to make such interpretive procedures explicit." We have attempted to make our interpretive procedures explicit by giving a clear definition of all the elements constituting the coding scheme used (cf. Chapter 4) and by providing the respective codes whenever an extract from the data is quoted.

In the data, an interactional negotiation device can be realized by one of the acts listed below. However, the mere occurrence of some of these acts does not necessarily initiate a 'negotiated interaction'. For example, 'repair' may occur in the feedback slot, close the exchange and not initiate any negotiation.

- 'repair',
- 'repair-initiation',
- 'comprehension check',
- 'prompt',
- 'cue',
- 'confirmation check',
- 'clarification request',
- 'clue',
- 'challenge', and
- 'acknowledge'.

These acts, which are defined and illustrated with examples in Chapter 4, might overlap with other acts since we (in contrast to Sinclair & Coulthard 1975) consider utterances multifunctional. Regarding the multifunctionality of utterances, Robinson (1985: 116) observes

> [i]t does seem that various attempts to diagnose functions [of language behaviour] have offered less than entirely satisfactory solutions. Sinclair & Coulthard (1975) faced the issue of plurality of functions of utterances (moves) but felt obliged to take refuge in requiring observers to recognize the primary function of an utterance. In describing the function of speech acts, Austin (1962) seems to emphasize the speaker's intention, while Searle (1975) includes the hearer's interpretation. Although it may be easier to describe speech acts from a single perspective, in reality all perspectives and possibilities must be incorporated into a

comprehensive account, and any selectivity can be justified only in terms of particular questions being addressed.

In the same direction, Long (1983c: 183) contends that interactional negotiation devices "often have multiple functions, and also multiple realizations, choice among which is not arbitrary." The multifunctionality of such devices as confirmation checks and clarification requests, which may simultaneously serve as corrective feedback, has been shown by Chun et al. (1982). In accordance with the foregoing discussion, Stubbs (1983: 169) argues that "it is possible to account for the coherence of the discourse only by supposing that utterances are interpreted simultaneously as acts of different kinds at different levels of abstraction." The next section attempts to account for teacher elicitation types, namely 'display' and 'referential' elicitations, two concepts which have been of great use in the analysis of the data and the interpretation of the results.

Teacher 'Elicitation' Types

L1 and L2 researchers have distinguished between different types of teacher 'elicitations'. Barnes' (1969) study on L1 classroom discourse distinguished between 'closed' and 'open-ended' questions; L2 researchers such as Naiman et al. (1978) and Bialystok et al. (1978) differentiated between 'specific' and 'general information' questions. Both of these distinctions discriminate between questions which expect a closed set of responses from those which do not control the nature and length of the expected response. More recently, and owing to the growing interest in communicative language teaching, a further distinction has been made between 'display' and 'referential' questions (Long & Sato 1983, Brock 1986, Pica & Long 1986). Our data show evidence of the occurrence of two types of teacher 'elicitations': 'display' elicitations , and 'referential' elicitations. These types of 'elicitations' are presented below with illustrations.

Display Elicitations
A 'display elicitation' is usually teacher-initiated and aims at eliciting information already known to her/him. The data show that within the scope of 'display elicitation' a distinction can further be made between 'display question' and 'model'.

Display Questions. Coulthard and Brazil (1981: 89) noted that display questions "are in some sense bizarre in that the questioner usually knows the answer already, while the answerer himself is often unsure and thus genuinely needs to be told whether the answer he has offered is the answer required." They are not genuine questions which seek information but, in Barnes' (1969) terms,

'pseudo-questions'. The teacher asks such questions to see whether pupils also
know the answer, as illustrated in the following example:

(7)
Teacher   -I- 1 T   : -> How do you read this number? (el.)
Elicit   -R- 2 P   : One hundred (rep.)
           -F- 3 T   : A Hundred or one hundred [1+] (eva.)
                        (1st grade - Lesson 2)

Models. A 'model' is an 'elicitation' or a type of prompt by the teacher. It aims
at eliciting an exact imitation of a previous utterance (see also Chaudron 1988:
45, and Van Lier 1988: 28). In the extract below, the initiating move is a 'model'
because it aims at eliciting an exact repetition of the model sentence provided by
the teacher.

(8)
Teacher   -I- 1 T   : -> I grind sugar cubes to get sugar powder (el.).
Elicit   Azerwal (nom.)
           -R- 2 P   : I grind sugar cubes to get sugar powder (rep.)
                        (3rd grade - Lesson 5)

Referential Elicitations
As Pica & Long (1986: 88) note, "[r]eferential questions are those to which the
speaker does not know the answer." In the TL classroom context, however,
'referential elicitations' are *not necessarily* genuine questions which really seek
information, because they mostly aim at eliciting language from pupils. Van Lier
(1988: 223) argues that "what distinguishes instructional questions from
conversational (non-instructional) ones is therefore not their referential or display
nature, but rather their *eliciting function* ." Anyway, as Chaudron (1988) notes,
referential questions may be either open or closed; whereas display questions
would tend to be closed. Furthermore, Brock (1986: 48) argues that "one can
reasonably assume that questions at low cognitive levels, asking for factual recall
or recognition, are display questions, while questions calling for evaluation or
judgement are likely to be referential questions." Consider the example below:

(9)
Teacher   -I- 1 T   : -> Do you think that a woman should do all the
Elicit   housework alone or should someone help her? (el.)
           -R- 2 P   : A woman shouldn't do all the housework alone (rep.)
           -F- 3 T   : yes (eva.)
                        (2nd grade - Lesson 2)

The teacher's 'elicitation' (1 T) in the above exchange is referential because the pupil's answer is not known to the teacher since it is concerned with opinion and based on judgement rather than "factual recall or recognition" (Brock 1986: 48).

TL Classroom Discourse Participants' Events

As shown in Boulima (1990), in a 'teaching of a text' lesson a distinction can be made between five participants' events: 'teacher events', 'pupil events', 'teacher-pupil events', 'text events', and 'disputable events'. These have been designed in line with Labov & Fanshel's (1977: 100) events which they define as follows:

A-events	: known to A, but not to B.
B-events	: known to B, But not to A.
AB-events	: known to both A and B.
O-events	: known to everyone present.
D-events	: known to be disputable.

This section attempts to present and discuss TL classroom discourse participants' events, as recorded in the data.

Teacher Event (T-event)
T-events are events to which the teacher "has privileged access, and about which he cannot reasonably be contradicted" (Stubbs 1983: 118). As the teacher is the primary knower of the target language in TL classrooms, any event that is concerned with the target language is a T-event. Consider the following extract:

(10)
Teacher -I- 1 T : What do we call the man who works in the customs? (el.)
Elicit   -R- 2 P1 : Customer. Customer (rep.)
         -F- 3 T : Customer (acc.). No (eva.). Customer (acc.). No (eva.).
                    Don't make this mistake (com.). The customs official.
                    The customs official (re.)
                    [   ]
          4 P1 :   Yes (ack.).
                    (3rd grade - Lesson 3)

The question the teacher asks in the above extract (1 T) is about a T-event because it is primarily concerned with the target language. One of the pupils comes up with a wrong answer (2 P1). The teacher negatively evaluates the reply, provides a 'comment' which informs the pupils that this is a mistake which they should not make, and then provides the correct reply through the act 'repair' (3 T) which is acknowledged (4 P1) by the same pupil who has given the incorrect answer.

Pupil Event (P-event)

P-events are events about which the pupil has privileged knowledge. Consider the following extract:

> (11)
> Re-   -I- 1 T   : <The teacher had asked pupils to make a sentence with
> initiate   'used to'>
>   -R- 2 P1 : My grandmother- before sleeping .. my grandmother used
>   to tell us stories but she doesn't tell us any more (rep.)
>   (3rd grade - Lesson 4)

In the above extract, P1 is required to make a sentence with 'used to'. He comes up with a sentence related to his personal experience, i.e., related to a P-event.

Teacher-Pupil Event (TP-event)

TP-events are events that are supposed to be known to both the teacher and the pupils, as illustrated in the following example:

> (12)
> Teacher -I- 1 T   : Where do they hold exhibitions? (el.) ..In many places in
> Elicit   Rabat but the famous place is-? (el.)
>   -R- 2 PP : In 'Bab Rouah' (rep.)
>   -F- 3 T   : At the 'Bab Rouah' gallery (eva./re.)
>   (2nd grade - Lesson 3)

The question the teacher asks in the above exchange concerns a TP-event, as both the teacher and pupils live in Rabat (Morocco) and know that the most famous place for exhibiting paintings is the 'Bab Rouah' gallery. Several pupils provide a correct reply (2 PP) which is repaired and positively evaluated by the teacher (3 T).

Text Event

Text events are events the knowledge of which is based on the comprehension of the text being studied. Consider the extract below:

(13)

Teacher	-I- 1 T	: Now (m.). Answer these questions using short form
Elicit		answers (s.).Was the writer's uncle amused when he
		heard the loud crash? (el.).. Raise your hands (cue)..
		Was the writer's uncle amused when he heard the loud
		crash? (el.) ... ... Fessriri (nom.)
	-R- 2 P	: Yes, he was (rep.)
	-F- 3 T	: Yes, he was [1+] (eva.).
Teacher	-I- 4 T	: Because-?
Elicit	-R- 5 P	: In the text it is said "It sounds as if the roof has fallen in!"
		exclaimed my uncle with a loud laugh (rep.)
	-F- 6 T	: Very good (eva.).. with a loud laugh (acc.). It means
		he was amused. He did not care for it. He was amused
		(com.)

(3rd grade - Lesson 1)

The above extract occurs after the pupils have read a text. The extract, as a whole, constitutes a 'text event' because successful interaction in this particular extract depends on the comprehension of the text being studied.

Disputable Event (D-event)
D-events have to do with matters that are disputable such as opinions. In the data, the teacher usually asks extended questions towards the end of the lesson. These are often concerned with pupils' opinions about a topic that has been dealt with during the lesson, as illustrated in the following example:

(14)

Teacher	-I- 1 T	: What do you think of smuggling? (el.)
Elicit	-R- 2 P1	: It's false (rep.)
Teacher	-I- 3 T	: It's- ? (re.ini.)
Initiated	-R- 4 P1	: It's a bad job. A bad job (rep.)
Negotiate	-F- 5 T	: Yes (eva.)

(3rd grade - Lesson 4)

The above extract starts with a teacher's question which aims at eliciting pupils' opinions about smuggling. This is a 'disputable event' since a pupil's opinion may be completely different from that of her/his peers or from that of the teacher. One of the pupils (P1) provides a reply which needs to be repaired (2 P1). Thus, the teacher performs a repair-initiation (3 T); then, the pupil provides a repaired reply (4 P1) which the teacher positively evaluates (5 T).

This section has portrayed the participants' events occurring in the data, namely 'teacher event', 'pupil event', 'teacher-pupil event', 'text event', and 'disputable event'. Understanding the difference between these events has been insightful for the analysis of the data and for the interpretation of the results.

Procedure Used in Analyzing Negotiated Interaction in the Data

The fifteen lessons constituting the data were transcribed and analyzed with regard to structure and function, using the 'Foreign Language Interaction Analysis System' (FLIAS) (cf. Chapter 4), adapted from Sinclair & Coulthard's (1975) system for analyzing classroom discourse. Then a mean of 243 teaching exchanges per lesson (3653 in all the data) were examined to distinguish negotiated from non-negotiated exchanges. The negotiated exchanges were focused on, analyzed and compared across the three proficiency levels of Moroccan secondary school EFL classes. Each exchange was coded in terms of two main variables: the function and the initiator (teacher or pupil) of the negotiation. The rationale behind examining these variables is that we presume that these are important factors affecting opportunities for target language acquisition.

The negotiated exchanges occurring in the data were compared qualitatively and quantitatively across proficiency levels. Accordingly, the number of negotiated exchanges was counted in each grade, percentages and means were computed. The same statistical procedure was used with the two basic negotiation categories recorded in the data (i.e., 'didactic' and 'conversational'), with their subcategories, and with teacher and pupil-initiated negotiations. Pupil-initiated negotiation was further focused on to spot what we have labelled 'disjunctive negotiation' and to investigate whether this type of negotiation is mitigated in terms of 'face-threat' (Brown & Levinson 1978) and whether and how this mitigation varies by proficiency level. Thus, the number, percentage, and mean of 'disjunctive negotiation', 'modulated' and 'unmodulated' negotiation have been computed and compared by grade.

Hypothesis testing procedures (factorial ANOVA and Pearson correlation) have been employed, using the SPSS and StatView programs, to determine to what extent the results are statistically significant. Each quantitative analysis has been followed by a qualitative one, to interpret and discuss the results of the statistical analysis. The significance or non-significance of the results of the statistical analyses have not always been taken at face value, because we are rather skeptical about statistical results, especially when they run counter to common sense. We believe that in human sciences, researchers should not be as strict as in hard sciences, with regard to the significance value (p-value), and that common sense and experience should, also, be relied upon in interpreting the results of the statistical analyses. In this connection, Von Raffler-Engel (1989: xx) notes that

> [s]ometimes appearances are deceiving. Impressive looking statistics are seldom verified, and detailed analysis has shown that a large number of statistics in psychology journals are faulty [...]. In market research faith in statistics is waning. One client is suing a marketing researcher on the basis of whose statistics he lost millions of dollars [...].
> Worse than the mistakes that can be corrected is the philosophy behind it all. The misconception that the methods of the hard sciences can be applied to the human sciences started with what Hall [...] calls the "narrow-pseudo rigor" of the structuralists.

Conclusion

This chapter has been concerned with the design of the empirical study undertaken in the present work and the method used in the analysis of the data. As to the design of the study, the chapter has described how the data have been collected and transcribed. It has also portrayed the subjects, the type of lesson recorded, the organization of the classroom where the data were collected, and the researcher's relation with the context investigated. With regard to the method of analysis, the chapter has presented the unit of analysis employed to analyze classroom interaction in the data, and has shown how the unit 'exchange', frequently, fails to fulfil the 'unit of analysis' function, which entails the introduction of the unit 'sequence'. The method used in identifying 'negotiated interaction' has also been briefly outlined. Additionally, certain concepts that have been insightful for the analysis of the data and for the interpretation of the results, namely teacher elicitation types, and TL classroom discourse participants' events, have been defined and illustrated with examples from the data.

Finally, the chapter has displayed the procedure followed in quantitatively and qualitatively analyzing 'negotiated interaction' in the data as a whole and by proficiency level. In the next chapter, the descriptive system (FLIAS), which has been used to code the data, structurally and functionally, is presented with illustrations from the data.

CHAPTER 4
Foreign Language Interaction Analysis System (FLIAS)

Introduction

This chapter presents the system of analysis used for coding and analyzing the data, namely 'Foreign Language Interaction Analysis System' (FLIAS) which is an adapted version of Sinclair & Coulthard's (1975) system[*]. Sinclair & Coulthard's (henceforth S & C) system has been selected among existing ones because it has proved to be one of the most adequate for handling classroom discourse, despite the criticisms voiced against it. Criticizing systems developed for analyzing SL classroom discourse for having borrowed most of their categories from systems designed to analyze content classroom discourse, Long (1983d: 9) observes that "[i]t is surprising that so much borrowings should have taken place when one considers that second language classrooms differ from most others in that language is both the vehicle and object of instruction."

> [A]doption of such categories assumes that they are relevant ones for the study of second language classrooms, too. If this were really the case, there would be no point in conducting classroom research on language learning at all [...]. It is generally recognized, after all, that second language instruction (and some first language teaching) is distinguished from content subject instruction by such characteristics as the provision of feedback on the formal correctness rather than the truth value of speech, and the relatively insignificant amount of information exchanged, i.e., genuine communication, in the target language (Long 1983d: 17).

---

[*] Reproduced by permission of Oxford University Press from Towards an Analysis of Discourse: The English Used by Teachers and Pupils by J. McH. Sinclair and R. M. Coulthard.

Yet, we believe that S & C's (1975) system was carefully elaborated, and with minor modifications it can perfectly cope with target language classroom discourse, though it was designed for analyzing content classroom discourse. This is indeed clearly stated by S & C (1975: 112), themselves, in the following quote: "Our system of analysis was designed to handle discourse produced in one type of classroom situation, although we have since discovered that with minor modifications it can handle a wide range of classroom situations." Attempting to use S & C's (1975) system in a previous study (Boulima 1990) of EFL classroom discourse, we realized that the system could not cope with all the data. Therefore, we introduced some changes and new categories into the system to render all the data analyzable within the framework of this system. The aim of this chapter is to present, in detail, this adapted version of S & C's system of analysis, arguing for the changes and the new categories and providing illustrations from the data.

Discourse Units in the 'FLIAS' System

The FLIAS system includes all the categories in S & C (1975) except for the exchanges 'repeat', 're-initiation (ii)', 'listing', and the act 'loop'. It makes some adaptations in the structure of some exchanges as well as the function of some acts, and introduces a number of new categories, namely the discourse unit 'sequence', the exchange 'negotiate', the acts 'repair', 'repair-initiation', 'comprehension check', 'confirmation check', 'clarification request', 'challenge', and the subcategories of the act 'acknowledge'. The FLIAS system is a hierarchical rank scale model, made up of six ranks. Moving from the top rank of the scale to the bottom, we have the following ranks which are hierarchically ordered and related to the rank below in a 'consist of' relationship:

Lesson
Transaction
(Sequence)
Exchange
Move
Act

The third discourse unit 'sequence' is optional. Thus, the structure of 'transaction' is expressed in terms of exchanges frequently (but not necessarily) forming a sequence. The six discourse units in FLIAS are presented below.

Lesson

The lesson is the highest unit of classroom discourse; it has a structure made up of transactions. In the present data, a lesson corresponds to the teaching and learning event which lasts from 45 to 50 minutes.

Transaction

Transaction is the second rank in the scale after 'lesson'. It is marked by boundaries and comprises one or more sequences and/or individual exchanges. It consists of a preliminary, a medial, and a terminal element. The medial element is realized by teaching exchanges such as 'inform', 'direct', or 'elicit' which may make up a sequence; whereas the preliminary and terminal elements, which mark the boundaries of transactions, are realized by boundary exchanges, usually marked by two types of moves: 'frame' and 'focus'.

Sequence

'Sequence' is a discourse unit which Boulima (1990) incorporated into S & C's system. It is the third rank in the scale after 'transaction' and has a structure made up of more than one teaching exchange, where the primary one is 'free' while the subsequent one(s) are 'bound' to or embedded in it (see Stubbs 1983 and Griffin & Mehan 1981), or where the primary and subsequent exchange(s) form a compound exchange. Sequence may have one of the following structures:

- $I [R (F)]^n (I) (R) (F)$
- $I R [I R (F)]^n (F)$
- $I R F [R (F)]^n$
- $I R F [I (R) (F)]^n$

'Sequence' is an optional discourse unit as transactions may comprise exchanges not forming a sequence, though this is very rare in the data. 'Sequence' - which can issue from 're-initiation', 'negotiation', or from a compound 'inform' or 'elicit' - has been introduced into the system of analysis because it offers insight into the interactional dynamics of some exchanges in TL classroom discourse. For example, the following interaction cannot be properly accounted for if we do not make use of a discourse unit larger than the exchange:

(15)
Teacher -I- 1 T   : You want to phone someone but you haven't got a
Elicit   telephone at home (s.). Where do you go? (el.)
         -R- 2 P1 : When I want to phone to someone (rep.)

[

```
Teacher  -I- 3 T   :                    To phone-? (re.ini.)
Initiated -R- 4 P1 : To phone someone, I go to the post's (rep.)
Negotiate

Teacher  -I- 5 T   : The post-? (re.ini.)
Initiated -R- 6 PP : Post office. Post office (rep.)
Negotiate
```
(2nd grade - Lesson 1)

The above datum undoubtedly stands as a distinctive discourse unit with functionally and structurally linked moves. However, the unit 'exchange' including only three moves, namely Initiation-Response-Feedback (IRF), cannot cope with the above extract because P1's response has been repaired, which engenders five moves besides the initiation move (1T). Such pieces of discourse are so frequent in the data that it is necessary to make use of a discourse unit larger than 'exchange' and smaller than 'transaction', namely 'sequence'.

Coulthard & Brazil (1981) and Sinclair & Brazil (1982) introduced the discourse unit 'sequence' (a series of bound exchanges) into their revised description of S & C's (1975) rank scale model. Sinclair & Brazil (1982: 52) maintain that structures larger than the exchange "may not always be prominent in all types of discourse, but they are certainly to be noted in the language of the classroom." They further argue that these structures arise "when a predictable routine is begun - perhaps a number of similar questions, or anything that participants recognize as forming a distinctive set of exchanges." Van Lier (1988) has also used the discourse unit 'sequence' in his analysis of repair in L2 classroom discourse. He notes that repair sequences are "made up of several teacher-learner dyads, each dyad can be extended beyond the basic three-turn format by a series of repairs which can occur during the learner's responding turn or in third place (the evaluation slot)" (Van Lier 1988: 206).

Exchange

Exchange is the fourth rank in the scale and has a structure expressed in terms of moves. There are two major classes of exchange: 'boundary' and 'teaching'.

Boundary Exchanges

"The function of boundary exchange is, as the name suggests, to signal the beginning or end of what the teacher considers to be a stage in the lesson" (S & C 1975: 49). A boundary exchange consists of two optional moves, namely 'frame' and 'focus', as the following example illustrates:

(16)
T: Frame : Now (m.)
      Focus : we're going to listen to the dialogue (ms.)
              (2nd grade - Lesson 5)

Teaching Exchanges
Teaching exchanges, on the other hand, "are the individual steps by which the lesson progresses" (S & C 1975: 49). A teaching exchange consists of three moves: 'Initiation', which is obligatory, 'Response' and 'Feedback', which are optional, as illustrated in the following example:

(17)
T : Initiation   : Was the writer's uncle amused when he heard the loud
                    crash? (el.) ... ... Fessriri (nom.)
P : Response : Yes, he was (rep.)
T : Feedback : Yes, he was [1+] (eva.)
                    (3rd grade - Lesson 1)

In FLIAS, there are three types of 'teaching' exchanges: 'free' exchanges (including 'elicit', 'inform', 'direct' and 'check'), bound exchanges (including 're-initiate', 'negotiate', and 'reinforce') and 'compound' exchanges (including 'compound elicit' and 'compound inform'). The difference between these three types of exchanges is that in 'free' exchanges there is always a head, that is to say, an initiating move; whereas in 'bound' exchanges the initiating move is usually not explicit and/or functionally bound to the preceding move and realized by acts such as 'nomination', 'prompt', and 'cue' - if the exchange is a 're-initiate' - and by 'repair', 'repair-initiation', 'comprehension check', 'confirmation check', 'clarification request', 'prompt', 'cue', 'clue', 'challenge', and 'acknowledge' - if the exchange is 'a negotiate'. The bound exchange is functionally closely related to the preceding exchange, as it functions to re-initiate or negotiate something stated in the preceding exchange. A compound exchange on the other hand, is an interrupted 'inform' or 'elicit' composed of closely related moves that cannot be analyzed properly if considered separately.

There are twelve teaching exchanges with specific functions and structures. Six of them are free (teacher 'inform', teacher 'direct', teacher 'elicit', teacher 'check', pupil 'elicit', and pupil 'inform'); four are bound ('re-initiate', 'reinforce', teacher-initiated 'negotiate', and pupil-initiated 'negotiate'); and two are 'compound' (compound teacher 'elicit' and compound teacher 'inform'). The twelve teaching exchanges are presented below, in terms of function and structure, and with illustrations from the data.

Free Exchanges
Teacher Inform. According to S & C (1975: 5O), "this exchange is used when the teacher is passing on facts, opinions, ideas, new information to the pupil"; pupils may respond by an 'acknowledge', but the teacher does not provide feedback. Thus, the structure S & C assigned to teacher inform is: I(R). However, in TL classroom discourse, it seems that teacher 'inform' is typical, because besides functioning to provide information, it typically functions to present new structures or vocabulary items in the fashion adopted by teachers in TL classes, as in the following 'inform' where the teacher presents the items to 'knock out' and to 'lie still':

(18)
Compound -I- 1 T : Listen (s.). If you saw the film yesterday.. At the end
Teacher   of the film- uh Boxing... when Champion knocked
Inform   out... the other ... To KNOCK OUT... when a boxer
                              gives a hit and= (i.)
                                                  [
        -R- 2 PP :   K O. K O. K O. <knock out. Knock out.
                           Knock out> (ack.)
        -I- 3 T : =the other falls. So he LAY STILL. Yes he LAY
                           STILL. He lay on the ground and couldn't move (i.).
                           (3rd grade - Lesson 2)

Thus, FLIAS also codes as teacher 'inform' all exchanges where the teacher is presenting new structures or vocabulary items. However, the structure it assigns to teacher 'inform' is not I(R), as in S & C's (1975) system, but rather I(R)(F), because an optional feedback may follow the optional response provided by the pupils, as the following example illustrates:

(19)
Teacher -I- 1 T : <The teacher draws the sea on BB, and indicates the
Inform   temperature at the sea: 10 degrees>. This is a sea (i.)
        -R- 2 PP : A sea (ack.)

Teacher -I- 3 T : And this is temperature: ten degrees (i.)
Inform -R- 4 P1 : It's cold (ack.)
        -F- 5 T : Yes (acc.)
                           (3rd grade - Lesson 4)

In the second 'inform' in the above example, the pupil provides an 'acknowledge' after the teacher's 'informative' to show that he is following what the teacher is saying. The teacher provides feedback through the act 'accept' to indicate that what the pupil has said is appropriate, and, probably, also to show her satisfaction of the fact that the pupil is paying attention. Indeed, the pupil's contribution "it's cold" looks like a pupil 'inform', but it is not, as it does not function to provide any new information. The same information is already provided by the teacher when she says that the temperature is ten degrees. The pupil's contribution (4 P1) is simply an exclamation by means of which he displays his understanding of the teacher's 'informative'; therefore, 4 P1 may be replaced by an interjection such as 'burr!' without causing its function to change.

Teacher Direct. This exchange is used by the teacher to get the pupil(s) to perform a nonverbal behaviour. Pupils respond by a 'react' act, which is a non-verbal act; and the teacher may provide feedback. The response is compulsory but the feedback is optional. Thus, the structure is IR(F). For example:

(20)
Teacher -I- 1 T   : Open your book uh.. passage 17 (d.)
Direct   -R- 2 PP   : (Activity) (rea.)
                                 (3rd grade - Lesson 2)

Teacher Elicit. It is "designed to obtain a verbal contribution from pupils" (S & C 1975: 51). It mostly functions to elicit information already known to the teacher. The teacher knows the answer but wants to discover whether pupils also know the answer. Having given their reply, pupils also want to know whether their answer was correct; therefore, they always expect an evaluation from the teacher. This renders feedback a compulsory element; and if it does not overtly occur, it is always covert in the initiation move of the subsequent exchange. Accordingly, the structure assigned for this type of exchange is IRF. Example:

(21)
Teacher   -I- 1 T : But what do they want to do? (el.)
Elicit   -R- 2 P : They want to get married (rep.)
                -F- 3 T : Yeah (eva.)
                                (1st grade - Lesson 4)

However, the teacher occasionally asks 'referential' questions (to which s/he does not know the answer). In the data, these questions are usually carried out through life-experience and opinion questions or through negotiating questions often realized by 'clarification request', 'confirmation check', or 'comprehension check'. Consider the referential question (1 T) in the following example:

(22)

Teacher -I- 1 T : -> What do you think of Ghandi's position uh uh
Elicit   Ghandi's ideas? (el.)
         -R- 2 P : He is not right (rep.)
         -F- 3 T : May be . It's your opinion (com.)
                   (2nd grade - Lesson 4)

S & C (1975: 4O) state that the act 'elicitation' is "realized by question"; but
in our data, and, no doubt, in TL classroom discourse in general, it seems that
teacher 'elicit' is typical. The teacher may perform an elicit not only by means of
a question, but also through directing several types of pattern drills to which
pupils respond by exactly repeating the model sentence provided by the teacher
(i.e., repetition drill), by making substitutions in it (i.e., substitution drill), by
changing it from one form to another (i.e., transformation drill), etc. Consider
the example below.

(23)

Teacher -I- 1 T: He/come/next week (el.)
Elicit   -R- 2 P: He'll come next week (rep.)
         -F- 3 T: Yes (eva.)
                   (1st grade - Lesson 3)

The teacher may also elicit pupils' replies by asking them to give their own
sentences using a vocabulary item or a structure which has just been taught. For
example:

(24)

Teacher -I- 1 T : Can you give an example using to 'collapse'? (el.)
Elicit   -R- 2 P : Many buildings collapsed in the Agadir earthquake (rep.)
         -F- 3 T : Earthquake (acc.). Very good (eva.)
                   (3rd grade - Lesson 1)

Teacher Check. This exchange is used by the teacher to check whether pupils
have got their books, whether they have finished a task, whether they can hear
what has been said, etc.; in other words, the teacher wants to ascertain whether
the lesson is progressing as expected. The questions used in 'check' exchanges
do not, simply and primarily, aim at *eliciting* language from the pupils but are
real questions to which the teacher does not know the answer. Consider 1 T in
the following example :

(25)
Check   -I- 1 T   : Did you hear what your friend said? (ch.)
         -R- 2 PP : No (rep.)
                [   ]
              3 PP : Yes (rep.)
                     (3rd grade - Lesson 1)

Pupil Elicit. In this exchange, it is the pupil who asks questions, and it is the teacher who replies; feedback does not occur for the pupil cannot evaluate the teacher's reply. The structure is I R. S & C (1975: 52) hold that children rarely ask questions, and when they do, they are mainly of the order "Do we put the date?" or "Can I go to the lavatory?" However, in the present data, pupil 'elicit' frequently occurs and is, sometimes, interesting and directly concerned with the content of the lesson. Consider the following example where the pupil's 'elicitation' is really communicative:

(26)
Pupil   -I- 1 P   : And you? <addressing the teacher> What do you think of
Elicit   smuggling? (el.)
              2 PP : (laughter)
         -R- 3 T   : I said smuggling is bad for the economy because, as you
                       said, if you don't pay the taxes to the customs, so you are
                       stealing (rep.)
                       (3rd grade - Lesson 3)

Pupil Inform. This exchange occurs when the pupil gives information which he thinks is relevant or interesting; the teacher usually provides feedback. The structure is I F, as S & C (1975) noted. In the following example, pupil 'inform' occurs immediately after teacher 'inform', and the information it contains is very relevant to what the teacher said in his 'inform'.

(27)
Teacher -I- 1 T   : In Tangier, may be two years or three years ago, a whole
Inform   building collapsed (i.)

Pupil   -I- 2 P   : And THIS year- THIS year in Casablanca. Casablanca (i.)
Inform   -F- 3 T   : In Casablanca (acc.). Yes (eva.)
                       (3rd grade - Lesson 1)

Bound Exchanges
S & C (1975) devised five bound exchanges ('re-initiate(i)', 're-initiate(ii)', 'listing', teacher 'repeat', and 'reinforce'). But in FLIAS, there are only four bound exchanges ('re-initiate', 'reinforce', teacher-initiated 'negotiate', and pupil-initiated 'negotiate').

Re-initiate. This exchange occurs when the teacher gets no response, a wrong, or an incomplete response to her 'elicitation', when she has asked a question which has more than one answer, or when she is eliciting repetitions of a model sentence. The teacher starts again using one or more of the following acts: 'prompt', 'nomination', and 'cue'. By means of these acts, the 'Re-initiate' exchange makes use of the same 'elicitation' as that of the previous exchange; and this is why it is bound to it. It is important to note here that the feedback move is non-occurring after no response, but essential after a wrong or an incomplete response. On the other hand, the initiating move is essential after no response but optional after a wrong or an incomplete response. Consider the following example, where the teacher performs a 'negotiate' and a 're-initiate' exchange before pupils can reply:

(28)
Teacher	-I-	1 T	: If you are ill, and you need some medicine, where must
Elicit			you go? (el.)
	-R-		: <No response>

Teacher	-I-	2 T	: Medicine, an aspirin or something else (cl.)
Initiated			
Negotiate			

Re-	-I-	3 T	: Where? Where? (p.)
initiate	-R-	4 PP	: Pharmacy (rep.)
	-F-	5 T	: Pharmacy [2] (eva.)
			(2nd grade - Lesson 1)

Consider the following datum which occurred while pupils were doing a multiple choice exercise, and where two wrong responses are given before an acceptable one is uttered:

(29)
Teacher	-I-	1 T	: Latifa (nom.). 'consulting him' means? (el.)
Elicit	-R-	2 P1	: Taking him in (rep.)
	-F-	3 T	: No (eva.)

Re-
initiate   -R- 4 P2 : Telling him off (rep.)
           -F- 5 T   : No (eva.)

Re-   -I- 6 T   : Nemawi (nom.)
initiate   -R- 7 P3 : Sending for him (rep.)
           -F- 8 T   : Yes (eva.). sending for him (acc.)
                       (3rd grade - Lesson 5)

Consider the example below where the teacher asks a question which has more than one response:

(30)
Teacher -I- 1 T   : Why didn't the writer's uncle spend much time in his
Elicit   cottage? (el.)
         -R- 2 P1   : The writer's uncle didn't spend much time in his cottage
                       because uh the cottage was not comfortable (rep.)
Re-   -I- 3 T   : And- ? (p.)
initiate -R- 4 P2   : Many of the windows were broken (rep.)
         -F- 5 T   : Many of the windows were broken [+1] (eva.)
Re-   -I- 6 T   : And- ? (p.)
initiate -R- 7 P3   : The roof leaked (rep.)
         -F- 8 T   : And the roof leaked [+1] (eva.)
Re-   -I- 9 T   : And- ? (p.)
initiate -R-10 P4   : He had just returned from abroad (rep.)
         -F-11 T   : Yes (eva.). He had just returned from abroad (acc.)
                       (3rd grade - Lesson 1)

What FLIAS has designated as 'Re-initiate' stands for three bound exchanges in S & C's (1975) system, namely 'Re-initiate(i)', 'Re-initiate(ii)', and 'listing'. S & C were more interested in structure than in function; that is why they differentiated between these three exchanges. But as FLIAS is more concerned with function than structure, it considers these three exchanges as one type of exchange, because they all function to re-initiate the same 'elicitation' uttered in the previous exchange.

Reinforce. It is an exchange bound to Teacher Direct. It occurs when the pupil has misunderstood a 'directive' or is slow or reluctant to react. The structure as stated by S & C (1975) is I R I^b R, where I^b is a bound initiation realized by 'clue', 'prompt' or 'nomination'. Example:

(31)
Teacher   -I- 1 T   : Open your copy books (d.)
Direct   -R- 2 PP : <Activity> (rea.)

Reinforce -I- 3 T   : I said open your copy books not your books (cl.)
            -R- 4 PP : <Activity> (rea.)
                        (1st grade - Lesson 4)

Teacher-Initiated Negotiate. When pupils cannot provide a reply or when the pupil's contribution contains a 'trouble source' (Schegloff et al. 1977), the teacher either repairs the 'trouble source', or initiates a repaired reply through acts like 'repair-initiation', 'confirmation check', 'clarification request', 'clue', etc. As pointed out in Chapter 3, these acts function as interactional negotiation devices. Consider the 'negotiate' exchange below.

(32)
Teacher   -I- 1 T   : What else do you do in the mosque? (el.)
Elicit   -R-   : <No response>

Re-   -I- 2 T   : You pray and- ? (p.)
initiate   -R- 3 P1   : I [raɪd] the *Qur'an* (rep.)

Teacher   -I- 4 T   : I- ? (re.ini.)
Initiated   -R- 5 P1   : I uh I [raɪd] (rep.)
Negotiate

Teacher   -I- 6 T   : You ride? (con. ch.)
Initiated   -R- 7 PP   : I [red]. I [red]. I [red] (rep.)
Negotiate   -F- 8 T   : READ (re.)
                         (1st grade - Lesson 1)

     The first reply (3 P1) offered by the pupil in the above extract is 'repairable' (see Schegloff et al. 1977) because it contains a pronunciation 'trouble spot'. To elicit a repaired reply from the same pupil, the teacher initiates a 'negotiate' exchange by means of a 'repair-initiation' (4 T). However, the pupil repeats the same error as in her previous reply (5 P1), so the teacher initiates another 'negotiate' exchange by means of a 'confirmation check' (6 T). Several pupils intervene, but they provide a reply which is also repairable (7 PP); thus, the teacher performs a third-turn 'repair' which closes the exchange.

Pupil-Initiated Negotiate. There are occasions where the pupil does not hear or does not understand what has been said. Therefore, s/he initiates a negotiate exchange by means of acts such as 'repair-initiation' in the case of problems of hearing and 'confirmation check' or 'clarification request' in the case of problems of understanding. Interestingly, there are also occasions where the pupil does not approve of the teacher's contribution. If the pupil is daring enough, s/he initiates a 'negotiate' to contest the teacher's contribution. The initiation is usually carried out through an act labelled 'challenge', which, in the data, is occasionally performed in Arabic or French, and can be either a question or a statement. The teacher usually provides a response or feedback to the pupil's 'challenge', depending on whether the 'challenge' is a question or a statement. Consider the example below where the first pupil-initiated 'negotiate' aims to confirm the pupil's understanding of the previous teacher utterance, whereas the second aims at contesting that same utterance.

(33)

Teacher	-I-	1 T	: What does she do after washing? (el.)
Elicit	-R-		: \<no response\>
	-F-	2 T	: Iron (re.)
Pupil	-I-	3 P1	: Iron? (con.ch.)
Initiated	-R-	4 T	: Yes. She irons the clothes (rep.)
Negotiate			
Teacher	-I-	5 T	: Repeat (el.)
Elicit	-R-	6 P1	: She irons the clothes (rep.)
			[
Pupil	-I-	7 P2	: No teacher (cha.)
Initiated			
Negotiate			
Teacher	-I-	8 T	: Don't you agree with me? (con.ch.). Aouad (nom.)
Initiated	-R-	9 P2	: Yes teacher (rep.)
Negotiate			
Teacher	-I-	10 T	: Why? (cla. req.)
initiated	-R-11	P2	: Teacher uh after washing- teacher uh uh \<switching to
Negotiate			Arabic\> *ka-t-nshr-um* \<she hangs them out\> (rep.)
		12 PP	: \<laughter\>
	-F-13	T	: Yes (acc.). But this is a long description. It will be a
			long description ... step by step (com.)
			(2nd grade - Lesson 2)

The extract above occurred while pupils were reading a series of pictures depicting the day of a housewife. The teacher performs an 'elicitation' which does not get a reply, possibly because the pupils do not know the word 'iron' or because of some ambiguity in the 'elicitation' itself if considered in terms of the series of pictures the pupils were reading. The picture of a woman washing clothes is followed by a picture of the same woman ironing them, but there is no picture of the woman hanging the clothes out to dry (see *Further Steps in English* 1986: 104, Student's Book). As the pupils cannot give a reply, the teacher performs a 'repair' in 2 T, thereby providing the reply she wanted to elicit. P1 initiates a negotiation (3 P1) to confirm her understanding of the teacher's contribution. However, in 7 P2, one of the pupils initiates another 'negotiate' exchange, by means of the act 'challenge', to reject the information provided by the teacher. Thus, in 8 T, the teacher initiates another 'negotiate' to repair the breakdown in communication. In 10 T, the teacher continues the negotiation further. P2 gives an acceptable reasoning which is accepted and commented upon by the teacher who thus closes the negotiation sequence.

A pupil-initiated 'negotiate' may also occur after another pupil's contribution containing a 'trouble source'. The initiating move provides a 'repair' to the 'trouble source'. If the 'repair' is appropriate, the teacher usually does not interfere; and the pupil responsible for the 'trouble source' usually comes up with a repaired reply. If the 'repair' is inappropriate, the teacher evaluates it and/or performs a 'repair-initiation'. But the teacher may postpone interfering to see if the pupil can give the correct reply in spite of the 'bad repair' (Hatch 1978: 415) offered to her/him. Consider 6 PP and 8 PP which are 'good' 'repairs' and 13 P3 which is a 'bad' 'repair', in the following example:

(34)
Teacher   -I- 1 T   : Where was the car parked? (el.)
Elicit   -R- 2 P1   : The car was parked outside the baker's (rep.)
            -F- 3 T   : Yes (eva.)
Re-   -I- 4 T   : Repeat (p.)
initiate   -R- 5 P2   : The car was outside (rep.)
                                  [
Pupil   -I- 6 PP :   Parked (re.)
Initiated   -R- 7 P2   : Parked uh uh uh (rep.)
Negotiate   ⌈
                                       ⌊
Pupil   -I- 8 PP   :   Outside the baker's (re.)
Initiated
Negotiate

Re-   -I- 9 T   : Well (m.). Now we are inside the classroom (cl.).
initiate   The car was- ? (p.)
             -R-10 P2   : Outside (rep.)

Teacher   -I- 11 T   : Outside what? (cla.req.)
Initiated   -R-12 P2   : The car was outside uh uh= (rep.)
Negotiate   ⌈
                                             ⌊
Pupil   -I- 13 P3 :   the park (re.)
Initiated   -R-14 P2   : =the park (rep.)
Negotiate

Teacher   -I- 15 T   : The- ? (re.ini.)
Initiated   -R-16 P1   : Baker's (rep.)
Negotiate   -F-17 T   : Yes (eva.)
                          (2nd grade - lesson 1)

Compound Exchanges
S & C (1975) distinguish between two types of exchanges: 'free' and 'bound'.
But in the present data, there are some exchanges which are neither 'free' nor
'bound'. To account for such exchanges, the system of analysis FLIAS
considers them as 'compound exchanges'. A compound exchange is usually an
interrupted teacher 'inform' or 'elicit' composed of closely related moves which
cannot be appropriately analyzed if considered separately. When the teacher is
performing an 'inform' or 'elicit', the pupil occasionally displays her/his
understanding of what has been said by means of the act 'acknowledge'. The
teacher either neglects the pupil's contribution and continues what s/he was
saying, or stops to provide feedback to what the pupil has just said, and then
proceeds with her initiation. This type of interaction constitutes a 'compound'
exchange, as illustrated in the examples below:

(35)
Compound -I- 1 T   : You have some problem. You have just had an
Teacher   accident= (s.)
Elicit   [
          -R- 2 P1 :   *Allah-y-hfed* (ack.) <Arabic interjection
                                meaning: 'May God protect us'>
          -I- 3 T   : =Where does the policeman take you? (el.)
          -R- 4 P2 : To the police station (rep.)
                      (2nd grade - Lesson 1)

(36)
Compound -I- 1 T   : But they WITNESSED= (i.)
Teacher   [
Inform   -R-2 P1 :   They were surprised (ack.)
            -I- 3 T   : =They WITNESSED ... they saw what happened (i.)
                         (2nd grade - Lesson 1)

(37)
Compound -I- 1 T   : Listen, I've got a friend. He isn't a good student,
Teacher   but he succeeded. He isn't a good student but he
Inform   succeeded. We can say= (s.)
                       [
          -R- 2 P1 :   He used to- (ack.)
                       [
              3 P2 :   He cheated (ack.)
          -F- 4 T   : Yes (acc.). May be he cheated (com.)
          -I- 5 T   : =So, although he is a bad student= (ack.)
                                              [
          -R- 6 PP :   a bad student (ack.)
          -I- 7 T   : =he succeeded (i.)
                       [
          -R- 8 PP : he succeeded (ack.)
                         (3rd grade - Lesson 3)

A compound exchange can also occur when a pupil is speaking and the
teacher wants to encourage her/him to go on by performing a 'conversational
continuant'. Consider the following example:

(38)
Re-   -I- 1 T   : <The teacher had asked pupils to give sentences using the
initiate   word 'cottage' which she had just explained>
                         Another example (p.)
          -R- 2 P1 : Every summer holiday, we uh our family spent uh uh
                         spends= (rep.)
                       [
          -I- 3 T   :   SPENDS. all right (eva./p.)
          -R- 4 P1 : =spends all the time in our cottage near the beach (rep.)
          -F- 5 T   : Okay (eva.)
                      _ (3rd grade - Lesson 1)

The above interactions might seem like instances of a 'free' exchange and a 'bound' exchange. However, this is not the case as the first exchange in each of these interactions is not 'free' because it contains only part of the 'head', namely the act 'elicitation' in the first extract, the act 'informative' in the second extract, and an act simultaneously functioning as 'evaluation' and 'prompt' in the third extract. On the other hand, the second exchange in each interaction is not 'bound' since it contains part of the 'head'. This shows the necessity of introducing the category 'compound exchange' in S & C's system.

Move

Move is the fourth rank in the scale, and has a structure expressed in terms of acts. A move is made up of one or more acts. As in S & C (1975), there are five classes of 'move' which realize two classes of 'exchange'. 'Frame' and 'Focus' moves realize boundary exchanges; whereas, 'Initiation', 'Response', and 'Feedback' moves realize teaching exchanges. These types of moves are defined below with illustrations from the data.

Frame
It is a move by means of which the teacher indicates that one stage in the lesson has ended and another is beginning. It is realized by a 'marker' followed by a short pause, for example: Right..

Focus
It frequently follows a framing move, and functions to tell the pupils "what is going to happen or what has happened" (S & C 1975: 45). Focusing moves have an optional 'marker' and 'starter', a compulsory 'metastatement' or 'conclusion', and an optional 'comment', for example:

(39)
T: Well (marker).
  You're going to listen to it again (metastatement). The last time (comment)
  (1st grade - Lesson 4)

Initiation
A teacher 'initiation' may aim at eliciting replies, directing actions or passing on information. A pupil 'initiation', on the other hand, functions to elicit a teacher reply or to pass on information the pupil thinks is relevant.

Response
This move depends on the preceding 'initiation'. There are three types of response; and each type is appropriate to the preceding 'initiation'. The responses appropriate to an 'informative', a 'directive', and an 'elicitation' are 'acknowledge', 'react', and 'reply', respectively.

Feedback
The function of the feedback move is mainly to let pupils know how well they have performed. 'Feedback' occurs not only after a pupil 'Response' but also after a pupil 'Initiation' when it is part of a pupil 'inform' or 'negotiate' exchange. It is realized by one or more of the following acts: 'repair', 'evaluate', 'accept', and 'comment', as illustrated in the following example:

(40)
Re-   -I- 1 T : <The teacher had asked pupils to give sentences using the
initiate   verb 'to dust' which she had just explained>
                    Yes (nom.)
         -R- 2 P1: Everyday *bba* <'father' in Moroccan Arabic> Omar dusts
                    the classroom (rep.)
         -F- 3 T : -> Yes. Okay (eva.) ... Everyday *bba* Omar dusts the
                    classroom (acc.). Yes but I still see much dust (com.)
                    (3rd grade - Lesson 1)

When a feedback move overtly consists of only 'repair' or 'comment', evaluation is then implicit and usually unfavourable. Consider the following example where 'comment' occurs in isolation and implies a negative evaluation.

(41)
Teacher -I- 1 T : Why did Carol go to the travel agent's? (el.)
Elicit   -R- 2 P : Because to ask for (rep.)
                              [
         -F- 3 T : ->   I see that you're very tired and you are
                    saying anything that comes to your mind (com.)
                    (1st grade - Lesson 5)

Act

Act is the unit at the lowest rank in the scale; it is the minimal discourse unit, and hence has no structure. S & C (1975) made use of twenty-two acts to account for classroom interaction. 'FLIAS' maintains all S & C's acts except for 'loop' (as the act 'repair-initiation' encompasses the function carried out by 'loop') and makes use of six new acts, namely 'repair', 'repair-initiation' 'comprehension check', 'confirmation check', 'clarification request' and 'challenge'; furthermore, it designs subcategories for the act 'acknowledge'. As in S & C (1975), each act stands for a function. However, while S & C (1975) consider or rather tend to imply that utterances have a single function, in the FLIAS system utterances are regarded as multifunctional. The same utterance may simultaneously fulfil a number of functions (see also Stubbs 1983, Brown and Yule 1983, Griffin and Mehan 1981).

The twenty-seven acts which have been used to code the data are presented below. The definitions of the twenty-one acts borrowed from S & C (1975) are based on the summary of acts they give on pages 40-44.

1) *Marker (m.)*
It is realized by a closed class of items such as: 'well', 'now', 'okay'. It functions to relate utterances to one another or to mark a boundary in the discourse.

2) *Starter (s.)*
It is realized by statement, question, command, or moodless item. Its function is to provide information about, or direct pupils' attention towards an area in order to facilitate the understanding of the teacher's subsequent contribution.

3) *Elicitation (el.)*
The function of this act is to request a linguistic response. In the data of the present study, there are several types of 'elicitation'; that which is realized by a 'model' or a 'call-word' when the teacher is directing a pattern drill; that which is realized by a 'display question' to which the teacher already knows the answer; and that which is realized by a 'referential question' to which the teacher does not know the answer. With the exception of some 'referential' questions which are really communicative, the common characteristic of these three types of 'elicitation' is that they all aim at *eliciting* language from the learner.

4) *Check (ch.)*
It is realized by *real* questions to which the teacher does not know the answer. Its function is to enable the teacher to check the progress of the lesson. As Sinclair & Coulthard (1975: 53) noted, "at some time in most lessons teachers feel the need to discover how well the children are getting on, whether they can hear," whether they have completed a task, whether they have got their textbooks etc. To do this, teachers perform a 'check', as in 1 T in the following extract:

(42)
Check   -I- 1 T   : -> Have you finished? (ch.)
        -R- 2 PP : Yes (rep.)
                    (3rd grade - Lesson 1)

5) *Directive (d.)*
It is realized by a command. Its function is to request a non-linguistic response.

6) *Informative (i.)*
It is realized by statement. Its function is to provide information. When it is a teacher 'informative', the only response is an acknowledgement of attention and understanding; whereas when it is a pupil 'informative', it is followed by feedback.

7) *Prompt (p.)*
It is realized by a closed class of items (for example, 'go on', 'come on', 'hurry up', 'and-?', 'or-?', 'yes-?', 'you ask about-?', 'make a sentence', etc.), by the teacher's repetition of her/his previous 'elicitation', or by the teacher's repetition of all or part of a pupil's utterance. It may perform one of the following three functions (1) to suggest that the teacher is no longer requesting a response but demanding one, (2) to encourage the pupil to go on with her/his utterance, or (3) to urge the pupil to give a complete sentence.

8) *Clue (cl.)*
It is realized by statement, command, question, or moodless item. Its function is to provide additional information to help the pupil answer the 'elicitation' or react properly to the 'directive'.

9) *Repair (re.)*
It is an act elaborated in accordance with the phenomenon of 'repair' in conversation, discussed by Schegloff et al. (1977). 'Repair' can be defined as "the treatment of trouble occurring in interactive language use" (Van Lier 1988: 183); it encompasses the notion of 'correction'. As Van Lier (1988: 183) observes, "repair is the generic term [...] correction is one type of repair." In 'FLIAS', 'repair' is used in its generic sense because besides the mere correction of errors, it functions to treat problems of speaking and understanding. Furthermore, it refers specifically to 'other-repair' rather than 'self-repair'. In the data, and apparently in all TL classroom discourse, the act 'repair' may be performed either by the teacher or by the pupil(s); it occurs after a 'trouble source' (Schegloff et al. 1977: 363), and functions to repair it.

The 'trouble source' may be either an 'audible' or a 'non-audible' error (Schwartz 1980: 138). 'Audible errors' are errors of *fact, reasoning* and *language*. As Van Lier (1988: 183) maintains "[e]rrors, whether of *fact* (e.g., stating that which is not the case) *reasoning* (defects of logic, argumentation, appraisals of cause-effect) or *language* (syntactic, phonological, stylistic, discoursal) indicate lack of competence in some respect." 'Non-audible errors', on the other hand, are due to problems of hearing and understanding the talk or to problems of speaking, namely 'word search' (Schegloff et al. 1977: 363). If the 'trouble source' is an 'audible error', the act 'repair' functions to correct the error (see example (32)); whereas, if the 'trouble source' is a 'non-audible error', specifically a 'word-search', 'repair' functions to supply the word(s) the pupil is searching for to complete his/her utterance (see example (34)). In the data, not all 'trouble sources' are followed by 'repair' or 'repair-initiation'; and 'repair' is not necessarily a 'good repair' but occasionally happens to be a 'bad repair' (Hatch 1978: 415) even when provided by the teacher as in example (89).

10) *Repair-initiation (re. ini.)*
This act - which functions to elicit a repaired reply - has been devised in agreement with what Schegloff et al. (1977) refer to as 'other-initiation of repair'. In the data, 'repair initiation' is usually performed by the teacher when the 'trouble source' is an 'audible error' (see examples (32) and (1)). The teacher either repeats the error with a rising tone or repeats the pupil's contribution stopping at the 'trouble source' to indicate the location of the error and to urge the pupil to complete the utterance, as in: he-? On the other hand, when the 'trouble source' is a 'non-audible error', it may be performed either by the pupil(s) as in (64) or by the teacher as in (62).

11) *Comprehension check (com. ch.)*
The teacher performs a 'comprehension check' to inquire whether the pupils have understood a previous utterance (see also Chaudron 1988: 45), as illustrated in 2 T in the extract below:

(43)
Teacher -I- 1 T   : Now (m.). She went to the travel agent's because she
Inform   wanted to ask about hotels. What does she want?
                       or what did she want? A room. Yes. A room in a hotel.
                       So she wanted to book a room in a hotel (i.)
Teacher -I- 2 T   : -> Do you know 'to book a room'? (com.ch.)
Initiated -R- 3 PP : No (rep.)
Negotiate

Teacher   -I- 4 T   : Well (m.). For example you phone a hotel and ask them
Inform   to book you a room for next week or next month (i.)
                                             [   ]
          -R- 5 P   :   Yes. Yes (ack.)
                      (1st grade - Lesson 5)

In the above extract, the 'comprehension check' occurs after a teacher 'inform' in which the teacher presents the phrase 'to book a room'. The teacher realizes that the phrase may not have been understood by the pupils; so, she initiates a 'negotiate' exchange by means of the act 'comprehension check', where she is genuinely seeking information so that she can decide whether to re-explain the phrase or not.

12) *Confirmation check (con. ch.)*
The speaker (teacher or pupil) performs a 'confirmation check' to inquire whether her/his understanding of her/his interlocutor's previous utterance is correct (see also Chaudron 1988: 45), as illustrated in 8 T in extract (33). The teacher may also perform a 'confirmation check' to inquire whether a pupil agrees with a proposition conveyed by one of the participants.

13) *Clarification request (cla. req.)*
The speaker (teacher or pupil) performs a 'clarification request' to ask for further information from the interlocutor about her/his previous utterance (see also Chaudron 1988: 45), as illustrated in 10 T in extract (33).

14) *Challenge (cha.)*
This act has been named after Labov & Fanshel's (1977) act 'challenge'. 'Challenge' in Labov & Fanshel (1977: 97) is "a speech act that asserts or implies a state of affairs that, if true, would weaken a person's claim to be competent in filling the role associated with a valued status." In the data, 'challenge' is a pupil's act. It follows a teacher's move, and functions to reject or contest the information provided in that move. Hence, when this act occurs, it may affect the teacher's power-status. Illustrations of this act are provided in examples (65), (33) and (89).

15) *Cue (cu.)*
It is realized by a closed class of items such as 'raise your hands', 'hands up'. Its function is to evoke a bid, thereby making pupils abide by the turn-taking pattern operating in classroom interaction.

16) *Bid (b.)*
It is realized by a closed class of verbal and non-verbal items such as 'Sir', 'Miss', 'Teacher', and a raised hand. Its function is to signal a desire to speak.

17) *Nomination (nom.)*
It is realized by a closed class of items such as pupils' names, 'you', 'yes'. Its function is to give permission to a pupil to speak.

18) *Reply (rep.)*
It is mainly performed by the pupil, but it may also be performed by the teacher. Its function is to provide a response to an 'elicitation'.

19) *React (rea.)*
It is performed by the pupil and realized by a non-linguistic action. Its function is to provide a response to a 'directive'.

20) *Comment (com.)*
It is performed by the teacher, usually in the feedback slot, and realized by a statement. It functions to exemplify, justify, and provide additional information.

21) *Accept (acc.)*
It is realized by a closed class of items such as 'yes', 'no', 'good', and repetition of the pupil's reply, all with neutral low fall intonation. Its function is to indicate that the teacher has heard or seen and that the 'reply', 'informative', or 'react' was appropriate.

22) *Evaluate (eva.)*
It is realized by words and phrases such as 'good', 'that's right', 'interesting', 'fine', 'yes', 'no', with a high falling intonation, and also by a repetition of the pupil's reply with either a high falling (positive evaluation) or a rising intonation (negative evaluation).

23) *Metastatement (ms.)*
It is realized by a statement which refers to some future time when what is described will occur. Its function is to help the pupils to see the structure of the lesson.

24) *Conclusion (con.)*
It is realized by a statement summarizing what has gone before. It is the converse of metastatement; its function is, again, to give the pupils an idea about the structure of the lesson.

25) *aside (z.)*
It is realized by an utterance not really addressed to the class. It covers instances where the teacher is talking to herself/himself, as in: "where did I put the chalk?"

26) *Silent stress (^)*
It is realized by a pause following a marker. Its function is to highlight the marker when it is serving as the head of a boundary exchange indicating a transaction boundary.

27) *Acknowledge (ack.)*
It is realized by a verbal or non-verbal signal confirming that the pupil is listening and understanding. The terms 'back-channel' (Yngve 1970, Duncan 1973) and 'listening response' (Erickson 1979, Van Lier 1988) have also been used by some scholars to refer to this speech act.

    According to S & C (1975: 50), in teacher 'inform' exchanges "pupils may, but usually do not make a verbal response to the teacher's initiation." In the present data, however, and seemingly in TL classroom discourse in general, a verbal 'acknowledge' from the pupils is very frequent. In a 'teaching of a text' lesson, most teacher 'informs' occur when the teacher is presenting a new structure or vocabulary item. This presentation may take various forms, all aiming at gaining pupils' attention and making them guess the rule of the structure or the meaning of the vocabulary item being taught.

    'Acknowledge' may overlap with the teacher's contribution because pupils usually do not wait until the teacher has finished the presentation but give cues of their understanding while s/he is speaking. In so doing, pupils intend to find out whether they have made the right guess if they are not sure, to display their knowledge at this very first stage if they are sure their guess is appropriate, or simply to show that they are following what the teacher is saying. Gaies (1983b) argues that in so doing pupils negotiate their intake. Interestingly, 'acknowledge' is occasionally called for by the teacher, namely by creating specific slots in her turn (see also Van Lier 1988: 116). The teacher may provide feedback for the pupils' interventions, as in 3 T in the following example:

(44)

Teacher	-I-	1 T	: Some years ago, something happened in India (s.). Gas leaked from a factory and many people died uh.. died and were injured etc. (i)
Inform			
	-R-	2 P1	: Blind (ack.)
	-F-	3 T	: Yes (eva.) People were blind because of the gas (com.)

                           (3rd grade - Lesson 1)

In the data, the act 'acknowledge' is occasionally performed in Arabic and/or in the pupil's second language, i.e. French, as in 2 P1 and 3 P2 in the example below:

(45)

Teacher	-I-	1 T	: Now (m.). We have a mosque and a church (i.)
Inform			<T. writes 'church' on BB.>
	-R-	2 P1	: *Église* <French word for 'church'> (ack.)
			[
		3 P2	: *L-kanisa* <Arabic word for 'church'> (ack.)
			(1st grade - Lesson 4)

In the data, 'acknowledge' may also occur after feedback, especially after the acts 'comment' or 'repair', as in the following examples:

(46)

Teacher	-I-	1 T	: If you want to buy books, where do you go? (el.)
Elicit	-R-	2 P1	: When I need some books, I go to the library (rep.)
	-F-	3 T	: Yes. library (acc.). But at the library, you can stay there to read or- (com.)
		4 PP	: -> Yes (ack.)
			(2nd grade - Lesson 1)

(47)

Teacher	-I-	1 T	: What do we call dollar, pound, French franc etc.? (el.)
Elicit	-R-	2 PP	: Money (rep.)
	-F-	3 T	: Money [2]. Money [2]. No (eva.)
Re-Initiate	-I-	4 T	: Especially, dollar, pound, French franc (cl.)
Re-Initiate	-I-	5 T	: Especially, dollar, pound, French franc (cl.)
	-R-		<no response from pupils>
	-F-	6 T	: Well (m.). It's hard currency (re.).
	-R-	7 PP	: Ah! *L- 'umla-ssa 'ba . L- 'umla-ssa 'ba* (ack.) <Arabic phrase for 'hard currency'>
			(3rd grade - Lesson 3)

Indeed, it may be argued that in the above extracts, the acts 'comment' or 'repair' along with the act 'acknowledge' following them constitute a "'Janus-faced' move, closing one exchange and opening the next" (Stubbs 1983: 132). They may be considered either a 'comment' or 'repair' followed by 'acknowledge', and part of the 'feedback' move, or an 'informative' followed by 'acknowledge', and part of a teacher 'inform' exchange. The first analysis is preferable for it is inappropriate to isolate an utterance for analysis without examining its relation to other utterances in the interaction (see also Schwartz 1980). The acts 'comment' and 'repair', in the previous example, are closely related to what has preceded, and cannot be analyzed appropriately if regarded as part of a subsequent 'inform'. A similar problem has already been pointed out by Coulthard (1977: 113), namely the problem of how to code a 'comment' that seems to drift into an 'inform'.

Apparently, pupils in TL classrooms are continuously trying to display their understanding of the teacher's contribution. Thus, 'acknowledge' may also occur after a 'starter' in a teacher 'elicit' or a teacher 'inform', generating a 'compound exchange'. Example:

(48)
Compound -I- 1 T   : OK. Now (m.). Listen, people don't want war= (s.)
Teacher   [
Elicit   -R- 2 PP :   Yes (ack.)
              -I- 3 T   : =What do they want? (el.)
              -R- 4 P   : Peace (rep.)
              -F- 5 T   : yes (eva.)
                          (2nd grade - Lesson 4)

Subcategories of the act Acknowledge. In TL classroom discourse, the act 'acknowledge' is typical. The pupil displays his understanding of the teacher's contribution using different strategies. Boulima (1990) found out that the different occurrences of this act would be better accounted for if subcategories of this act were developed. The system of analysis FLIAS makes use of six subcategories of this act. Gaies (1983b) (cf. Chapter 2) studied 'learner feedback' in ESL classroom discourse, and devised subcategories of the 'reacting move'. Some of these subcategories have been very useful for describing different types of 'acknowledge'. Thus, four of Gaies's (1983b) subcategories were borrowed by FLIAS and used as subcategories of 'acknowledge'; two others were added. The six subcategories of 'acknowledge' are presented below with definitions and examples. With respect to the first four subcategories, the definitions given here are based on those provided by Gaies (1983a: 200).

a) *Comprehension signal.* The pupil indicates that a preceding teacher utterance has been understood, using non-verbal signals or verbal ones such as 'yes' (see examples (46) and (48)).

b) *Confirmation by repetition.* By repeating a single word or an entire utterance, the pupil signals comprehension or non comprehension, or tests whether he has correctly heard the teacher's utterance (see examples (19) and (49)).

(49)
Compound -I- 1 T   : We can say: I was watching TV= (i.)
Teacher   [
Inform   -R- 2 PP :   TV (ack.)
             -I- 3 T   : =meanwhile my brother was doing his homework (i.)
                     (3rd grade - Lesson 2)

c)*Confirmation by paraphrase.* The pupil indicates comprehension by paraphrasing a word or an utterance produced by the teacher, as in 2 P in the following example:

(50)
Teacher -I- 1 T : We can say for example that the weather in Rabat is damp;
Inform   whereas in Marrakesh it's not damp (i.)
        -R- 2 P : Hot (ack.)
        -F- 3 T : Not hot (eva.)
                 (3rd grade - Lesson 1)

d) *Utterance completion.* The pupil signals comprehension by anticipating the rest of a teacher's utterance, as in 4 P1 and 4 P2 in the following example:

(51)
Compound -I- 1 T   : There were some people there= (i.)
Teacher   [
Inform   -R- 2 P1 :   Yes (ack.)
             -I- 3 T   : =They saw- =(i.)
                                  [
             -R- 4 P1 :   Mr. Barki (ack.)
                                [   ]
                5 P2 :   The man (ack.)
             -F- 6 T   : =the incident (re.)
             -I- 7 T   : They saw the incident. Well (i.)
                                       [
             -R- 8 P1 :   But didn't do anything (ack.)
             -F- 9 T   : Yes (eva.)
                     (2nd grade - Lesson 1)

e) Confirmation by translation. The pupil indicates comprehension by translating a word or utterance, produced by the teacher, into a language that classroom participants also know. In the present data, pupils makes use of Arabic or French for this purpose, as illustrated in 2 PP, 5 PP and 8 P in the following example:

(52)
Teacher -I- 1 T   : <pointing to a picture> Here is the COURTYARD (i.)
Inform -R- 2 PP : L-khassa. L-khassa <Arabic word for 'fountain'> (ack.)
        -F- 3 T   : No (eva.)
Teacher -I- 4 T   : This is a fountain <pointing to the fountain> (i.)
Inform -R- 5 PP : Fontaine <French word for 'fountain'> (ack.)

Teacher -I- 6 T   : And this is a COURTYARD (i.). In our school there's a
Inform   courtyard. At ten o'clock during the break you don't leave
                      the school .. You stay at school in the courtyard (com.)
        -R- 7 PP : Courtyard (ack.)
            8 P   : Wst-e-ddar <Arabic phrase meaning 'hall'> (ack.)
                      (1st grade - Lesson 1)

f) Adding relevant information. The pupil indicates comprehension by supplying information in agreement with the teacher's contribution. This is usually carried out through shouted out words or phrases because the pupil does not have time to produce a full sentence, as illustrated in the first 'acknowledge' in the following example:

(53)
Compound -I- 1 T   : SMUGGLE .. Take something which is forbidden.
Teacher   You hide it and take it to another country to sell it
Inform   there (i.). OK (m.). For example you take gold=
                                                              [
        -R- 2 P1 : ->   Drugs (ack.)
        -I- 3 T   : =and you sell it in Algeria or=
                                      [   ]
        -R- 4 P1 :   Abroad (ack.)
        -I- 5 T   : =in Spain (com.)
                      (3rd grade - Lesson 3)

These subcategories of the act 'acknowledge' have given much insight into the data and have been useful in distinguishing between informative and non-informative 'acknowledge'. Informative 'acknowledge' includes the four subcategories: 'confirmation by paraphrase', 'utterance completion', 'confirmation by translation', and 'adding relevant information'. On the other hand, non-informative 'acknowledge' encompasses the two subcategories: 'comprehension signal' and 'confirmation by repetition'.

List of All Acts

The acts which have been used to code the data are listed below with their abbreviations:
1) marker (m.)
2) starter (s.)
3) elicitation (el.)
4) check (ch.)
5) directive (d.)
6) informative (i.)
7) prompt (p.)
8) clue (cl.)
9) repair (re.)
10) repair-initiation (re.ini.)
11) comprehension check (com. ch.)
12) confirmation check (con. ch.)
13) clarification request (cla. req.)
14) challenge (cha.)
15) cue (cu.)
16) bid (b.)
17) nomination (nom.)
18) reply (rep.)
19) react (rea.)
20) comment (com.)
21) accept (acc.)
22) evaluate (eva.)
23) metastatement (ms.)
24) conclusion (con.)
25) aside (z.)
26) silent stress (ˆ)
27) acknowledge (ack.)

Conclusion

This chapter has presented, in detail, the system used to code and analyze the data, namely 'Foreign Language Interaction Analysis System' (FLIAS), providing illustrations from the data, and arguing for the changes and the categories Boulima (1990) introduced into Sinclair & Coulthard's system. 'FLIAS' is, to a great extent, an adequate system for handling TL classroom discourse, since it has enabled us to code all the data, and has facilitated the analysis of 'negotiated interaction'. The next three chapters present and discuss the results of the empirical study undertaken in the present work. Chapter five focuses on the discourse functions of 'negotiated interaction'. Chapter six shows how frequent 'negotiated interaction' is in the data and compares its frequency by proficiency level. Chapter seven endeavours to tackle 'negotiated interaction' in relation to the notion of unequal-power discourse usually ascribed to classroom discourse.

CHAPTER 5
Discourse Functions of Negotiation
in the TL Classroom

Introduction

The literature on negotiated interaction has mainly been concerned with a particular type of negotiation, namely the negotiation of meaning. However, as Aston (1986: 135) observes "not all conversational trouble concerns issues of comprehensibility, even though that is clearly a major difficulty in LL [learner-learner] and NL [native-learner] interaction." Hence, an interesting question to ask is "what discourse functions does negotiated interaction fulfil in the TL classroom?" The present chapter captures the most outstanding discourse functions of negotiation in the TL classroom. After a preliminary analysis of the data, several functions have been identified. These lead to two main types of negotiation: *didactic* and *conversational* .

Didactic Negotiation

Introduction

The pedagogic orientation of TL classroom interaction warrants the occurrence of didactic negotiation which aims at the resolution of interactional problems specific to the TL classroom. The resolution process results in four didactic negotiation genres: 'medium-oriented negotiation', 'comprehension check-oriented negotiation', 'turn-taking-oriented negotiation', and 'complete sentence-oriented negotiation'. These are presented below with illustrations from the data.

Medium-Oriented Negotiation

This negotiation genre aims to repair errors related to the medium of interaction. It is an exchange or a sequence of exchanges aiming at the resolution of a 'trouble source' (Schegloff et al. 1977) caused by misuse of the forms and/or functions of the target language, as in the following examples:

(54)
Re-   -I- 1 T   : <The teacher had asked pupils to give sentences using
initiate   'to tell tales'> Yes (nom.)
            -R- 2 P1 : When I was very- when I was very young my
                         grandmother tell me
                                        [
Teacher   -I- 3 T   : ->   told (re./p.)
Initiated   -R- 4 P1 : told me some tales (rep.)
Negotiate   -F- 5 T   : Some tales [1+] (eva.)
                         (3rd grade - Lesson 1)

In the above extract, the negotiation is triggered by the grammatical error (tell) in the pupil's reply (2 P1). The teacher undoubtedly understood the message; so there is no breakdown in communication. However, she initiates a negotiate exchange by an act simultaneously functioning as a 'repair' and a 'prompt' (3 T). Through this act, the teacher directs the pupil's attention to the grammatical error by repairing it, and prompts him to restart his utterance at the point where the 'trouble source' occurred.

(55)
Re-   -I- 1 T   : <The teacher had asked pupils to give sentences using
initiate   the verb 'to leak'> (el.)
            -R- 2 P1 : In the present= (rep.)
                                        [
Teacher   -I- 3 T   : ->   In the present? (con. ch.)... PrisoN.
Initiated   PrisoN (re./p.)
Negotiate   -R- 4 P2 : In jail (ack.)
            -F- 5 T   : Yes (eva.) in jail (acc.) or in prison (com.)
Re-   -I- 6 T   : Yes (p)
initiate   -R- 7 P1 : =In jail, the [seilin]= (rep.)
                                        [
Teacher   -I- 8 T   : ->   the ceiling (re./p.)
Initiated   -R- 9 P1 : =leak= (rep.)
Negotiate   ⌈
                         ⌊
Teacher   -I- 10 T : ->   leaks (re./p.)
Initiated   -R-11 P1 : =in the [hi:vər] <French word for winter pronounced
Negotiate   as if it were an English word> (rep.)

Teacher   -I- 12 T   : -> in the winter (re./p.)
Initiated   -R-13 P1   : in the winter (rep.)
Negotiate -F-14 T   : All right (eva.).. in the winter (acc.)
                          (3rd grade - Lesson 1)

The above extract contains a series of 'medium-oriented negotiations' initiated by the teacher to repair P1's reply which contains many 'trouble sources' caused by the pupil's limited proficiency in English. The first teacher-initiated negotiation is triggered by a lexical error in the pupil's reply: he misuses the word 'present' to mean 'prison'. The second negotiation is triggered by the pupil's mispronunciation of the word 'ceiling'. The third negotiation is triggered by a morphological error, as the pupil uses the verb 'leak' without the third-person singular marker 's'. The last negotiation is triggered by another lexical error due to an interference from the pupil's second language French: he uses the French word 'hiver' (winter) pronounced as if it were an English word.

It might be argued that the negotiation triggered by the 'trouble source' "present" occurring in the pupil's turn 2 P1 is a 'meaning-oriented negotiation' rather than a 'medium-oriented negotiation'. However, since the teacher does not wait for the pupil to answer her 'confirmation check' "in the present?" but immediately corrects the 'trouble source', we are confident in arguing that there has been no breakdown in communication, though such a 'trouble source' might cause nonunderstanding in ordinary conversation and even in classroom interaction.

(56)
Teacher   -I- 1 T   : Next question (el.)
Elicit   -R- 2 P1   : Why Jane won't be there? (rep.)

Teacher   -I- 3 T   : -> It's a QUESTION (cl.)
Initiated   -R- 4 P1   : Why won't Jane be there? (rep.)
Negotiate -F- 5 T   : Yes (eva.)
                          (1st grade - lesson 5)

In the above extract, the 'teacher-initiated negotiate' is triggered by the pupil's repairable utterance in 2 P1, which is an uninverted question with rising intonation. The teacher initiates a negotiation by providing a 'clue' to the pupil. This is followed by a correct reply from the pupil (4 P1) which is positively evaluated by the teacher. Zamel (1981) refers to the type of information provided in 3 T of the above extract as 'informational feedback' because it provides information which is useful for the pupil in confirming or rejecting his hypotheses about the target language.

In the three extracts cited above, the teacher's acts 'repair-initiation', 'repair', 'confirmation check', and 'clue' function to provide what Schachter (1984, 1986) refers to as 'negative input'. That is to say, "information provided to the learner that her utterance was in some way insufficient, deviant, unacceptable or not understandable" (Schachter 1986: 215). This metalinguistic information relating to the correctness of learners' production is, according to Schachter (1986), available both directly (through corrections) and indirectly (through confirmation checks, clarification requests, and failures to understand).

Such metalinguistic information, according to Schachter (1984, 1986) and Swain (1985), helps the L2 learner to confirm or reject the hypotheses s/he is making about the language; and this is likely to have an impact on the development of her/his interlanguage, shaping it towards target language norms. On the same wavelength, Chaudron (1988: 134) points out that "[t]he information available in feedback allows learners to confirm, disconfirm, and possibly modify the hypothetical, "transitional" rules of their developing grammars." In contrast, Krashen (1982a) belittles the importance of metalinguistic feedback and considers correction not only useless for acquisition but also dangerous as it may lead to a negative affective response. According to him, the only data necessary are the actually occurring linguistic forms provided by the native speaker in communicative situations. Similarly, according to Flynn (1983), the only input necessary for the learner is the actually occurring linguistic forms, 'negative input' excluded. On the basis of findings of several studies of negotiated interaction (cf. Chapter 2), we assume that what Schachter (1984, 1986) calls 'negative input' is a key variable in TL development. As the above examples illustrate, by initiating a 'medium-oriented negotiation', the teacher attempts to help the pupil overcome a speaking problem (see 'helping' in Van Lier 1988), and this, as Van Lier (1988: 120) contends, "may be a significant pedagogical feature of L2 discourse."

It is worth noting that when the teacher interrupts to prompt or help the pupil to come up with the appropriate contribution, as in the above extracts, s/he has no intention of taking the floor nor of stopping the turn in progress. Pupils seem to understand this for they always proceed with the reply immediately after the teacher's *prompting* or *helping* (realized by means of acts such as 'repair', 'repair-initiation', 'clue' or 'confirmation check'). This suggests that there is an unstated communicative convention at work which the pupils seem to have internalized.

As the above extracts illustrate, 'medium-oriented negotiation' frequently occurs in intra-turn position. In this case, it is subservient to the turn in progress, because it functions to facilitate the development and supervise the formulation of that turn. The repair sequences resulting from a teacher initiation of a 'medium-oriented negotiation' can be regarded, to quote Van Lier (1988:

207), "as annoying hiccups in the interaction." As Van Lier (1988: 207-8) further argues,

> [i]t appears that certain types of repair need to be done in appropriate slots, in separate turns, while others are done within the turn in which the trouble occurs. The former generally deal with problems of hearing or understanding the talk, and with matters relating to content, whereas the latter deal with 'helping out' with speaking problems, and occur immediately after the trouble spot, without waiting for the turn to end.

Schegloff et al. (1977) assert that 'intra-turn repair' does not occur in NS-NS everyday conversation; and McHoul (1990) reports its absence also in L1 classrooms. On the basis of this evidence, it may be argued, along with Van Lier (1988), that 'intra-turn repair' is a TL classroom specific way of repairing.

When teacher repair occurs in intra-turn position, it may deny the pupil the opportunity to do self-repair which, according to Van Lier (1988: 211), is "probably an important learning activity." Indeed, though we recognize the importance of 'negative input', we would agree with Van Lier that "some delay of other-repair (both initiation and error-replacement) may be beneficial, since it would promote the development of self-monitoring and pragmatic adjustment which is essential to competence in the target language" (Van Lier 1988: 211).

In the data, most medium-oriented negotiation sequences are initiated by the teacher, as can be seen in the above examples. However, this type of negotiation may also be initiated by a pupil, usually as a reaction to another pupil's repairable contribution or when the pupil wants to inquire about an item or an aspect related to the form of the target language. Consider the examples below:

```
(57)
Re-        -I- 1 T   : <The teacher had asked pupils to answer the question:
initiate               "Where do you go if you want to buy some meat?> (el.)
                       Aouad (nom.)
           -R- 2 P1  : If we need to buy some meat to put it on Couscous, I
                       go to the butcher (rep.)
Pupil      -I- 3 PP  : -> Butcher'S. Butcher'S (re.)
Initiated  -R- 4 P1  : Butcher's (rep.)
Negotiate  -F- 5 T   : Yes (eva.)
                       (2nd grade - lesson 1)
```

In the above extract, several pupils initiate a negotiation (3 PP) to repair the 'trouble source' "butcher" occurring in 2 P1. The initiation of the negotiate exchange is realized by the act 'repair' which is acknowledged by the pupil for

he repeats the form provided by the pupils (i.e., butcher's). This is followed by
a positive evaluation from the teacher who thereby closes the exchange.

(58)
Re-   -I- 1 T   : <The teacher had asked pupils to transform some
initiate   sentences using 'unless'> Romani (nom.)
              -R- 2 P1 : If he doesn't drink this, he won't recover .. Unless he
                          drink this he (rep.)
                                        [
Teacher -I- 3 T   :   He drinks (re./p.)
Initiated
Negotiate

Pupil   -I- 4 P1 : Drinks? (con. ch.)
Initiated -R- 5 T   : Yes (rep.)
Negotiate

Teacher
Initiated -R- 6 P1 : drinks this he won't recover (rep.)
Negotiate
                    (3rd grade - lesson 5)

In the above extract, the pupil has to transform the sentence "If he doesn't
drink this, he won't recover" using the conjunction 'unless'. Her reply in 2 P1
contains a language error, namely the omission of the third-person singular
marker in "he drink." This brings about a 'teacher-initiated negotiate' functioning
to repair the trouble source and prompt the pupil to proceed with her reply
incorporating the repair. The following 'pupil-initiated negotiate' is embedded in
the 'teacher-initiated negotiate'. The pupil initiates this negotiate exchange in
order to elicit a confirmation of the teacher's repair before she proceeds with her
reply. This may be considered an 'appeal for assistance', in the sense of Tarone
(1980, 1981), which the L2 learner uses as a communication strategy to avoid or
repair troubles of communication.

Comprehension Check-Oriented Negotiation

'Comprehension check-oriented negotiation' is an exchange or a series of
exchanges initiated by the teacher by means of the act 'comprehension check' in
order to check whether pupils have understood a previous utterance and/or
whether they are following what's going on, as in the following examples:

(59)

Teacher -I- 1 T : And we can speak as well of uh ... If you wash your
Inform   clothes and you put them on the washing line and there
                     is no sun shining.. you take them off but they are still
                     damp. If you wear damp clothes, you'll get ill (i.).=
                                                            [   ]
        -R- 2 P :   ill. Yes (ack.)
        -I- 3 T : =They are not really wet but they are damp (com.)
Teacher -I- 4 T : -> Do you know what is 'wet'? (com. ch.)
Initiated -R- 5 PP : Yes. Yes (rep.)
Negotiate

Teacher -I- 6 T : If you go outside in the rain, you'll get wet. But if you
Inform   put your clothes on the washing line, you wait for two
                     days and there is no sun shine and you take them and
                     they are still damp. There is some water in them but just
                     a little and if you wear them you'll get ill (i.).
                     (3rd grade - Lesson 1)

The above extract starts with a 'Teacher Inform' where the teacher is trying
to explain the word 'damp'; but while she is explaining she uses the word 'wet'.
As she wants to make sure that pupils know this word, she initiates a
'comprehension check-oriented negotiation' (4 T). Though the pupils reply with
an affirmation (5 PP), the teacher gives an 'inform' where she reviews the
meaning of the word 'wet' before using it to explain the word 'damp' (6 T).
   'Comprehension check-oriented negotiation' is typical of classroom
interaction, where the teacher needs to continuously check whether learners
comprehend and follow what's going on in each classroom activity. This type of
negotiation saliently indicates the teacher's attempt, on the one hand, to make
sure pupils understand what's going and, on the other hand, to avoid
conversational trouble.
   Early (1985) found that in content classrooms 'comprehension checks'
occurred significantly more frequently than other negotiating questions, namely
'confirmation checks' and 'clarification requests'. Similarly, both Long & Sato's
(1983) and Pica & Long's (1986) studies found that while 'comprehension
checks' were the least frequent in dyadic NS-NNS conversations, they were the
most frequent in L2 classroom interaction, in comparison with 'confirmation
checks' and 'clarification requests'. Long (1983b: 219) argues that
'comprehension checks' will occur more frequently when the major flow of
information is from teacher to students, whereas 'confirmation checks' and
'clarification requests' will occur more frequently when there is a two-way flow

of information. We were also interested in investigating the frequency of 'comprehension check-oriented negotiation' in order to provide further support to the findings of these studies. The result of this investigation is revealed in Chapter six.

The other two types of didactic negotiation to be described are respectively concerned with organizing pupil participation in TL classroom interaction and making pupils speak in complete sentences. Chaudron (1977: 32) considered 'speaking out of turn' and 'not speaking in complete sentences' as errors of L2 classroom interaction and discourse. Sinclair and Coulthard (1975: 51) pointed out that "so important is feedback that if it does not occur we feel confident in saying that the teacher has withheld it for some strategic purpose." As Sacks (1972: 31) pointed out, "the resulting silence will be taken as notable - a rejoinder in its own right, a silence to be heard." Thus, the teacher may refrain from giving an evaluative feedback following a pupil reply, in order to remind the pupil(s) that a rule of TL classroom interaction has been violated (cf. the 'turn-taking rule' and the 'complete sentence rule' in the following two sections). Violation of these rules may, though not necessarily, result in negotiation. When negotiation does occur, the teacher will usually explicitly remind the pupils of the rules by such cues as "Raise your hand" and "a complete sentence, please," which results in two types of negotiation: 'turn-taking-oriented negotiation' and 'complete sentence-oriented negotiation'.

Turn-Taking-Oriented Negotiation

In all forms of spoken discourse, there are conventions about who speaks when (Schegloff & Sacks 1974). In the classroom, the teacher has the right to speak whenever she wants to; but the pupils do not have such a right. In principle, they are not supposed to speak unless the teacher allocates a turn to them. Sinclair & Coulthard (1975: 113) noted that "'[s]houting out' or 'calling out' was proscribed even when the answer was correct. Pupils who made an answering move when a preliminary bid followed by teacher nomination was required were told "can't hear you if you shout"", which implies that the teacher refrains from giving an evaluation after shouted out replies. This is also true for the present data; the teacher withholds feedback as a means of sanctioning the pupil(s) for having violated the 'turn-taking rule' operating in classroom discourse. Accordingly, an explicit reminder of what this rule prescribes usually follows the 'shouted out' reply, for example: "Raise your hand," "Don't speak all at the same time," and "If you don't raise your hand, I can't hear you." Following a shouted out reply, such cues or simply ignoring the reply and nominating a particular pupil to speak, usually initiate what we refer to as 'turn-taking-oriented negotiation'. Consider the following extract:

(60)
Teacher	-I- 1 T	: Now (m.). Exercise 5 ... Choose the best explanation
Elicit		according to the context (s.). 'Leak'.. What does it
		mean? (el.)
	-R- 2 P1	: Let the rain in (rep.)

Teacher	-I- 3 T	: -> Jeddoub (nom.)
Initiated	-R- 4 P2	: It means. was in bad condition (rep.)
Negotiate		

Pupil	-I- 5 PP	: Let the rain in. Let the rain in (re./rep.)
Initiated		
Negotiate	-F- 6 T	: Was in bad condition (acc.). No (eva.)

Pupil	-I- 7 PP	: Let the rain in (re./rep.)
Initiated		
Negotiate		

Teacher	-I- 8 T	: -> Raise your hand (cu.) .. yes (nom.)
Initiated	-R- 9 P3	: Leak is. let the rain in (rep.)
Negotiate	-F-10 T	: Let the rain in (acc.).Yes. Very good (eva.). If you
		say that the roof is leaking .. it means that it lets the
		rain in (com.)
		(3rd grade - Lesson 1)

In the above extract, the teacher refrains from providing feedback after the first correct reply (2 P1) to her 'elicitation' because she intends to produce 'a silence to be heard' (Sacks 1972), as the pupil has spoken out of turn. By withholding feedback, she aims at reminding the pupil that he has violated a classroom interactional convention, and that as a result he is deprived of knowing whether the reply he has given is a correct one. By nominating another pupil to answer the question (3 T), she initiates a 'turn-taking-oriented negotiation' to suggest that an interactional problem has arisen and that resolving it necessitates ignoring the reply which was given out of turn and re-initiating the exchange once again (see also McHoul 1978).

Being incorrect, the reply in 4 P2 engenders a 'pupil-initiated negotiation' aiming to repair the trouble source in 4 P2. The repair in 5 PP, which simultaneously functions as a reply to the teacher's question, is also not evaluated, because the 'turn-taking rule' prescribes speaking one at a time (see Mehan 1979 and Van Lier 1988). Apparently, the pupils are so involved in the interaction and so eager to repair the 'trouble source' occurring in 4 P2 that they forget about the 'turn-taking rule' and do not even wait till the teacher has evaluated the reply in 4 P2. As a result, the teacher ignores their contribution though it is a correct reply to her question, and instead reacts to the reply in 4 P2 by negatively evaluating it.

However, as the teacher does not explicitly remind the pupils of the 'turn-taking rule', several pupils violate the rule for the third time, and come up with the reply in 7PP. At that time, besides refraining from providing an evaluative feedback, the teacher reminds them of the convention: "Raise your hand," which explicitly informs the pupils that they should not speak unless they are allocated a turn by the teacher, and that they should speak one at a time - 'the one floor law' (Van Lier 1988: 98).

In our attempt to investigate whether the 'turn-taking rule' is a powerful rule operating in EFL classroom discourse (cf. Boulima 1990), we found that there is a strong positive correlation between the violation of this rule and the teacher refraining from providing evaluative feedback ($r = 0.772$, $p<.05$). Yet, as Griffin and Mehan (1981: 201) point out, there are occasions where this rule fails to operate: "[w]hen the called out answers attain the uniformity of a choral response, when an unexpected individual calls out, when a valuable answer is called out, the teacher may act as if the rule is not there." Furthermore, Schinke-Llano (1983: 149) points to 'directed' and 'non-directed' interactions in classroom discourse. "Directed interactions are those characterized by the teacher's turn-taking with a single student [...]. Non-directed interactions, on the other hand, are those characterized by the involvement of many students or the entire class." 'Non-directed' interactions necessarily imply the violation of the 'one-at-a-time' convention prescribed by the 'turn-taking rule', operating in classroom interaction.

Such factors as those pointed out by Griffin and Mehan (1981) and Schinke-Llano (1983), and which prevent the 'turn-taking rule' from operating, do not necessarily suggest that this rule is not powerful, but rather that there is some flexibility in terms of pupil participation in TL classroom discourse (see also Van Lier 1988: 137), and that teacher initiation of 'turn-taking-oriented negotiation' is a technique which is used by teachers to regulate pupil participation in classroom discourse.

Complete Sentence-Oriented Negotiation

Nystrom (1983) directs attention to another rule of classroom interaction which, this time, is typical of TL classroom discourse. That is the 'complete sentence rule' implying that, in the TL classroom, pupils are supposed to answer in complete sentences (see also Mehan 1974). This rule also operates in the present data; the teacher occasionally refrains from evaluating the pupil's reply or, in

Sinclair & Coulthard's (1975) terms, 'withholds feedback' when the pupil fails
to answer in a complete sentence. The sanctions that are issued from the
violation of the 'complete sentence rule' explicitly inform the pupil of what the
rule prescribes. Hence, the teacher usually comes up with such remarks as:
'make a sentence', 'I want a complete sentence', and 'a sentence please'.
Consider the following extract:

> (61)
> Teacher   -I- 1 T   : What did he promise him? (el.)
> Elicit   -R- 2 P1   : Not to say anything (rep.)
>
> Teacher   -I- 3 T   : -> Make a sentence (p.)
> Initiated -R- 4 P1   : He promised not to say anything to the customs (rep.)
> Negotiate -F- 5 T   : Yes (eva.)
>   (3rd grade - Lesson 3)

In the above extract, the first reply provided by the pupil (2 P1) is not
evaluated by the teacher because the pupil has not answered in a complete
sentence. Accordingly, the teacher initiates a 'complete sentence-oriented
negotiation' (3 T) in order to remind the pupil of the 'complete sentence rule' and
prompt him to answer the question using a complete sentence. Hence, the pupil
reformulates his reply using a complete sentence (4 P) which is positively
evaluated by the teacher (5 T).

Conclusion

The types of negotiations described above are *didactic* because they are
pedagogic in orientation. Such negotiations are typical of TL instructional
discourse where learners continuously struggle with their interlanguage in order
to use the target language accurately and where the teacher or, at times, other
learners, strive(s) to help them with their speaking problems, which results in
what we have labelled as 'medium-oriented negotiation'. The other three types of
didactic negotiation are exclusively teacher-initiated and concern the teacher's
responsibility to check pupils' comprehension of the target language samples
occurring in classroom interaction, to organize pupil participation in classroom
discourse, and to make pupils speak in complete sentences. These are,
respectively, 'comprehension check-oriented negotiation', 'turn-taking-oriented
negotiation', and 'complete sentence-oriented negotiation'.

Nonetheless, in addition to didactic negotiation, the data reveal the
occurrence of another type of negotiation - which we refer to as 'conversational
negotiation' - that is common to all face-to-face interaction and that addresses

various problems of communication, including problems of hearing, understanding, and sustaining the conversation. McHoul (1990) asserts that in classrooms teacher and learner roles are clearly defined, so that it is the learner who has the trouble, and the teacher who repairs it. In the data, this is, to a large extent, true for 'didactic' but not for 'conversational' negotiation, since in 'conversational negotiations', the teacher may also be the participant who has the trouble; and the resolution may be done by either the teacher or the pupil(s), or by both parties cooperatively.

Conversational Negotiation

Introduction

What Schachter (1984: 172) views "as equally important as sources of negative input, is a whole set of response types, ranging from explicit corrections at one end of a continuum, through confirmation checks and clarification requests, to [...] failures to understand at the other end." Thus, with this expanded view of negative input, the widely held claim concerning the lack of availability of negative input (Day et al.'s (1984) study shows that 90% of all occurring errors are not corrected) "is severely weakened, and may well be untenable" (Schachter 1984: 176). Interestingly, according to Schachter (1984) the least explicit type of negative input is the most efficient in terms of interlanguage development towards target language norms. She writes:

> The most obvious source of negative data, explicit correction, is also the least serious in terms of the intelligibility factor and thus, one might argue, is the least efficacious as a source of negative input. The explicit correction [...] is meant to convey the message that the conversational partner knows exactly what message was transmitted by the learner but is unwilling to accept it in the form in which it was transmitted (Schachter 1984: 172).

In contrast to 'didactic negotiation', 'conversational negotiation' is an exchange or a series of exchanges aiming at the resolution of the sort of conversational problems that may occur in any face-to-face interaction, including NS-NS conversation. It is triggered by problems such as non-/mishearing, non/incomplete understanding, and 'schema mismatch', but also by the interlocutors' attempts to repair the meaning conveyed in a previous turn, their desire to reach an agreement on a given 'disputable' proposition, express surprise concerning the content of a previous utterance, sustain the conversation, and display their satisfactoriness of the talk. This leads to seven kinds of negotiation, namely 1)'hearing-oriented negotiation', 2) 'meaning-oriented negotiation', 3) 'content-oriented negotiation', 4) 'general knowledge-oriented negotiation', 5) 'agreement-oriented negotiation', 6) 'surprise display-oriented negotiation', and 7) 'conversational continuant'. These negotiation genres are described below with illustrations from the data.

Hearing-Oriented Negotiation

'Hearing-oriented negotiation' is an exchange or a series of exchanges oriented towards the resolution of a 'trouble source' due to mishearing or nonhearing. Needless to say, hearing problems are frequent in any face-to-face interaction, and TL classroom interaction is no exception. On the contrary, it is more liable to problems of hearing due to the use of the foreign language, the sounds of which the pupils are not yet familiar with, and due to the background noise caused by the class while one of the participants is speaking. Consider the following examples:

(62)
Teacher   -I- 1 T   : How often does she wash the windows? (el.)
Elicit   -R- 2 P1 : She washes the windows once a month (rep.)

Teacher   -I- 3 T   : -> She washes the windows-? (re.ini.)
Initiated -R- 4 P1 : Once a month (rep.)
Negotiate -F- 5 T   : Once a month (acc.). Yeah (eva.)
                     (1st grade - Lesson 3)

In the above extract, the teacher does not hear part of the pupil's utterance (2 P1); therefore, she initiates a 'hearing-oriented negotiation' by means of the act 'repair-initiation' (3 T) (see also Schegloff et al. 1977, Schwartz 1980, and Van Lier 1988). The pupil provides a reply (4 P1) which the teacher accepts and evaluates in 5 T.

(63)
Teacher   -I- 1 T   : Who wants to repeat what Laarbi said? (el.).
Elicit   Mr Halim (nom.)
          -R- 2 P1 : Laarbi said that if he could a job in town, he would
                     <unint.> (rep.)
Teacher   -I- 3 T   : -> What? (re. ini.) I don't hear anything (com.)
Initiated -R- 4 P1 : Laarbi said that if he could a job in town, he
Negotiate   <unint.> (rep.)

```
Teacher     -I- 5 T   : -> He-? (re. ini.)
Initiated
Negotiate

Teacher     -I- 6 T   : -> What would he do? (re. ini./ cl.)
Initiated   -R- 7 P1  : He would study in the evenings (rep.)
Negotiate   -F- 8 T   : Yes (eva.).. He would study in the evenings (acc.)
                        (2nd grade - lesson 3)
```

The above extract occurred when the pupils were doing a 'reported speech' exercise. The extract starts with a 'Teacher Elicit' where the teacher asks a pupil to report what Laarbi said; that is to report the sentence: "If I can get a job in town, I will study in the evenings." The pupil gives a reply which is unintelligible mainly because it is spoken in a low voice but also because of the background noise. Therefore, the teacher initiates a 'hearing-oriented negotiation' (3 T) to let the pupil know that she could not hear the reply. The pupil gives the reply a second time but it is still unintelligible. Hence, the teacher initiates another 'hearing-oriented negotiation' (5 T) to which the pupil does not provide a reply, probably because he presumes that there is something wrong with his answer. Accordingly, the teacher initiates a third 'hearing-oriented negotiation' (6 T) which, by virtue of containing the modal verb 'would', also functions as a 'clue' to the pupil to help him come up with the correct reply. As a matter of fact, following this 'clue', the pupil gives the correct reply and in an audible and intelligible voice, this time.

Hence, we might conclude that in the above extract, the pupil is not sure of the correctness of his reply; therefore, he keeps giving it in a low voice (2 P1) (4 P1) despite the teacher's explicit comment "I don't hear anything" (3 T). What's more, the pupil refrains from giving a reply after the teacher's 'hearing-oriented negotiation' in 5 T, probably because the teacher uses a tactic, namely "He-?" that is usually used in a 'medium-oriented negotiation', when the pupil's reply contains a language error. However, when the teacher initiates the negotiation by means of a 'repair-initiation' which also functions as a 'clue', i.e., "What would he do?", the pupil could come up with the correct reply. The teacher's implicit 'clue' in 6 T has certainly functioned as 'informational feedback', in the sense of Zamel (1981), which has helped the pupil to confirm or reject the hypotheses he has made about the way the sentence in question should be reported. This informational feedback has certainly either given him more self-confidence to utter the reply in an audible voice (in case his original reply was correct) or provided him with additional information which helped him to come up with the correct reply (in case his original reply was incorrect).

The hearing-oriented negotiations in the above extracts are all initiated by the teacher. Yet, the data show that this type of negotiation is not typically teacher-initiated but may also be pupil-initiated. Consider the following example:

(64)
Teacher   -I- 1 T   : He couldn't spend an hour without smoking (i.)
Inform

Pupil   -I- 2 P   : -> Spend what? (re. ini.)
Initiated   -R- 3 T   : An HOUR. ONE HOUR (rep.)
Negotiate
                    (3rd grade - Lesson 5)

In the above extract, it is the pupil who mishears the teacher's utterance in 1 T. The pupil initiates a 'hearing-oriented negotiation' by means of the act 'repair-initiation' (2 P). The teacher, therefore, provides a repaired reply (3 T) where she first emphasizes the pronunciation of the 'trouble source' (AN HOUR), and then rephrases the utterance, also pronouncing it with emphasis (ONE HOUR).

Sinclair & Coulthard (1975) note that in their data, there are no examples of a pupil admitting not to have heard the teacher. Conversely, as the above extract reveals, in the present data, there are instances where a pupil admits, by means of a 'hearing-oriented negotiation', not to have heard or to have misheard what the teacher said. This discrepancy between Sinclair & Coulthard's (1975) and our data is probably due to the fact that their study involved primary school pupils whereas ours involved secondary school pupils aged between 15 and 20. Because of this age factor, it may be argued that the power relation in the context where Sinclair & Coulthard's (1975) data were collected was more asymmetric than in the context of the present data, so that acknowledging to have misheard or not heard the teacher is, no doubt, more 'face-threatening' (cf. Brown & Levinson 1978) in the former than the latter context.

Meaning-Oriented Negotiation

In recent years, discussions of negotiation of meaning have become common in second language acquisition literature; hence, the terminology used to refer to the phenomenon has likewise flourished. Unfortunately, as Gass & Varonis (1991: 123) observe,

> there is little consistency between and even within authors concerning such terms as "miscommunication", "misunderstanding", and "communication breakdown." For example, what Tannen (1975) refers to as "communication mix-up", Gumperz and Tannen

(1979) refer to variously as "misunderstanding" or "miscommunication", Thomas (1983) as "pragmatic failure", and Milroy (1984) as "communicative breakdown" [...] while [...] we use the term "negotiated communication."

Accordingly, as Gass & Varonis (1991: 123) further point out, "this literature is particularly difficult to interpret because different researchers are using different terms for the same phenomenon, on the one hand, and the same term for different phenomena, on the other." With regard to the term negotiation, we have attempted to make our terminological position clear by using 'negotiated interaction' as a generic term which encompasses different negotiation genres distinguished on the basis of their discourse function. We occasionally make use of such terms as 'communication breakdown', 'miscommunication' and 'misunderstanding', but they are used interchangeably to refer to a problem of understanding.

'Meaning-oriented negotiation' is an exchange or a series of exchanges aiming at confirming or clarifying the meaning of an utterance, or at repairing a proposition conveyed in a previous turn. 'Meaning-oriented negotiation' that is concerned with confirming or clarifying the meaning of an utterance includes exchanges that involve indications of real or feigned nonunderstandings and subsequent negotiations of meaning. Feigned nonunderstanding is a strategy used by the teacher to incite the pupil "to try out means of expressions and see if they work" (Swain 1985: 249). As for 'meaning-oriented negotiation' concerned with repairing a proposition conveyed in the previous turn, it also does not necessarily involve genuine problems of understanding. Excluding the 'word search' negotiation, this type of negotiation is concerned with errors of *fact* about either a *T-event* or a *P-event* (cf. Chapter 3), in other words, events that are part of the personal experience of either the teacher (T-event) or the pupil (P-event). If the negotiation is about a T-event, it is usually the teacher who performs the act 'repair'; whereas if it is about a P-event, it is usually the pupil who repairs the interactional problem by the act 'repair' which may simultaneously function as a 'challenge' to the teacher. When a problem of understanding is at issue, the negotiation addresses not only 'actual' but also 'potential' breakdowns of the communication (cf. Long 1981, Varonis & Gass 1985b, and Aston 1986). Negotiation routines in 'meaning-oriented negotiation' may be carried out by such acts as 'confirmation check', 'clarification request', 'repair', 'clue', and 'challenge'. Consider the following example:

(65)
Re-   -I- 1 T   : <The teacher had asked pupils to give examples using
initiate   'to care for something'> mhm (nom.)
             -R- 2 P1   : I don't care the sport because= (rep.)

```
                                              [
Teacher    -I- 3 T   :                   I don't care FOR sport (re./p.)
Initiated  -R- 4 P1  : =I don't care for sport because I'm ill (rep.)
Negotiate  -F- 5 T   : I'm ill [4] (eva.). Now (m.). Listen to me (s.)
                       when you say 'I don't care' it means this is your
                       nature (com.)
Pupil      -I- 6 P1  : -> It's MY nature (cha.)
Initiated
Negotiate


Teacher    -I- 7 T   : -> You don't like sport? (con. ch.)
Initiated  -R- 8 P1  : Yes
Negotiate  -F- 9 T   : Oh yes, that's right (acc.). But you mustn't say
                       because I'm ill (com.)
                                          [
           -R-10 P2  :               don't like it (ack.)
           -F-11 T   : Or, I don't care for sport THESE days because I'm
                       ill (re.)
Pupil      -I- 12 P1 : -> ALL days teacher (cha./re.)
Initiated  -F-13 T   : Yes (acc.). You don't care for sport because=
Negotiate                                        [      ]
           -R-14 P1  :                          NEVER (ack.)
           15 T      : =you don't like it (com.).
Pupil      -I- 16 P1 : -> BECAUSE I'm ILL teacher (cha./re.)
Initiated  -F-17 T   : Oh yes. because you are ill (acc.) ... Okay. if you
Negotiate              like (com.)
                       (3rd grade - Lesson 1)
```

In the above extract, which is a case of 'incomplete understanding' wherein "one or more participants perceive that something has gone wrong" (Milroy 1984: 15), the pupil's move in 6 P1 reveals that the teacher has not completely understood what the pupil is attempting to convey. Hence, a series of teacher and pupil initiated negotiations follow in order to negotiate the meaning of the pupil's utterance given in 4 P1 and resolve the understanding problem. However, apparently, the negotiation sequence is closed without the teacher really understanding what the pupil means.

After the lesson had been over, we (who also had doubts about what the pupil meant) consulted the teacher and the pupil to check whether an understanding had really been reached. The teacher acknowledged not to have really understood what the pupil meant; therefore, the pupil stated, using his mother tongue this time, that he had had a heart disease for years, that this prevented him from practising sport, and that in this way he came not to care for sport. On the basis of this information, we came to understand that in the above extract, since the pupil did not know the English phrase 'heart disease', he kept repeating that he was 'ill'; and it is this word which has created the ambiguity in his contribution. Further, the student's limited proficiency in the medium of the interaction prevented him from taking a complete turn to explain what he meant; therefore, he kept 'stepping in sideways' (Scarcella & Higa 1981) providing challenge acts while the teacher was speaking.

'Meaning-oriented negotiation', as pointed out by Gass & Varonis (1991: 127), "may ultimately result in transmission of the intended message or may instead result in a lack of understanding." The above extract shows that no understanding has been reached in spite of the series of negotiation exchanges. In principle, the negotiation of meaning has the effect of producing comprehensibility (cf. Varonis & Gass 1985b, Aston 1986); yet, this function

> conflicts with evidence that 'non-understanding routines' are frequently unsuccessful in this respect. In repair sequences, participants often appear to follow Fillmore's (1979) strategy of feigning understanding[as in the above extract], rather than indicating that the procedures have failed to achieve comprehension and that yet further reparatory work is called for. In such cases, to use Garfinkel's (1967) terms, we may say that a formal rather than a substantive understanding is achieved, so that participants go through the formal motions of acting as if they had understood, regardless of whether they have in substance [see also McCurdy 1980] (Aston 1986: 133).

Accordingly, Aston (1986: 134) argues that "[i]n order to show that a greater frequency of negotiation entails more input being made comprehensible, it would be necessary to have information on the frequency with which such negotiation achieves substantive understanding." Though it is beyond the scope of the present study to address this relevant and interesting issue, we believe that even in those cases where 'meaning-oriented negotiation' does not result in comprehension, the particular interaction in which learners are involved in this type of negotiation is likely to have a role in enhancing TL acquisition. As can be witnessed in the above extract, the pupil is trying hard to make his output comprehensible, as in 6 P1 (It's MY nature), 12 P1 (ALL days teacher), 14 P1 (NEVER), 16 P1 (Because I'm ILL teacher) which are all 'repair' and 'challenge' acts uttered with an emphasized item. One function of such output is that "it provides the opportunity for meaningful use of one's linguistic resources" (Swain 1985: 248), and hence "extends the linguistic repertoire of the learner as he or she attempts to create precisely and appropriately the meaning desired" (Swain 1985: 252). This type of interaction where the teacher provides 'negative input' (Schachter 1984, 1986), and where learners struggle to make output comprehensible is, no doubt, crucial for TL development.

Interestingly, Schachter (1984) argues that the least explicit type of 'negative input', in other words 'failures to understand' (as is the case in the above extract) is the most efficient in terms of interlanguage development towards target language norms. Like Schachter (1984) and Swain (1985), we believe that in signalling problems of accessibility by means of such acts as 'clarification requests' and 'confirmation checks', or problems of acceptability by means of such acts as 'repair' and 'clue', the teacher may be providing learners with both metalinguistic information about their interlanguage and the target language as well as opportunities for confirming or rejecting the hypotheses they are making about the target language, shaping interlanguage grammar towards target norms.

Nevertheless, many model-oriented linguists such as Dulay & Burt (1974), Krashen (1981a), Ritchie (1978), Flynn (1983), and Bialystok (1978) claim that language learners do not receive and further do not need metalinguistic information. Brown & Hanlon (1970), an L1 study which is almost universally cited as evidence that language learners do not receive metalinguistic information in their input, investigated the reaction of adults to deviant utterances in child L1 learners' speech, and found that the ungrammatical utterances received as much approval as the grammatical ones. As Schachter (1986: 220) argues, "[f]or the model-oriented linguists to use this study as the sole basis for claims regarding the nonavailability of metalinguistic information is foolhardy," for according to Brown & Hanlon (1970), metalinguistic information simply meant 'corrections'; yet, metalinguistic information is also transmitted in such indirect indications of disapproval as confirmation checks, clarification requests, misunderstandings, failures to understand, failures to respond, surprise, laughter etc.

Studies concerned with the negotiation of meaning in NS-NNS interaction consider hearing problems as nonunderstanding problems (e.g., Scarcella & Higa 1981, Varonis & Gass 1985b, Bremer et al. 1988, Deen & Van Hout 1991). However, we have opted for distinguishing between the two, and thereby between 'hearing-oriented negotiation' and 'meaning-oriented negotiation'. In the first type of negotiation, the listener does not hear the words or part of the words uttered by the speaker, and hence a verbatim repetition of the speaker's utterance is sufficient to resolve the problem; whereas in the second type of negotiation, the listener hears everything but still has problems of understanding, and therefore more clarification is often needed to restore the understanding problem.

Admittedly, it is sometimes difficult to decide whether the negotiation is caused by a hearing or an understanding problem, as in the case of mishearing which results in misunderstanding. Yet, examples of this type hardly ever occur in the data. In coding the data as one or another type of negotiation, we have always relied on the whole interaction to find out whether the interlocutors are negotiating a hearing or a meaning problem. In other words, there might be a problem of mishearing in a given extract, but if the hearing problem is not negotiated, and the interlocutors focus on the 'trouble source', as a meaning rather than a hearing problem, the negotiation is not coded as a 'hearing-oriented negotiation' but rather as a 'meaning-oriented negotiation'. Consider the following example:

(66)

Re- initiate	-I- 1 T	: <The teacher had asked pupils to make a sentence using 'used to'>
	-R- 2 P1	: My grandmother- Before sleeping my grandmother used to tell us stories but she doesn't tell us any more (rep.)
Teacher Elicit	-I- 3 T -R- 4 P1	: Why? (el.) : Stories (rep.)
Teacher Initiated Negotiate	-I- 5 T	: Because now you watch television (re.)
Pupil Initiated Negotiate	-I- 6 P1 -F- 7 T	: No. because now she is very old (cha./re.) : She is very old (acc.). She can't- uh (com.). Okay (eva.)

(3rd grade - Lesson 4)

In the above extract, the pupil is asked to make a sentence using the structure 'subject/used to do something'. The pupil comes up with an acceptable reply (2 P1); but the teacher does not provide an evaluative feedback because he wants to ask a subordinate question (3 T) to get further information about the proposition conveyed in the pupil's contribution. The pupil *mishears* the question and gives an irrelevant reply (4 P1). Instead of focusing on the hearing problem, asking the question once again, and leaving the pupil to reply, the teacher deals with the 'trouble source' in 4 P1 as a meaning 'trouble source', and hence initiates a 'meaning-oriented negotiation' by means of the act 'repair'.

As maintained by Schwartz (1980: 151) "repair is a process of negotiation, involving speakers conferring with each other to achieve understanding." Actually, the teacher's contribution in 5 T is a 'repair' to the 'trouble source' in 4 P1 but also a tentative answer to the 'referential question' in 3 T. Yet, since the question in 3 T is concerned with a P-event (cf. Chapter 3), and since the pupil disapproves of the proposition conveyed in 5 T, he initiates a 'meaning-oriented negotiation' via an act which simultaneously challenges the teacher's 'repair' and repairs the information it conveys (6 P1). The teacher accepts the 'challenge', starts a 'comment' which he immediately cuts off, then evaluates the pupil's contribution, thereby closing the exchange (7 T).

Hence, though the above extract contains a problem of mishearing (as the pupil's reply in 4 P2 illustrates), the negotiation as performed by the interlocutors does not address the hearing but rather the meaning problem which results, in the first negotiate exchange, from the pupil's irrelevant reply (4 P1), and in the second negotiate exchange from the teacher inappropriately substituting for the pupil in answering a purely P-event question, namely why the pupil's grandmother does not tell him stories any more. Accordingly, the two negotiate exchanges in the above extract are not coded as 'hearing-', but rather as 'meaning-' oriented negotiations, though they occur after a hearing problem.

Setting a clearcut distinction between 'medium-oriented' and 'meaning-oriented' negotiation has also been problematic, since it is at times difficult to decide whether a negotiation is triggered by misuse of a linguistic item or simply by failure to convey the desired meaning. Actually, misuse of the forms and/or functions of the target language may result in problems of understanding, and hence may trigger a negotiation sequence that is difficult to code as to whether it is a medium- or a meaning-oriented negotiation. Taking into consideration the pedagogic orientation of TL classroom interaction, we opted for coding as 'medium-oriented' any negotiation sequence following a pupil's contribution that contains an error of the forms and/or functions of the target language, when the negotiation seems to address the error, and even when it is not clear whether this negotiation overlaps with a problem of understanding. The rationale behind such a seemingly arbitrary decision is that in the data, the teacher rarely has problems understanding pupils' contributions containing a language error. This is evident from the fact that if the teacher's 'repair-initiation' does not result in the pupil's adequate repair of her/his own utterance, the teacher hardly ever fails to provide an outright correction of the error, hence restoring both the form and the meaning of the pupil's contribution. Consider the following example:

(67)
Teacher   -I- 1 T   : Why do women want to work? (el.)
Elicit   -R- 2 P1 : Because if they stay at home they feel born and uh

Teacher   -I- 3 T   : -> They feel-? (re. ini.)
Initiated   -R- 4 P1 : Born (rep.)
Negotiate -F- 5 T   : Bored (re.)
                       (2nd grade - Lesson 2)

In the above datum, the negotiation is triggered by the grammatical error (i.e., "born") in the pupil's reply. The occurrence of such an error in L2 learner speech is likely to cause miscommunication, especially in ordinary conversation when learners are interacting with native speakers or other nonnative speakers of English. However, given that the above extract occurs in an EFL classroom context where the teacher has acquired considerable experience and skill in decoding learners' interlanguage, and where the teacher belongs to the same cultural environment as the pupils, it is likely that there has been no breakdown in communication. But, still, because of the pedagogic orientation of L2 classroom interaction, the teacher initiates a negotiate exchange by means of the act 'repair-initiation' (3 T) which aims at eliciting a repaired reply. However, as the student is unable to come up with an adequate repair for she repeats the same 'trouble source' (4 P1), the teacher closes the negotiate exchange by providing a 'repair' (5 T).

Gass & Varonis (1984: 85) argue that

> the listener's familiarity with the topic of discourse greatly facilitates the interpretation of the entire message. In addition, such variables as familiarity with a particular speaker, with others of an interlocutor's language background, and with other nonnative speakers also increase the comprehensibility of the discourse.

The above example, along with Gass & Varonis' (1984) results, reaffirm the importance of interlocutor familiarity and support Labov & Fanshel's (1977) finding that "most of the information needed to interpret actions is already to be found in the structure of shared knowledge and not in the utterances themselves (Labov & Fanshel 1977: 82).

Content-Oriented Negotiation

In the type of lesson constituting the data (teaching of a text), learners have to listen to or read a passage, or at times read a picture and then answer the instructor's questions (Wh, true/false, multiple choice questions etc.). The reading of the text may result in noncomprehension or misinterpretation, especially as pupils are not yet proficient in the target language. 'Content-oriented negotiation' is an exchange or a series of exchanges whereby the teacher and the pupil(s) act jointly to clarify the content of the text being studied or the picture(s) being read to the satisfaction of both parties (see also 'negotiation of content' in Rulon & McCreary 1986), as in the following examples:

(68)
Direct   -I- 1 T   : Now (m.). Read the text again and answer the
                          questions you have on your book. 'True' or 'False'
                          and justify. You say 'True' why? 'False' why? (d.)
             -R- 2 PP   : Yes (ack.) <Activity> (rea.)
                          <After approximately ten minutes>
Teacher   -I- 3 T   : Now (m.). The first one (el.)
Elicit   -R- 4 P1   : Ghandi wants the British governor to leave his house
                          .. False (rep.)
             -F- 5 T   : False [1+] (eva.)
Teacher   -I- 6 T   : Why? (el.)
Elicit   -R- 7 P1   : Because Ghandi wants the British governor to leave
                          India (rep.)
             -F- 8 T   : To leave India (acc.). Yes (eva.)
Pupil   -I- 9 P2   : -> Teacher (b.). It's true (cha.)
Initiated
Negotiate

Pupil   -I- 10 PP : -> It's false (re.)
Initiated
Negotiate

Direct   -I- 11 T   : Well (m.). Let him express himself (d.)

Teacher   -I- 12 T   : -> Why is it true? (cla. req.)
Initiated   -R-13 P2   : Because to leave India. Because uh because uh
Negotiate

Teacher   -I- 14 T   : Yes? (p.)
Initiated   -R-15 P2   : Because Ghandi uh because Ghandi is under the
Negotiate   enemy occupation (rep.)

Teacher   -I- 16 T   : Under- ? (re. ini.)
Initiated   -R-17 P2   : The enemy occupation (rep.)
Negotiate   -F-18 T   : Yes [1-] (acc.)

Teacher   -I- 19 T   : -> But does he want him to leave his
Initiated   HOUSE? (con. ch.)
Negotiate   -R-20 PP   : No (rep.)
             21 P3   : He wants to meet him in the court (rep.)
             -F-22 T   : mhm [1-] (acc.)

Teacher   -I-23 T   : -> But-? (cl./p.)
Initiated   -R-24 P4   : Ghandi wants the British to leave India (rep.)
Negotiate   -F-25 T   : To leave India (acc.). Yes (eva.)

Pupil   -I- 26 P5 : -> It's true because house in this sentence has the
Initiated   meaning of India because we have "it is time you reco-
Negotiate   gnized you're masters in someone else's home" (cha.)
             -R-27 P2   : Yes (ack.)
             -F-28 T   : Well (m.). Listen it's not really
                                                      [
Pupil   -I- 29 P5 : ->   it has another meaning (cha.)
Initiated   -F-30 T   : Yes [1-] (acc.).If you take it like this.
Negotiate   ⌈
                                                      ∟
Pupil   -I- 31 P5 : ->   Yes it's true (cha.)
Initiated   -F-32 T   : But it's not really true because what is meant here is
Negotiate   not Ghandi's house but India. So it's the country of
                        India and not Ghandi's house. Home here has the
                        meaning of country (com.)
                        (2nd grade - Lesson 4)

The above extract occurred while pupils were doing a comprehension task
which usually follows the reading of a text. Two statements were written on the
black-board, and pupils had to find out whether they were true or false according
to the text. A pupil gives a correct reply (2 P1) which is positively evaluated by
the teacher (3 T). Then, the teacher asks the pupil to justify his reply. The pupil
gives a justification (5 P1) which the teacher accepts and evaluates positively (6
T). However, another pupil (P2) seems to disagree with the reply provided by
P1 and to have another interpretation of the text; so he performs a 'challenge' (9
P2) to contradict the teacher's evaluation. The negotiation continues, with the
participation of several pupils, through several exchanges . Finally the teacher,
apparently, manages to convince the pupil who initiated the first negotiation (P2)
that, contrary to 'home', the word 'house' cannot be used to mean country and
hence, the statement "Ghandi wants the British governor to leave his house" is
false according to the text.

(69)
Re-   -I- 1 T   : <The teacher had asked pupils to read some pictures
initiate   using the passive voice> Yes Hajji (nom.)
             -R- 2 P1   : The window has been opened (rep.)
             -F- 3 T   : Yes (eva.)

```
Pupil      -I- 4 P2  : -> No broken (cha./re.)
Initiated   -R- 5 PP  : Broken. Broken (ack.)
Negotiate  -F- 6 T   : Broken (acc.). Not opened. Broken (com.)
                       (2nd grade - lesson 5)
```

The above extract occurs while the pupils are doing an exercise in which they have to read some pictures using the passive voice. P1 gives a reply that is correct in terms of form but inappropriate in terms of content as the picture in question shows a window that has been broken not opened. The teacher who is certainly more concerned with the correct use of the passive voice, inadvertently, positively evaluates the reply. However, a pupil (P2) who is daring enough to challenge the teacher's evaluation initiates a 'content-oriented negotiation' to repair the proposition conveyed in 2 P1. Several pupils acknowledge the repair provided by P2; the teacher accepts the repair and provides a 'comment' to stress that the correct reply is 'broken' not 'opened', and thereby closes the exchange.

```
(70)
Teacher    -I- 1 T   : <The teacher had asked pupils to find out whether two
Elicit                 statements were true or false according to the text
                       being studied and to justify their answers> (el.)
           -R- 2 P1  : Because the tricks were in no way remarkable (rep.)
Teacher    -I- 3 T   : -> So. Is it true? (con. ch.)
Initiated   -R- 4 P1  : It's false (rep.)
Negotiate  -F- 5 T   : It's false because the tricks were in no way remarkable
                       (acc.). Yes [1+] (eva). They weren't attractive or
                       interesting (com.).
Teacher    -I- 6 T   : The second one (el.)
Elicit

Pupil      -I- 7 P2  : -> So why he had given him money? (cla.req./cha.)
Initiated   -R-       : <No response>
Negotiate  -F- 8 T   : Yes (acc.)

Teacher    -I- 9 T   : -> Why? (cla. req.) <addressed to the whole class>
Initiated
Negotiate

Pupil      -I-10 P2  : -> Why he had given the man some money? (cla.req/
Initiated              cha.)
Negotiate  -F-11 T   : Yes (acc.)
```

```
Teacher    -I-12 T    : -> Why did he give the man some money? (cla.req.).
Initiated                 That's a good question (com.)
Negotiate  -R-13 P3   : Because he is like a beggar (rep.)
           -F-14 T    : He is like a beggar (acc.). Yes [1+](eva.)
                        (3rd grade - Lesson 2)
```

The teacher had asked pupils to find out whether two statements were true or false according to the text being studied. The first one, which engenders the negotiation sequence in the above extract, reads: "Robert threw some money in the old man's hat because he enjoyed the monkey's tricks." The first 'negotiate' exchange is initiated by the teacher's 'confirmation check' in 3 T, as P1 provides a justification without stating whether the statement is true or false. Then, P1 provides a reply which is accepted, positively evaluated, and commented upon by the teacher who thereby closes the exchange.

In 6 T, the teacher moves to the second statement and performs an 'elicitation'. However, one of the pupils (P2) is daring enough to re-open the previous exchange and initiate a negotiation by means of an utterance which overtly acts as a 'clarification request' (7 P2). But given the choice of the word "So" with which P2 starts his utterance, the challenging intonation of the utterance, and the asymmetrical power relations of the classroom context, it is sound to argue that 7 P2 simultaneously and covertly functions as a 'challenge' to the teacher.

The teacher seems to appreciate P2's contribution for he accepts it and uses the same clarification request to check whether the other pupils know the answer (10 T) to P2's clarification request; but, he gets no reply. This gives P2 more confidence to re-initiate the negotiate by the same 'clarification request', challenging the whole class for they apparently do not know the answer to a question that is very relevant to their judging the statement in question as true or false. The teacher accepts P2's contribution once again, initiates another negotiate exchange using the same 'clarification request' performed previously by the pupil, and evaluates P2's contribution as a "good question" that is worthy of being answered. At this point, one of the pupils (P3) provides a tentative answer which is accepted and positively evaluated by the teacher (15 T).

Indeed the negotiation does not stop here but goes further through several exchanges that are not cited in the above extract. By the end of the negotiation the pupils find out with the help of the teacher that Robert, one of the characters of the story reported in the text being studied, put some money in the old man's hat not because he enjoyed the monkey's tricks, but because he thought the monkey was dead as the latter lay still and the old man began to weep. The following extract is another illustration of 'content-oriented negotiation'.

(71)

Teacher	-I- 1 T	: Choose the best answer... The writer didn't go to bed
Elicit		immediately after supper because: One [...] Two [...]
		Three [...] Four [...] (s.). What is the best answer? (el.)
	-R- 2 P1	: He wanted to hear all his uncle's exciting stories (rep.)
Teacher	-I- 3 T	: -> Is it correct? (con. ch.)
Initiated	-R- 4 PP	: Yes (rep.)
Negotiate	-F- 5 T	: Yes. it's correct (eva.)
		(3rd grade - Lesson 1)

In the above extract, the teacher asks a multiple choice question (1 T). P1 gives a correct reply (2 P1). However, instead of evaluating the reply and closing the exchange, the teacher initiates a negotiation to check whether the other pupils agree that the reply given in 2 P1 is correct according to the text being studied. In 4 PP, the pupils reply with an affirmation which is followed by an evaluative feedback which simultaneously functions to positively evaluate the reply in 2 P1 and that in 4 PP. See also extract (72) below.

(72)

Teacher	-I- 1 T	: Why are they very excited (el.). Mesbah (nom.)
Elicit	-R- 2 P1	: They're excited because Brian and Mary have decided
		to get married there next month (rep.)
Teacher	-I- 3 T	: -> What does it mean THERE? (cla. req.)
Initiated	-R- 4 P1	: In Marbury (rep.)
Negotiate	-F- 5 T	: In Marbury [1+] (eva.)
		(1st grade - Lesson 5)

The above extract starts with a teacher 'elicitation' followed by a pupil's reply (2 P1) that is correct according to the text being studied. However, the teacher refrains from providing an evaluative feedback but instead initiates a 'content-oriented negotiation' so as to request a clarification of the referent 'there', occurring in the pupil's reply (2 P1) but lacking an antecedent. By so doing, the teacher wants to check whether the pupil has understood the text being studied or is simply reproducing the phrases mentioned in the text without comprehending what they refer to. The pupil gives a reply (4 P1) which is positively evaluated by the teacher (5 T).

As Rulon & McCreary (1986: 195) argue, "negotiation of content, like negotiation of meaning, may be essential to the promotion of interaction necessary for successful second language acquisition." Indeed, research related to the negotiation of content is becoming more and more essential as there is a continual increase in the number of nonnative speakers attending universities where English is the medium of instruction. Since the tasks these students are ordinarily requested to perform focus primarily on content and are integrated into the lesson as a whole, it is important to ascertain the most effective means of discussing this content (Rulon & McCreary 1986: 195).

General Knowledge-Oriented Negotiation

'General knowledge-oriented negotiation' is an exchange or a series of exchanges performed by the interlocutors (when no understanding problem is at issue) to negotiate general knowledge. 'General knowledge-oriented negotiation' is always concerned with negotiating the acceptability of a proposition concerned with TP-events (cf. Chapter 3), in other words, events that are supposed to be known to both the teacher and the pupils. Accordingly, pupils may repair other pupils' contributions and may possibly challenge the teacher if there is a mismatch between their own knowledge and the expressed proposition.

Bremer et al. (1988: 144) point to how 'schema mismatch' and 'lack of world knowledge' may play a role in problems of understanding in NS-NNS interaction. However, in the data, 'general knowledge-oriented negotiation' involves no problems of understanding, since 'schema mismatch' in this kind of negotiation does not cause a problem of 'accessibility' but rather one of 'acceptability'; in other words, the hearer understands but does not accept the proposition conveyed in the interlocutor's utterance. Such a definition might cause a problem as to the distinction between 'meaning-oriented negotiation' that is concerned with errors of *fact* and 'general knowledge-oriented negotiation'. Yet, the difference between the two is that the former is concerned with either T-events or P-events, whereas the latter is concerned with facts related to TP-events, i.e., general knowledge (cf. Chapter 3).

On the other hand, the definition provided here for 'general knowledge-oriented negotiation' might seem to overlap with that of 'agreement-oriented negotiation' (presented in the next section), since both of them are concerned with a problem of 'acceptability' concerning the content of a former utterance. However, the difference between these two types of negotiation is that the former is concerned with a 'TP-event'; whereas the latter is concerned with a 'disputable event' (cf. Chapter 3) such as opinions. Therefore, acceptability might not be reached in 'agreement-oriented negotiation'; while it should, in principle, be achieved in 'general knowledge-oriented negotiation', because there is only one resolution for the problematic proposition since it is concerned with general knowledge.

(73)
Teacher   -I- 1 T   : Do you know another leader. another leader who was
Elicit   like Ghandi? (el.)... Yes (nom.)
           -R- 2 P1   : Allal El Fassi (rep.)
           -F- 3 T   : ... Well (s.). Yes [1-] (acc.)

Re-   -I- 4 T   : Yes (nom.)
initiate   -R- 5 P2   : Omar El Mokhtar (rep.)

Teacher   -I- 6 T   : -> He was peaceful? (con. ch.) <addressed to the
Initiated   whole class>
Negotiate -R- 7 PP   : No (rep.)
           -F- 8 T   : No (acc.)

Re-   -I- 9 T   : Yes (nom.)
initiate   -R- 10 P3   : Mao Tse-Tung

Teacher   -I- 11 T   : -> Mao Tse-Tung. Was he peaceful? (con.ch.)
Initiated -R- 12 PP   : No (rep.)
Negotiate -F- 13 T   : No (acc.)
                       (2nd grade - lesson 4)

The above extract starts with a teacher 'elicitation'. P1 gives a reply which
is, after some hesitation, accepted by the teacher. The same 'elicitation' is re-
initiated by the teacher's nomination of another pupil to give another reply. P2's
reply triggers a 'general knowledge-oriented negotiation' initiated by the teacher
through the act 'confirmation check' (6 T). Several pupils disconfirm P2's reply;
the teacher accepts the pupils' contribution and re-initiates the 'elicitation' once
again. P3 provides a reply which triggers another 'general knowledge-oriented
negotiation' initiated by the teacher (11 T). Several pupils disconfirm P3's reply;
the teacher accepts their contribution, and thereby closes the exchange.

(74)
Teacher -I- 1 T   : Do you remember Africa Cup? (el./s.)
Elicit   -R- 2 PP : Yes. Yes (rep.)

Teacher -I- 3 T   : Where was Morocco uh the Moroccan team playing? (el.)
Elicit   -R- 4 PP : In Casa (rep.)

Teacher -I- 5 T   : And the Algerian team? (el.)
Elicit   -R- 6 P1 : In Casa (rep.)

```
Pupil     -I-  7 PP  : In Rabat. In Rabat (re.)
Initiated -F-  8 T   : In Rabat (acc.). Yes (eva.)
Negotiate
                      (3rd grade - lesson 2)
```

The above extract starts with a 'referential question' functioning simultaneously as an 'elicitation' for the pupils' reply and as a 'starter' for the next 'elicitation'. The interaction progresses smoothly in a linear fashion until P1 replies to the teacher's third 'elicitation'. This reply triggers a 'general knowledge-oriented negotiation' initiated by several pupils via the act 'repair'. The teacher accepts and positively evaluates the pupils' repair, and hence closes the exchange.

```
(75)
Re-        -I-  1 T   : Can you give me another sentence (p.)
initiate   -R-  2 P1  : Giralda is a minaret in Spain (rep.)
           -F-  3 T   : mhm (acc.) .. NO (eva.). There is NO minaret in
                        Spain (com.)
Pupil      -I-  4 P1  : -> <unint> Giralda in Spain (cha.)
Initiated  -F-  5 T   : NO (eva.) ... Moroccan minaret=
Negotiate                                              [
           6 PP   :                              Yes (ack.)
           7 T    : =The mosque has got a minaret. The church hasn't got
                    any minaret (com.)
                      (1st grade - lesson 1)
```

The above extract starts with a re-initiation of a previous 'elicitation' in which the teacher asks the pupils to give a sentence using the word 'minaret'. P1 gives a reply (2P1); the teacher accepts it but changes her mind after less than one second pause. Hence, she negatively evaluates the reply and provides a comment explaining why the pupil's reply is unacceptable (3T). Nevertheless, since the pupil's contribution is concerned with general knowledge, that is with a TP-event, and since the pupil seems confident in the correctness of the information conveyed in her reply, she initiates, via the act 'challenge', a 'general knowledge-oriented negotiation' (4 P1) in order to negotiate the acceptability of her reply. However, the teacher rejects the pupil's contribution and provides a comment (7 T) which further emphasizes the inappropriateness of the pupil's reply.

The above extract might seem as an instance of misunderstanding due to the teacher and pupil's schema mismatch; however, we consider it an example of 'general knowledge-oriented negotiation' because the problem actually triggering the negotiation is not one of accessibility but of acceptability. The teacher's 'comment' "there is no minaret in Spain" (3 T) reveals that she has understood the pupil's reply but refuses to accept it. On the other hand, the pupil's initiated negotiation "Giralda in Spain" (4 P1) does not aim at making her contribution more comprehensible for the teacher, but rather at negotiating acceptability.

Yet, given that 'Giralda' (in Seville, Spain) was indeed a mosque with a minaret, and is now restored in such a way that its minaret has become the tower of the cathedral built in the place of the ancient mosque, it is worth pointing out that the teacher's comments (3 T, 5 T, 7 T) are not sufficiently informational, in Zamel's (1981) sense, so as to let the pupil know why her reply is unacceptable according to the teacher. Indeed, the feedback provided by the teacher (3 T, 7 T) may possibly reveal that she has never heard of such a monument.

(76)
Teacher   -I- 1 T   : But there is another problem concerning smuggling (s.).
Elicit   Who smuggles? (el.)
          -R- 2 P   : Poor (rep.)
Teacher   -I- 3 T   : -> Do you think only poor people smuggle? (con. ch.)
Initiated -R- 4 PP : No. No (rep.)
Negotiate
                    (3rd grade - Lesson 3)

In the above extract, the teacher initiates a 'general knowledge-oriented negotiation' by means of a 'confirmation check' (3 T). The use of 'only' in "Do you think that only poor people smuggle" suggests that the teacher has some scepticism about the pupil's reply in 2 P. This indirect or, in Brown & Levinson's (1978) terms, 'off-record' negative feedback may be considered a 'mitigating move' (Kasper 1989: 52) through which the teacher avoids giving an outright direct rejection of the reply in 2 P. The pupils' reply (4 PP) to the teacher's confirmation check seems to be in line with the teacher's unexpressed but implicit schemata. Hence, the negotiation exchange is closed by the pupils, apparently, accepting the teacher's implicit proposition that smuggling is practised not only by poor people but by rich people as well.

Widdowson (1983) regards the discourse process as a negotiation designed to achieve a convergence of worlds, where interlocutors' concern is not only with the mutual accessibility, but also with the mutual acceptability of those worlds. Widdowson (1983) captures the procedures which service these two requirements by noting that

> [it] is the co-operative imperative which impels people to put their schemata into contact with others, and there are procedures available to service this impulse. These co-operative procedures are

concerned with making information accessible, with clarifying its relationship with existing schemata, building up frames of reference, indicating which routine is in operation and so on, all the time working towards a satisfactory convergence of the worlds so that understanding can be achieved (Cited in Aston 1986: 137).

As pointed out when we were discussing 'meaning-oriented negotiation', negotiated interaction does not necessarily produce a substantive understanding, (see also McCurdy 1980, Aston 1986). In the same way, 'general knowledge-oriented negotiation' does not necessarily produce a substantive acceptance of the information which the interlocutors appear to have accepted by the end of the negotiation. To quote Aston (1986: 139), what the negotiation appears to achieve "is a formal display of the convergence of participants worlds."

Agreement-Oriented Negotiation

Schegloff et al. (1977) have shown how other-corrections in repair often imply disagreement rather than non-understanding (see also Gaskill 1980). In the present study, 'agreement-oriented negotiation' is an exchange or a series of exchanges in which the participants (teacher and pupil(s)) aim at reaching an agreement concerning a 'disputable event' (cf. Labov & Fanshel 1977: 100) such as opinions, as in the extracts below:

(77)

Teacher Initiated Negotiate	-I- 1 T	: \<After a female pupil had said that the husband should help his wife with the housework, the teacher asked the following question to a male pupil\> -> Do you agree with her? Are you going to help your wife with the housework? (con.ch.)
	-R- 2 P1	: No (rep.)
Teacher Initiated Negotiate	-I- 3 T	: -> Why? Why not? (cla. req.)
Teacher Initiated	-I- 4 T	: -> Do you think that the man shouldn't do the housework? (con. ch.)
Negotiate	-R- 5 P1	: Teacher .. the woman must do the housework (rep.)
Teacher	-I- 6 T	: The woman-? (re. ini.)
Initiated Negotiate	-R- 7 P1	: should do everything in the house (rep.)

Teacher   -I- 8 T   : -> Why? (cla. req.)
Initiated
Negotiate

Teacher   -I- 9 T   : -> Well (m.). A man is stronger than a woman and he
Initiated   can do the housework better than a woman (s.). Don't
Negotiate   you think so? (con. ch.)
             -R-10 P1 : Yes teacher (rep.)
                         (2nd grade - lesson 2)

The above extract, which occurred in a class of male and female pupils, contains a series of teacher-initiated negotiations where the teacher, who is female, is trying to negotiate an agreement on the proposition: "the husband should help his wife with the housework," suggested by a female pupil in a previous turn. Given the cultural context of the participants (Moroccan culture), this proposition constitutes, from an acceptability standpoint, a knot in the discourse; therefore, some retrospective action is required before the discourse can proceed any further. The teacher takes the lead to untie the 'acceptability knot', and hence initiates several 'agreement-oriented negotiations' by the act 'confirmation check'. Interestingly, though P1 has stated that he will not help his wife with the housework (2 P1), that "the woman must do the housework" (5 P1), and that "the woman should do everything in the house" (7 P1), the teacher seems to have affected his position for he apparently agrees with her by the end of the extract.

This is revealing in terms of the power factor operating in classroom discourse, and, accordingly, in concert with the notion of the classroom being a setting of unequal-power discourse. The pupil seems to surrender when he gets involved in an argumentation with the teacher, certainly because of the politeness factor (for it is thought to be improper to go on arguing with the teacher, who is supposed to be the knowledgeable participant in the classroom) but, no doubt, also because of his limited proficiency in the target language, which probably discourages him from proceeding with the argumentation. However, it is sound to argue that the pupil's display of agreement, in the above extract, is not *actual* but rather *formal*. It may also be argued that what he really agrees upon is not that the husband should help his wife with the housework but rather that the man is stronger than the woman and that he can do the housework better than the woman; but "can" by no means implies "should."

As has been illustrated in the discussion of 'meaning-oriented negotiation', negotiation routines do not necessarily produce a substantive understanding (see also McCurdy 1980, Aston 1986, and Gass & Varonis 1991). Likewise, where agreement is at issue, negotiation does not necessarily produce substantive agreement (see also Aston 1986). Frequently, what it appears to achieve is "a formal display of the convergence of participants' worlds" (Aston 1986: 139).

```
(78)
Teacher  -I-  1 T   : Do people really want war? (el.)
Elicit    -R-  2 PP  : No. they don't want (rep.)
          -F-  3 T   : No. they don't (re.). Yes (eva.)
Pupil    -I-  4 P1  : People die (i.)
Inform


Teacher  -I-  5 T   : Do they want war? (el.)
Elicit    -R-  6 P1  : No. they don't (rep.)
          -F-  7 T   : No. they don't [1+] (eva.)
Pupil    -I-  8 P2  : -> Some peoples WANT [wær] (cha.)
Initiated -F- 9 T   : WAR (re.)
Negotiate
```

(2nd grade - Lesson 4)

The above extract starts with a question that relates to a 'disputable event' (cf. Labov & Fanshel 1977). Several pupils provide a reply (2 PP). The teacher repairs the form of the reply, then provides a positive evaluation (3 T). One of the pupils provides an inform (4 P1) which is ignored by the teacher who instead wants the pupil to answer the previous elicitation, apparently to see whether the pupil is able to give a correct short form answer. The pupil provides a reply (6 P1) which is positively evaluated (7 T) by the teacher, who thereby closes the exchange. However, P2 re-opens the exchange, initiating an 'agreement-oriented negotiation' by the act 'challenge' (8 P2) and providing an information contrary to that positively evaluated by the teacher. As the 'challenge' (8 P2) contains a pronunciation 'trouble source', the teacher repairs it, and closes the exchange without dwelling on the 'agreement-oriented negotiation' initiated by the pupil and without pushing down the exchange any further (9 T). This certainly reveals teacher power in classroom discourse.

```
(79)
Teacher  -I-  1 T   : Who can give a sentence with 'weep'? (el.)
Elicit    -R-  2 P1  : The woman weeps for nothing (rep.)
          -F-        <laughter>
Teacher  -I-  3 T   : Do you agree with him? (con.ch.) <addressed to the
Initiated            class>
Negotiate -R- 4 P2  : Yes yes it's correct (rep.)
```

Teacher   -I- 5 T   : Do you agree with him? (con.ch.) <addressed to a
Initiated   female pupil>
Negotiate -R- 6 P3   : No (rep.)
               -F- 7 T   : Nobody weeps for nothing (com.). Nobody weeps for
                             nothing (com.)
                             (3rd grade - lesson 2)

The above extract occurs after the teacher has explained the lexical item 'to weep'. The teacher asks the pupils to give a sentence using this item so that she can check whether they have understood. One of the male pupils came up with the sentence "the woman weeps for nothing" (2 P1). Instead of providing an evaluative feedback to the pupil's contribution, close the exchange, and move to another pupil to elicit another sentence, the teacher chooses to dwell on the pupil's disputable proposition and initiate an 'agreement-oriented negotiation'. Thereby, he creates what Varonis & Gass (1985b: 73) label 'a vertical sequence in a horizontal progression'; in other words, he pushes the conversation downwards in order to act upon what he perceives as a 'trouble source' (i.e., the pupil's proposition) and repair the trouble before the interaction can proceed any further. The teacher closes the sequence by providing a comment which rejects the pupil's proposition conveyed in 2 P1.

Surprise Display-Oriented Negotiation

As has been pointed out by Schegloff et al. (1977), repair procedures (or interactional negotiation devices) are often employed where there is no 'hearable error'. Similarly, Goffman (1981: 272) has argued that these procedures can be used to focus on a 'remarkable' rather than a 'faultable' matter, and in this way create a topic of talk. On the same wavelength, Corsaro (1977) draws attention to the way negotiating devices like 'clarification requests' may simply reveal surprise rather than problems of understanding or agreement. The present data confirms the above observations, among other things, by virtue of the occurrence of what we have labelled 'surprise display-oriented negotiation'. Varonis & Gass (1985b) consider 'surprise indicators' as 'conversational continuants' (cf. the following section). However, we distinguish between the two, for 'surprise indicators' in the data do not necessarily function to sustain conversation, but rather and primarily to indicate surprise.

'Surprise display-oriented negotiation' is an exchange or a series of exchanges initiated by one of the participants in order to express surprise regarding the content of a previous speaker's contribution. Consider the following examples:

(80)

Teacher	-I- 1 T	: When do you go to the mosque? (el.)
Elicit	-R- 2 P1	: [fridei] <meaning Friday> (rep.)
Teacher	-I- 3 T	: On-? (re. ini.)
Initiated	-R- 4 PP	: Tomorrow (rep.)
Negotiate	5 P2	: Everyday (rep.)
Teacher	-I- 6 T	: -> Everyday?! (con. ch.)
Initiated	-R- 7 P3	: No (rep.)
Negotiate	8 P2	: Everyday (rep.)
	9 P3	: Tomorrow (rep.)
	10 P2	: Everyday (rep.)
Teacher	-I- 11 T	: Repeat please (p.)
Initiated	-R-12 P2	: Everyday evening (rep.)
Negotiate		
Teacher	-I- 13 T	: -> You go to the mosque?! (con. ch.)
Initiated	-R-14 P2	: Yes (rep.)
Negotiate	-F-15 T	: So .. you are a good Muslim (com.)

(1st grade - lesson 1)

The above extract contains two 'surprise display-oriented negotiations', each initiated by the teacher by means of a 'confirmation check' (6 T, 13 T). It might be argued that labelling these negotiations as 'surprise display-oriented negotiation' adds a superfluous category since these negotiations could well be considered as 'meaning-oriented negotiations'. However, because of the exclamatory intonation of these 'confirmation checks' and the teacher's and pupils' shared knowledge that it is very rare for pupils to go to the mosque everyday, we are confident in categorizing the above two negotiations as 'surprise display-oriented negotiations' rather than 'meaning-oriented negotiations'. Moreover, the 'comment' "So.. you are a very good Muslim" (15 T) provided by the teacher gives further support to the fact that the previous confirmation checks (6 T, 13 T) are oriented towards expressing surprise rather than resolving a problem of understanding.

(81)

Re-	-I- 1 T	: <The teacher had asked pupils to give examples of the
initiate		things that taste good>
	-R- 2 P1	: Couscous tastes good (rep.)
	-F- 3 T	: Yes (eva.)

```
Re-        -I- 4 T   : What else? (p.)
initiate    -R-      : <No response>

Re-        -I- 5 T   : Don't you know any other delicious things? (p.)
initiate    -R- 6 P2 : Woman (rep.)

Teacher    -I- 7 T   : -> Do you eat woman?! (con. ch.)
Initiated   -R- PP   : <laughter>
Negotiate      8 P1  : Shu wld lhram  <Arabic interjection meaning: 'See the
                       bastard!'> (ack.)
NB. P1 is a girl whereas P2 is a boy.
                       (2nd grade - lesson 2)
```

The above extract contains a 'surprise display-oriented negotiation' initiated by the teacher by means of a 'confirmation check' (7 T) which functions to express the teacher's surprise at the proposition conveyed in P2's reply. Actually, as the pupil (P2) does not reply to the 'confirmation check' in 7 T, it might be argued that 7 T is no more than an evaluative feedback in question form since it implicitly lets the pupil know that his reply is unacceptable. However, as 7 T does not function to close the exchange (for the teacher may expect the pupil to simply reply: "no"), we consider the feedback move as nonoccurring (after 6 P2) but its function as covert in the initiating move (7 T) "Do you eat woman?!" of the following exchange. See also example (82) below.

```
(82)
Teacher  -I- 1 T   : Should the woman do all the housework in your
Elicit               opinion? (el.)
         -R- 2 P1  : She should do the housework alone (rep.)
Teacher  -I- 3 T   : So .. you think that the woman SHOULD do
Initiated            all  (con. ch.)
Negotiate            [
         -R- 4 P1  :     Yes teacher (rep.)
Teacher  -I- 5 T   : -> Yes?! You agree with this?! (con. ch.)
Initiated -R- 6 T  : Yes (rep.)
Negotiate
```

                       (2nd grade - lesson 2)

The above extract contains two teacher-initiated negotiations. The first one is a 'meaning-oriented negotiation' whereby the teacher wants to make the pupil confirm or disconfirm the teacher's understanding of the reply. This is evident from the tone of the utterance and the teacher's emphasis of "SHOULD" (3 T) to make sure that the pupil did not say "shouldn't". However, given that P1 is a female pupil, the teacher who is also female is astonished at P1's reply (4 P1) to the 'confirmation check'. Therefore, the teacher initiates another negotiate exchange which does not aim at negotiating meaning nor at reaching agreement, but rather at expressing surprise; hence, the second negotiate is coded as a 'surprise display-oriented negotiation'. Goffman (1981: 272) argues that interactional negotiation devices (e.g., 'confirmation checks' and 'clarification requests') can be used to focus on a 'remarkable' rather than a 'faultable' matter, and in this way create a topic of talk. As a matter of fact, this is what happened in the exchanges following the above extract. The teacher found the pupil's proposition 'remarkable' and therefore focused the interaction on it for the following five exchanges (not quoted here), by urging the pupil to answer the questions "Aren't you going to work later? You are studying now, don't you want to work?"

Conversational Continuant

Varonis & Gass (1985b) seem to "have trouble in distinguishing nonunderstanding routines (which negotiate meaning) from conversational continuants (which they consider do not)" (Aston 1986: 133). Further, echoing Chun et al. (1982), they suggest that occasionally the two functions of negotiating meaning and continuing the conversation may simultaneously be performed. Scarcella & Higa (1981) do attempt to systematically differentiate between these two functions; therefore, they classify some procedures as 'negotiating meaning' and others as 'keeping the conversation going'. "But again the distinction is not clear-cut: other-repetitions, for instance appear under both headings" (Aston 1986: 133).

> The result of these ambiguities is that it is not clear (remaining within the terms of these studies) to what extent the greater frequency of the procedures coded actually implies greater negotiation of meaning, and to what extent it merely indicates more work being performed to keep the conversation going. It certainly points to a need to achieve a clearer account of the discourse functions of these procedures (Aston 1986: 133).

The present data reveal the occurrence of two types of 'conversational continuant': 'prompt' (performed by the teacher) and 'acknowledge' (performed by the pupil). 'Prompt' never negotiates meaning; whereas 'acknowledge', whose primary function is to sustain the conversation and display pupil attention, may implicitly negotiate meaning but not in the sense of a 'meaning-oriented negotiation' which explicitly addresses actual or potential problems of understanding.

Actually, in 'conversational continuant', we are dealing with a special kind of negotiation, one by means of which the hearer sustains the conversation by encouraging and/or cooperating in the production of the turn in progress, but without attempting to repair or initiate a repair of an utterance in that turn. As Varonis & Gass (1985b: 86) observe, "negotiation may strengthen the social or interpersonal dimension of an interaction by acting as a conversational continuant." Conversational continuants or what Van Lier (1988), following Erickson (1979), calls 'listening responses' "do not seek the floor, but merely acknowledge, express approval, understanding, etc." (Van Lier 1988: 115). In some accounts of turn-taking, conversational continuants are not considered turns in themselves (e.g., Oreström 1983) but rather as 'turn lubricators' (cf. Van Lier 1988). As maintained by Van Lier (1988: 116), conversational continuants or

> [l]istening responses fulfil an important function in verbal
> .interaction, in conversation as well as in lectures, debates, interviews,
> etc. (see Erickson 1979, Schegloff 1981). They are typically
> demonstrations of approval, attention, encouragement,
> understanding. Their character is supportive or neutral as regards
> the turn in hand, and in that sense they may facilitate that turn's
> development ('lubricate' it), and may boost its duration and
> smoothness.

In the TL classroom context, we can distinguish between two types of conversational continuants, namely 'teacher conversational continuant' and 'pupil conversational continuant'. These are presented below with illustrations from the data. It is noteworthy that though 'conversational continuants' result in a 'negotiated exchange', in coding the data we opted for not labelling the exchange initiated by a 'conversational continuant' as a 'negotiate exchange' for the sake of differentiating between negotiation that explicitly aims at resolving an interactional problem (i.e., the types of negotiation that have been presented in the preceding sections) and the negotiation which aims at sustaining the conversation (i.e., the kind of negotiation being presented here).

Teacher Conversational Continuant
Teacher conversational continuant is a teacher move which encourages the pupil to go on with her/his utterance. In this way, it constitutes affective support to the pupil on the floor. It is usually carried out by the act 'prompt' or by the acts 'accept' and/or 'evaluate' which simultaneously function as a 'prompt'. Consider 3 T and 7 T in the following extract:

(83)
Re-   -I- 1 T   : <The teacher had asked pupils to make a sentence using
initiate   to 'leak'> mhm (nom.)

           -R- 2 P1   : Yesterday- yesterday.. I bought uh uh bottles of milk uh
                        uh bottles of milk but=
                                              [
           -I- 3 T   : ->   very good (eva./p.) yes (acc./p.)
           -R- 4 P1   : =but bottles=
                                     [
Teacher   -I- 5 T   :   a bottle (re.)
Initiated -R- 6 P1   : =one bottle was uh uh -there is a small hole uh hole=
Negotiate   [
           -I- 7 T   : ->   yes (eva./p.)
           -R- 8 P1   : =and milk began to leak (rep.)
           -F- 9 T   : To leak (acc.). Very good (eva.)
                         (3rd grade - Lesson 1)

In the above extract, 3 T and 7 T are 'conversational continuants' encouraging the pupil to go on with his utterance, since he is hesitating and searching for his words (consider uh uh in 2 P1 and 6 P1). But in this particular extract teacher conversational continuants also function to provide 'intra-turn positive feedback' (Boulima 1990) that occurs while the pupil's reply is still in progress and lets the pupil know that his reply is potentially good. Apparently, the teacher predicts that the reply will be a 'good' one; hence, she provides premature evaluations (3 T and 7 T) which simultaneously function to encourage the pupil to go on with his reply. This is obvious in 3 T where the teacher uses the phrase 'very good' to evaluate the pupil's utterance and at the same time prompt him to go on. The choice of words used in this conversational continuant (namely 'very good', an evaluative phrase that is very rare in the data and used only if the teacher really approves of the reply) shows that this conversational continuant also carries an evaluative function. However, since it is intra-turn and does not close the exchange, this evaluation is not coded as occurring in the feedback slot but in the initiating move of the following bound exchange.

As for 7 T in the above extract, one may argue that it is no more than a 'back-channel' (Yngve 1970, Duncan 1973, Brown & Yule 1983) which only functions to "indicate to the person that he should continue" (Brown & Yule 1983: 92). However, given the classroom context and given the high falling tone of 7 T which shows strong agreement (see Sinclair & Coulthard 1975: 62), we opted for coding it as an 'evaluate' which simultaneously functions as a 'prompt' for the pupil to go on.

Sinclair & Coulthard (1985: 93) argue that "a teacher can say 'yes' in one way to mean 'you're right' and in another way to mean 'go on'." Conversational continuants which do not carry an evaluative function also occur in the data. They are usually performed by repeating part of the pupil's utterance or by means of a 'yes' or 'mhm' uttered in a rising tone. Consider 4 T in the following example:

```
(84)
Re-        -I- 1 T   : <The teacher had asked pupils to give sentences using
initiate                the verb 'to collapse'>
           -R- 2 P1  : The government collapses=
                                          [
           -I- 3 T   : ->                         Yes [3] (p.)
           -R- 4 P1  : =collapses many house in order to build uh many old
                        houses uh in order (rep.)
                                       [
           -F- 5 T   :                     Yes (acc.). But we don't say the
                        government collapses many old houses (com.)
                                    [
            6 PP     :                 collapses (ack.)
Pupil      -I- 7 P1  : What we say? (cla. req.)
Initiated  -R- 8 T   : Okay (s.). We speak of 'to collapse' when it happens
Negotiate               suddenly (com.). Yes? (com.ch.) Whereas the govern-
                        ment knocks down .. All right? 'To collapse' is about
                        something which collapses by itself not somebody
                        collapses it .. Not somebody knocks it down (com.)
                        (3rd grade - Lesson 1)
```

Uttered in a low rising tone, 3 T in the above extract is a 'prompt' which encourages the pupil to go on with his reply. The teacher certainly has doubts about what the pupil wants to say; therefore, she refrains from giving a prompt which simultaneously functions as an 'intra-turn positive evaluation' as in the preceding example.

As has been noted above, conversational continuants are performed not only by the teacher but also by the pupils. But if 'teacher conversational continuant' usually carries the function of an 'intra-turn positive evaluation' and/or, at least, a prompt to go on, 'pupil conversational continuant', on the other hand, usually functions as an 'acknowledge' indicating understanding, and hence sustaining the interaction; and when it occurs in intra-turn position, it implicitly prompts the speaker to go on.

Pupil Conversational Continuant

'Pupil conversational continuant' is in line with what Gaies (1983b) refers to as the reacting move of learner feedback. It can be defined as unelicited information provided by the pupil(s) to the teacher about the comprehensibility and usefulness of the teacher's or another pupil's ongoing utterance(s). It is always carried out by the act 'acknowledge' (cf. Chapter 4) which is used by the pupils to display their understanding and negotiate their intake (see also Gaies 1983b). The act 'acknowledge' is also comparable to what Varonis & Gass (1985b) refer to as 'conversational continuant', functioning to keep the conversation going in nonnative/nonnative conversations. As Scarcella & Higa (1981) argue, sustaining the conversation is an aspect of negotiation which enables the learner to maintain a conversation long enough to obtain sufficient comprehensible input for language development.

In the data, 'Pupil conversational continuant' usually occurs after a teacher utterance, but may also occur after another pupil utterance. The pupil provides an 'acknowledge' to show that s/he is paying attention and/or to negotiate her/his understanding of what the speaker is saying, as in extract (53) which is reproduced below.

```
Compound -I- 1 T    : SMUGGLE .. Take something which is forbidden.
Teacher               You hide it and take it to another country to sell it
Inform                there (i.). OK (m.). For example you take gold=
                                                            [
   -R- 2 P1 : ->                                  Drugs (ack.)
   -I- 3 T    : =and you sell it in Algeria or=
                          [        ]
   -R- 4 P1 :                      Abroad (ack.)
   -I- 5 T    : =in Spain (com.)
                  (3rd grade - Lesson 3)
```

In the above extract, the teacher is performing an 'inform' in which he is explaining the word 'to smuggle'. While the teacher is speaking, one of the pupils shouts out words that indicate his understanding (2 P1, 4 P1); and in this way, he negotiates his intake. Consider also the following extract:

```
(85)
Teacher -I- 1 T    : Well (m.). Here we have a WEDDING in MARBURY
Inform               (s.) A WEDDING is a marriage .. ceremony (i.)
                                        [      ]    [       ]
   -R- 2 PP : ->                        Ah Ah.     Yes. Yes (ack.)
```

```
Teacher -I- 3 T   : And MARBURY is (i.)
Inform                         [
        -R- 4 P  : ->                   a hotel (ack.)
        -F- 5 T  : No (eva.). It's an English village (re.)
                    (1st grade - Lesson 4)
```

In the above extract, the teacher is explaining the title of the text she is going to teach: "A wedding in Marbury." She first starts by explaining the word 'wedding' which the pupils seem to have understood quickly since they provide an 'acknowledge' (2 PP), functioning as a conversational continuant, to display their understanding and thereby inform the teacher that there is no need to dwell on the explanation of that item. Thus, the teacher moves to the explanation of the word 'Marbury'; but before she has explained what it means, one of the pupils attempts to guess the meaning of the word and complete the teacher's utterance (4 P). Yet, her guess is incorrect, and therefore negatively evaluated by the teacher (5 T) who then provides a repair which simultaneously functions to complete her 'informative' started in 3 T. Consider also extract (37) which is reproduced below.

```
Compound -I- 1 T   : Listen, I've got a friend. He isn't a good student,
Teacher               but he succeeded. He isn't a good student but he
Inform                succeeded. We can say= (s.)
                      [
        -R- 2 P1 :    He used to- (ack.)
                      [
           3 P2 :     He cheated (ack.)
        -F- 4 T  : Yes (acc.). May be he cheated (com.)
        -I- 5 T  : =So, although he is a bad student= (ack.)
                                  [
        -R- 6 PP :                a bad student (ack.)
        -I- 7 T  : =he succeeded (i.)
                      [
        -R- 8 PP :    he succeeded (ack.)
                    (3rd grade - Lesson 3)
```

In the above extract, the teacher is performing an 'inform' to explain the use of the conjunction 'although'. But, as soon as he has finished the 'starter' (1 T), two pupils simultaneously try to guess what the teacher is going to say (2 P1 & 3 P2), and in this way are performing a conversational continuant and negotiating their intake. The teacher starts to present the sentence with 'although' in 5 T; but, once again, the teacher's utterance overlaps with the contribution of several pupils (6 PP & 8 PP) who are trying to display and negotiate their understanding by attempting to complete the teacher's utterance.

In classroom talk, conversational continuants may at times be seen to be elicited, called for, or expected by the teacher. That is, the teacher may create specific slots in her/his turn to invite learners to provide conversational continuants. Consider extract (51), reproduced below, where the conversational continuant is elicited:

```
Compound  -I- 1 T   : There were some people there= (i.)
Teacher                                          [
Inform     -R- 2 P1 :                             Yes (ack.)
           -I- 3 T   : =They saw- =(i.)
                                   [
           -R- 4 P1 :              Mr. Barki (ack.)
                                   [        ]
               5 P2 :              The man  (ack.)
           -F- 6 T   : =the incident (re.)
           -I- 7 T   : They saw the incident. Well (i.)
                                                     [
           -R- 8 P1 :                                But didn't do anything (ack.)
           -F- 9 T   : Yes (eva.)
                       (2nd grade - Lesson 1)
```

In 3 T and 7 T of the above extract, the teacher creates slots in her utterances in order to invite pupils to provide an 'acknowledge', in other words, a 'conversational continuant' which displays their attention to what the teacher is saying and their understanding of the text which they have listened to previously. 4 P1 and 5 P1 are tentative completions to the teacher's utterance, but which were covertly negatively evaluated by the teacher's 'repair' in 6 T. The teacher creates a second slot in her utterance in 7 T which is followed by a pupil's tentative completion (8 P1). The teacher positively evaluates the pupil's contribution, hence closing the exchange (9 T).

Varonis & Gass (1985b: 82) argue that "[i]n many instances, a particular exchange is ambiguous with regard to whether it is truly an example of a conversational continuant or whether it is an indicator of nonunderstanding. In fact, in some instances it may serve both functions simultaneously." Consider 4 P1 and 5 P2 in the above extract, which are meant as 'conversational continuants' by the pupils who perform them, but which turn out to be indicators of nonunderstanding. Further, Varonis & Gass (1985b: 82) note that "[t]here are clearly instances when one member of a conversational dyad tries to appear relevant and knowledgeable by using continuing devices in just those situations when there has been no understanding, but when one is trying to hide the lack of understanding," as in the following example cited in Varonis & Gass (1985b: 82), and which is not taken from a witnessed conversation, but is as Varonis & Gass (1985b: 82) observe, "plausible and probably common in discourse":

    Guest : I generally weave using warp way stripes.
-> You   : Oh, warp way stripes.
    Guest : They have wonderful dynamism, yet such simplicity.
-> You   : Yes. Dynamic yet simple.
    Guest : The color possibilities seem almost limitless once you've
                mastered the basic technique.
-> You   : Limitless possibilities!

Likewise, in classroom discourse, pupils may repeat what the teacher has said, not because they understand it and thereby implying that the teacher may go on with her utterance, but on the contrary because they don't understand it and thereby indicating that the particular utterance being repeated is unfamiliar and hence its pronunciation needs to be practised and its meaning needs to be explained. Consider the following extract:

(86)
Teacher -I- 1 T   : Please books and copybooks shut (d.)
Direct   -R-   <Activity> (rea.)

Focus   -I- 2 T   : Well (m.). The title of our lesson today is ...'a wedding
                        in Marbury' 'a wedding in Marbury' (ms.)
                        <T. writes this title on BB>
         -R- 3 PP : <laughter because PP don't understand the title>
         -F- 4 T   : Yes I know (com.) ... Of course you don't know what
                        it means (com.)
Teacher -I- 5 T   : 'A wedding in Marbury' (s.). So let's listen to the
Direct   cassette recorder or the tape recorder
         -R-   <the class is listening to the tape> (rea.)
Teacher -I- 6 T   : A wedding (i.)
Inform   [
         -R- 7 P1 : ->   A wedding (ack.)
                             [
             8 P2 : ->   A wedding (ack.)
         -F- 9 T   : You don't know what it means (com.)
Teacher -I-10 T   : Okay (m.). Well (s.). Do you remember 'looking for a
Elicit   flat'? (el.).. Brian and Mary (cl.)

```
            -R-11 PP : Yes (rep.)
            -F-12 T  : Yes [1-] (acc.)
 Teacher    -I- 13 T : Are they married? (el.)
 Elicit
                      (1st grade - Lesson 4)
```

The above extract occurred at the very beginning of a lesson. Although laughter in other instances in the present data may indicate understanding, the pupils' laughter in 3 PP is metalinguistic information that the teacher's previous utterance "a wedding in Marbury" (2 T) has not been understood (see Schachter 1986 where laughter is also considered as an indirect indication of nonunderstanding). Furthermore, the pupils' repetition of the word 'wedding' (7 P1 & 8 P2) does not indicate that they have understood what it means but on the contrary that they have not. In the Moroccan context, as in EFL classroom contexts in general, where there is no or very little chance for pupils to learn or practise English outside the classroom, the teacher usually has a fair knowledge of what words and structures pupils already know; and therefore, most of the time, s/he can correctly guess whether the 'acknowledge' is one displaying understanding or nonunderstanding. Furthermore, the paralinguistic cues accompanying the 'acknowledge' may be very informative for the teacher in this regard. Yet, it is a fact that extracts like the above are very rare in the data; in other words, when 'acknowledge' occurs it usually aims at displaying understanding.

'Pupil conversational continuant' certainly indicates pupil attentiveness and involvement in classroom interaction; and attentiveness and involvement in the discourse by all participants is, no doubt, the *sine qua non* of successful communication. Stevick (1976, 1980, 1981) rightly contends that it is precisely active involvement that facilitates acquisition because it 'charges' the input and allows it to 'penetrate' deeply. In Stevick's framework, the charge comes from the hearer rather than from the speaker source, that is to say, from the learner rather than from the teacher in TL classroom contexts.

Nonetheless, we would agree with Van Lier (1988: 219) that 'pupil conversational continuants' are always "subservient to a teacher-controlled activity, i.e., they are *reactive* rather than *proactive*. They give evidence of some negotiation, but only in terms of surface aspects of an on-going activity. They do not aim to shape that activity, [...]." It is precisely this characteristic that differentiates pupil conversational continuant from pupil-initiated negotiation; the latter explicitly aims at resolving an interactional problem and may contribute to shaping an ongoing activity.

Conclusion

This chapter has been concerned with two main types of negotiation occurring in TL classroom discourse, namely 'didactic negotiation' and 'conversational negotiation'. As the names suggest, the first type of negotiation is typical of TL classroom interaction; whereas the second is common to all face-to-face interaction. 'Didactic negotiation' encompasses four genres, namely 'medium-oriented negotiation', 'comprehension check-oriented negotiation', 'turn-taking-oriented negotiation', and 'complete sentence-oriented negotiation'. As for 'conversational negotiation', it encompasses seven genres, namely 'hearing-oriented negotiation', 'meaning-oriented negotiation', 'content-oriented negotiation', 'general knowledge-oriented negotiation', 'agreement-oriented negotiation', 'surprise display-oriented negotiation', and 'conversational continuant'.

Negotiated interaction aims at locating and dealing with actual or potential trouble sources related to 'accessibility' or 'acceptability' (see also Widdowson 1983 and Aston 1986). Nonetheless, some sort of negotiation can also occur when no trouble is at issue, as is the case in most 'conversational continuants'. This type of negotiation mainly functions to sustain the conversation by encouraging and/or cooperating in the production of the ongoing turn, with no attempt to repair it. Hence, such negotiation implicitly functions to maintain rapport and lower the 'affective filter' (Krashen 1982a) in TL classroom interaction. There are two types of 'conversational continuant': 'teacher conversational continuant' and 'pupil conversational continuant'.

The task of differentiating between certain genres of 'didactic negotiation' and 'conversational negotiation' has not been without difficulties. This is due to the fact that, occasionally, it is difficult to ascribe the negotiation to a single discourse function, since in certain exchanges it is the concurrence of several factors which triggers the negotiation. To prevent the overlap of these negotiation genres in our coding of the data, we elaborated a clearcut operational definition for each negotiation genre, focusing on the function rather than the trigger of the negotiation since we were particularly concerned with the *discourse function* of the negotiation.

CHAPTER 6
Frequency Distribution of Negotiation
in the TL Classroom

Introduction

How frequent is negotiated interaction in TL classroom discourse; and does this frequency vary by proficiency level? We seek to investigate these questions in order to confirm or disconfirm, on the one hand, Pica's (1987) claim that there is a relative absence of negotiated interaction in the ESL classroom, and, on the other hand, Brock (1986), Rulon & McCreary (1986) and Bremer et al.'s (1988) assertion that the higher the learners' linguistic proficiency, the less negotiation occurs. We also aim to find out what functions mostly characterize EFL classroom discourse negotiations in Moroccan secondary schools, and whether this varies by proficiency level.

Hence, four main quantitative analyses are carried out in this chapter. First, the frequency of negotiated and non-negotiated exchanges, in the data, is investigated. Second, negotiated exchanges are focused on; and the frequency of didactic and conversational negotiation is computed. Third, didactic negotiation is further examined by computing the frequency of each 'didactic negotiation' genre. Finally, conversational negotiation is further examined by investigating the frequency of each 'conversational negotiation' genre. These quantitative analyses are accompanied with qualitative ones to explain and discuss the quantitative findings.

Frequency of Negotiated and Non-negotiated Exchanges

Negotiated and non-negotiated exchanges have been computed in each lesson; and their frequency has been compared in the data as a whole and by grade. The results are presented and discussed below.

Table 4: Summary statistics for negotiated vs. non-negotiated exchanges by grade

| Grades | | Teaching exchanges | | Totals |
		Negotiated	Non-negotiated	
1st G.	n	817	486	1303
	%	62.70	37.30	100
	X	163.40	97.20	130.30
2nd G.	n	1066	356	1422
	%	74.96	25.04	100
	X	213.20	71.20	142.20
3rd G.	n	640	288	928
	%	68.96	31.04	100
	X	128	57.60	92.80
Totals	n	2523	1130	3653
	%	69.07	30.93	100
	X	168.20	75.33	121.77

n : sample size
% : row percentage
X : observed mean

As illustrated in Table 4 and Figure 7, there is a preference for negotiated exchanges over non-negotiated ones. The notion of 'preference' is not intended, here, as a psychological claim about the teacher's or pupils' desires, "but as a label for a structural phenomenon very close to the linguistic concept of *markedness* " (Levinson 1983: 332-3). As Gaskill (1980: 126) noted, the term 'preference' "does not refer to a personal or psychological inclination or to any standard of what is considered polite or proper. The term 'preference' is used to describe organizational properties of a given phenomenon in conversation."

As the above Table shows, there are 2523 negotiated exchanges in the data while there are only 1130 non-negotiated ones (F= 22.807, df= 1, p= .000). The statistical significance of this result implies that there is a certain dynamism in the interaction process in TL classrooms. This dynamism, reflected in the predominance of negotiated over non-negotiated exchanges, leads to a discourse structure that is far more complex and unpredictable than the oversimplified and rigid structure suggested by Sinclair & Coulthard (1975) for analyzing classroom interaction, namely an initiating move opening the exchange, a responding move, and an evaluative feedback move closing the exchange. Yet, given that Sinclair & Coulthard's (1975) system of analysis has proved to be one of the most adequate systems for coding and analyzing classroom discourse, we reckon that the structures resulting from negotiated interaction can be better accounted for by adapting Sinclair & Coulthard's (1975) model in such a way as

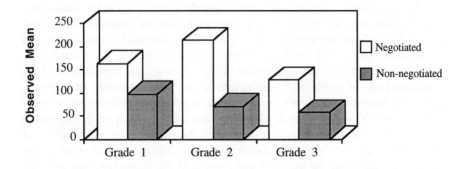

Figure 7: Negotiated vs. non-negotiated exchanges by grade

to cope with the prevailing occurrence of negotiated interaction. Actually, this is what we have done in the coding and analysis of the data (cf. Chapter 4).

As Varonis & Gass (1985b: 73) observe, in negotiated interaction, "the conversational flow is marred by numerous interruptions. These may be seen as vertical sequences in a horizontal progression." Negotiated interaction in TL classrooms also results in a structure resembling the vertical constructions Varonis & Gass (1985b) found in nonnative/nonnative conversations and Scollon (1979) found in mother-child interaction or the so-called scaffolded interaction that Hawkins (1988) found in elementary school ESL classrooms with Low English Proficient Children (see also Hatch 1983a: 165-173).

Since the interactions in the present data occur in teacher-fronted classrooms and mainly between teacher and pupil(s) - two participants with largely different proficiencies in the target language - the predominance of negotiated exchanges sustains the finding that "when participants have little shared background (be it cultural, linguistic, or personal), the conversation is likely to be peppered with interruptions for clarification of content or language form" (Gass and Varonis 1991: 122). Accordingly, the present study leads to a different conclusion from that drawn by researchers like Long & Sato 1983, Pica & Doughty 1985, Doughty & Pica 1986, Pica & Long 1986, Pica 1987 (cf. Chapter 2), namely that there is a relative lack of negotiated interaction in the ESL classroom. This mismatch between the results of these studies and ours may be explained by the fact that we have a wider and more comprehensive view of what might be regarded as negotiated interaction. These studies coded as negotiation sequences only those exchanges through which learners and teachers check the understanding and genuinely seek clarification of each other's messages. Thus, while these studies are restricted to the negotiation of meaning, we coded as a 'negotiated exchange' a wide range of negotiated talk ranging from medium-, meaning-, content-, to agreement-oriented negotiation, etc. (cf. Chapter 5).

Long (1983b), Long & Sato (1983), and Pica (1987) consider "classrooms [...] less than optimal environments for successful second-language acquisition" (Pica 1987: 17) by virtue of the relative absence (as attested in their studies) of negotiation sequences held to foster successful SL/FL comprehension, production, and ultimately acquisition. Thus, the statistical significance of the predominance of negotiated interaction in our data naturally triggers the pedagogic question: what does the high frequency of negotiated interaction imply from an acquisitional point of view? As discussed in Chapter 5, negotiated interaction is multifunctional. It negotiates the accuracy of the medium of interaction (see also 'comprehensible output' in Swain 1985) as well as the comprehensibility of the meaning and content of the interaction (see also 'the negotiation of meaning' in Varonis & Gass 1985b and 'the negotiation of content' in Rulon & McCreary 1986). It also functions to negotiate for agreement, to regulate pupil participation to make it comply with TL classroom rules of interaction. Finally, it serves to sustain the interaction, maintain rapport, and lower the 'affective filter' (Krashen 1982a).

As argued in Chapter 5, all these functions have a role in creating a favourable context for acquisition, by rendering the teacher's input more comprehensible (meaning-oriented negotiation), the pupils' output more comprehensible (meaning-oriented negotiation) and more accurate (medium-oriented negotiation), the pupils' intake more pupil-controlled (pupil conversational continuants), the content of the interaction more comprehensible (content-oriented negotiation), classroom interaction more dynamic and more communicative through the processes of the above mentioned negotiation genres and through discussion oriented activities, as in 'agreement-oriented negotiation'. Last but not least, negotiated interaction, no doubt, contributes to lowering the *affective filter,* by means of teacher and pupil conversational continuants. The affective dimension of foreigner talk discourse has been considered an important variable in the acquisition process (cf. Smith 1971, MacFarlane 1975, Vigil & Oller 1976, Zamel 1981, Krashen 1982a).

Accordingly, the high frequency of negotiated interaction in the data implies that the conditions in which learning can occur are created, that pupils are given the opportunity to achieve successful comprehension and production of new vocabulary items and structures and, as a result, that the context in which the data have been collected is favourable for learners' interlanguage development towards target language norms. Hence, the data refute Pica's (1987: 17) suggestion that classroom activities "offer students little opportunity to move beyond their current level of comprehension or production."

However, following Aston (1986: 140), one may argue that "it is not simply or even primarily the frequency but above all the social context of negotiation which influences acquisition," a context to which the initiation of negotiated interaction "is reflexively related, both mirroring and constructing participants' definitions of the situation." Since this issue is dealt with in Chapter 7, where negotiated interaction is tackled in terms of the power factor operating in classroom discourse, suffice it to say, here, that a context where pupil-initiated negotiation is possible is already a context where the 'affective filter' is lowered; otherwise pupils will give no cues as to the comprehensibility of input, feign understanding even if they don't understand, feign agreement even if they don't agree, and refrain from taking the initiative of repairing each other's utterances or challenging a proposition conveyed by the teacher.

Returning back to the results in the above Table, an observation that is not without importance can be made; it concerns the disparity among the three grades in terms of the total number of teaching exchanges in each grade. The frequency of teaching exchanges slightly tends to increase from first (n= 1303), to second grade (n= 1422), but seems to noticeably decrease in the third grade (n= 928). This may imply that there is a trend for more verbal interaction in the first and second grades than in the third grade. However, such a conclusion should not be taken at face value since the variance of the total number of teaching exchanges across the three grades is not statistically significant (F= 2.809, df= 2, p= .100). The non-significance of this finding suggests that there is more variability between the lessons of the same grade than between the lessons of different grades.

As for the frequency distribution of negotiated and non-negotiated interaction by grade, the findings reveal that the variance is not noticeably important. Though the frequencies displayed in the above Table (n= 817 vs. n= 486 in the first grade, n= 1066 vs. n= 356 in the second, and n= 640 vs. n= 288 in the third) show that the preference for negotiated over non-negotiated interaction is highest in the second grade and lowest in the first grade, two-factor analysis of variance has shown that these findings are not statistically significant (F= 2.344, df= 2, p= .118).

Furthermore, though a comparison of the total number of negotiated exchanges occurring in each grade reveals that the highest frequency of negotiated interaction is recorded in the second grade (n= 1066), whereas, the least frequency is witnessed in the third grade (n= 640), one-factor analysis of variance has shown that these findings are not statistically significant (F= 1.483, df= 2, p= .266). Hence, the seeming variability among the first, second, and third grade, in terms of the frequency distribution of negotiated interaction, may simply be due to the non-significant variability among the three grades, in terms of the total number of teaching exchanges occurring in each grade.

On the basis of these findings, we cannot support the claim made by Brock (1986), Rulon & McCreary (1986), and Bremer et al. (1988) that the more advanced L2 learners are, the less likely it is for negotiation to occur. It is worth noting that the concern in Brock (1986) has been with the negotiation of meaning in ESL classroom interaction; in Rulon and McCreary (1986), it has been with both the negotiation of meaning and content in ESL classroom interaction; and in Bremer et al. (1988), concern has been with the negotiation of meaning in NS-NNS interaction. Yet, the three studies reach the same conclusion, namely that it is likely for negotiation to be less frequent in interactions involving advanced learners.

However, Deen & Van Hout (1991), who were also concerned with the negotiation of meaning in NS-NNS interaction, give an argument that is out of tune with the conclusion of the above studies. They write:

> It is likely that in interaction with more advanced non-native speakers more attempts to negotiate meaning, resulting in clarification sequences, are made because the likelihood of successful negotiation is greater. In the interaction between a native speaker and a real beginner in a target language many factual or potential nonunderstandings may remain implicit (Deen & Van Hout 1991: 124).

The non-significant variance of the frequency of negotiated interaction across beginning, intermediate, and advanced classes disconfirms both conflicting claims advanced in the above studies. This non-significant variance may be explained by the fact that EFL teacher-fronted classroom interaction, of which the data is one example, being controlled by the teacher (through teacher 'elicitations', teacher 'informatives', teacher choice of topic, teacher choice of text, etc.), the difficulty of teacher talk, of text, of topic, and thereby of the interaction as a whole is adjusted to the proficiency level of the class. Hence, each proficiency level is involved in accessible but challenging tasks which call for a comparable amount of negotiated interaction in the three proficiency levels. Accordingly, we would argue that, in TL classroom discourse, pupils' proficiency level has no effect on the frequency of negotiated interaction.

The present section has been concerned with the frequency distribution of negotiated in comparison with non-negotiated exchanges in the data as a whole and by proficiency level. The results reveal a significant preference for negotiated over non-negotiated interaction but a non-significant variance between the frequency of these two variables by proficiency level. In the following section, TL classroom negotiation is dealt with in more detail: the frequency distribution of its two major functional categories (i.e., didactic and conversational negotiation) is focused on.

Frequency of Didactic and Conversational Negotiation

This section investigates the frequency distribution of didactic in comparison with conversational negotiation in the data as a whole and by grade, in order to find out what sort of negotiation characterizes the data, and whether pupils' proficiency level impacts on the occurrence of those two major types of TL classroom negotiation. The rationale behind such an investigation is to ascertain whether the occurring negotiations are mainly oriented towards the resolution of problems that are specific to classroom interaction or also towards the resolution of those problems that are common to any face-to-face interaction. Put otherwise, the study is interested in finding out whether pupils are as frequently engaged in the sort of negotiations occurring outside the classroom as they are engaged in those negotiations typical of the 'black box' (i.e., the classroom, cf. Long 1983d), and which they will hardly ever encounter outside the classroom. The results are exposed and discussed below.

Table 5: Summary statistics for didactic vs. conversational negotiation by grade

Grades		Negotiated interaction		
		Didactic	Conversational	Totals
1st G.	n	375	442	817
	%	45.90	54.10	100
	X	75	88.40	81.70
2nd G.	n	379	687	1066
	%	35.55	64.45	100
	X	75.80	137.40	106.60
3rd G.	n	178	462	640
	%	27.81	72.19	100
	X	35.60	92.40	64
Totals	n	932	1591	2523
	%	36.94	63.06	100
	X	62.13	106.07	84.10

n : sample size
% : row percentage
X : observed mean

As illustrated in Table 5 and Figure 8, there is a preference for conversational negotiation (n= 1591) over didactic negotiation (n= 932), in the data as a whole and in all three grades (n= 442 vs. n= 375 in the first, n= 687 vs. n= 379 in the second, and n= 462 vs. n= 178 in the third) (F= 10.139, df= 1, p= .004). The statistical significance of this finding implies that in the data, pupils are more often engaged in those negotiations common to ordinary conversation and involving the negotiation of matters such as 'meaning', 'content', and 'agreement' than in TL classroom specific negotiations, of which the negotiation of the form of the target language is the most important. Hence, it might be argued that negotiated interaction, as witnessed in the data, is more oriented towards developing pupils' target language *use* rather than *usage* (cf. Widdowson 1972, 1978), and, as a result, seems to provide learners with the opportunity to practice some of the skills needed to cope with the communication requirements of the world outside the 'black box' (Long 1983d).

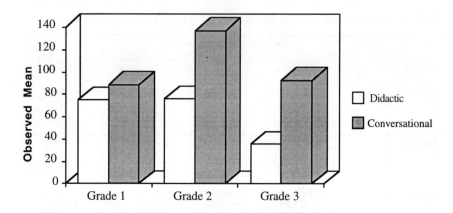

Figure 8: Didactic vs. conversational negotiation by grade

Thus, it may be argued that despite being teacher-fronted, lessons where conversational negotiation predominates over didactic negotiation are on the whole communicatively-oriented, since conversational negotiation cannot be conducted in the mechanical Stimulus-Response-Reinforcement process advocated by some methods of language teaching. A communicatively-oriented lesson is one which provides an atmosphere in which genuine and meaningful communication can take place comfortably; one which recognizes the teaching of *communicative competence* as its primary goal. Sociolinguists, such as Hymes (1972), have attempted to show what the development of communicative competence may involve; and second language acquisition researchers (such as

Munby 1978, Brumfit & Johnson 1979, Canale & Swain 1980, Johnson & Morrow 1981, and Canale 1983) have come up with insightful descriptions in terms of second language learning, and have given examples of possible classroom applications.

Current research in applied linguistics maintains that it is beneficial for learners of a target language to be exposed and actively involved in spontaneous, genuine, and meaningful communication in that language (Canale & Swain 1980, Johnson & Morrow 1981, Brumfit 1984, Allwright 1984). It follows, therefore, that teachers should provide learners with opportunities to engage in spontaneous, genuine, and meaningful communication if learners are to discover the linguistic, sociolinguistic, and pragmatic rules necessary for target language comprehension and production. Learners should experience doubt and uncertainty, and learn how to make appropriate linguistic, content, and pragmatic choices. Actually, though classroom conversational negotiation is meaningful, whether all conversational negotiation genres, as perceived by the present study, are genuine is a debatable issue, by virtue of the predominance of teacher-initiated negotiation (cf. Chapter 7) and display elicitations (see subsequent section). Indeed, since the teacher is basically the knowledgeable participant in classroom discourse, a teacher-initiated negotiation is mostly carried out by a display elicitation, the answer of which is already known to the teacher. This state of affairs might imply that most teacher-initiated negotiations are far from being genuine.

Paulston (1974) differentiates between meaningful and communicative interaction. Speech, in the former, is described as contextually relevant; whereas, in the latter, it is described as bearing information unknown to the hearer. Thus, according to advocates of communicative methodology, communicative interaction, by definition, involves genuine and authentic interaction. However, to quote Van Lier (1988: 29), L2 classroom-oriented researchers

> have failed to consider the communication potential of the L2 classroom *itself* and the authentic resources for interaction it has to offer. Classroom authenticity may not exactly mirror world authenticity, but there may be sufficient correlates for the former to be viable as a training ground for the latter.

Indeed, target language classrooms "can never just be a replica of the outside world" because they are "a shortcut to language learning, and to be this they must be different from what goes on outside. In some ways, they must economize, concentrate and cut corners" (Van Lier 1988: 179).

The issue of authentic and genuine communication is closely related to that of 'information gap' in L2 communicative methodology. Morrow (1981), following Johnson (1979), claims that in real life, there is always a transfer or exchange of information between people; in other words, communication always aims at bridging an information gap. According to Morrow (1981: 62), "[t]his concept of information gap seems to be one of the most fundamental in the whole area of communicative teaching." However, following Van Lier (1988), we would argue that the idea that 'information gap' is a prerequisite for communication to occur is the most pervasive assumption in L2 methodology. As Van Lier (1988: 29) contends,

> if we examine the purposes and contexts of most of our verbal interaction during an average day, we will probably come to the conclusion that the transmission of information is a very minor concern compared to such vital tasks as creating and maintaining social relationships, establishing accommodation between speaker and hearer, getting people to do things for us, making sense of the situation we are in, creating a good impression of ourselves, and so on.

In answer to this criticism, Morrow (1981) would claim that all depends on what we mean by 'information'; in the situations described by Van Lier (1988) in the above quotation, communication is taking place, but "the information which is transferred is of the 'interpersonal' social type rather than the 'ideational' (factual)" (Morrow 1981: 62).

In the same train of thought, Pica (1987), argues that for target language classrooms to become optimal environments for successful language acquisition, "what is needed are activities whose outcome depends on information exchange and which emphasize collaboration and an equal share of responsibility among classroom participants" (Pica 1987: 17). She further contends that

> [a]lthough activities with a built-in requirement for information exchange are widely espoused in methods literature and have enjoyed a long tradition in communicative language teaching [...], they should not be confused with the more well-known information gap activities. In these latter activities, one participant holds all information necessary for completing a task and the other participant must work to elicit it. Although this kind of activity could promote interactional modification moves towards achieving input comprehensibility, there is the danger that participants could fall into the unequal role relationship characterizing much of classroom discourse, since information is elicited and supplied rather than exchanged and shared (Pica 1987: 17-18).

Furthermore, Pica (1987: 4) notes that

[n]either the need for mutual understanding nor the opportunity to restructure interaction to meet this need is inherent to a language-learning environment. These circumstances arise as learners and their interlocutors often engage in a two-way flow of communication in which each processes something that the other wants or needs and has a right to request and a responsibility to share.

Drawing from empirical data on NS-NNS conversation occurring in settings outside the classroom, Pica (1987: 4) describes "how unfamiliar linguistic material becomes comprehensible to learners and their interlocutors when they modify and restructure their interaction." She highlights the importance of these modifications in terms of the acquisition process. Hence, she argues that the two-way flow of communication which is characteristic of NS-NNS interaction and which seems to be lacking in SL classroom interaction is a *sine qua non* for negotiated interaction to occur, in other words, a necessary condition for learners to progress beyond their current level of comprehension and production and thereby for acquisition.

Conversely, as illustrated by the statistically significant predominance of 'conversational negotiation' over 'didactic negotiation' in the present data, it might be argued that the one-way flow of information, characteristic of the lessons constituting the data (as illustrated in the following section), does not hamper the occurrence of 'conversational negotiation'. This provides further support for Gass & Varonis' (1985b) finding which refutes Long's (1983c) prediction that the one-way flow of information is a hindrance to the occurrence of negotiated interaction. Hence, following Gass & Varonis (1985b), it may be argued that the kind of information exchange (i.e., whether there is a one-way or a two-way flow of information) is not the only determining factor of negotiated interaction.

To investigate whether an increase in the flow of information going from pupil to teacher would have an effect on the frequency of conversational negotiation, the study computed the correlation between conversational negotiation and pupil replies to referential elicitations, on the one hand, and between conversational negotiation and pupil informative acts, on the other hand. The results reveal a moderate positive correlation in the first investigation ($r= .534$, $df= 13$, $p= .05$), but a non-significant positive correlation in the second investigation ($r= .234$, $df= 13$, $p> .10$). This leads to the conclusion that an increase in information flowing from pupil to teacher might contribute to increasing the frequency of conversational negotiation, which would make classroom interaction sound more unclassroom-like and more communicative.

The predominance of 'conversational negotiation' in the data also disconfirms Long's (1983b: 218) claim that "the SL classroom offers very little opportunity to the learner to communicate in the target language or to hear it used for communicative purposes by others." Yet, it is important to note that 'conversational negotiation', in the present study, covers a wider range of negotiation than the negotiation of meaning as perceived by Long (1983a, b, c), Gass & Varonis (1985b), and Pica (1987). But, as discussed in Chapter 5, negotiation - in the sense of *modified interaction* (cf. Long 1981, 1983a, b, c) leading to *metalinguistic information* (cf. Swain 1985, Schachter 1984, 1986) - that renders teachers' input and learners' output more comprehensible and more acceptable, and that is accordingly necessary for learners' interlanguage development towards target language norms is, certainly, not restricted to the negotiation of meaning.

Indeed, as Allwright (1984a: 162-3) argues "the role of general classroom interaction as communication practice has gone largely unnoticed in the methodological literature. It has always seemed to create special communication exercises, as if communication was not already taking place in any form." In 'conversational negotiation', the focus is put on the truth value of speech and the communicative value of the interaction itself, and mainly on solving communication problems. It is assumed that learners acquire the target language by using it in conversation (cf. the 'scaffolding principle' in Hatch 1978 and Chaudron 1988). As Hatch (1978: 404) puts it "[o]ne learns how to do conversation, one learns how to interact verbally, and out of this interaction syntactic structures are developed." Such a reasoning rests on the psychological argument that

> the process of communication is, in an important sense, a learning process. We learn *by* communicating, especially in language learning where (the argument runs) it is by *using* the means of communication, in solving communication problems, that we not merely practise communicating but also *extend* our command of the means of communication, the language itself (Allwright 1984: 157).

However, the preference for conversational negotiation, in the data, by no means suggests that 'didactic negotiation' is neglected. The frequencies related to 'didactic negotiation' (n= 375 in the first grade, n= 379 in the second, and n= 178 in the third) as displayed in the above Table show that 'didactic negotiation' is also important. Yet, as indicated by the analysis of variance between the frequency of 'didactic' and 'conversational' negotiation in each grade (n= 375 vs. n= 442, in the first grade; n= 379 vs. n= 687, in the second grade; and n= 178 vs. n= 462, in the third grade), there is a statistically significant higher preference for 'conversational' over 'didactic' negotiation in the second and third grade, in comparison to the first grade (F= 3.208, df= 2, p= .058) (cf. Figure

8). Accordingly, and bearing in mind that 'medium-oriented negotiation' is the most frequent genre of 'didactic negotiation' (78.86%) (see subsequent section), it may be argued that in more proficient classes, far more emphasis is put on 'fluency' than 'accuracy' and on meaningful interaction than error treatment.

'Accuracy work' aims at developing pupils' ability to produce grammatically correct sentences. Accuracy, to quote Brumfit (1984: 52), "reflects a concern that has always been strong in the history of language teaching, which will result in usage, rather than use of language in the classroom." However, as Brumfit (1984: 52) argues, over-use of accuracy work "will impede successful language development." 'Fluency work', on the other hand, aims at developing pupils' ability to communicate a message with ease, not necessarily using perfect intonation, vocabulary, or grammar, but not using utterances likely to cause a breakdown in communication (cf. Brumfit 1984, Richards et al. 1985).

Thus, the tendency for 'didactic negotiation' to have the least frequency in the third grade (n= 375 in the first, n= 379 in the second, and n= 178 in the third) may suggest that developing pupils' accuracy is deemed more important in beginning and intermediate classes than in advanced classes, probably because the former have not yet mastered the elementary basics of the linguistic form of the target language. This coincides with the assumption that 'accuracy' is to a great extent necessary for 'fluency' (cf. Brumfit 1984). In this connection, Morrow (1981: 65) notes that "grammatical and phonological mistakes hamper communication, and enough of them - especially in the wrong place - can totally destroy it."

The tendency for 'didactic negotiation' to have the least frequency in the third grade may either suggest that pupils in advanced classes make less mistakes, as to the forms and functions of the target language, than beginning and intermediate classes, or that certain pupils' mistakes, in advanced classes, are perceived by classroom participants no more than 'performance mistakes' (i.e., mistakes due to carelessness, lack of attention, or limited fluency in the target language) and hence not worthy of repair. Anyway, in advanced classes, accuracy work, in the sense of error treatment or medium-oriented negotiation, seems to be deemed less essential or perhaps less necessary than in beginning and intermediate classes.

This state of affairs is reminiscent of Swain's (1985: 249) assertion that the immersion students constituting the subjects of her study "do not demonstrate native-speaker productive competence" partly because they are

> not being "pushed" in their output. That is to say, the immersion students have developed, in the early grades, strategies for getting their meaning across which are adequate for the situation they find themselves in: they are understood by their teachers and peers.

There appears to be little social or cognitive pressure to produce
language that reflects more appropriately or precisely their
intended meaning: there is no push to be more comprehensible
than they already are. That is, there is no push for them to analyze
further the grammar of the target language because their current
output appears to succeed in conveying their intended message. In
other words, [...], they no longer receive much negative input
(Swain 1985: 249).

In the same way, in our data, the apparently decreasing frequency of
'didactic negotiation' in advanced classes might imply that in these classes pupils
receive less 'negative input' as to the appropriateness of their output, in terms of
the forms and functions of the target language. This might engender
'fossilization' (cf. Selinker 1972, Vigil & Oller 1976, Selinker & Lamendella
1979, Brown 1987). Krashen (1985: 43) argues that "[most] adult second-
language acquirers 'fossilize', that is, they stop short of the native speaker level
of performance in their second language."

[f]ossilizable linguistic phenomena are linguistic items, rules and
subsystems which speakers of a particular NL [native language] will
tend to keep in their IL [interlanguage] relative to a particular TL
[target language], no matter what the age of the learner or amount
of explanation and instruction he receives in the TL (Selinker
1972: 215).

Describing the process of fossilization in interlanguage development,
Brown (1987: 186) argues that "the internalization of incorrect forms takes place
by means of the same learning processes as the internalization of correct forms,
but we refer to the latter [...] as 'learning'" while the former is called
'fossilization'. In other words, as Allwright & Bailey (1991: 93) note, "learning
correctly consists of internalising appropriate forms of the target language, while
fossilisation is the consistent use of recognisably erroneous forms."

While it is not yet clear why fossilization does occur, some researchers (for
example, Brown 1987 and Vigil & Oller 1976) contend that fossilization is
related to the type of feedback target language learners receive. Yet, as Chaudron
(1988) observes, for the information available in feedback to have an impact on
the learner's hypothetical rules of his developing grammar, the learner should
pay attention to and be ready for that information. Vigil & Oller (1976) dealt with
this issue of readiness and attention. They emphasized pragmatic interaction
factors which serve to either 'reinforce' or 'destabilize' the learner's hypothetical
rules, and viewed feedback as having a primary role in the fossilization of these
rules. According to them, target language learners get at least two types of
feedback from their interlocutors. The first is 'cognitive feedback' (i.e., the

positive or negative information about learners' output, which usually leads to information about target language forms). The second is 'affective feedback' (i.e., the positive, neutral, or negative affective support provided by the interlocutor and signals about the interlocutor's desire to continue the conversation; see the 'motivational function' of feedback in Annett 1969) (see also Chaudron 1988 and Allwright & Bailey 1991). Allwright & Bailey (1991: 94) contend that

> [b]oth types of feedback ['cognitive' and 'affective'] are simultaneously supplied to language learners by their interlocutors in most communicative settings. As the learners test their hypotheses about how to communicate in the target language, the people they are talking to respond, usually with both cognitive and affective feedback.

Interestingly, according to Vigil & Oller (1976: 281),

> the tendency towards fossilization of either correct or incorrect forms is governed by feedback principally on the cognitive dimension. However, if feedback: on the affective dimension is not predominantly as expected, and predominantly positive, the feedback on the cognitive dimension will lose much of its force.

Accordingly, the prevention of fossilization of erroneous forms depends on the provision of clear cognitive information about the problems in learners' output. But to make sure that conversation will be sustained, cognitive feedback must go hand in hand with positive affective feedback; otherwise, learners may interpret cognitive feedback as a sign of 'failure', and may refrain from taking risks. In this connection, Smith (1971: 23-26) argues that "risks taken depend upon the price paid for making errors [...]. If the cost is too high, few risks will be taken." Nonetheless, in Vigil & Oller's (1976) model, positive feedback must not be so supporting and encouraging that learners see no point in altering their inaccurate or inappropriate output.

Vigil & Oller's (1976) feedback model has been criticized by Selinker & Lamendella (1979: 368) who maintain that "[f]ossilization in interlanguage learning *cannot* be accounted for solely (or even primarily) in terms of a need for particular sorts of feedback." Similarly, Krashen (1985) seems to have a completely different view from that of Vigil & Oller (1976) about what might cause fossilization. He argues that fossilization may be caused by several factors, but that insufficient quantity of comprehensible input is the most obvious cause. He excludes the importance of error correction and cognitive or informational feedback in preventing fossilization. He writes:

> The common view that lack of error correction and focus on form
> in early language teaching is responsible for fossilization is not
> predicted by the theory [Krashen's]: the theory maintains that the
> cause is lack of good comprehensible input (Krashen 1985: 48).

Although we do recognize the importance of 'comprehensible input' in the
process of TL acquisition, we do not exclude the importance of 'negative input',
which encompasses error correction and 'informational feedback'. As discussed
in Zamel (1981), 'informational feedback', occurring after a learner's erroneous
utterance, informs the learner (explicitly or implicitly) why her/his reply is
wrong. It continues to process information so that the hypotheses the learner is
testing are confirmed or rejected. According to Zamel (1981: 146),

> when an error occurs, the feedback should point out where the
> disparity between the response and the desired response lies [...].
> Feedback which points out the disparity transmits new information
> to the student's underlying processes, allowing the student to
> perceive why the response is incorrect [...]. Such feedback thus
> deals with the error effectively.

To illustrate this, she provides the following example:

Student : There is a hat on her head.
Teacher : Yes, there is a hat. But, is it on the man or the woman?
Student : The man ... OK ... there is a hat on his head
              (Zamel 1981: 146).

However, this by no means suggests that we advocate loading feedback
with too much information, neither do we advocate systematic error correction.
On the contrary, we sustain the view which recommends that teachers should
react tactfully to pupils' errors, knowing when to correct and when not to
correct, and when and how to do error treatment. Therefore, we utterly disagree
with researchers such as Dulay, Burt, and Krashen (1982: 35) who maintain that
"[a]lthough students say that they want correction (Cathcart and Olson 1976) and
teachers try to provide as much as they can, *it is all too obvious to both teachers
and students that errors are often impervious to correction* " (emphasis added).
Actually, researchers who exclude the importance of error correction in target
language acquisition seem to ignore that by refraining altogether from correcting
errors, teachers would deprive learners from, at least, knowing that they have
used an erroneous form. These researchers seem to ignore that the incorporation
of correct forms in interlanguage grammar is a long-term rather than a short-term
process.

As the literature on interlanguage suggests, it is not always evident that a
language learner who is continuously exposed to the target language will steadily

advance in her/his proficiency in that language. It might even be argued, following Corder (1971) and Krashen (1985), that the language learner's motivation to develop her/his interlanguage grammar towards target language norms wanes once this grammar achieves sufficient development as to enable her/him to communicate her/his purposes adequately, and this may be another cause of fossilization.

It is noteworthy that the learners involved in the present study were learning English in an 'extreme foreign language situation' (Krashen 1985: 46). This implies that the only comprehensible input they receive comes from the teacher and classmates, both nonnative speakers of English. Such input, 'interlanguage talk', as Krashen (1985: 47) argues, is "filled with errors," and hence may cause fossilization of erroneous forms in learners' interlanguage.

On the basis of considerations like Swain's (1985) claim that her subjects do not show native-speaker productive competence partly because they are not being "pushed" in their output, Vigil & Oller's (1976) emphasis on the importance of feedback in preventing fossilization, Corder's (1971) and Krashen's (1985) claim that learners' motivation decreases when they have sufficient tools to communicate in the target language, and Krashen's (1985) contention that 'extreme foreign language situations' are more liable contexts for fossilization, it may be argued that the decreasing frequency of didactic negotiation (but more precisely of 'medium-oriented negotiation'; see subsequent section) in favour of conversational negotiation - recorded in the data in more proficient classes - renders the danger of fossilization more real for advanced EFL learners in Moroccan secondary schools. In comparison to beginning and intermediate, advanced learners seem to receive the least amount of 'negative input' about the accuracy and appropriateness of their output. This may be inferred from the significant disparity between the frequency of didactic and conversational negotiation in the third grade (27.81% vs. 72.19%, respectively) in comparison to (45.90% vs. 54.10% in the first grade and 35.55% vs. 64.45% in the second grade) (see also subsequent section).

To provide further support for the above findings, the frequency distribution of didactic negotiation across the three grades has been considered in isolation from conversational negotiation. This distribution has been computed in terms of the total number of didactic negotiation occurring in the data as a whole. The results reveal an apparent variability between the three grades, especially as one moves from second to third grade (n= 375 in the first grade, n= 379 in the second grade, and n= 178 in the third grade). However, the one-factor analysis of variance has shown that this result is not statistically significant (F= 2.462, df= 2, p= .127). Likewise, the variability recorded between the three grades, in terms of the frequency distribution of conversational negotiation regardless of didactic negotiation (n= 442 in the first grade, n= 687 in the second, and n= 462 in the third) is not statistically significant (F= 2.025, df= 2, p= .175). These apparent variances may simply be due to the non-significant variance between the total number of teaching exchanges occurring in each grade.

To summarize and conclude, one might venture to argue that the significant (F= 3.208, df= 2, p= .058) tendency for 'didactic negotiation' to decrease in favour of 'conversational negotiation', in third grade classes, might imply the danger of fossilization of the linguistic forms acquired in lower grades and accordingly no or less development of advanced pupils' interlanguage grammar towards native-speaker competence. Yet, the tendency for 'conversational negotiation' to significantly increase, to the detriment of 'didactic negotiation', in more proficient classes (54.10% vs. 45.90 in the first grade; 64.45% vs. 35.55% in the second grade; and 72.19% vs. 27.81% in the third grade) might just as well imply that the more proficient classes are, the more meaningful and communicative TL classroom interaction becomes, and as a result the more opportunity is given for learners to indulge in meaningful and sometimes authentic interactions that learners are more likely to encounter outside the 'black box' (Long 1983d), when interacting with speakers of English.

This creates the following paradox: "in order to become a competent member of·a speech community, one must participate in the affairs of that community" (Van Lier 1988: 184). This necessarily implies that learners should be involved in what we have labelled 'conversational negotiation'. However, "in order to develop communicative competence one must learn to use the language code the way it is supposed to be used" (Van Lier 1988: 184). And this by no means discards the importance of what we have labelled 'didactic negotiation', and more precisely of 'medium-oriented negotiation', which constitutes 78.86% of the total number of 'didactic negotiation' (see subsequent section). To resolve this paradox, it might be suggested that a balance should be struck between didactic and conversational negotiation in each of the three grades.

Yet, a crucial question is: how can this so-called 'balance' be achieved, given that the occurrence of 'didactic' or 'conversational' negotiation is not necessarily controlled by the teacher, but also by many other factors such as the type of 'trouble source', the focus of the activity, the degree of pupil 'initiative', etc.? Indeed this is a complex issue where different variables enter into play. The present study, not being designed to account for such an issue, can but leave this question unanswered since a conclusive answer is not available at this point.

The focus of the present section has been to examine the frequency of 'didactic negotiation' in comparison with 'conversational negotiation' in the data as a whole and by grade. The study has found a significant predominance of 'conversational' over 'didactic' negotiation in the whole data. As for how the frequency of these binary features of classroom negotiation compare by grade, the results reveal a significantly higher preference for 'conversational' over 'didactic' negotiation in intermediate and advanced classes than in beginning classes. This suggests that pupils' proficiency level has an impact on the organizational properties of didactic and conversational negotiation. In the next two sections, the frequency of each 'didactic' and 'conversational' negotiation genre is examined, in the data as a whole and by proficiency level.

Frequency of Didactic Negotiation Genres

The aim of this section is to investigate the frequency of the four didactic negotiation genres, in the data as a whole and by proficiency level to find out what type of didactic negotiation(s) mostly characterize(s) the data, and whether the frequency of these genres varies by proficiency level. The results are displayed in the subsequent Table:

Table 6: Summary statistics for didactic negotiation genres by grade.

Grades		Didactic negotiation				Totals
		MON	CCON	CSON	TTON	
1st G.	n	301	08	26	40	375
	%	80.27	02.13	06.93	10.67	100
	X	60.20	01.60	05.20	08	18.75
2nd G.	n	304	07	56	12	379
	%	80.21	01.85	14.77	03.17	100
	X	60.80	01.40	11.20	02.40	18.95
3rd G.	n	130	17	11	20	178
	%	73.03	09.55	06.18	11.24	100
	X	26	03.40	02.20	04	08.90
Totals	n	735	32	93	72	932
	%	78.86	03.43	09.98	07.73	100
	X	49	02.13	06.20	04.80	15.53

MON   : 'medium-oriented negotiation'
CCON   : 'comprehension check-oriented negotiation'
CSON   : 'complete sentence-oriented negotiation'
TTON   : 'turn-taking-oriented negotiation'
n   : sample size
%   : row percentage
X   : observed mean

As Table 6 and Figure 9 indicate, there is a noticeable and significant (F= 40.083, df= 3, p= .000) preference for 'medium-oriented negotiation' (78.86%)

over the other didactic negotiation genres. This is predictable in TL classrooms where one of the primary roles of the interaction is to ascertain the accurate use of the language. Hence, it may be argued that 'medium-oriented negotiation' is the typical didactic negotiation genre. In the second place, comes the frequency of 'complete sentence-oriented negotiation' (09.98%) which implies that teachers occasionally perceive pupils' not speaking in complete sentences as an error of TL classroom interaction or even as an improper use of the target language. In the third place, comes the frequency of 'turn-taking-oriented negotiation' (07.73%) which suggests that, in the data, as in most teacher-fronted classrooms, teachers occasionally consider pupils' speaking out of turn or all at the same time a violation of a classroom convention (see also Chapter 5).

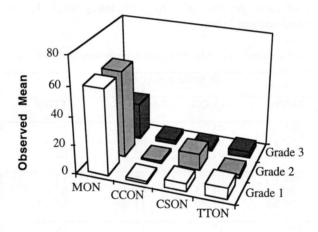

Figure 9: Didactic negotiation genres by grade

However, a striking finding is related to the noticeable low frequency (03.43%) of 'comprehension check-oriented negotiation'. On the basis of findings of studies like Early (1985), Long & Sato (1983), and Pica & Long (1986) which record a high frequency of 'comprehension checks' in both content and L2 classroom discourse, we expected to find a high frequency of 'comprehension check-oriented negotiation' in the data. However this turned out not to be the case. The discrepancy between our results and those of these studies may be due to the fact that we did not count as negotiation devices 'comprehension checks' such as OK? yes? mhm? which the teacher produces while talking without waiting for the pupils' reply. These acts do not trigger a 'comprehension check-oriented negotiation' for the teacher never waits for a reply and pupils never provide a verbal reply. Therefore, a considerable number of these acts may simply be functioning as 'fillers'. Yet, the non-occurrence of verbal replies does not necessarily imply that the teacher does not receive non-verbal replies to her 'comprehension checks'. However, since the data were audio- rather than video-recorded, the study has no basis for judging whether these 'comprehension checks' are genuine ones or no more than 'fillers'.

Long (1983b) contends that 'comprehension checks' will occur more frequently when the major flow of information is from teacher to students. The low frequency of 'comprehension check-oriented negotiation' in our data by no means indicates that, in the lessons investigated, the major flow of information is not from teacher to students. This seems clear in the high frequency of display in comparison to referential elicitations (cf. Chapter 3) and of teacher informative acts (i.e., teacher 'informative', 'clue', 'repair', and 'comment') in comparison with pupil informative acts (i.e., pupil 'informative', 'challenge', and informative 'acknowledge'). It is worth noting that a pupil 'repair' addressed to another pupil is not counted as an informative act in this particular investigation because it does not contribute to the information flowing from pupil to teacher but rather from pupil to pupil. When pupil 'repair' occurs after a teacher utterance, it simultaneously functions as a challenge, and contributes to the information flowing from pupil to teacher. Consider the subsequent Tables:

Table 7: Summary statistics for display vs. referential elicitations by grade

Grades		Elicitations		Totals
		Display	Referential	
1st G.	n	1208	68	1276
	%	94.67	05.33	100
	X	241.60	13.60	127.60
2nd G.	n	1064	240	1304
	%	81.60	18.40	100
	X	212.80	48	130.40
3rd G.	n	579	209	788
	%	73.48	26.52	100
	X	115.80	41.80	78.80
Totals	n	2851	517	3368
	%	84.65	15.35	100
	X	190.07	34.47	112.27

n : sample size
% : row percentage
X : observed mean

Table 8: Summary statistics for teacher vs. pupil informative acts by grade

Grades		Informative Acts (IA)		Totals
		Teacher IA	Pupil IA	
1st G.	n	311	26	337
	%	92.28	07.72	100
	X	62.20	05.20	33.70
2nd G.	n	391	42	433
	%	90.30	09.70	100
	X	78.20	08.40	43.30
3rd G.	n	419	86	505
	%	82.97	17.03	100
	X	83.80	17.20	50.50
Totals	n	1121	154	1275
	%	87.92	12.08	100
	X	74.73	10.27	42.50

n : sample size
% : row percentage
X : observed mean

As Tables 7 and 8 show, and as illustrated in Figures 10 and 11, there is a preference for the one-way flow of information, that is from teachers to pupils. This is evident in the statistically significant predominance of 'display elicitations' (n= 2851) over 'referential elicitations' (n= 517) (F= 69.648, df= 1, p= .000) and also in the statistically significant predominance of 'teacher informative acts' (n= 1121) over 'pupil informative acts' (n= 154) in the data as a whole (F= 198.786, df= 1, p= .000). These findings imply, to quote Pica & Long (1986: 93) that "teachers are 'knowers' whose primary function is to give information and to test whether students have received it by asking them to display their new knowledge."

However, a finding that is not without importance is that as one moves from beginning, to intermediate, to advanced classes, one records a slight but significant decrease in 'display elicitations' (n= 1208 in the first grade, n= 1064 in the second, and n= 579 in the third), in favour of 'referential elicitations' (F= 3.229, df= 2, p= .057), and also a slight but significant increase in 'pupil informative acts' (n= 26 in the first grade, n= 42 in the second, and n= 86 in the third) (F= 4.531, df= 2, p= .021). Interestingly, this coincides with the finding reported in the previous section, namely that the more proficient the class is, the more preference there is for 'conversational negotiation', in other words, the

more tendency there is for classroom talk to become more 'unclassroom-like'
and more communicatively-oriented.

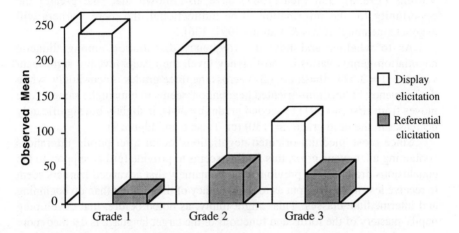

Figure 10: Display vs. referential elicitations by grade

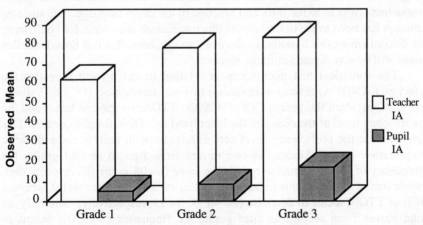

Figure 11: Teacher informative acts (IA) vs. pupil informative acts (IA) by grade

These findings suggest that, as pupils get more proficient in the target
language, classroom interaction slightly tends towards the two-way flow of
information held by Long (1980) and Long and his associates (Long 1983b,
Long & Sato 1983, Pica & Long 1986) to be a necessary condition for the

'negotiation of meaning' which, in turn, is held to be a prerequisite for target language development. Studies of task type such as Duff (1986), Gass & Varonis (1985a), and Pica (1987) have also shown that "the greater the opportunity for the information to be bidirectional, the more learners will negotiate meaning" (Gass & Varonis 1991: 136).

As to whether and how the frequency distribution among didactic negotiation genres varies by proficiency level, the results reveal a significant variance (F= 3.524, df= 2, p= .037) across the three grades. Accordingly, while the frequency of 'medium-oriented negotiation' seems to remain the same as one moves from first (n= 301) to second grade (n= 304), it slightly but significantly decreases in the third grade (n= 130) (cf. Table 6 and Figure 9).

Since most 'medium-oriented negotiations' occur after pupils' utterances containing a language error, this finding seems to provide further support to the conclusions drawn in the previous section, namely that advanced learners seem to receive less negative input as to the accuracy of their output than do beginning and intermediate classes. This, might imply, as noted before, that developing pupils' mastery of the forms and functions of the target language is deemed more essential or more necessary in beginning and intermediate than in advanced classes. However, since the frequency of pupil utterances containing a language error is a variable that certainly affects the frequency of 'medium-oriented negotiation', it may be argued that the low frequency of 'medium-oriented negotiation' in the third grade may simply be due to the fact that advanced pupils make less errors as to the form and function of the target language. Yet, since no attempt has been made to investigate this issue, there is no basis for confirming or disconfirming this hypothesis. Suffice it to say, here, that it is hoped that this issue will be investigated in future research.

The statistical test undertaken in relation to the present investigation (factorial ANOVA) reveals a significant *two-way interaction* (F= 2.627, df= 6, p= .028) between the genres CCON, CSON, TTON, on the one hand, and the proficiency level of the class, on the other hand (cf. Table 6 and Figure 9). This implies that the proficiency level acts differently with each of these didactic negotiation genres. Hence, as one moves from first to second grade, the frequency of CCON seems to remain the same (n= 08 vs. n= 07, respectively), while that of CSON seems to increase (n= 26 vs. n= 56, respectively), whereas that of TTON seems to decrease (n= 40 vs. n= 12, respectively). Similarly, as one moves from second to third grade, the frequency of CCON seems to increase (n= 07 vs. n= 17, respectively), while that of CSON seems to decrease (n= 56 vs. n= 11, respectively), whereas that of TTON seems to increase (n= 12 vs. n= 20, respectively).

To shed light on what this two-way interaction means, it is proper to briefly explain how the statistical test used works. Two-way analysis of variance has computed the effect of the proficiency level factor, the effect of the didactic negotiation factor, and the effect of a combination of these two factors. The first two effects represent the *main effect* whereas the combination effect represents the *interaction effect*.

> [W]henever we have a strong interaction effect, we cannot consider the main effect as important. The interaction effect overrides the main effect. [...]. whenever the interaction is significant, researchers must qualify their claims about the importance of the *independent variables* (Hatch & Farhady 1982: 158-9) (emphasis added).

On the basis of these considerations, it may be argued that the apparently significant (F= 3.524, df= 2, p= .037) difference in the frequencies of CCON, CSON, and TTON across the three grades may simply be due to the fact that one of these genres has a high frequency in a particular grade but a low frequency in the other grades. More precisely, the recorded significant variance of these genres across the three grades may not be due to an impact of the proficiency level factor, but rather to the high frequency of CSON, in comparison to CCON and TTON, in the second grade (cf. Table 6 and Figure 9).

The question rises: how can the high frequency of 'complete sentence-oriented negotiation' (CSON), in the second grade, be accounted for? This high frequency may imply that in beginning classes, teachers accept some pupils' replies though not formulated in a complete sentence, in order to encourage pupils to participate notwithstanding their low competence in the target language. However, in the second grade, teachers seem to constrain pupils more often to speak in complete sentences instead of utterances or single words, as a means of giving them more productive practise in the target language. Yet, when pupils reach the third grade, the teacher puts less constraint on them to speak in complete sentences probably as a means of rendering classroom interaction more communicative and spontaneous and less mechanical. Apparently, in the third grade, the teacher presumes that pupils have acquired sufficient competence in the target language to allow them to express themselves as people do in everyday conversation, i.e., to speak in sentences, utterances, or single words.

Though these arguments may sound acceptable, the occurrence of 'complete sentence-oriented negotiation' depends first and foremost on whether the 'complete sentence rule' (cf. Chapter 5) has been violated. So, there may be more violation of this rule in the second than in the first and third grade. To investigate this issue, the total number of violations of the 'complete sentence rule' has been computed in each grade and compared to the frequency of 'complete sentence-oriented negotiation'. Consider the following Table:

Table 9: Summary statistics for 'complete sentence-oriented negotiation' in relation to the violation of 'the complete sentence rule' by grade.

Grades		CSR violated	CSON
1st G.	n	78	26
	%	100	33.33
	X	15.60	05.20
2nd G.	n	112	56
	%	100	50
	X	22.40	11.20
3rd G.	n	95	11
	%	100	11.58
	X	19	02.20
Totals	n	285	93
	%	100	32.63
	X	19	06.20

CSR	: complete sentence rule
CSON	: 'complete sentence-oriented negotiation'
n	: sample size
%	: row percentage
X	: observed mean

As the above Table reveals, when the percentage of 'complete sentence-oriented negotiation' has been computed in terms of the total number of violations of 'the complete sentence rule', the following results have been obtained: the highest frequency of 'complete sentence-oriented negotiation' occurs in the second grade, i.e., 50.00%, in comparison with 33.33% in the first grade, and 11.58% in the third. These findings seem to sustain the hypothesis that second grade pupils are more constrained to speak in complete sentences than first or third grade pupils. However, since these findings are not statistically significant (F= 2.134, df= 2, p= .161), it is likely that other variables, besides the proficiency level of the class, are at work in TL classroom interaction and seem to affect the frequency of 'complete sentence-oriented negotiation'.

One possible intervening variable is teacher style. It might be argued that teacher initiation of a 'complete sentence-oriented negotiation' also depends on teacher style which in turn largely depends of the TL teaching method used. If the teacher is more of an advocate of the audio-lingual method, s/he would be more inclined to emphasize the 'complete sentence rule'. On the other hand, if s/he is more of an advocate of communicative language teaching, s/he would not stress such a rule. This reasoning is based on the fact that contrary to

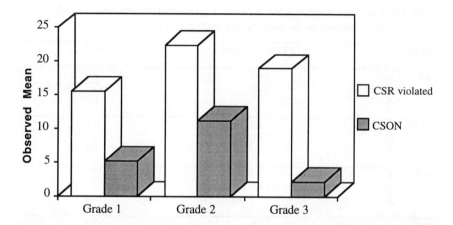

Figure 12: 'Complete sentence-oriented negotiation' (CSON) in relation to the violation of the 'complete sentence rule' (CSR) by grade

communicative language teaching where meaning is paramount, the audio-lingual method, being based on a behaviourist-structuralist approach to second language teaching, attends to structure and form more than meaning and function (cf. Finocchiaro and Brumfit 1983 for a comparison between audio-lingual and communicative language teaching).

It is worth pointing out that when the present data were collected, communicative language teaching was highly recommended in EFL classrooms in Morocco. However, since the teachers involved in the study had been taught English themselves via the audio-lingual method, and later had been trained to teach English using this method which was in vogue for a long time in Morocco, it is, as the data reveal, at times difficult for teachers to get rid of their habit of making pupils speak in complete sentences.

As Table 6 shows, in contrast to the high frequency of 'complete sentence-oriented negotiation' in the second grade (n= 56), there is a low frequency (n= 12) of 'turn-taking-oriented negotiation' in the same grade. This might suggest that teachers are more lenient in applying the 'turn-taking rule' with second grade pupils. Yet, to better understand the importance teachers attribute to the 'turn-taking rule' in each grade, we thought it was relevant to compute the frequency of 'turn-taking-oriented negotiation' in terms of the total number of violations of this rule. Consider Table 10:

Table 10: Summary statistics for 'turn-taking-oriented negotiation' in relation to
the violation of the 'turn-taking rule' by grade

Grades		TTR violated	TTON
1st G.	n	145	40
	%	100	27.59
	X	29	08
2nd G.	n	87	12
	%	100	13.79
	X	17.40	02.40
3rd G.	n	88	20
	%	100	22.73
	X	17.60	04
Totals	n	320	72
	%	100	22.50
	X	21.33	04.80

TTR	: turn-taking rule
TTON	: 'turn-taking-oriented negotiation'
n	: sample size
%	: row percentage
X	: observed mean

As Table 10 and Figure 13 illustrate, when 'turn-taking-oriented negotiation'
has been computed in terms of the total number of violations of the 'turn-taking
rule', the following results have been obtained: the least frequency of 'turn-
taking-oriented negotiation' occurs in the second grade (13.79%), in comparison
to 27.59% in the first grade, and 22.73% in the third grade. These percentages
might imply that teachers are more lenient about the 'turn-taking rule' in the
second grade. However, given that these results are not at all statistically
significant (F= .001, df= 2, p= .999), it is sound to argue that the frequency of
'turn-taking-oriented negotiation' is governed by factors other than the
proficiency level of the class. Indeed, it is difficult to capture the variables which
might impact on the occurrence or non-occurrence of a 'turn-taking-oriented
negotiation'. Such variables as those pointed out by Griffin and Mehan (1981)
and Schinke-Llano (1983), discussed in Chapter 5, may be powerful factors
affecting the frequency of 'turn-taking-oriented negotiation'. Accordingly, the
'turn-taking rule' may fail to operate when the violation coincides with a choral
or valuable response, when the response is given by an unexpected individual,
or when the interaction is 'non-directed'.

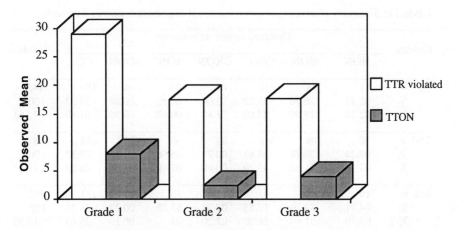

Figure 13: 'Turn-taking-oriented negotiation' (TTON) in relation to the violation of the 'turn-taking rule' (TTR)

The aim of this section has been to investigate the frequency of didactic negotiation genres in the data as a whole and by grade, in order to find out what genre is predominant in TL classroom discourse and whether and how the proficiency level of the class has an impact on the occurrence of these didactic negotiation genres. The results reveal that 'medium-oriented negotiation' is the most frequent in the data as a whole and in all three grades, and hence is the typical genre of didactic negotiation. The results also reveal a significant two-way interaction between the proficiency level and 'comprehension check-oriented negotiation', 'complete sentence-oriented negotiation', and 'turn-taking-oriented negotiation'. Given this two-way interaction, only lukewarm claims could be made about the effect of the proficiency level.

The next section analyzes the frequency distribution among 'conversational negotiation' genres in the data as a whole and by grade, and attempts to qualitatively account for this distribution.

Frequency of Conversational Negotiation Genres

In the present section, the frequency of 'conversational negotiation' genres is investigated in the data as a whole and by grade, in order to find out which genres mostly characterize TL classroom talk, and whether their frequency is in any way affected by the proficiency level of the class. The results of this investigation are given and discussed below. Consider Table 11:

Table 11: Summary statistics for conversational negotiation genres by grade

Grades		HON	MON	CON	GKON	AON	SDON	CC	Totals
				Conversational negotiation					
1st	n	11	118	138	09	03	04	159	442
	%	02.49	26.70	31.22	02.04	00.68	00.90	35.97	100
	X	02.20	23.60	27.60	01.80	00.60	00.80	31.80	12.63
2nd	n	36	208	246	02	39	15	141	687
	%	05.24	30.28	35.81	00.29	05.68	02.18	20.52	100
	X	07.20	41.60	49.20	00.40	07.80	03	28.20	19.63
3rd	n	19	158	81	11	15	01	177	462
	%	04.11	34.20	17.53	02.38	03.25	00.22	38.31	100
	X	03.80	31.60	16.20	02.20	03	00.20	35.40	13.20
Ts.	n	66	484	465	22	57	20	477	1591
	%	04.15	30.42	29.23	01.38	03.58	01.26	29.98	100
	X·	04.40	32.27	31	01.47	03.80	01.33	31.80	15.15

HON   : 'hearing-oriented negotiation'
MON   : 'meaning-oriented negotiation'
CON   : 'content-oriented negotiation'
GNON : 'general knowledge-oriented negotiation'
AON   : 'agreement-oriented negotiation'
SDON : 'surprise display-oriented negotiation'
CC   : 'conversational continuant'
n   : sample size
%   : row percentage
X   : observed mean
Ts.   : Totals

The first striking observation we can make from the results in the above Table is that almost 90% of the conversational negotiation in the data is shared by three genres only, namely 'meaning-oriented negotiation', 'content-oriented negotiation', and 'conversational continuants', with more or less 30% of frequency for each. The remaining 10% is shared by the other four genres, namely 'hearing-oriented negotiation', 'general knowledge-oriented negotiation', 'agreement-oriented negotiation', and 'surprise display-oriented negotiation'. Accordingly, the question arises: why bother to study such phenomena that rarely occur in the data, and no doubt rarely occur in TL classroom discourse in general? The answer is, to quote Van Lier (1988: 2), because "[t]he particular is [...] as relevant as the general" since "[t]he first concern must be to analyse the data *as they are* ."

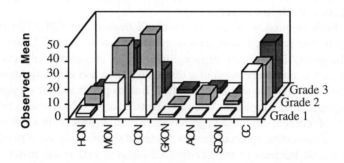

Figure 14: Conversational negotiation genres by grade

How can the high frequencies of 'meaning-oriented negotiation', 'content-oriented negotiation', and 'conversational continuant' be accounted for? And what implications may the predominance of these negotiation genres, in TL classroom discourse, have as far as acquisition is concerned? On the other hand, how can the low frequency of the other four genres be explained? And what does it imply from an acquisitional standpoint?

The high frequency of 'meaning-oriented negotiation' (30.42%) can be accounted for by pupils' limited proficiency in the target language which creates problems of understanding either on the part of the teacher or on the part of the learner. It is worth noting that when the learner displays a problem of understanding, genuine nonunderstanding is at play; whereas, when it is the teacher who indicates a problem of understanding, it may be either genuine or feigned nonunderstanding. Feigned nonunderstanding is a tactic used by the teacher to incite the pupil, who has given a repairable contribution, to try out other means of expression to convey the meaning intended. 'Meaning-oriented negotiation' also occurs when the hearer (teacher or pupil) perfectly understands what the speaker (teacher or pupil) is trying to convey, but due to some conversational trouble, the hearer repairs the proposition conveyed. Owing to pupils' limited proficiency, such acts as confirming, clarifying, and repairing frequently occur in the data, which warrants the high frequency of 'meaning-oriented negotiation'. As discussed in Chapter 5, "[t]his adjustment-in-interaction may be crucial to language development" (Van Lier 1988: 180).

The finding that 'meaning-oriented negotiation' is frequent in the data further refutes Pica's (1986, 1987) and Long's (1983b) claim that the SL classroom is a less than favourable context for the negotiation of meaning, and as a result a less than favourable context for SL acquisition (see Chapter 5). Hence, if the theory claiming that negotiation of meaning is a *sine qua non* for target language development is valid, the present finding provides further support for Van Lier's (1988: 213) claim that "second language development can and does occur in classrooms" (sic).

The high frequency of 'content-oriented negotiation' (29.23%) may be explained by the type of lesson recorded: teaching of a text (cf. Chapter 3) as well as the pupils' limited proficiency. Since one of the primary objects of this type of lesson is comprehension of a text, much time and effort are devoted to the comprehension of the text being studied. But, as pupils are not yet proficient in the language, many problems of comprehension arise, which results in a high frequency of 'content-oriented negotiation'. Rulon & McCreary (1986) found that learners interacting in small groups produced significantly more negotiation of content than learners in teacher-fronted classes; yet, as the results of the present investigation show, teacher-fronted classes also produce a considerable amount of 'content-oriented negotiation'. And since the negotiation of content is also "essential to the promotion of interaction necessary for successful second language acquisition" (Rulon & McCreary 1986: 195), it may be argued that teacher-fronted classrooms do not hamper the occurrence of 'content-oriented negotiation', nor do they hamper SL/FL acquisition.

The high frequency of 'conversational continuants' (29.98%) which, as noted in Chapter 5, include both pupil and teacher conversational continuants, may be justified as follows: having a limited proficiency in the target language, pupils attempt to adjust teacher input by providing cues of their understanding or non-understanding. Similarly, being aware of pupils' limited proficiency, the teacher frequently provides back-channel cues to encourage them to proceed with their utterance. Pupil conversational continuants reveal pupil *initiative* and *involvement* which are crucial variables for L2 development (cf. Stevick 1976, 1980). Further, because they are supportive in nature, both teacher and pupil conversational continuants may contribute to lowering the *affective filter* during classroom interaction, and accordingly create a favourable affective environment for target language acquisition.

In short, the high frequency of 'meaning-oriented negotiation', 'content-oriented negotiation' and 'conversational continuants', in the data, reveals that teacher-fronted classrooms by no means hinder the sort of interaction claimed to promote target language acquisition (cf. Hatch 1978, Pica 1986, 1987, Varonis & Grass 1985a, b, c, Long 1980, Rulon & McCreary 1986, and Gaies 1983b).

Going back to the results in the above Table, how can the very low frequency of 'hearing-oriented negotiation' (04.15%), 'general knowledge-oriented negotiation' (01.38%), 'agreement-oriented negotiation' (03.58%), and 'surprise display-oriented negotiation' (01.26%) be accounted for? And what implications does this low frequency have for target language acquisition?

The low frequency of 'hearing-oriented negotiation' may be explained in three ways. The first explanation is related to the 'turn-taking rule'. Since this rule, which implies the 'one floor law' (cf. Van Lier 1988), seems to be operating in the lessons studied, and since teachers do their best to keep pupils quiet while one participant is speaking, very few occasions of mishearing or non-hearing occur. The second explanation is related to the direction of discourse. Since discourse in the lessons investigated is mainly between teacher and pupils, and rarely involves pupil-pupil interaction, pupils do not necessarily initiate a 'hearing-oriented negotiation' when they do not hear each other's contributions because they perceive the teacher as the main participant supposed to hear a pupil's contribution in order to be able to evaluate it. Actually, aside from instruction, the primary role of teachers, especially in teacher-fronted classrooms, is often considered to be the provision of feedback. Fanselow (1987: 267) claims that "[b]y definition, to teach is to provide feedback."

If the second explanation is valid, reflecting what is really going on in TL teacher-fronted classrooms, this state of affairs might have regrettable repercussions on target language development, because pupils can learn from each other's contributions and from each other's mistakes as much as they can learn from the teacher's instruction or feedback. And if learners do not initiate a 'hearing-oriented negotiation' when they do not hear each other's contributions, they certainly deprive themselves of an important source of input.

The third explanation for the low frequency of 'hearing-oriented negotiation' may be the power factor operating in classroom discourse. Classroom interaction is an instance of unequal-power discourse characterized by the asymmetrical role relations of its participants. Accordingly, pupils may perceive their initiation of a 'hearing-oriented negotiation', when they do not hear a teacher's contribution, as 'face-threatening' (Brown & Levinson 1978), because pupils are supposed to be attentive to what the teacher is saying. Displaying non-hearing of what the teacher has said may imply non-attentiveness, and hence may result in reproof from the teacher. Therefore, pupils may refrain from initiating a negotiation exchange for the sake of saving face. If this explanation is valid, this state of affairs may also jeopardize pupils' target language development, for it deprives them from receiving as much comprehensible input as provided by the teacher.

The low frequency of 'general knowledge-oriented negotiation' in the data (01.38%) may simply be due to the fact that the participants, being members of the same group and cultural community, have much shared personal and cultural background to reduce schema mismatches, and accordingly, reduce 'general knowledge-oriented negotiations'. This provides further support to Gass & Varonis's (1991: 122) suggestion that "when participants have little shared background (be it cultural, linguistic, or personal), the conversation is likely to

be peppered with interruptions for clarification of content or language form."
Yet, when schema mismatches arise, it is crucial to initiate a negotiation,
because, if successful, the negotiation will resolve the mismatch, put classroom
participants on the same wavelength, and hence make the discourse proceed
smoothly. However, if the negotiation is not successful, as in extract (75),
reproduced below, it can but induce pupil frustration and confusion.

Re-	-I- 1 T	: Can you give me another sentence (p.)
initiate	-R- 2 P1	: Giralda is a minaret in Spain (rep.)
	-F- 3 T	: mhm (acc.) .. NO (eva.). There is NO minaret in Spain (com.)
Pupil	-I- 4 P1	: -> <unint> Giralda in Spain (cha.)
Initiated	-F- 5 T	: NO (eva.) ... Moroccan minaret=
Negotiate		[
	6 PP	: Yes (ack.)
	7 T	: =The mosque has got a minaret. The church hasn't got any minaret (com.)

(1st grade - lesson 1)

Given the asymmetrical power relations between teacher and pupils, P1 in
the above extract could not insist further on negotiating acceptability for her
reply. Nonetheless, it was apparent for the researcher (who was present during
the lesson) that the pupil was not convinced of the teacher's proposition.

As for the low frequency of 'agreement-oriented negotiation' in the data
(03.58%), it may be explained by the fact that since it is the teacher who has
control over the topic of interaction, s/he usually keeps the discussion of
'disputable events' till the end of the lesson, after the main activities involved in
the 'teaching of a text' have come to an end (i.e., teaching structures, teaching
vocabulary, listening to or reading a text, and doing comprehension and
language exercises). This results in teachers usually finding themselves with no
or very little time left for the post-reading/post-listening activity involving pupils
in 'agreement-oriented negotiation'. Therefore what usually happens in EFL
classrooms in Morocco is that teachers start this activity in a teacher-fronted
classroom session; but because of time constraints, they keep it for a 'debate'
group work activity. Such group work gives pupils the opportunity to express
their standpoints about a question that was at issue in a previously studied text,
and practise the vocabulary items, and possibly also, the structures they have
learnt in the previous 'teaching of a text' lesson.

This by no means implies that 'agreement-oriented negotiation' never occurs
in the middle of a 'teaching of a text' activity. However, this is very rare since
pupils, during this activity, are primarily required to display their understanding

of the structures, vocabulary items, and the text taught. Pupils seem to understand the rules of the game; so, even if one participant does not agree with a proposition expressed in a previous turn, s/he generally does not react because s/he knows that the activity the class is involved in is focused on the structures, the vocabulary and the 'text' being studied rather than on debating disputable issues. This state of affairs may hamper pupils' involvement in and spontaneous reactions to what is going on. And, as has repeatedly been claimed in TL acquisition research, involvement in and spontaneous participation to the discourse may be crucial variables affecting target language development (cf. Stevick 1976, 1980, Allwright 1984a).

Finally, the low frequency of 'surprise display-oriented negotiation' (01.26%) may also be interpreted in terms of the shared cultural and personal knowledge between teachers and pupils. Since both of them belong to the Moroccan culture, instances of surprise concerning a particular proposition rarely occur. The low frequency of this negotiation genre may also be due to the predominance of 'display elicitations' the answers of which are already known to the teacher. In other words, since the teacher already knows the answer, there is little opportunity for her/him to hear something that would surprise her/him. Actually, in the data, all instances of 'surprise display-oriented negotiation' are initiated by the teacher and occur when the information is flowing from pupils to the teacher, that is, in the context of a 'referential elicitation' or a 'pupil informative act'.

The only explanation that can be given for the fact that no instance of 'surprise display-oriented negotiation' has been initiated by pupils in the data has to do with the power factor. Since the interaction is mainly between teacher and pupils rather than among pupils, expressing surprise vis-à-vis a proposition made by the teacher may be "face-threatening" (Brown & Levinson 1978). Accordingly, pupils refrain from initiating a 'surprise display-oriented negotiation' for the sake of "face-saving" (Goffman 1967, Brown & Levinson 1978).

Although factors like the shared background and personal knowledge, the predominance of 'display elicitations', and the asymmetrical power relations seem to hamper the occurrence of 'surprise display-oriented negotiation', pupils' limited proficiency in the foreign language is a factor that may bring about such a negotiation. Given their limited proficiency in the target language, pupils may come up with some strange propositions like the one in extract 56, namely 'women are delicious'. Such a proposition, as discussed in Chapter 5, has triggered a 'surprise display-oriented negotiation', initiated by the teacher by means of the 'confirmation check' "do you eat woman?!" (sic).

This kind of negotiation has at least two functions: on the one hand, it informs the pupil that his utterance is unacceptable since the word 'delicious' can

218 NEGOTIATED INTERACTION

be attributed only to eatable things; on the other hand, it reduces tension by introducing laughter in the classroom. Such a negotiation may incite pupils to pay more attention to what is going on, in order not to be deprived from the pleasure of understanding a surprising proposition, a joke, or a humorous comment made by one of the participants. Yet, although these surprising and/or humorous contributions probably have the effect of lowering the *affective filter* by reducing the tension of teacher-fronted classrooms, if they are ironical, they might have the reverse effect.

On the whole, 'surprise display-oriented negotiation' introduces some spontaneity and authenticity in TL classroom discourse and involves pupils in a sort of interaction that is not very different from ordinary conversation. Therefore, encouraging pupils to react spontaneously to classroom talk, for instance by expressing surprise at a surprising contribution, can but be beneficial to pupils' productive competence.

The statistical analysis factorial ANOVA reveals a significant variance in the frequency distribution among conversational negotiation genres ($F= 24.875$, $df= 6$, $p= .000$). As to how this distribution varies by proficiency level, factorial ANOVA also reveals a significant variance across the three grades ($F= 3.644$, $df= 2$, $p= .030$), which may imply that the proficiency level of the class has an impact on the frequency distribution among these genres. However, the statistical analysis also reveals a significant *two-way interaction* ($F= 2.164$, $df= 12$, $p= .021$) between conversational negotiation genres and the proficiency level of the class. Bearing in mind that "the interaction effect washes out the main effect" (Hatch & Farhady 1982: 159), we conclude that the proficiency level has no effect on the frequency of conversational negotiation genres. To investigate whether this conclusion is valid, one-factor analysis of variance was computed. The results were non-significant for any of the conversational negotiation genres. The non-significance of these results provides further support for the above conclusion and implies that there is more variance among the lessons belonging to the same grade than among those belonging to different grades.

A possible explanation for the finding that the proficiency level of the class has no impact on the frequency distribution among the seven conversational negotiation genres may be related to the nature of conversational negotiation itself. Conversational negotiation is oriented to problems of the talk, problems that may also arise in everyday conversation, namely problems of hearing, understanding meaning and content, sustaining the conversation, agreeing etc. Hence, it may be proper to argue that a comparable number of these problems arises in the three grades, which results in a comparable frequency of conversational negotiation genres across these grades, because, no matter what the proficiency level of the class is, solving these problems is necessary if the interaction is to proceed smoothly.

The aim of this section has been to find out what discourse function of conversational negotiation is predominant in the data, and whether the proficiency level of the class has an impact on the frequency distribution among conversational negotiation genres. The results reveal that the most frequent functions of conversational negotiation are 'meaning-oriented negotiation', 'content-oriented negotiation', and 'conversational continuant'. These constitute 90% of the total frequency of conversational negotiation occurring in the data; the remaining 10% is shared by the other four genres. On the other hand, no impact of the class proficiency level has been recorded.

Conclusion

This chapter has investigated the frequency distribution of negotiated interaction in the data as a whole and by proficiency level. The aim has been three-fold: to find out how frequent negotiated interaction is in the data, what discourse functions of negotiation mostly characterize the data, and whether and how the frequency of the different functions of negotiated interaction varies by proficiency level. Accordingly, four main quantitative analyses have been undertaken. The first computed the frequency of negotiated and non-negotiated exchanges, the second computed the frequency of didactic and conversational negotiation, the third computed the frequency of didactic negotiation genres, and the fourth computed the frequency of conversational negotiation genres.

The results reveal a significant preference for negotiated exchanges over non-negotiated ones, a preference for conversational over didactic negotiation, a preference for 'medium-oriented negotiation' over the other didactic negotiation genres, and a preference for 'meaning-oriented negotiation', 'content-oriented negotiation', and 'conversational continuant' over the other conversational negotiation genres. As to whether and how the degree of these preferences varies by proficiency level, the study reveals a non-significant variance concerning the preference for negotiated over non-negotiated exchanges by proficiency level, a significantly higher preference for conversational over didactic negotiation in intermediate and advanced classes than in beginning classes, a significantly higher preference for 'medium-oriented negotiation' in beginning and intermediate than in advanced classes, but a non-significant impact of the proficiency level on the frequency of conversational negotiation genres.

The chapter has also attempted to provide explanations for the results of each quantitative analysis. In the next chapter, negotiated interaction is discussed in relation to the notion of unequal-power discourse.

CHAPTER 7
Negotiation in a Setting of Unequal-Power Discourse

Introduction

> No natural speech utterance is ever made in a linguistic vacuum.
> Each is enriched and empowered by a social history that considers
> the relationships of class, status, power, and solidarity, and a
> linguistic history that includes culturally specific rules of discourse
> (Labov & Fanshel 1977), politeness (Brown & Levinson 1978),
> conversational maxims (Grice 1975, Keenan 1976), conversational
> inference (Gumperz & Tannen 1979), and patterns of
> interpretation (Tannen 1981a) (Gass & Varonis 1991: 121).

Like any instructional setting, the TL classroom is "a venue for the exercise of power" (Van Lier 1988: xi). The asymmetrical power and role relations of the teacher and learners and the pedagogical orientation of interaction are reflected in the verbal behaviour of the participants, and accordingly, make TL classroom discourse different from ordinary conversation in informal settings. The question arises: in what way could the initiation of negotiated interaction be interpreted given that the classroom is a setting of unequal-power discourse?

In this chapter, negotiated interaction is discussed with regard to the notion of 'unequal-power discourse' (Hatch & Long 1980); therefore, two main investigations are undertaken. On the one hand, we examine the frequency of teacher- in comparison with pupil-initiated negotiation to show how the initiation of negotiation is revealing in understanding the exercise of power through discourse in TL classrooms. Accordingly, all negotiated exchanges are investigated with regard to their discourse function and to who initiates the negotiation. On the other hand, pupil-initiated negotiation is further focused on in order to shed more light on pupil negotiation of power. Hence, we examine the frequency of what we have labelled pupil-initiated *disjunctive* negotiations and investigate whether and how these 'face-threatening' (Brown & Levinson 1978) negotiations are 'modulated' (Schegloff et al. 1977, Gaskill 1980) by the pupil. Simultaneously, we attempt to qualify the results in terms of the widely held claim that the classroom is a context of unequal-power discourse.

Initiating Negotiation or Negotiating Power?

The present section aims at examining the frequency of teacher- in comparison with pupil-initiated negotiation, to give an idea about how the initiation of negotiation might shed light on the exercise of power in TL classroom discourse. With this aim in mind, the various negotiation genres are tackled in terms of who (teacher or pupil) mostly initiates the negotiation.

Teacher- vs. Pupil-initiated Negotiation

This section investigates the frequency of teacher-initiated negotiation in comparison with pupil-initiated negotiation in order to test the hypothesis that the teacher, by virtue of her/his social and linguistic powerful status, is the initiator par excellence of negotiation in TL classroom discourse. The section also aims to find out whether the frequencies of teacher- and pupil-initiated negotiation vary by proficiency level in order to test the hypothesis that teacher control wanes in more proficient classes. The results are given and discussed below.

Table 12 : Summary statistics for teacher- vs. pupil-initiated negotiation by grade

Grades		Negotiated interaction		Totals
		T-initiated	P-initiated	
1st G.	n	588	229	817
	%	71.97	28.03	100
	X	117.60	45.80	81.70
2nd G.	n	861	205	1066
	%	80.77	19.23	100
	X	172.20	41	106.60
3rd G.	n	396	244	640
	%	61.87	38.13	100
	X	79.20	48.80	64
Totals	n	1845	678	2523
	%	73.13	26.87	100
	X	123	45.20	84.10

n : sample size
% : row percentage
X : observed mean

As illustrated in Table 12 and Figure 15, there is a significant preference for teacher- over pupil-initiated negotiation in the data (n= 1845 vs. n= 678, respectively) (F= 25.939, df= 1, p= .000). This seems to further confirm the claim that the classroom is a context of unequal-power discourse. Teacher-initiated negotiation probably reflects teacher control; whereas pupil-initiated negotiation probably reflects pupil initiative. As Van Lier (1988: 178) notes,

> [t]he teacher controls classroom interaction, undoubtedly, almost all the time. This is not necessarily a negative comment, since without this control there might be no lesson or, to come back to Stevick's terms, without control there might be no initiative. By looking at the places in a lesson where control can be usefully relaxed to allow more initiative, the teacher can work towards achieving a balance between these two forces, and steer a course between ritual and free-for-all.

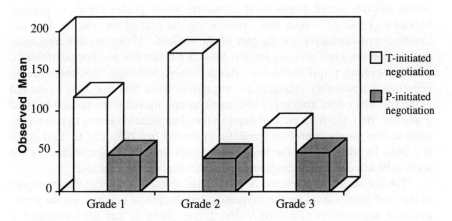

Figure 15: Teacher- vs. pupil-initiated negotiation by grade

Actually, pupil-initiated negotiation, though low in the data (26.87%), in comparison to teacher-initiated negotiation, should be given much consideration, for it reveals that "learners are not wholly under the control of the teacher" (Allwright 1980: 166). It also reveals what pupils are doing to ensure the accurate use of the target language, to ensure their understanding both of participants' contributions and of the text being studied, and to sustain the conversation. Accordingly, pupil-initiated negotiation reveals what pupils are doing to manage their own and one another's learning. This seems to support Allwright's (1984a: 156) assertion that "we can no longer see teachers simply as teachers, and learners simply as learners, because both are, for good or ill, 'managers of learning'."

Taylor (1983: 75) argues that a communicatively-oriented lesson, which is by definition student- rather than teacher-centred "does not require that the teacher abdicate authority in the classroom." Stevick (1980: 19), who addresses this issue by distinguishing between teacher control and student initiative, contends that

> 'initiative' and 'control' are not merely two directions along a single dimension. That is to say, 'control' on the part of the teacher does not interfere with 'initiative' on the part of the student: when the teacher tightens her 'control' of what is going on, she need not cut into the student's 'initiative'; often, in fact, she will actually increase it. Similarly, insufficient 'control' by the teacher may reduce or paralyze the 'initiative' of the student.

As shown in Table 12 and Figure 15, the frequency distribution of teacher- versus pupil-initiated negotiation across the three grades seems to support Stevick's (1980: 19) claim that "'control' on the part of the teacher does not interfere with 'initiative' on the part of the student." However, this frequency distribution does not seem to support Stevick's claim that teacher control will, often, increase pupil initiative. Accordingly, although teacher-initiated negotiation noticeably increases as one moves from first (n= 588) to second grade (n= 861), and noticeably decreases as one moves from second to third grade (n= 396), the frequency of pupil-initiated negotiation seems to remain the same as one moves from first (n= 229), to second (n= 205), and to third grade (n= 244). In other words, the frequency of pupil-initiated negotiation does not seem to be affected by the frequency of teacher-initiated negotiation.

The statistical test (factorial ANOVA) has revealed a non significant impact of the proficiency level on the frequency distribution of teacher- versus pupil-initiated negotiation (F= 2.617, df= 2, p= .094). It has also revealed a significant *two-way interaction* between the proficiency level and these two variables (F= 3.667, df= 2, p= .041). Given that "the interaction effect overrides the main effect" (Hatch & Farhady 1982: 158), it may be argued that the significant variance (F= 25.939, df= 1, p= .000) recorded between the frequency of teacher-initiated negotiation in comparison with pupil-initiated negotiation in the data as a whole, may simply be due the fact that teacher-initiated negotiation has a noticeably high frequency in the second grade (n= 861). This suggests that there is a positive interaction between teacher-initiated negotiation and the second grade. In other words, teacher-initiated negotiation is significantly preferred in the second grade, but not in the other grades.

The significant *interaction* effect also means that the proficiency level has a different effect on the frequency distribution between teacher- and pupil-initiated negotiation across the three grades. As pointed out earlier, while the frequency of teacher-initiated negotiation seems to vary from one proficiency level to another (n= 588 in the first grade, n= 861 in the second, and n= 396 in the third), that of pupil-initiated negotiation seems not to be affected by the proficiency level factor (n= 229 in the first grade, n= 205 in the second, and n= 244 in the third).

To further investigate whether this apparent variance in the frequencies of teacher-initiated negotiation and pupil-initiated negotiation by grade is significant, one-factor ANOVA was computed for each of these variables in isolation from the other. The results reveal a significant variance for teacher-initiated negotiation (F= 3.966, df= 2, p= .048), which shows that teacher-initiated negotiation significantly has the highest frequency in the second grade and the lowest in the third grade. However, one factor ANOVA reveals an utterly non-significant variance in the frequency of pupil-initiated negotiation by grade (F= .104, df= 2, p= .902). Hence, if the claim, made earlier, that pupil-initiated negotiation reflects pupil initiative is valid, it may be argued that the proficiency level has no effect on pupil 'initiative' but it does have an effect on teacher control.

The question arises: how can this differential effect of the proficiency level on the frequency distribution of teacher- and pupil-initiated negotiation be explained? The non-variant frequency of pupil-initiated negotiation across the three grades may be explained as follows: given that TL teacher-fronted classrooms are controlled by the teacher, by means of teacher 'elicitations', teacher 'informatives', teacher choice of text, etc., the difficulty of the interaction is probably adjusted to the proficiency level of the class. Thus, each proficiency level is required to perform an accessible but challenging task, which brings about a comparable amount of pupil interactional problems, and, consequently, a comparable amount of pupil-initiated negotiation. The non-variant frequency of pupil-initiated negotiation by grade may also imply that the 'affective filter' (Krashen 1982a) is equally lowered, in the three grades, to allow pupil initiative.

On the other hand, the significant variance in the frequency of teacher-initiated negotiation by grade, which implies that the teacher exerts the most 'control' in the second grade but the least 'control' in the third grade, may suggest that teachers perceive their control of pupil contributions as more necessary for target language development with intermediate than with beginning and advanced classes. Hence, in the second grade, they take the lead in negotiating any problem that may arise be it didactic or conversational.

In the first grade, teachers seem to moderate their control in order to encourage pupils to contribute to the discourse, since pupils have very limited competence in the target language. In the second grade, teachers seem to tighten their control of what is going on in order to incite pupils to pay more attention to the main aspects seeming to trigger most interactional problems. These aspects, as discussed in Chapter 6, are related to the forms and functions of the target language (cf. 'medium-oriented negotiation'), the meaning of teacher as well as pupil contributions (cf. 'meaning-oriented negotiation'), and the comprehension of the text being studied (cf. 'content-oriented negotiation'). In the third grade, however, the teacher lessens her control, probably, because s/he perceives that pupils' lexical and grammatical systems in the target language are sufficiently developed to let them manage the conversation themselves. In other words, having acquired an advanced competence in the target language, pupils are given more opportunity to do self-repair in terms of form and to initiate conversational negotiation themselves. In short, such adjustments in the discourse characteristics of teacher talk, across the three grades, might imply that teachers deem their tightening control, in the second grade, to be more crucial for target language development than in other grades. However, teacher control cannot properly be explained without accounting for the quality of teacher-initiated negotiation. This issue is investigated in the following sections.

The present section has computed teacher- in comparison with pupil-initiated negotiations in the data as a whole and by proficiency level, in order to find out who mostly initiates the negotiation and whether this varies by proficiency level. The results show that the significant preference for teacher- over pupil-initiated negotiation may simply be due to the high preference for teacher- over pupil-initiated negotiation in the second grade. To better understand the distribution of teacher-initiated in comparison with pupil-initiated negotiation by grade, it is essential to investigate the frequency of these two variables in terms of the major categories of negotiated interaction (i.e., 'didactic' and 'conversational') and their various discourse functions. This is considered in the following sections.

Teacher- vs. Pupil-initiated Didactic Negotiation

This section aims at investigating the frequency of teacher- in comparison with pupil-initiated didactic negotiation, in order to test the hypothesis that the teacher, by virtue of her/his higher linguistic competence is the initiator par excellence of didactic negotiation and the hypothesis that teacher control decreases in more proficient classes. In view of these aims, teacher- and pupil-initiated didactic negotiation have been computed in the data as a whole and by proficiency level. The results are presented and discussed below. Consider the subsequent Table:

Table 13 : Summary statistics for teacher-initiated vs. pupil-initiated didactic negotiation by grade

Grades		Didactic Negotiation		Totals
		T-initiated	P-initiated	
1st G.	n	303	72	375
	%	80.80	19.20	100
	X	60.60	14.40	37.50
2nd G.	n	351	28	379
	%	92.61	07.39	100
	X	70.20	05.60	37.90
3rd G.	n	161	17	178
	%	90.45	09.55	100
	X	32.20	03.40	17.80
Totals	n	815	117	932
	%	87.45	12.55	100
	X	54.33	07.80	31.07

n : sample size
% : row percentage
X : observed mean

As Table 13 and Figure 16 show, there is a significant (F= 37.048, df= 1, p= .000) preference for teacher-initiated over pupil-initiated didactic negotiation (n= 815 vs. n= 117, respectively). This is to be expected in TL classrooms where the teacher's primary role is to ensure the accurate and appropriate use of the target language by means of 'medium-oriented negotiation'. This finding seems to further emphasize the image of the teacher as an authority figure. Paradoxically, it also seems to suggest that the teacher is "a 'facilitator' [...] who responds to the students' emerging language needs" (Taylor 1983: 76).

The percentage (12.55%) of pupil-initiated didactic negotiation, though low, is suggestive, for it implies that even though didactic negotiation is pedagogic in orientation, pupils manage to have a share in its initiation, mainly by providing corrective feedback to one another's 'repairable' contributions. This suggests that, in the data, the teacher is not the only classroom participant who may provide corrective feedback, although traditionally this is regarded to be exclusively the teacher's business. This finding seems to refute Sinclair & Brazil's (1982: 58) claim that "pupils have a very restricted range of verbal functions to perform. *They rarely initiate, and never follow up* (emphasis added)." By providing corrective feedback to one another's 'repairable' contributions, pupils do initiate and do follow up, but, of course, not in the sense of providing an explicit evaluation of the 'repairable' reply.

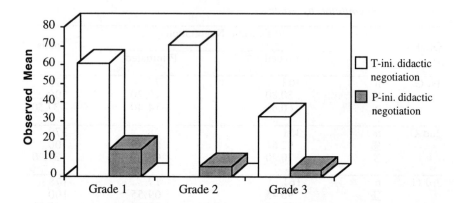

Figure 16: Teacher- vs. pupil-initiated didactic negotiation by grade

The occurrence of pupil-initiated didactic negotiation is out of tune with the "traditional view of teaching and learning which conceptualizes classroom instruction as the conveyance of information from the knowledgeable teacher to the 'empty' and passive learner" (Chaudron 1988: 10). It implies that pupils contribute to managing classroom interaction and, accordingly, to one another's learning (see also Allwright 1984a). This state of affairs contributes to moderating the idea that the teacher is the knowledgeable participant in TL classroom interaction.

As to how the frequencies of teacher- versus pupil-initiated didactic negotiation vary by proficiency level, the results illustrated in Table 13 and Figure 16 (n= 303 vs. n= 72 in the first grade, n= 351 vs. n= 28 in the second, and n= 161 vs. n= 17 in the third) reveal a significant tendency towards variance (F= 3.012, df= 2, p= .068). Specifically, the disparity between the frequencies of teacher- and pupil-initiated didactic negotiation seems more evident in the second grade. This further sustains the finding, recorded in the previous section, that there is a positive *interaction* between teacher-initiated negotiation and the second grade; in other words, teachers seem to overlook fewer interactional problems in this grade than in the other grades.

This section has investigated the frequency of teacher- in comparison with pupil-initiated didactic negotiation, in the data as a whole and by proficiency level, so as to find out who mostly initiates the negotiation and whether this varies by proficiency level. The results reveal a significant preference for teacher- over pupil-initiated didactic negotiation, and a significant tendency towards variance of this preference by proficiency level. Teacher-initiated didactic negotiation seems to be mostly preferred in the second grade. The frequency distribution of teacher- in comparison with pupil-initiated conversational negotiation is investigated in the following section.

Teacher- vs. Pupil-initiated Conversational Negotiation

Is teacher 'control' also preferred to pupil 'initiative' in terms of the initiation of 'conversational negotiation'? And are teacher 'control' and pupil 'initiative' affected by the proficiency level of the class?. The answers to these questions are given and discussed below. Consider the following Table:

Table 14: Summary statistics for teacher- vs. pupil-initiated conversational negotiation by grade

Grades		Conversational Negotiation		Totals
		T-initiated	P-initiated	
1st G.	n	285	157	442
	%	64.48	35.52	100
	X	57	31.40	44.20
2nd G.	n	510	177	687
	%	74.24	25.76	100
	X	102	35.40	68.70
3rd G.	n	235	227	462
	%	50.87	49.13	100
	X	47	45.40	46.20
Totals	n	1030	561	1591
	%	64.74	35.26	100
	X	68.67	37.40	53.03

n : sample size
% : row percentage
X : observed mean

There is a statistically significant (F= 10.872, df= 1, p= .003) preference for teacher-initiated over pupil-initiated conversational negotiation in the data. As Table 14 and Figure 17 show, there are almost twice as many teacher-initiated as pupil-initiated conversational negotiations (n= 1030 vs. n= 561, respectively). This seems to further emphasize the notion of teacher 'control' in TL classroom discourse.

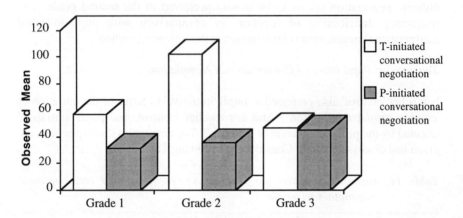

Figure 17: Teacher- vs. pupil-initiated conversational negotiation by grade

However the percentage (35.26%) of pupil-initiated conversational negotiation is revealing especially if compared to that of pupil-initiated didactic negotiation (12.55%) (see also Figure 18). It suggests that when it comes to non-didactic talk, learners become largely responsible for their learning, by attempting to negotiate interactional problems and sustain the conversation. In this way, they negotiate for more comprehensible input and control their intake.

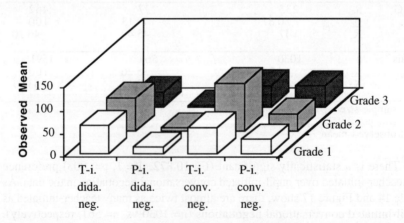

Figure 18: Teacher- vs. pupil-initiated 'didactic' and 'conversational' negotiation by grade

The assumption that there is a close relationship between initiative and learning, or at least opportunities for learning, is obvious in Seliger's (1983) distinction between 'High Input Generators' and 'Low Input Generators'. The results of the present investigation reveal that pupils take more initiative, produce more output, and hence generate more input when problems of the talk are at issue than when problems of TL forms are at issue. The relatively high percentage of pupil-initiated conversational negotiation (35.26%) implies that the affective environment in the classrooms where the data were collected is optimal for encouraging pupil 'initiative' (Stevick 1980), 'intake control' (Gaies 1983), and ultimately acquisition.

To increase pupil initiative, advocates of communicative language teaching stress the importance of psychological factors in the classroom. Littlewood (1981), for instance, contends that since the developmental processes of communicative ability occur inside the learner, the latter's psychological state is a crucial factor in helping or hampering them. The development of communicative skills, therefore,

> requires a learning atmosphere which gives [...] [learners] a sense of security and value as individuals. In turn, this atmosphere depends to a large extent on the existence of interpersonal relationships which do not create inhibitions, but are supportive and accepting [...]. [C]ommunicative teaching methods leave the learner scope to contribute his own personality to the learning process. They also provide the teacher with scope to step out of his didactic role in order to be a 'human among humans' (Littlewood 1981: 93-4).

The frequency distribution between teacher- and pupil-initiated conversational negotiation by grade seems to reveal a noticeable variance (n= 285 vs. n= 157 in the first grade, n= 510 vs. n= 177 in the second grade, and n= 235 vs. n= 227 in the third grade). However, this variance is not statistically significant (F= 2.744, df= 2, p= .084). The statistical test also reveals a significant *two-way interaction* (F= 4.005, df= 2, p= .032). Given that "the interaction effect washes out the main effect" (Hatch & Farhady 1982: 159), this finding implies that the significant (F= 10.872, df= 1, p= .003) variance between the frequency of teacher- and pupil-initiated conversational negotiation in the data as a whole is simply due to the fact that teacher-initiation of conversational negotiation is highly preferred in the second grade (n= 510 vs. n= 177, respectively). This further sustains the claim made in earlier sections, that there is a positive interaction between teacher-initiated negotiation and the second grade.

To further support this claim, one-factor ANOVA was computed for the frequency of teacher-initiated conversational negotiation by proficiency level. The results were highly significant (F= 5.286, df= 2, p= .023), which implies that the frequency of teacher-initiated conversational negotiation is indeed high with second grade classes. This further supports the suggestion made earlier, namely that teachers seem to exert more 'control' with intermediate classes than with beginning or advanced classes, possibly because they perceive their tightening 'control' with intermediate classes as more beneficial for pupils' target language development.

The aim of the present section has been to ascertain whether there is a preference for teacher- over pupil-initiated conversational negotiation in the data, and whether this varies by proficiency level. The results reveal a significant preference for teacher-initiated conversational negotiation but also a significant *two-way interaction effect*. This interaction effect means that the recorded significant preference for teacher-over pupil-initiated conversational negotiation in the data may simply be due to the high preference for teacher-initiated conversational negotiation in the second grade.To find out whether there is any relationship between the discourse function of the negotiation and the occurrence of teacher- or pupil-initiated negotiation, all negotiated exchanges have been investigated in terms of who initiates the negotiation and in terms of the function of the negotiation. The results are given and discussed in the following two sections.

Teacher- vs. Pupil-initiated Didactic Negotiation Genres

Our concern in the present section is to further investigate the frequency of teacher- versus pupil-initiated didactic negotiation, by focusing on each of its functions and examining who typically initiates the negotiation in the data as a whole and how this compares by proficiency level. The aim is to find out whether there is a relationship between the discourse function and the initiator (teacher or pupil) of the negotiation, in other words, whether there is a difference between teacher 'control' and pupil 'initiative' when different didactic negotiation genres are involved. The results of these investigations are given and discussed below.

The main observation that can be made from Table 15 and Figure 19 below is that 'comprehension check-oriented negotiation', 'complete sentence-oriented negotiation' and 'turn-taking-oriented negotiation' are typical teacher-initiated negotiations which pupils never initiate. This implies that there are some TL classroom conventions at work which pupils seem to understand and comply

Table 15: Summary statistics for teacher- vs. pupil-initiation of didactic negotiation genres by grade

Grades		MON		CCON		CSON		TTON		Totals
		T-ini.	P-ini.	T-ini.	P-ini.	T-ini.	P-ini.	T-ini.	P-ini.	
1st G.	n	229	72	08	00	26	00	40	00	375
	%	61.07	19.20	02.13	00	06.93	00	10.67	00	100
	X	45.80	14.40	01.60	00	05.20	00	08	00	09.38
2nd G.	n	276	28	07	00	56	00	12	00	379
	%	72.82	07.39	01.85	00	14.77	00	03.17	00	100
	X	55.20	05.60	01.40	00	11.20	00	02.40	00	09.48
3rd G.	n	113	17	17	00	11	00	20	00	178
	%	63.48	09.55	09.55	00	06.18	00	11.24	00	100
	X	22.60	03.40	03.40	00	02.20	00	04	00	04.45
Totals	n	618	117	32	00	93	00	72	00	932
	%	66.31	12.55	03.43	00	09.98	00	07.73	00	100
	X	41.20	07.80	02.13	00	06.20	00	04.80	00	07.77

MON   : 'medium-oriented negotiation'
CCON : 'comprehension check-oriented negotiation'
CSON : 'complete sentence-oriented negotiation'
TTON : 'turn-taking-oriented negotiation'
T-ini. : teacher-initiated
P-ini. : pupil-initiated

n : sample size
% : row percentage
X : observed mean

with. Pupils seem to understand that the initiation of these negotiations are part of the teacher's role as a teacher. Indeed, violating such a convention might bring about reproof from the teacher because it implies that pupils are either unaware of classroom cultural conventions or are deliberately attempting to reverse the status and role relationships in the classroom. This finding, no doubt, further reveals the asymmetrical role relations between the teacher and pupils. It, probably, also reveals pupils' acknowledgement of the teacher's authority and of TL classroom cultural rules.

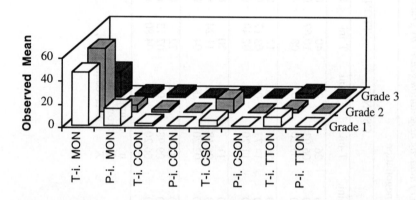

Figure 19: Teacher- vs. pupil-initiation of didactic negotiation genres by grade

As to 'comprehension check-oriented negotiation', since interaction in a teacher-fronted classroom is mainly between teacher and pupils rather than among pupils themselves, it is unlikely for the pupil to initiate this didactic negotiation genre while talking to the teacher. Pupil initiation of this kind of negotiation would imply either that the teacher is not paying attention to what the pupil is saying or that the pupil underestimates the knowledge and professional experience of the teacher (see also Pica 1987).

Similarly, it is unlikely for the pupil to initiate a 'complete sentence-oriented negotiation' while talking to the teacher, because pupils seem to understand that if the teacher resorts to such an artificial discourse rule as the 'complete sentence rule' (cf. Chapter 5), it is only for the sake of making pupils practice the target language by inciting them to produce longer stretches of talk. Pupils seem to understand that the teacher need not respect such a rule since s/he is proficient in the target language. They are, no doubt, aware that the teacher does not respect such a rule in her/his own contributions.

Likewise, the pupil cannot initiate a 'turn-taking-oriented negotiation' while interacting with the teacher because the latter is supposed to have an unconditioned right to the floor. Allwright (1980: 170) found out that "[t]he teacher does almost all the interrupting, and is even among those guilty of turn stealing."

In short, it would be 'face-threatening' (Brown & Levinson 1978) for the pupil to initiate one of these three didactic negotiations. To do so would suggest that s/he has no knowledge of classroom cultural rules (put bluntly, that s/he is a classroom 'cultural monster') or that s/he deliberately chooses to transgress these rules.

As for 'medium-oriented negotiation', there is a significant ($F= 31.063$, $df= 1$, $p= .000$) preference for teacher- over pupil-initiated 'medium-oriented negotiation' in the data ($F= 618$ vs. $n= 117$, respectively). This, as pointed out earlier, is to be expected in TL classroom discourse where one of the teacher's vested responsibilities is to ensure the accurate and appropriate use of the target language. The statistical test (factorial ANOVA) computed to investigate the variance in the frequency distribution between teacher- and pupil-initiated 'medium-oriented negotiation' by proficiency level also reveals a significant variance ($F= 3.683$, $df= 2$, $p= .040$). This variance is greatest in the second grade and least in the third ($n= 229$ vs. $n= 72$ in the first grade, $n= 276$ vs. $n= 28$ in the second, and $n= 113$ vs. $n= 17$ in the third). This implies that the discrepancy between teacher 'control' and pupil 'initiative' with regard to the form of the target language is highest in the second grade and lowest in the third grade. This finding further supports the claim made earlier, namely that the teacher seems to perceive her control of pupils' contributions in the second grade as most crucial for pupils' target language development.

When one-factor ANOVA was computed to investigate whether the frequency distribution of teacher-initiated 'medium-oriented negotiation' in isolation from that of pupil-initiated 'medium-oriented negotiation' significantly varies by proficiency level, the results revealed a non-significant variance ($F= 3.022$, $df= 2$, $p= .086$). However, as the p-value ($p= .086$) reveals, there seems to be a tendency for teacher-initiated 'medium-oriented negotiation' to vary by proficiency level and to be the least frequent in the third grade, which implies that the teacher tends to exert the least 'control' over the form of pupils' contributions in the third grade. This further supports a previous claim (cf. Chapter 6), namely that in advanced classes there seems to be the least focus on 'accuracy', in comparison with beginning and intermediate classes.

As Table 15 and Figure 19 illustrate, the frequency of pupil-initiated 'medium-oriented negotiation' seems to vary by proficiency level ($n= 72$ in the first grade, $n= 28$ in the second, and $n= 17$ in the third). However, one-factor ANOVA has revealed that this seeming variance is not statistically significant

(F= 2.327, df= 2, p= .140), which implies that there is more variance between the lessons of the same grade than between the lessons of different grades. Therefore, it may be argued that the proficiency level factor has no effect on the amount of 'medium-oriented negotiation' initiated by the pupils. In other words, pupil 'initiative' with regard to the negotiation of the forms of the target language is not affected by the proficiency level of the class. This may probably suggest that, in all three grades, pupils seem to give the same importance to accuracy. Hence, in all three grades, whenever a 'repairable' utterance - in terms of form - is produced, pupils will provide 'repair' if they are aware of the 'trouble source', if they know how to repair it, and, of course, if the teacher has not already repaired it. Yet, overlap, occasionally, does occur between teacher and pupil repair.

The present section has aimed at examining the four functions of didactic negotiation with regard to who mostly initiates the negotiation in the data, and how this varies by proficiency level. The results suggest that three didactic negotiation genres (namely 'comprehension check-oriented negotiation', 'complete sentence-oriented negotiation', and 'turn-taking-oriented negotiation') are never initiated by the pupil, and, therefore, may be considered typical teacher-initiated negotiations. On the other hand, the results concerning 'medium-oriented negotiation' reveal that there is a significant preference for teacher- over pupil-initiation of this negotiation genre in the data, and that this preference is highest in the second grade and least in the third grade. Accordingly, it has been argued that insufficiency of 'medium-oriented negotiation' in the third grade renders advanced classes more vulnerable to 'fossilization' than beginning or intermediate classes.

Teacher- vs. Pupil-initiated Conversational Negotiation Genres

This section investigates the seven conversational negotiation genres detected in the data in terms of who (teacher or pupil) mostly initiates the negotiation, in the data as a whole and by proficiency level. The purpose of this investigation is to capture the typical functions of teacher- and pupil-initiated conversational negotiations, to find out whether there is any relationship between the discourse function and the initiator of the negotiation and whether this varies by proficiency level. In other words, the aim is to ascertain whether and how the amount of teacher 'control' and pupil 'initiative' vary when various functions of conversational negotiation are involved. The results are presented and discussed below.

Table 16: Summary statistics for teacher- vs. pupil-initiation of conversational negotiation genres by grade

Grades		HON		MON		CON		GKON		AON		SDON		CC		Totals
		T-i	P-i	T-i	P-i	T-i	P-i	T-i	P-i	T-i	P-i	T-i	P-i	T-i	P-i	
1st G.	n	08	03	97	21	96	42	08	01	03	00	04	00	69	90	442
	%	01.81	00.68	21.95	04.75	21.72	09.50	01.81	00.23	00.68	00	00.90	00	15.61	20.36	100
	X̄	01.60	00.60	19.40	04.20	19.20	08.40	01.60	00.20	00.60	00	00.80	00	13.80	18.00	06.31
2nd G.	n	29	07	184	24	200	46	02	00	29	10	15	00	51	90	687
	%	04.22	01.02	26.79	03.49	29.11	06.70	00.29	00	04.22	01.46	02.18	00	07.42	13.10	100
	X̄	05.80	01.40	36.80	04.80	40	09.20	00.40	00	05.80	02	03	00	10.20	18	09.81
3rd G.	n	12	07	118	40	60	21	10	01	10	05	01	00	24	153	462
	%	02.60	01.51	25.54	08.66	12.99	04.55	02.16	00.22	02.16	01.08	00.22	00	05.19	33.12	100
	X̄	02.40	01.40	23.60	08	12	04.20	02.00	00.20	02	01	00.20	00	04.80	30.60	06.60
Totals	n	49	17	399	85	356	109	20	02	42	15	20	00	144	333	1591
	%	03.08	01.07	25.08	05.34	22.38	06.85	01.26	00.12	02.64	00.94	01.26	00	09.05	20.93	100
	X̄	03.27	01.13	26.60	05.67	23.73	07.27	01.33	00.13	02.80	01	01.33	00	09.60	22.20	07.58

HON   : 'hearing-oriented negotiation'
MON   : 'meaning-oriented negotiation'
CON   : 'content-oriented negotiation'
GKON   : 'general knowledge-oriented negotiation'
AON   : 'agreement-oriented negotiation'
SDON   : 'surprise display-oriented negotiation'
CC   : 'conversational continuant'
T-i   : teacher-initiated
P-i   : pupil-initiated
n   : sample size
%   : row percentage
X̄   : observed mean

As Table 16 shows, there is a significant (F= 7.969, df= 1, p= .009) preference for teacher- over pupil-initiated 'hearing-oriented negotiation' in the data (n= 49 vs. n= 17, respectively). This seems to further reveal the asymmetrical power relationship between teacher and pupils in TL classroom discourse. Hence, it may be argued that teachers initiate 'hearing-oriented negotiation' whenever they do not hear a pupil's contribution, which further illustrates teacher control of what is being said. However, pupils do not seem to have such control or rather such initiative, probably because of the power factor operating in classroom discourse. As pointed out previously (cf. Chapter 6), pupils may refrain from initiating 'hearing-oriented negotiation' because their admitting not to have heard what the teacher has said may be 'face-threatening' (Brown & Levinson 1978) since it may suggest non-attentiveness, and hence may result in reproof from the teacher.

As to how the frequencies of teacher- vs. pupil-initiated 'hearing-oriented negotiation' vary by proficiency level, the results reveal a significant variance (F= 3.805, df= 2, p= .037). As Table 16 and Figure 20 show, while the first and third grades reveal a similar variance between the frequency of teacher- and pupil-initiated 'hearing-oriented negotiation', the second grade reveals the largest variance between these two variables (n= 08 vs. n= 03 in the first grade, n= 29 vs. n= 07 in the second, and n= 12 vs. n= 07 in the third). This might suggest that teacher 'power' is most evident in the second grade, since pupil-initiated 'hearing-oriented negotiation' does not increase in the same degree as teacher-initiated 'hearing-oriented negotiation', from first to second grade. This further sustains the finding that the teacher seems to exert more 'control' over pupils' contributions in the second grade than in the two other grades.

As for the frequency distribution between teacher- and pupil-initiated 'meaning-oriented negotiation' in the data, the statistical test (factorial ANOVA) reveals a significant preference for teacher over pupil initiation of this negotiation genre (F= 73.115, df= 1, p= .000). As revealed in Table 16 and Figure 20, the frequency of teacher-initiation far exceeds that of pupil-initiation of 'meaning-oriented negotiation' (n= 399 vs. n= 85, respectively), which suggests that in spite of evidence of cooperation from pupils, the heaviest responsibility for the negotiation of meaning in TL classroom discourse clearly lies with the teacher. This seems to sustain Scarcella & Higa's (1981: 410) assertion that

> [o]ne of the most salient features of negotiation work is that it is not always evenly distributed among conversational partners. Specifically, the more competent speaker (socially, cognitively, or linguistically) generally assumes a greater responsibility for [...] establishing understanding.

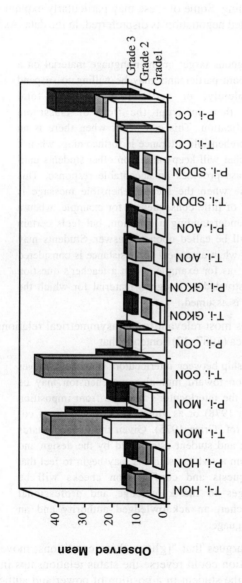

Figure 20: Teacher- vs. pupil-initiation of conversational negotiation genres

This asymmetrical aspect of negotiation work further supports the idea that the TL classroom is a context of unequal-power discourse. Pica (1987) directs attention to several reasons which seem to cut down opportunities for classroom participants to negotiate meaning. Some of these may particularly explain why pupil-initiated 'meaning-oriented negotiation' is dispreferred, in the data. As Pica (1987: 12) points out,

> when faced with ambiguous target or interlanguage material on a particular topic, classroom participants may be willing to suspend comprehension completely, or settle for less than total understanding, rather than interrupt the flow of classroom discourse to seek clarification. This can occur when there is an expectation that a comprehensible utterance is forthcoming, when it is assumed that the teacher will keep calling on other students until one member of the class provides an acceptable response. This situation can also arise when the incomprehensible message is deemed unimportant or of little consequence, for example, when a student has difficulty understanding a question, but feels certain that another student will be called upon to answer. Students may also avoid seeking help when an appeal for assistance is considered a sign of incompetence, as for example, when a teacher's question refers to previously instructed or assigned material for which the students' accountability is assumed.

Furthermore, and perhaps most relevant to the asymmetrical relationship between teacher and pupils, Pica (1987: 12) contends that

> when the status relationship between interlocutors is unequal, moves to restructure interaction toward mutual comprehension may be perceived as threats to the interlocutor's freedom from imposition (cf. Brown & Levinson 1978) or as violation of principles of co-operative conversation (cf. Grice 1975). Given the unequal status relationships of teacher and student established by the design and organization of classroom activities, students may begin to feel that their clarification requests and confirmation checks will be perceived as challenges to the knowledge and professional experience of the teacher, an acknowledged authority and an expert on the target language.

Pica (1987: 12) further argues that "[g]iven these conditions, moves to restructure classroom interaction could reverse the status relationships in the classroom and thereby place the student in a position of power and authority over their teacher." Hence, she concludes that "[i]t is perhaps not unfair to say that, [...], classrooms are still considered less than optimal environments for successful second-language acquisition" (Pica 1987: 117).

We utterly disagree with Pica (1987) on these two considerations for we believe that pupil-initiated moves to restructure interaction *cannot* reverse the status relationship in the classroom. The asymmetrical power and role relationships in the classroom do not solely stem from the interactive behaviour of participants, but mainly from the institutionalized situation in which the interaction takes place. Hence, pupil-initiated moves to negotiate meaning might have the effect of moderating teacher power but can never reverse the power status relationships in the classroom. Paradoxically, the main problem concerning the conception of power in classroom discourse stems from the widely accepted view that power in such an institutionalized situation is an a priori established social fact by the asymmetrical social status and role relationship between the teacher and pupils. Differences in rights, duties and obligations are known in advance and any deviation from the stereotype of classroom discourse (for example by a pupil's attempt to initiate a negotiation exchange) is seen as exceptional, abnormal or even far reaching, since, according to Pica (1987: 12), it "could reverse the status relationships in the classroom."

No matter what effect pupil initiation of 'meaning-oriented negotiation' might have on the power status of classroom participants, the crucial effect of these moves is that they bring about not only more 'comprehensible input' (Krashen 1982a) but more 'comprehensible output' (Swain 1985) as well. And as pointed out throughout the present work, these are key variables in target language acquisition. These pupil moves, which are real attempts at genuine communication, reveal pupils' active involvement in classroom interaction. Such involvement facilitates language acquisition (cf. Stevick 1976, 1980, 1981) and "real attempts at real communication [...] are in the last resort the most productive events for language learners" (Allwright 1980: 185). Hence, contrary to Pica's (1987) above claim, we believe together with Van Lier (1983: 3) that "classrooms are [indeed] viable places for language learners to spend time in" (sic).

The frequency of pupil-initiated 'meaning-oriented negotiation', though low in comparison to teacher-initiated 'meaning-oriented negotiation' in the data (n= 85 vs. n= 399, respectively), does indicate that teacher power is not absolute. It shows that teacher power is not so strong as to hamper pupils, altogether, from negotiating for meaning, i.e., displaying their nonunderstanding of a previous contribution or repairing that contribution if it is 'repairable' in terms of meaning. Indeed, though the teacher is the typical initiator of 'meaning-oriented negotiation', for understanding to be achieved (when there is a problem of understanding), it has to be jointly managed between the teacher and pupil(s).

Hence, it may be argued that the management of understanding, which is probably an indicator of 'power' and 'control' in TL classroom discourse, is a negotiated process between the teacher and pupils. Such classroom negotiations, to quote Allwright (1980: 166), "are directly or indirectly concerned, potentially at least, with all aspects of the management of learning."

However, this by no means suggests that there are no pupils who would feign understanding when they don't understand, because revealing non-understanding may be embarrassing and, accordingly, 'face-threatening' (Brown & Levinson 1978). Therefore, it is essential that teachers attempt to provide an affective environment in which the negotiation of meaning is possible, i.e., allowed and even encouraged. Bremer et al. (1988: 3), among others, direct attention to "the role that unequal distribution of power can play in hindering clarification of nonunderstanding."

As to the impact of the proficiency level on the frequency distribution between teacher- and pupil-initiated 'meaning-oriented negotiation', the statistical test (factorial ANOVA) revealed a significant variance by grade (F= 4.524, df= 2, p= .022). The statistical test also revealed a significant *two-way interaction* (F= 5.111, df= 2, p= .014) between the proficiency level factor and the initiation of 'meaning-oriented negotiation' factor. This significant *interaction* effect implies that the significant variances recorded between the frequency of teacher and pupil-initiated 'meaning-oriented negotiation' in the data as a whole (F= 73.115, df= 1, p= .000) and by grade (F= 4.524, df= 2, p= .022) may simply be due to the fact that teacher-initiated 'meaning-oriented negotiation' is significantly high in the second grade. As Table 16 and Figure 20 reveal, the variance between teacher- and pupil-initiated 'meaning-oriented negotiation' is the greatest in the second grade, in comparison to the other grades (n= 97 vs. n= 21, in the first grade, n= 184 vs. n= 24, in the second, and n= 118 vs. n= 40, in the third). This further sustains the finding that teacher 'control' of classroom discourse seems to be greatest in the second grade.

The frequency distribution between teacher- and pupil-initiated 'content-oriented negotiation' seems to tell the same story, though there is no significant *two-way interaction effect*. The statistical test (factorial ANOVA) revealed a significant preference for teacher- over pupil-initiated 'content-oriented negotiation ' (F= 10.229, df= 1, p= .004) in the data as a whole (n= 356 vs. n= 109 respectively). This implies that the responsibility for the resolution of problems related to the comprehension of the text being studied mainly lies with the teacher. This further supports Scarcella & Higa's (1981: 410) assertion that "the more competent speaker (socially, cognitively, or linguistically) generally assumes a greater responsibility for [...] establishing understanding." Rulon & McCreary (1986) found that students, in group work, initiated significantly more negotiation of content than in teacher-fronted classes (for a review of this study, see Chapter 2). Attempting to explain this finding, they argue that

> [p]erhaps the teacher's "discussion" following the lecture cleared up any misunderstanding they might have had about the lecture's content and so there was no need to request clarification. On the other hand, perhaps misunderstandings continued to exist, but the students did not, as a result of the "audience effect" (Barnes 1973), feel confident enough to make their need for clarification known in such a large "audience" (Rulon & McCreary 1986: 194).

Yet, the frequency of pupil-initiated 'content-oriented negotiation' in the data (n= 109) is revealing. Besides showing pupil 'initiative' (cf. Stevick 1980), it suggests that pupils are not unhealthily affected by the 'authoritative figure' (Long et al. 1976) of the teacher nor by the 'audience effect' (Barnes 1973) of the teacher-fronted classroom. Although, it is a widely held claim that "[b]oth teaching and learning in the teacher-fronted classroom can be an extremely stressful experience" (Rulon & McCreary 1986: 184), the relatively high frequency of pupil-initiated 'content oriented negotiation', recorded in the data, might suggest that learning, in teacher-fronted TL classrooms, is not that stressful.

As for the effect of the proficiency level on the frequency distribution between teacher- and pupil-initiated 'content-oriented negotiation', the statistical test (factorial ANOVA) has revealed a significant variance by grade (F= 3.532, df= 2, p= .004). As Table 16 and Figure 20 show, this variance is highest in the second grade, in comparison with the other grades (n= 96 vs. n= 42 in the first grade, n= 200 vs. n= 46 in the second, and n= 60 vs. n= 21 in the third). This seems to further substantiate the finding that teacher 'control' is greatest in the second grade.

However, an increase in teacher 'control' does not seem to interfere with, or more precisely reduce, pupil 'initiative'. Thus, as illustrated in Figure 20, though teacher-initiation of 'content-oriented negotiation' noticeably increases from first to second grade, pupil-initiation of the same negotiation genre seems to remain the same. However, a decrease in teacher 'control' seems to bring about a decrease in pupil 'initiative', in terms of the negotiation of content. Hence, as can be seen in Figure 20, as one moves from second to third grade, one records a noticeable decrease in teacher-initiated 'content-oriented negotiation' but also a slight decrease in pupil-initiated 'content-oriented negotiation'. This seems to support Stevick's (1980: 19) statement that "insufficient 'control' by the teacher may reduce or paralyze the initiative of the student."

With regard to 'content-oriented negotiation', Stevick's claim implies that if the teacher does not take the lead in negotiating the comprehension of the content being discussed mainly via 'clarification requests' and 'confirmation checks' about pupils' contributions, students might be discouraged from negotiating content themselves. This might be explained in terms of the asymmetrical power, role relations, and discourse rules operating in the classroom. Pupils seem to acknowledge that it is the teacher who should direct the discourse and that they should follow the example of the teacher. Thus, if the teacher seems to dwell on an issue (be it the form of the target language, the meaning of participants' contributions, the comprehension of the text, etc.), they usually tend to do the same; if the teacher seems to consider a given issue as unimportant, they also usually tend to do the same.

As for the frequency distribution between teacher- and pupil-initiated 'general knowledge-oriented negotiation' in the data, the statistical test (factorial ANOVA) revealed a non-significant difference between the frequencies of these two variables ($F= 1.906$, $df= 1$, $p= .180$), despite the seeming preference for teacher-initiation of this negotiation genre, as revealed in the above Table ($n= 20$ vs. $n= 02$). This finding implies that the teacher is not the initiator par excellence of 'general knowledge-oriented negotiation' in TL classroom discourse, which sounds logical since this negotiation genre is a TP-event (cf. Chapter 3) rather than a T-event; i.e. it is a speech event concerned with information that is supposed to be known to both the teacher and pupils. Such finding is revealing for it implies that when the teacher is not the primary knower of a speech event, s/he is not necessarily the typical initiator of the negotiation. The finding seems to sustain Woken & Swales' (1989) and Zuengler's (1989a, 1989b) claim that differences in language proficiency are by no means sufficient to explain dominance, active involvement, and the extent of conversational participation in foreigner talk discourse (i.e., discourse involving nonnative speakers); knowledge of the discourse domain is also an important variable.

As to the impact of the proficiency level on the frequency distribution between teacher- and pupil-initiated 'general knowledge-oriented negotiation', the statistical test (factorial ANOVA) also revealed a non-significant variance between the frequencies of these two variables by grade ($F= .394$, $df= 2$, $p= .679$). The non-significance of the seeming variance, between the frequencies of these two variables by grade, as displayed in the above Table ($n= 08$ vs. $n= 01$ in the first grade, $n= 02$ vs. $n= 00$ in the second, and $n= 10$ vs. $n= 01$ in the third) (see also Figure 20) means that there is more variance among the lessons of the same grade than among the lessons of different grades.

The finding that the proficiency level has no impact on the variance between teacher- and pupil-initiated 'general knowledge-oriented negotiation' may be due to the fact that general knowledge has nothing to do with participants' proficiency in the target language. However, it could be argued that a participant with a higher proficiency in the target language and a higher general knowledge would tend to initiate more 'general knowledge-oriented negotiations'. This, no doubt, explains the high (though non-significant) frequency of teacher- in comparison with pupil-initiated 'general knowledge-oriented negotiation' in the data as a whole. The teacher, by virtue of her/his higher proficiency in the target language, her/his higher level of education, and experience, is in a better position than pupils to initiate such negotiations.

Interestingly, the statistical test (factorial ANOVA) also revealed a non-significant variance between the frequencies of teacher- and pupil-initiated 'agreement-oriented negotiation' in the data (F= 1.436, df= 1, p= .242). The non-significance of this variance implies that, despite the apparent difference between the frequencies of these two variables (n= 42 vs. n= 15, respectively), the teacher and pupils act as one population with regard to the initiation of 'agreement-oriented negotiation'. A possible explanation for this state of affairs is that since 'agreement-oriented negotiation' is concerned with 'disputable events' rather than with events directly linked with the target language (as in medium-, meaning-, content-oriented negotiation), the teacher is not necessarily its typical initiator.

Nonetheless, what has been said for 'general knowledge-oriented negotiation' goes also for 'agreement-oriented negotiation', namely that a participant with a higher proficiency in the target language is likely to take the lead in initiating the negotiation because of her/his ease of expression in the target language. This, possibly, explains the high but non-significant preference for teacher-initiated 'agreement-oriented negotiation' in the data. Yet, the non-significant preference for teacher-initiation of both 'general knowledge-oriented negotiation' and 'agreement oriented negotiation' might imply that teacher 'control' and 'power' seem to wane when the speech event is not directly concerned with target language comprehension or production.

As for variance in the frequency distribution between teacher- and pupil-initiated 'agreement-oriented negotiation' by grade, the above Table seems to show that it is greatest in the second grade (n= 03 vs. n= 00 in the first grade, n= 29 vs. n= 10 in the second, and n= 10 vs. n= 05 in the third) (see also Figure 20). However, this result is statistically non-significant (F= 1.986, df= 2, p= .159), which means that the proficiency level of the class has no effect on the frequencies of teacher- and pupil-initiated 'agreement-oriented negotiation', in other words on teacher 'control' and pupil 'initiative' with regard to this type of negotiation. This state of affairs may be due to the fact that the initiation of 'agreement-oriented negotiation' is not primarily dependent on participants' proficiency in the target language since this negotiation genre is concerned with 'disputable events' rather than with events primarily related to the comprehension or production of the target language.

The results for 'surprise display-oriented negotiation' were significant, in terms of who typically initiates the negotiation both in the data as a whole (F= 23.529, df= 1, p= .000) and by proficiency level (F= 9.588, df= 2, p= .001). However, the statistical test (factorial ANOVA) also revealed a significant *interaction* (F= 9.588, df= 2, p= .001) between the proficiency level and who initiates the negotiation. As illustrated in Table 16 and Figure 20, there is a preference for teacher over pupil-initiated 'surprise display-oriented negotiation' in the data (n= 04 vs. n= 00 in the first grade, n= 15 vs. n= 00 in the second, and n=01 vs. n= 00 in the third). The statistical significance of this finding suggests that since most teacher-fronted TL classroom interaction is between teacher and pupils rather than among pupils themselves, pupils may be inhibited from expressing surprise with regard to a teacher's proposition, due to the asymmetrical power relations. Indeed, it seems paradoxical to maintain that pupils are inhibited from expressing surprise with regard to a teacher's proposition when the data reveal the occurrence of pupil 'challenge' of teacher contributions (cf. Chapter 4 and 7). The explanation of this paradox may lie in the fact that 'surprise display-oriented negotiation' usually brings about laughter and may imply ridicule, and hence if initiated by the pupil may sound more offensive, less serious, and less lesson-oriented than 'challenge'. As a result, pupils may refrain from initiating this negotiation genre for fear this would result in reproof from the teacher.

Since the results reveal a significant *two-way interaction* effect, and since "[t]he interaction effect washes out the main effect" (Hatch & Farhady 1982: 159-60), it may be argued that the preference for teacher- over pupil-initiated 'surprise display-oriented negotiation', in the data, is mainly due to the fact that there is a positive *interaction* between teacher-initiation of this negotiation genre and the second grade. In other words, the frequency of teacher-initiated 'surprise display-oriented negotiation' happens to be noticeably high in the second grade, which brings about the significant result concerning the variance between the frequencies of teacher- and pupil-initiated 'surprise display-oriented negotiation', both in the data as a whole and by grade. The high frequency of teacher-initiated 'surprise display-oriented negotiation', in the second grade, may be another indicator of teacher 'control' and 'power' which seem to be greatest in this grade.

By initiating 'surprise display-oriented negotiation', the teacher may exert a negative psychological effect on the pupil whose contribution has triggered surprise. Paradoxically, since such a negotiation usually brings about pupils' laughter, it may contribute to lowering the 'affective filter' (Krashen 1982a) in the classroom, and may motivate pupils to be more attentive to what is going on (see also Chapter 6). Accordingly, it may be contended that teacher-initiated 'surprise display-oriented negotiation' is more beneficial for the 'audience' than for the pupil involved in the negotiation. Nonetheless, if the classroom climate is positive, the occurrence of such a negotiation may have no negative psychological effect on the pupil whose contribution has triggered the negotiation, and, thus, may be beneficial for her/his target language development.

The last subcategory of conversational negotiation to be discussed in terms of who initiates the negotiation is 'conversational continuant'. As Table 16 and Figure 20 show, there is a noticeable preference for pupil over teacher 'conversational continuant' in the data (n= 333 vs. n= 144, respectively). Interestingly, this result is statistically highly significant (F= 7.813, df= 1, p= .010), which might paradoxically imply that pupils work harder than the teacher to sustain the conversation, and, in this way, reveal their 'initiative' (Stevick 1980), or, put bluntly, exercise some power over the teacher and some 'control' over the interaction. This seems to be out of tune with Scarcella & Higa's (1981: 410) claim that "the more competent speaker (socially, cognitively, or linguistically) generally assumes a greater responsibility for sustaining the conversation."

The discrepancy between our findings and those of Scarcella & Higa (1981) may be due to a difference in the coding scheme. Scarcella & Higa (1981) used two measures to account for native speaker work to sustain the conversation, namely 'rhetorical questions' and other 'repetition', and four measures to account for nonnative speaker work, namely 'stepping in sideways', self and other 'repetition', 'topic initiation and topic shift', and 'conversational fillers'. Nonetheless, since the present data is pedagogically oriented, different strategies from those reported by Scarcella and Higa (1981) have been found to primarily function to sustain the conversation. As pointed out in Chapter 5, 'teacher conversational continuant' mainly functions to encourage the pupil to go on with her/his utterance while 'pupil conversational continuant' mainly functions to reveal that the pupil(s) is (are) following and understanding what is being said, and in this way incite(s) the speaker (mainly the teacher) to go on. Hence, it may be concluded that since Scarcella and Higa's (1981) data (NS-NNS interaction) are different from ours (TL classroom interaction), and since the coding schemes used in both studies are different, it is not surprising that the results should be different.

The only explanation that can be offered to the paradoxical finding that pupils work harder than teachers to sustain the conversation is that when pupils are motivated to learn the target language, when they are involved in the interaction, they may assume a greater responsibility for sustaining the conversation than the teacher, the competent speaker linguistically. Viewed from another standpoint, the above finding may have nothing to do with pupil motivation to learn the target language, but may simply be related to their motivation to participate in classroom interaction by virtue of a favourable affective environment or interesting topics introduced by the teacher. 'Motivation' (Gardner 1985), 'involvement' (Stevick 1980), and 'participation' (Seliger 1983) have been considered key variables in target language acquisition (see also Allwright & Bailey 1991).

The type of pupil 'control' revealed in the preference for pupil over teacher 'conversational continuant', in the data, is similar to what Gaies (1983b) refers to as 'learner intake-control'. By providing 'conversational continuants', pupils negotiate the nature of the input provided to them and hence control their intake. Another interesting observation, with regard to the notions of 'control' and 'power' in TL classroom discourse, concerns the overlap of pupil 'conversational continuant' with teacher speech: a considerable number of these pupil moves occur while the teacher's contribution is still in progress; such simultaneous speech might have the effect of moderating teacher 'control'. O'Barr (1982), whose main concern was courtroom rather than classroom discourse, found that in all instances involving overlap between the lawyer's and the witness' speech, the audience perceived the lawyer's control of the situation as low and that of the witness as high. O'Barr (1982) concludes that a lawyer is perceived to lose control whenever simultaneous speech occurs in the courtroom.

Though classroom discourse resembles courtroom discourse, by virtue of being an institutional talk and by virtue of the asymmetrical power and role relationships of its participants, it differs from it, among other things, by virtue of its pedagogical orientation. However, this difference by no means suggests that some of the findings of the former might not be insightful in interpreting the findings of the latter, and vice versa, specifically in terms of the exercise of 'power' through discourse. Therefore, one might venture to argue that the overlap of 'pupil conversational continuants' with teacher speech, recorded in the data, reveals some sort of pupil 'control' to the detriment of teacher 'control' over the interaction.

Paradoxically, as pointed out in Chapter 5, this sort of pupil 'control' or rather pupil 'initiative' is occasionally invited by the teacher. This seems in line with what Watts (1991) calls 'collaborative floor construction' which implies that

> the hearers are on the same floor as the speaker, since they may be
> expected to produce relevant responsive behaviour during the
> activity. For instance, in a lecture the lecturer appears to have the
> floor to her/himself, but the audience have the obligation to
> respond appropriately during or at the end of the speech event [...].

Failure to produce this response indicates a deliberate withholding of an obligation. It implies that the audience was not really on the floor. Thus, although the lecturer may have been listened to, the message conveyed by the audience is the opposite" (Watts 1991: 44).

Furthermore, this overlap implies that despite being teacher-fronted, the lessons constituting our data differ from traditional lessons where the convention seems to prescribe that when the teacher is talking, the pupils must listen and not say a word, and that if they want to intervene, they should wait for transitional points in the discourse, perform a 'bid', and wait to be allocated a turn by the teacher (Sinclair & Coulthard 1975, McHoul 1978). The overlap of pupil 'conversational continuants' with teacher speech seems to substantiate Allwright's (1980) and Van Lier's (1988) claim that there is some flexibility in terms of participation in classroom discourse.

Returning back to the results displayed in Table 16 and graphed in Figure 20, it can be seen that the discrepancy between the frequencies of teacher and pupil 'conversational continuant' is greatest in the third grade, in comparison with the other grades (n= 69 vs. n= 90 in the first grade, n= 51 vs. n= 90 in the second, and n= 24 vs. n= 153 in the third). However, this variance is highly non-significant (F= .213, df= 2, p= .810), which implies that the proficiency level of the class has no effect on the frequency distribution between teacher and pupil 'conversational continuant' in the data.

The finding that the frequency of teacher 'conversational continuant' does not vary by grade seems to be out of tune with the claim made throughout the foregoing discussion, namely that teacher 'control' seems to be mostly evident in the second grade. A possible explanation for this mismatch in the results may be that, in the second grade, the teacher is more concerned with repairing pupils' contributions than encouraging them to go on with their utterances. In other words, since the teacher seems to perceive her 'control' over second grade pupils' contributions as most beneficial for TL development, when a pupil, in this grade, is producing an utterance, the teacher will usually keep interrupting to repair form or meaning; and in this way, opportunities for teacher 'conversational continuants' to occur are lessened. Van Lier (1988: 119) contends that "*intra-turn repair/repair initiation* includes brief requests for clarifications, replacement of errors, and also instances of prompting and helping. Like listening response they are subservient to the turn in progress, but unlike them they alter that turn." Accordingly, it may, in the long run, be argued that by interrupting to repair pupils' utterances, the teacher is simultaneously sustaining the conversation.

This section has examined each conversational negotiation genre in the data with regard to its predominant initiator. The results related to 'hearing-oriented negotiation', 'meaning-oriented negotiation', 'content-oriented negotiation', and 'surprise display-oriented negotiation' reveal a significant preference for teacher- over pupil-initiation and a higher preference in the second grades in comparison with the other grades. Conversely, the results related to 'general knowledge-oriented negotiation' and 'agreement-oriented negotiation' reveal that there is no variance between the frequency of teacher- and pupil-initiation in the data nor by proficiency level. Interestingly, the results for 'conversational continuants' give evidence of a significant preference for pupil- over teacher- 'conversational continuant', yet a non-significant effect of the proficiency level. We have also attempted to qualify each finding in terms of the power factor widely claimed to be operating in classroom discourse. The claim made in this section is that teacher power in TL classroom discourse is a negotiated process between the teacher and pupils (see also Mehan 1974a and Allwright 1980). Pupil negotiation of power in TL classroom discourse is further researched in the following section.

More on Pupil Negotiation of Power in TL Classroom Discourse

Introduction

In this section, we briefly shed light on what we have labelled pupil-initiated 'disjunctive negotiations', in order to find out whether and how these 'face-threatening:' (Brown & Levinson 1978) negotiations are 'modulated' (Schegloff et al. 1977, Gaskill 1980) by the pupil, in the data.

Van Lier's (1988) framework for analyzing repair in SL classroom discourse distinguishes between 'conjunctive' and 'disjunctive' repair. The first one "is designed to help, enable, support," whereas the second one "is designed to evaluate, challenge, contest" (Van Lier 1988: 189). Such a distinction seems to apply for the negotiated exchanges occurring in our data as well. Hence, following Van Lier (1988), it may be argued that a movement from 'conjunctive' to 'disjunctive' negotiation "implies two things: firstly, increasing status- or role-marking or inequality, and secondly, increasing likelihood of threat of face" (Van Lier 1988: 190).

A pupil-initiated 'disjunctive negotiation' is usually initiated by the act 'challenge' (cf. Chapter 4) which is designed to contest or reject a teacher's previous contribution. In accordance with contextual appropriacy, such a 'face-threatening act' as pupil challenge of teacher contribution should be 'modulated' in terms of face-threat. However, because of their limited linguistic and pragmatic competence, pupils usually sound domineering when performing such an act. This seems to further sustain Thomas' (1984: 226) claim that "nonnative speakers often seem inappropriately over-assertive or domineering when talking English."

Pupil-initiated 'Disjunctive Negotiation'

Stressing teacher power in classroom discourse, Edmondson (1981: 90) points out that "what counts as a 'correct' pupil-response is determined by the teacher: if 'wrong' answers are 'accepted' by the teacher, they thereby become by definition 'right' answers." Conversely, though very rare in our data, the occurrence of pupil 'challenge' of teacher contributions seems to be out of tune with this claim by Edmondson (1981). Consider extract (69) which is reproduced below.

Re-	-I- 1 T	: <The teacher had asked pupils to read some pictures
initiate		using the passive voice> Yes Hajji (nom.)
	-R- 2 P1	: The window has been opened (rep.)
	-F- 3 T	: Yes (eva.)
Pupil	-I- 4 P2	: -> No broken (cha./re.)
Initiated	-R- 5 PP	: Broken. Broken (ack.)
Negotiate	-F- 6 T	: Broken (acc.). Not opened. Broken (com.)
		(2nd grade - lesson 5)

Contrary to Edmondson's (1981) claim, the above extract reveals that what counts as a 'correct' pupil-response is not necessarily always determined by the teacher, and if 'wrong' answers are 'accepted' by the teacher, they do not necessarily become by definition 'right' answers. Consider also the 'challenge' in the extract below.

(87)

Re-	-I- 1 T	: <The teacher had asked pupils to give sentences
initiate		following the model sentence "when I get sleepy, I
		have a shower">
	-R- 2 P1	: When I get tired after months of work, I have a
		holiday (rep.)
	-F- 3 T	: Yes (eva.)
Re-	-I- 4 T	: Assmi (nom.)
initiate	-R- 5 P2	: When I have .. when I get dirty I have a bath (rep.)

```
Teacher    -I- 6 T   : I have-? (re. ini.)
Initiated   -R- 7 P2  : a bath (rep.)
Negotiate  -F- 8 T   : a bath (acc.). No (eva.)

Pupil      -I- 9 P2   : -> DIRTY, teacher <challenging tone> (cha.)
Initiated
Negotiate

Teacher    -I- 10 T  : Dirty? (con.ch.) Dirty or thirsty? (cla.req.)
Initiated   -R-11 P2  : Dirty (rep.)
Negotiate  -F-12 T   : Yes (eva.)

Re-        -I- 13 T  : Repeat. Repeat (p.). Yes (eva.)
initiate    -R-14 P2  : When I get dirty I have a bath (rep.)
           -F-15 T   : Yes (eva.)
                     (2nd grade - lesson 5)
```

The interactional problem in the above extract is caused by the teacher mishearing 'dirty' in 5 P2 as 'thirsty'; therefore, she negatively evaluates the reply given in 5 P2. However, P2 is daring enough to initiate a negotiation exchange (9 P2) by means of the act 'challenge', in order to negotiate for the acceptability of her reply. As the above extract reveals, she succeeds in this endeavour. Hence, contrary to Edmondson's (1981) claim, the above extract shows that pupils are not passive recipients of the knowledge provided by the teacher, and that if 'correct' answers are 'rejected' by the teacher, they do not necessarily become by definition 'wrong' answers. It shows that pupils are able to negotiate for the acceptability of their replies even when this necessitates challenging the status of the teacher as the knowledgeable participant in classroom interaction, with all the embarrassment and face-threat this might imply.

Similarly, Richards & Skelton's (1989) data give evidence of the occurrence of pupil challenge of teacher contribution even in a traditional 'grammar' teacher-fronted lesson. Therefore, they conclude that "there is evidence to suggest that a focus on language as subject provides a fertile source of accidental moments where communicative exchanges arise naturally" (Richards & Skelton 1989: 235). Consider the following extract, quoted from Richards & Skelton (1989), which resembles many of the extracts involving pupil-initiated 'disjunctive negotiation' in our data (cf. extracts (33), (68), (70), (88))

T : now there is no word like whose which we're talking about and if
    we'd wanted to say something like the roof of the house we'd
    have to do it this way ... John's house ... sorry
                                    [
S6:   its which its
T : not ... very good idea but not quite ... John's house ... the roof
    of which ... the only way we can do it is to say the roof of which
    ... OK ... the roof of which
                     [
S6:   so can say John's hou- John's house ... er ... which
    its door is broken
T : no you can't
S6: why? ((Slightly demanding. Suppressed laughter from other Ss,
    slightly nervous laughter from T))
T : in fact because we don't ... we have to say John's house of which
    the door is broken ... allright ... or John's house which has a
    broken door ... we'd probably ... we'd probably avoid this
    ((mumbling from class)) because it's rather long and heavy ...
    when ... if you can't turn it round and say it another way we'd
    have to say the roof of which the door of which
S4: yes ... we can't say John's house of which the roof needs ... er
                                                                      [
T :   no ... er
    ... we don't do that Abdullah ... we say John's house the roof of
    which
    (quoted from Richards & Skelton, 1989: 236-7)

Commenting on the above extract, Richards & Skelton (1989: 237) observe
that

> the teacher fails in her role as arbiter of correctness - she is
> betrayed into confusion and contradiction by the unexpected
> pressure which has been brought to bear. Ironically, it is a student
> who comes to her rescue, repeating her initial mistake in a form
> which invites her to draw a clear contrast with the correct form.
> [...]. It is this conflict between the teacher's attempt to confine the
> lesson within predetermined limits and the students attempts to
> direct attention elsewhere which provides the source of so much
> interaction.

As Stubbs (1983: 134) points out, "it is quite possible that the teacher and pupils
may have different views about how the discourse could and should develop."

Pupil 'challenge' of teacher contributions is very rare in the data. Out of the 2523 negotiated exchanges occurring in the data, only 33 (i.e., 01.31%) are initiated by pupil challenge, and thereby constitute pupil-initiated 'disjunctive negotiations'. This seems to sustain Sinclair & Coulthard's (1975: 130-1) claim that "the teacher's orientation is rarely challenged." Interestingly, the data reveal that the more proficient pupils are, the more liable they are to challenge teacher contributions. Consider the results reported in the Table below, and graphed in Figure 21.

Table 17: Summary statistics for pupil 'challenge' by grade

Grades		Pupil 'challenge'
1st G.	n	01
	%	03.03
	X	00.20
2nd G.	n	15
	%	45.45
	X	03
3rd G.	n	17
	%	51.52
	X	03.40
Totals	n	33
	%	100
	X	02.20

n : sample size
% : row percentage
X : observed mean

As illustrated in Table 17 and Figure 21, pupil 'challenge' significantly (F= 8.291, df= 2, p= .005) increases in intermediate and advanced classes (n= 01 in the first grade, n= 15 in the second, and n= 17 in the third). This may be explained in terms of pupils' productive competence. The more proficient pupils are, the more confident they are in their interlanguage, and hence, the more self confident and daring they are to produce 'challenge', that is to question the truth value and validity of a teacher's contribution.

Van Lier (1988: 123) argues that "initiative is expressed in two ways: through retrospective and through prospective actions, that is, by acting on prior talk and by influencing future talk." Pupil 'challenge' undoubtedly reveals pupil initiative for it acts on a previous teacher contribution, initiating thereby a negotiation exchange to resolve an interactional problem and make the teacher

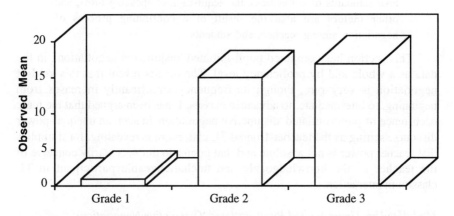

Figure 21: Pupil 'challenge' by grade

and pupil(s) speak on the same wavelength.

On the basis of recommendations from communicative language theory, we assume, following Stevick (1980), Allwright (1984a), and Van Lier (1988), that pupil initiative is crucial for target language acquisition. Accordingly, pupils who dare challenge teacher contributions are, to quote Seliger (1983), 'high input generators' who contribute to the management of learning. They are affected neither by the 'authoritative figure' of the teacher (Long et al. 1976) nor by the 'audience effect' (Barnes 1973) of the teacher-fronted classroom, since they venture to perform such a 'face-threatening act' (Brown & Levinson 1978) as 'challenge'.

Despite its low frequency in the data, the mere occurrence of pupil 'challenge', in such an unequal-power discourse setting as the TL classroom, implies that pupils no longer take for granted the traditional view which conceptualizes the teacher as the 'knowledgeable', 'infallible' and 'unchallengeable' participant in classroom interaction. On the contrary, as the present data illustrate, teacher contributions are questioned and negotiated, whenever necessary, rather than taken for granted. On the basis of this consideration, we can conclude, along with Long (1983d), Mehan (1974), and Allwright (1980), that the teacher's power in TL classroom discourse is not absolute but rather subject to negotiation. In this connection, Long (1983d: 11) maintains that

> '[u]nequal-power' discourse, of which the classroom is one setting,
> is marked among other ways by the teacher's predetermined ability
> to control topic and speaker. However, this power is not absolute;
> Mehan (1974) and Allwright (1980), among others, have shown

how standards of correctness, the acquisition of speaking turns, and other factors are also the result of a continuing process of negotiation among teachers and students.

This section has computed pupil-initiated 'disjunctive negotiation', in the data as a whole and by proficiency level. The results reveal that this kind of negotiation is very rare, though its frequency significantly increases from beginning, to intermediate, to advanced classes. It has been argued that the mere occurrence of pupil-initiated 'disjunctive negotiation' in such an unequal-power discourse setting as the teacher-fronted TL classroom is revealing, for it implies that teacher power is not absolute and that pupils do not necessarily conceive of the teacher as the knowledgeable and unchallengeable participant in TL classroom interaction.

Modulated vs. Unmodulated Pupil-initiated 'Disjunctive Negotiations'

To what extent are pupil-initiated 'disjunctive negotiations' mitigated in the data as a whole and by proficiency level? And how is this mitigation or modulation carried out?

Similar to Brown & Levinson's (1978) terms 'on-record' and 'off-record' are Schegloff et al.'s (1977) terms 'modulated' and 'unmodulated'. According to them, modulated repair (which may also encompass expressions of disagreement) appears to display uncertainty as a means of mitigating face-threat when other-correction is given or disagreement expressed. Gaskill (1980) also makes use of these terms in his study of corrections in native speaker-nonnative speaker conversations. He defines modulation as follows: "Modulation occurs in the correction being done as a question and/or in conjunction with such utterances as 'I think' [...] and 'Y'mean'. Thus, the other-correction is really saying something like "Did you mean to say Y instead of X?" (Gaskill 1980: 127).

Surprisingly, in the present data, modulation is very rarely resorted to if we consider how pupil 'challenge' is performed and formulated. Pupil 'challenge' (i.e., 'repair' of a teacher's contribution or expressions of disagreement with her/him) is usually abrupt and 'on-record', to use Brown & Levinson's (1978) term, and hence may be judged as impolite (cf. Leech 1983) by those unaccustomed to talking to nonnative speakers. This unintentional impoliteness, caused by lack of modulation, reveals pupils' 'pragmatic failure' (Thomas 1983) which is certainly due to their limited linguistic and pragmatic competence in the target language. Consider Table 18 below.

Table 18: Summary statistics for modulated vs. unmodulated pupil challenge

Grades		Pupil 'challenge'		Totals
		Modulated	Unmodulated	
1st G.	n	00	01	01
	%	00	100	100
	X	00	00.20	00.10
2nd G.	n	00	15	15
	%	00	100	100
	X	00	03.00	01.50
3rd G.	n	05	12	17
	%	29.41	70.59	100
	X	01	02.40	01.70
Totals	n	05	28	33
	%	15.15	84.85	100
	X	00.33	01.87	01.10

n : sample size
% : row percentage
X : observed mean

As Table 18 and Figure 22 show, there is a significant (F= 19.236, df= 1, p= .000) preference for unmodulated over modulated pupil 'challenge' in the data (n= 28 vs. n= 05, respectively). The statistical test (factorial ANOVA) also showed that there is a significant effect (F= 8.291, df= 2, p= .002) of the proficiency level. As Table 18 shows, there is a noticeable variance between the frequency of modulated and unmodulated challenge from one grade to another (n= 00 vs. n= 01 in the first grade, n= 00 vs. n= 15 in the second, and n= 05 vs. n= 12 in the third). However, since there is also a significant *two-way interaction* effect (F= 5.382, df= 2, p= .012), the significant variance recorded by grade may simply due to the high frequency of modulated challenge in the third grade.

The recorded lack of modulation in expressing such a face-threatening act as pupil 'challenge' of teacher contribution is first and foremost due to pupils' limited linguistic and pragmatic competence. This finding is in line with Beebe & Takahashi's (1989a, 1989b) that Japanese ESL speakers' directness is partly due to the fact that they are using a second language in which they are not yet proficient. As Beebe & Takahashi (1989b: 119) argue, there is "further evidence that ESL speakers from countries other than Japan sound blunt and direct [...] apparently due to lack of native speaker competence in the social rules of speaking." Consider extract (88) below.

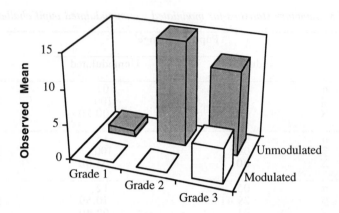

Figure 22: Modulated vs. unmodulated challenge by grade

(88)

Teacher	-I-	1 T	: Mr Barki said that he was a business man .. He often had to go abroad and that he-? (el.)
Elicit			
	-R-	2 P1	: He always be punctual (rep.)
	-F-	3 T	: He always be [1-] (acc.). No (eva.)

Re-initiate	-R-	4 P2	: Must. Must (rep.). We don't change must (i.)

Teacher-initiated	-I-	5 T	: You don't change must? (el.)
	-R-	6 P2	: Yes (rep.)
Negotiate		7 P3	: Had to be (rep.)
	-F-	8 T	: That he had to be punctual (eva./re.).That he had to be punctual (eva./re.)

Pupil-initiated	-I-	9 P2	: -> Teacher (b.).. We don't change 'must' (cha.)
	-F-	10 T	: No (eva.). Must changes ... ... He had to- ... 'Must' in the past is 'had to'. 'Must' in the past is 'had to'. In reported speech you say 'had to' (com.)
Negotiate			(2nd grade - Lesson 3)

In the above extract, the pupils are required to transform the sentence 'I must always be punctual' (part of a reported speech exercise on their textbook) from direct to reported speech. A pupil gives a wrong reply (2 P1) which is negatively evaluated by the teacher (3 T). Then, another pupil (P2) shouts out the incorrect reply 'must. must', meaning that this is the word needed so that

P1's reply becomes correct; furthermore, he wrongly argues that 'must' does not change when transforming a sentence from direct to reported speech (4 P2). The correct reply is provided by the third pupil (7 P3), and positively evaluated by the teacher (8 T). But, though the focus is on a T-event (i.e., a speech event where the teacher is supposed to be the primary knower since it is concerned with knowledge of the target language), P2 is daring enough to challenge the teacher's positive evaluation of the previous reply by the blunt and unmodulated assertion: "Teacher.. We don't change must" (9 P2). To end up this negotiation, the teacher provides a feedback (10 T) which negatively evaluates the 'challenge' provided by P2 and explains that 'must' in the past is 'had to'. Consider also the blunt and unmodulated challenges in extract (68) reproduced below:

| Direct | -I- 1 T | : Now (m.). Read the text again and answer the questions you have on your book. 'True' or 'False' and justify. You say 'True' why? 'False' why? (d.) |
| | -R- 2 PP | : Yes (ack.) <Activity> (rea.) |

<After approximately ten minutes>

Teacher	-I- 3 T	: Now (m.). The first one (el.)
Elicit	-R- 4 P1	: Ghandi wants the British governor to leave his house .. False (rep.)
	-F- 5 T	: False [1+] (eva.)
Teacher	-I- 6 T	: Why? (el.)
Elicit	-R- 7 P1	: Because Ghandi wants the British governor to leave India (rep.)
	-F- 8 T	: To leave India (acc.). Yes (eva.)
Pupil Initiated Negotiate	-I- 9 P2	: -> Teacher (b.). It's true (cha.)
Pupil Initiated Negotiate	-I- 10 PP	: -> It's false (re.)
Direct	-I- 11 T	: Well (m.). Let him express himself (d.)
Teacher Initiated Negotiate	-I- 12 T	: -> Why is it true? (cla. req.)
	-R-13 P2	: Because to leave India. Because uh because uh

```
              -I- 14 T    : Yes? (p.)
              -R-15 P2    : Because Ghandi uh because Ghandi is under the
                            enemy occupation (rep.)
Teacher       -I- 16 T    : Under- ? (re. ini.)
Initiated     -R-17 P2    : The enemy occupation (rep.)
Negotiate     -F-18 T     : Yes [1-] (acc.)

Teacher       -I- 19 T    : -> But does he want him to leave his
Initiated                   HOUSE? (con. ch.)
Negotiate     -R-20 PP    : No (rep.)
              21 P3       : He wants to meet him in the court (rep.)
              -F-22 T     : mhm [1-] (acc.)
Teacher       -I- 23 T    : -> But-? (cl./p.)
Initiated     -R-24 P4    : Ghandi wants the British to leave India (rep.)
Negotiate     -F-25 T     : To leave India (acc.). Yes (eva.)

Pupil         -I- 26 P5   : -> It's true because house in this sentence has the
Initiated                   meaning of India because we have "it is time you reco-
Negotiate                   gnized you're masters in someone else's home" (cha.)
              -R-27 P2    : Yes (ack.)
              -F-28 T     : Well (m.). Listen it's not really
                                                    [
Pupil         -I- 29 P5   : ->                        it has another meaning (cha.)
Initiated     -F-30 T     : Yes [1-] (acc.).If you take it like this.
Negotiate                                           ⌈
                                                    ⌊
Pupil         -I- 31 P5   : ->                        Yes it's true (cha.)
Initiated     -F-32 T     : But it's not really true because what is meant here is
Negotiate                   not Ghandi's house but India. So it's the country of
                            India and not Ghandi's house. Home here has the
                            meaning of country (com.)
                            (2nd grade - Lesson 4)
```

    Takahashi & Beebe's (1987) study of refusals in ESL Japanese talk showed
that "higher proficient Japanese ESL speakers were more indirect in their
refusals than lower proficiency Japanese who tended more frequently to say
bluntly: "I can't." Similarly, in the present data, as the above Table reveals,
when pupils reach an advanced level in English, their 'challenge' of teacher
contributions, occasionally, appears less direct, that is 'modulated' in Schegloff
et al.'s (1977) sense. Consider extract (70) reproduced below:

Teacher	-I- 1 T	: <The teacher had asked pupils to find out whether two statements were true or false according to the text being studied and to justify their answers> (el.)
Elicit		
	-R- 2 P1	: Because the tricks were in no way remarkable (rep.)
Teacher	-I- 3 T	: -> So. Is it true? (con. ch.)
Initiated	-R- 4 P1	: It's false (rep.)
Negotiate	-F- 5 T	: It's false because the tricks were in no way remarkable (acc.). Yes [1+] (eva). They weren't attractive or interesting (com.).
Teacher	-I- 6 T	: The second one (el.)
Elicit		
Pupil	-I- 7 P2	: -> So why he had given him money? (cla.req./cha.)
Initiated	-R-	: <No response>
Negotiate	-F- 8 T	: Yes (acc.)
Teacher	-I- 9 T	: -> Why? (cla. req.) <addressed to the whole class>
Initiated		
Negotiate		
Pupil	-I-10 P2	:-> Why he had given the man some money? (cla.req/ cha.)
Initiated		
Negotiate	-F-11 T	: Yes (acc.)
Teacher	-I-12 T	: -> Why did he give the man some money? (cla.req.). That's a good question (com.)
Initiated		
Negotiate	-R-13 P3	: Because he is like a beggar (rep.)
	-F-14 T	: He is like a beggar (acc.). Yes [1+](eva.) (3rd grade - Lesson 2)

In the above extract, pupil 'challenge' or disagreement is expressed indirectly and with deference through the factual question "So why he had given him money?" (7 P2). Beebe & Takahashi (1989a, 1989b) studied disagreement as a 'face-threatening act' in Japanese ESL speakers speaking to American English speakers. They found that there is a preponderance of hinting behaviour, usually through factual questions, in data involving lower status Japanese people speaking to higher status American interlocutors. They write:

> In most, not all cases, it [factual question] has been a strategy that a
> lower status Japanese used in English to avoid telling something
> face-threatening to a higher status person. The seemingly factual

question is part of a hinting strategy designed to promote self
discovery by the higher status person, thereby letting the lower
status person off the hook for telling them something they don't
want to hear (Beebe & Takahashi 1989b: 104).

The extract below contains examples of both modulated and unmodulated
pupil 'challenge'. The extract occurred while the class was doing a vocabulary
multiple choice question exercise after reading a text.

(89)

Teacher	-I- 1 T	: Number 3: to become aware of? (el.)
Elicit	-R- 2 P1	: Noticed (rep.)
	-F- 3 T	: No (eva.)
Re-initiate	-R- 4 P2	: Crushed (rep.)
	-F- 5 T	: No (eva.)
Re-initiate	-R- 6 PP	: Tasted. Tasted (rep.)
	-F- 7 T	: Don't speak at the same time (com.)
Re-initiate	-I- 8 T	: Abdou (nom.)
	-R- 9 P3	: Tasted (rep.)
	-F-10 T	: No (eva.)
Re-initiate	-R-11 P4	: Crushed (rep.)
	-F-12 T	: No (eva.). Become aware of .. HEARD (re.)
Pupil Initiated Negotiate	-I- 13 P1	: -> Teacher please. 'become aware of' it means that uh <switching to French> *on a conscience .. avoir conscience de ..C'est pas entendre* <One is aware. To be aware of .. It's not to hear> (cha.)
	-F-14 T	: Well (m.). He heard. He heard (re.). He wasn't okay. He wasn't uh uh. He heard (re.)
Pupil Initiated Negotiate	-I- 15 P1	: -> It doesn't mean noticed? (cha./el.)
	-R-16 T	: It can- can- it can mean noticed in another context but here uh= (rep.)
		[
Pupil Initiated Negotiate	-I- 17 P1	: -> Here it means? <challenging tone> (cha./el.)
	-R-18 T	: =Here- Here- He was like sleeping and he heard (rep.) <T. reading>: "He became aware of the unpleasant feel and smell of his body" (s.). Well (m.). Became aware of .. NOTICED (rep.)

Pupil   -I- 19 PP : -> No. Heard. Heard. Heard (cha.)
Initiated
Negotiate

Teacher   -I- 20 T   : <T. reading>: "I became aware of the unpleasant feel
Initiated   and smell of my body" (s.)
Negotiate   [
            -R-21 P1 :   Noticed (ack.)
            -F-22 T   : Yes (acc.). Here it's noticed (com.)
              23 P1   : [Ha::] <raising her arms indicating victory>
              24 T   : It's noticed. Sorry in the text it is noticed.
                        So it's noticed not heard (com.)
                        (3rd grade - Lesson 5)

In the above extract, though 13 P1 and 19 PP are direct or 'on-record' challenges, 15 P1 and 17 P1 are, to echo Beebe & Takahashi (1989b), seemingly factual questions which might reveal that clarification is being directly requested, not disagreement being indirectly suggested. However, if we take into consideration the paralinguistic features (intonation and facial expressions) accompanying these two utterances (15 P1 and 17 P1), there is no doubt that they are indirect disagreements with the teacher's proposition and even challenges to the teacher's status as the knowledgeable participant with regard to aspects related to the target language. Another interesting conclusion to be made about the above extract is that the teacher's power is undoubtedly threatened to a certain extent. This is reflected in the way she has lost her casualness; she hesitates, repeats words, and makes a lot of false starts (see 14 T, 16 T, 18 T and 24 T).

As the above extracts illustrate, the device of asking seemingly factual questions to indirectly express disagreement with a previous teacher proposition is the main device by means of which pupil 'challenge' is modulated in the data. This provides further support for Beebe & Takahashi's (1989a, 1989b) findings concerning the use of factual questions as a means of mitigating disagreement, in order to reduce face-threat.

The aim of the present section has been to investigate how and to what extent pupil-initiated 'disjunctive negotiation' is modulated in the data as a whole and by proficiency level. The results show that asking seemingly factual questions is a device used by the pupils to modulate their challenges to teacher contributions. The results also reveal a significant preference for unmodulated over modulated challenges. This has been explained by the pupils' limited linguistic and pragmatic competence in the target language. In accordance with this interpretation, the data show that some modulation does occur in advanced classes.

Conclusion

This chapter has researched two issues. First, it has examined each negotiated exchange in the data, as to who initiates the negotiation (teacher or pupil) and what function the negotiation performs. The aim is to find out whether the teacher is the initiator par excellence of negotiated interaction in TL classroom discourse, whether and how this is affected by a change in the function of the negotiation, and whether and how this is affected by a change in the proficiency level of the class. Such investigations were carried out in the prospect that the results might illuminate the understanding of how power through discourse is negotiated in TL classroom interaction. Second, the chapter has focused on what we have labelled pupil-initiated 'disjunctive negotiation'. This face-threatening negotiation has been investigated in terms of its frequency in the data as a whole and by proficiency level, and in terms of whether and how its initiating move (usually carried out by the act 'challenge') is modulated, and whether and how this varies by proficiency level.

The results of the first investigation reveal that the seeming preference for teacher- over pupil-initiated negotiation in the data may simply be due to the high preference for teacher- over pupil-initiated negotiation in the second grade. Accordingly, it has been argued that teacher power seems to be most evident in the second grade. Actually, when the main categories of negotiated interaction, namely didactic and conversational negotiation, have been investigated, it has been found that the high preference for teacher- over pupil-initiated negotiation in the second grade tends to be significant with respect to didactic negotiation, but is highly significant with respect to conversational negotiation. On the other hand, on the basis of the relatively high frequency of pupil-initiated negotiation in the data, it has been argued that teacher power, in TL classroom discourse, is far from being absolute. The exercise of power through discourse, specifically with regard to resolving interactional problems, is rather a negotiated process between the teacher and pupils (see also Mehan 1974a and Allwright 1980).

The results of the second investigation reveal that pupil-initiated 'disjunctive negotiations' are very rare in the data. Nonetheless, their frequency significantly increases as one moves from beginning, to intermediate, to advanced classes. This has been interpreted in terms of pupils' greater confidence in their interlanguage which urges them to challenge rather than take for granted a teacher's proposition seeming to mismatch their schema. Furthermore, it has been argued that the mere occurrence of pupil 'challenge' in classroom discourse is suggestive with regard to the notion of unequal-power discourse. It reveals that teacher power is not absolute and that pupils do not consider the teacher as the unchallengeable participant in classroom interaction.

As to whether and how pupil 'challenge' is modulated, the results reveal that there is a significant preference for unmodulated over modulated challenges. This has been explained in terms of pupils' insufficient linguistic and pragmatic competence in the target language. Yet, the data show that pupils in advanced classes, contrary to beginning and intermediate classes, occasionally modulate their challenges by making them sound as factual questions, asking for factual information, rather than as direct disagreements with or blunt rejections of a teacher's previous contribution.

CHAPTER 8
Conclusion

This chapter summarizes the findings and draws some conclusions. Attention is also directed to the limitations of the study and to the implications of its findings for three fields of inquiry 1) TL teaching and teacher training, 2) TL classroom discourse analysis, and 3) sociolinguistics. Before closing this chapter, some suggestions for further research are made.

Summary of Findings

Before summarizing the findings, it is relevant to restate the research questions which the study aimed to answer. Our investigation of negotiated interaction in EFL classroom discourse, in Moroccan secondary schools, has been framed by the following questions:
1. What are the main discourse functions of 'negotiated interaction' in EFL classroom discourse, in Moroccan secondary schools?
2. How frequent is 'negotiated interaction' in EFL classroom discourse in Moroccan secondary schools, and does this frequency vary by proficiency level?
3. In what way could the initiation of 'negotiated interaction' be interpreted in view of the fact that the EFL classroom is a setting of unequal-power discourse?

To provide answers to these questions, qualitative and quantitative analyses of 'negotiated interaction' have been undertaken, with the three proficiency levels compared as to each investigation. The results are summarized below.

With regard to the first research question, the data reveal that a distinction can be made between two types of negotiation: *didactic* and *conversational*, the first being typical of TL classroom interaction while the second being common to all face-to-face interaction. Within 'didactic negotiation', a distinction has further been made between four negotiation genres, namely
- 'medium-oriented negotiation',

- 'comprehension check-oriented negotiation',
- 'turn-taking-oriented negotiation', and
- 'complete sentence-oriented negotiation'.

On the other hand, within 'conversational negotiation', a distinction has further been made between the following negotiation genres:
- 'hearing-oriented negotiation',
- 'meaning-oriented negotiation',
- 'content-oriented negotiation',
- 'general knowledge-oriented negotiation',
- 'agreement-oriented negotiation',
- 'surprise display-oriented negotiation', and
- 'conversational continuant'.

With regard to the second research question, a preference for negotiated over non-negotiated interaction and a preference for 'conversational' over 'didactic' negotiation has been recorded in the data. Furthermore, within the scope of 'didactic negotiation', a preference has been recorded for 'medium-oriented negotiation' over the other didactic negotiation genres. On the other hand, within the scope of 'conversational negotiation', a preference has been recorded for 'meaning-oriented negotiation', 'content-oriented negotiation' and 'conversational continuant'.

As to the effect of the proficiency level on the preference organization of 'negotiated interaction', it has been found that the extent of preference for 'negotiated' over 'non-negotiated' interaction does not significantly vary by proficiency level. When the frequencies of 'didactic' and 'conversational' negotiation have been compared by proficiency level, a significantly higher preference for 'conversational' negotiation has been witnessed in intermediate and advanced than in beginning classes. When the frequencies of didactic negotiation genres have been compared by grade, a significantly higher preference for 'medium-oriented negotiation' has been recorded in beginning and intermediate classes. On the other hand, the preference organization of conversational negotiation genres proved to be unaffected by the proficiency level factor. The frequency distribution of all the discourse functions of negotiated interaction, in the data as a whole and by proficiency level, is summarized in Table 19:

As Table 19 reveals, the most outstanding discourse functions of negotiated interaction are 'medium-', 'meaning-', 'content'-oriented negotiation, and 'conversational continuant'. Yet, 'medium-oriented negotiation' has significantly the highest frequency (F= 27.302 , df= 10, p= .000) in the data. This seems warranted in TL classrooms where the most problematic aspect of the interaction is the form of the language of communication.

Table 19: Summary statistics for the overall discourse functions of negotiated interaction by grade

		NEGOTIATED INTERACTION											
		DIDACTIC NEGOTIATION				CONVERSATIONAL NEGOTIATION							Totals
Grades		MON	CCON	CSON	TTON	HON	MEON	CON	GKON	AON	SDON	CC	
1st G.	n	301	08	26	40	11	118	138	09	03	04	159	817
	%	36.84	00.98	03.18	04.90	01.35	14.44	16.89	01.10	00.37	00.49	19.46	100
	X	60.20	01.60	05.20	08	02.20	23.60	27.60	01.80	00.60	00.80	31.80	163.40
2nd G.	n	304	07	56	12	36	208	246	02	39	15	141	1066
	%	28.52	00.65	05.25	01.12	03.38	19.51	23.08	00.19	03.66	01.41	13.23	100
	X	60.80	01.40	11.20	02.40	07.20	41.60	49.20	00.40	07.80	03	28.20	213.20
3rd G.	n	130	17	11	20	19	158	81	11	15	01	177	640
	%	20.31	02.66	01.72	03.12	02.97	24.69	12.65	01.72	02.34	00.16	27.66	100
	X	26	03.40	02.20	04	03.80	31.60	16.20	02.20	03	00.20	35.40	128
Totals	n	735	32	93	72	66	484	465	22	57	20	477	2523
	%	29.13	01.27	03.69	02.85	02.62	19.18	18.43	00.87	02.26	00.79	18.91	100
	X	49	02.13	06.20	04.80	04.40	32.27	31	01.47	03.80	01.33	31.80	168.20

MON   : 'medium-oriented negotiation'
CCON : 'comprehension check-oriented negotiation'
CSON : 'complete sentence-oriented negotiation'
TTON : 'turn-taking-oriented negotiation'

HON   : 'hearing-oriented negotiation'
MEON : 'meaning-oriented negotiation'
CON   : 'content-oriented negotiation'
GNON : 'general knowledge-oriented negotiation'
AON   : 'agreement-oriented negotiation'
SDON : 'surprise display-oriented negotiation'
CC   : 'conversational continuant'

n : sample size
% : row percentage
X : observed mean

With regard to the third research question, it has been argued that the initiation of 'negotiated interaction' might reveal a way of exercising power and dominance through discourse in the TL classroom. Therefore, teacher- and pupil-initiated negotiations have been computed in the data as a whole and by proficiency level. Furthermore, to find out whether there is any relationship between the function and the initiator of the negotiation, each teacher- and pupil-initiated negotiation has been marked in terms of its discourse function. The results reveal that the recorded preference for teacher- over pupil-initiated negotiation may simply be due to the high preference for teacher- over pupil-initiated negotiation in the second grade. Indeed, the results concerning 'didactic negotiation' suggest that there is a preference for teacher- over pupil-initiated negotiation in the data as a whole while those concerning 'conversational negotiation' suggest that the recorded preference may simply be due to the high preference for teacher- over pupil-initiated negotiation in the second grade.

The results concerning the relationship between the function and the initiator of the negotiation reveal that within the scope of 'didactic negotiation', the negotiation genres 'comprehension check-', 'complete sentence-', and 'turn-taking-' oriented negotiation are never initiated by the pupil, and hence may be considered typical teacher-initiated negotiations. 'Medium-oriented negotiation' is, occasionally, initiated by the pupil, but teacher-initiation is significantly preferred; the results further show that this preference is highest in the second grade and lowest in the third grade. Within the scope of 'conversational negotiation', the results reveal that teacher-initiation is preferred to pupil-initiation of the negotiation genres 'hearing-', meaning-', 'content-', and 'surprise display-' oriented negotiation and that this preference is highest in the second grade. On the other hand, the results related to 'general knowledge-' and 'agreement-' oriented negotiation show that there is no significant difference between the frequency of teacher- and pupil-initiation in the data as a whole and across the three proficiency levels. Interestingly, pupil-initiated 'conversational continuant' has been found to be preferred to teacher-initiated 'conversational continuant', with no significant variance across the three proficiency levels.

Given that the third research question is concerned with the exercise of power and dominance through discourse in the TL classroom, the study has been interested in further focusing on the negotiations initiated by the 'powerless' participant in classroom discourse. Hence, 'pupil-initiated negotiations' have been examined to pinpoint what we have labelled 'disjunctive negotiation' which aims to reject or contest (i.e., 'challenge') a previous teacher contribution. The results of this investigation have shown that pupil-initiated 'disjunctive negotiations' are very rare in the data, but their frequency significantly increases in intermediate and advanced classes. We were also interested in finding out whether and how these pupil-initiated 'disjunctive negotiations' are modulated, i.e., mitigated in terms of 'face-threat', in the data as a whole, and how this varies by proficiency level. The data give evidence of a preference for unmodulated over modulated negotiation. Furthermore, no modulation ever occurs in the 'disjunctive negotiations' initiated by beginning and intermediate pupils; but it, occasionally, does occur in those initiated by advanced pupils. When modulation occurs, it is carried out via the strategy of making 'challenges' sound as factual questions.

While presenting the above findings, we attempted to, simultaneously, draw some conclusions with regard to four main concerns 1) the functional structure of TL classroom discourse, 2) the kind of TL classroom interactions that are most favourable for TL development 3) the effect that the proficiency level can have on the interactive behaviour of TL classroom participants, and 4) the implications that negotiated interaction may have for the claim that the classroom is a setting of unequal-power discourse. These conclusions are summarized in the section below.

Conclusions

The conclusions drawn from the above findings are summarized in the following points:

1. By virtue of the predominance of negotiated over non-negotiated interaction in the data, it may be argued that the functional structure of a teaching exchange in TL classroom discourse is far more complex than the basic structure IRF elaborated by several scholars (Sinclair & Coulthard 1975, Mishler 1972, Mehan 1979, 1985) for analyzing classroom interaction. Negotiated interaction in the data reveals either of the following structures:

- $I [R (F)]^n (I) (R) (F)$
- $I R [I R (F)]^n (F)$
- $I R F [R (F)]^n$
- $I R F [I (R) (F)]^n$

2. On the basis of discussions in Schachter (1984, 1986), Swain (1985), Van Lier (1988), Stevick (1976, 1980), Krashen (1982a), Rulon & McCreary (1986), Bremer et al. (1988), and Gaies (1983b) concerning the importance, for target language development, of such variables as 'negative input', 'comprehensible input', 'comprehensible output', 'repair', 'involvement', 'learner intake-control', and 'lowering the affective filter', it has been argued that almost all the negotiation genres witnessed in the data have the effect of prompting TL acquisition, since they constitute the type of interaction most favourable for TL development. As a whole, they function to render teacher

input and pupil output more comprehensible, pupil output more accurate, intake more pupil-controlled, the content being studied more comprehensible, and the interaction more spontaneous and communicative. Yet, the effect of 'turn-taking'- and 'complete sentence'-oriented negotiation on the promotion of acquisition is doubtful, since these two didactic negotiation genres are mainly oriented towards regulating pupil participation rather than resolving problems of the talk or sustaining the conversation.

3. In accordance with "the theory that more negotiated interaction would enhance L2 acquisition" (Chaudron 1988: 130), the predominance of negotiated interaction in the data suggests that teacher-fronted classrooms are not unfavourable environments for pupil interlanguage development towards target language norms.

4. The preference for 'conversational' over 'didactic' negotiation in the data implies that the negotiations occurring in teacher-fronted EFL classroom interaction, in Moroccan secondary schools, are more oriented towards resolving those interactional problems that are common to any face-to-face interaction. These negotiations are more directed towards promoting pupils' *use* but do not neglect *usage* (Widdowson 1972, 1978). This suggests that EFL teaching in Moroccan secondary schools tends to be communicative in orientation.

Yet, since the present data proved to be an instance of one-way flow of information, the preference for 'conversational' over 'didactic' negotiation suggests that the one-way flow of information does not hamper the occurrence of 'conversational negotiation' which is, in many ways, comparable to what Long (1983c) and Pica (1987), among others, refer to as the negotiation of meaning. Such a conclusion is out of tune with Long (1983c) and Pica's (1987) claim that the one-way flow of information is a hindrance to the negotiation of meaning to occur. Nonetheless, on the basis of the moderate positive correlation recorded between the frequencies of conversational negotiation and replies to referential elicitations, we argue that increasing information flow from pupil to teacher might bring about more conversational negotiation.

As to the effect of the proficiency level factor, the finding that there is a higher preference for 'conversational' over 'didactic' negotiation in intermediate and advanced classes suggests that in these classes more emphasis is put on meaningful interaction than on error treatment. On the other hand, the tendency for 'didactic negotiation' to have the least frequency in advanced classes may be explained in two ways: either pupils in these classes produce less errors of form, or classroom participants perceive these errors as no more than 'performance mistakes', and hence not worthy of repair. On the basis of suggestions in Swain (1985), Vigil & Oller (1976), Corder (1971) and Krashen (1985) concerning *fossilization*, it has been argued that the decreasing frequency of 'medium-oriented negotiation', in advanced classes, might imply the potential of 'fossilization' in these classes (cf. Chapter 6 for discussion).

5. The high preference for teacher- over pupil-initiated negotiation in the second grade implies that teachers exert the highest 'control' over classroom talk in this grade. This has been explained by teachers' possible conception that such control of intermediate pupils' contributions is more beneficial for interlanguage development in intermediate classes than in beginning or advanced classes.

The significant finding that the frequency of pupil-initiated negotiation does not vary by proficiency level reveals that pupils in the three grades seem to take the same amount of initiative to repair 'troubles' of the form of the target language, to resolve interactional problems and to sustain the conversation. That is to manage learning and negotiate power in classroom interaction.

The percentage of pupil-initiated negotiation (26.87%), in the data, though low in comparison to teacher-initiated negotiation has been claimed to be important since it reveals that the exercise of power through discourse is a negotiated process between the teacher and pupils, that teacher power is not absolute, and that teacher 'control' is not as powerful as to hinder pupil-initiated negotiation. Pupil-initiated negotiation shows that pupils are not unhealthily impressed by the 'authoritative figure' of the teacher (Long et al. 1976) and the 'audience effect' (Barnes 1973) of teacher-fronted classrooms.

Furthermore, pupil-initiated negotiation reveals what pupils are doing to manage classroom interaction and thereby their own and peers' interlanguage development. The relatively high frequency of pupil-initiated negotiation both within the scope of 'didactic' and 'conversational' negotiation reveals that teaching and learning in the context investigated has nothing to do with the "traditional view of teaching and learning which conceptualizes classroom instruction as the conveyance of information from the knowledgeable teacher to the «empty» and passive learner" (Chaudron 1988: 10). However, the high percentage of pupil-initiated 'conversational negotiation' (35.26%) in comparison with pupil-initiated 'didactic negotiation' (12.55%) implies that pupils take more 'initiative' when problems of the talk are involved than when problems of the forms of the target language are involved.

Concerning the relationship between the function and the initiator of the negotiation, the finding that three types of 'didactic negotiation' are never initiated by the pupil, namely 'comprehension check-oriented negotiation', 'complete sentence-oriented negotiation' and 'turn-taking-oriented negotiation', suggests that there are some classroom cultural rules at work which pupils seem to have internalized and comply with. On the other hand, the preference for teacher- over pupil-initiated negotiation with regard to 'medium-', 'hearing-', 'meaning-', 'content-' and 'surprise display-'oriented negotiation implies that the responsibility for the resolution of interactional problems related to such aspects of the talk lies with the teacher. This highlights the nature of negotiation work (see also Scarcella & Higa 1981) in TL classrooms, and, hence, further supports the idea that the TL classroom is a context of unequal-power discourse. However, the non-preference for teacher- over pupil-initiated negotiation with regard to 'general knowledge-' and agreement-'oriented negotiation, together with the preference for pupil 'conversational continuant' imply that when the negotiation is not directly concerned with the comprehension or the production of the target language, the teacher is not the typical initiator of the negotiation. In other words, teacher 'control' seems to decrease when the speech event is not directly concerned with target language comprehension or production.

Additionally, the preference for pupil 'conversational continuant' over teacher 'conversational continuant' suggests that pupils exercise considerable control over the interaction, the kind of control Gaies (1983b) labels 'learner intake-control'. Further, since pupil 'conversational continuant' implies pupil 'initiative' (Stevick 1976, 1980) and is an indicator of pupil 'involvement' (Stevick 1976, 1980), its high frequency in the data suggests that pupils in TL classrooms contribute to the management of their own and peers' learning.

6. The finding that pupil-initiated 'disjunctive negotiation' is very rare, in the data, seems to provide further support for the claim that the classroom is a setting of 'unequal-power discourse' (Hatch & Long 1980). Nevertheless, the mere occurrence of pupil-initiated 'disjunctive negotiation' implies that pupils do not view the teacher as the 'unchallengeable' participant in classroom discourse. On the other hand, the finding that this type of pupil-initiated negotiation seems to increase in more proficient classes indicates that the more proficient pupils are, the more daring they become to challenge teacher contributions, in other words to initiate 'disjunctive negotiation'. The initiation of such negotiation implies pupil 'initiative' and suggests that the initiator of the negotiation is far from being impressed by the 'authoritative figure' of the teacher or the 'audience effect' of the teacher-fronted classroom, since s/he ventures to perform such a face-threatening act as pupil 'challenge' of teacher contribution.

7. The finding that there is a preference for unmodulated over modulated pupil-initiated 'disjunctive negotiation'and that there is no instance of 'modulation' (Schegloff et al. 1977, Gaskill 1980) in both beginning and intermediate classes may reveal pupils' 'pragmatic failure' (Thomas 1983). Such 'pragmatic failure' is unquestionably due to pupils limited linguistic and pragmatic proficiency in the target language, or in Beebe & Takahashi's (1989b: 119) words, "due to lack of native speaker competence in the social rules of speaking."

Limitations

No matter how acceptable the above conclusions might sound, they should not be taken at face value. Rather, the results should be interpreted with caution and with the following limitations in mind:

1. The fundamental limitation stems from the fact that the data have been collected by audio- rather than video-recording. Hence, in the analysis of the data, we have had no access to non-verbal cues accompanying participants' contributions nor to the non-verbal interaction which might occur independently from the verbal interaction. As in any face-to-face interaction, a considerable part of TL classroom interaction, is performed non-verbally (silence, grunts, gestures, facial expressions such as nods, shaking head, frowns, grimaces, etc.). Saville-Troike (1987: 105) stresses

> the extent to which adequate description and interpretation of the process of communication and its development require attention to the meaning and functions of extralinguistic aspects, perhaps as much as to verbal codes [...]. These aspects are not mere accompaniments of spoken language, but their communicative import may indeed outweigh the referential meaning conveyed by the linguistic code if conflicting signals are involved. To ignore them in the study of communicative interaction, then, is to risk limiting our understanding of the processes involved in the achievement of successful communication - even with a common linguistic code.

Since the data have been collected by audio- rather than video-recording, we have failed to account for "the meaning and functions of extralinguistic aspects" (Saville-Troike 1987: 105) involved in negotiated interaction. This might have had the effect of limiting our "understanding of the process involved [in negotiated interaction and] in the achievement of successful communication" (Saville-Troike 1987: 105) in the context investigated.

Stressing the importance of video-recording in the study of face-to-face interaction, Van Lier (1988: 238) argues that "[v]ideo recording is preferable, since non-verbal behaviour is important for analysis. Of course, the purpose of the analysis will determine how important visual information is; at the very least it is extremely helpful, at times it may be indispensable." Nevertheless, due to the practical problems involved in video-recording, and to its clear effect on increasing the 'observer's paradox' (Labov 1972), we contented ourselves with audio-recording. Yet, to make up for this limitation, we were all the time present while the data were being collected, observing how EFL classroom lessons are being accomplished, and taking as many field notes as possible, including relevant non-verbal behaviour which might help in the analysis of the recorded talk. As a matter of fact, most of these field notes have been of great use in understanding what was going on, especially when verbal behaviours seemed insufficient to capture certain aspects of negotiated interaction.

2. Another important limitation is related to the design of the study. Our findings concerning negotiated interaction across the three proficiency levels are the result of an 'apparent-' rather than a 'real-' time study. A real-time study would require a design comparing the lessons of the same teachers and the same pupils across the three proficiency levels. However, it is very difficult, if not impossible, to put such a design into practice since teachers never keep the same pupils for three years, as some pupils fail, others succeed, and teachers are usually assigned different classes from those they had the previous year. In view of these considerations, an apparent-time study has been undertaken, assuming that this might shed light on how negotiated interaction is accomplished and how this develops from beginning, to intermediate, to advanced classes. Extraneous variables that might affect the results of such an apparent-time study have been controlled. Thus, in each grade, different teachers, different classes from different schools, and female and male teachers and pupils were involved. Moreover, the same teacher-fronted activity (teaching of a text) was carried out (with more or less the same procedure) in all the fifteen lessons constituting the data. Hence, it is sound to argue that our results and conclusions reflect, to a large extent, what is really going on in TL classroom discourse.

3. Another limitation stems from the fact that we did not account for an important issue, namely whether the tendency of the frequency of 'medium-oriented negotiation' to be lower with advanced than with beginning or intermediate classes is due to the occurrence of fewer errors in terms of the form of the target language. Accounting for this question would have given more insight into how 'medium-oriented negotiation' works by proficiency level. It would have enabled us to draw more valid conclusions concerning the possibility of 'fossilization' which we have hypothesized to represent a potential threat for advanced classes. However, because the study has not been designed, from the outset, to account for this question, undertaking such a task implied recoding all the data with regard to whether pupils' contributions contain a 'trouble source' in terms of form, whether the 'trouble source' is ignored or followed by a 'medium-oriented negotiation', whether this negotiation is teacher- or pupil-initiated, and how these issues vary by proficiency level. Undertaking such a

task seemed to imply indulging in a study that can stand by itself; therefore, we suggest this relevant issue for further research.

4. Another important limitation is that we did not go beyond talk to consult ethnographic knowledge. We could have invited the teacher and the pupil(s) involved in a particular negotiated interaction to comment together or independently upon the recorded material. These comments would certainly have constituted an important source of information which would have given much insight into the data. Though we were aware of the importance of such extra information, the practical difficulties involved in this task made us refrain from undertaking such an endeavour. The main difficulty stems from the fact that teachers and pupils are never free during school hours; and it is not easy to get hold of them out of school hours.

Implications for Applied Linguistics and Sociolinguistics

Implications for TL Teaching and Teacher Training

"'[I]mplications' are often expressed in the form of injunctions, appeals to teachers to do something different" (Allwright 1984a: 166). Before moving to such injunctions, this section starts by pointing to an implication of the findings for target language pedagogy *as things are* in EFL classrooms, in Moroccan secondary schools.

Negotiated interaction involves learners in the management of their own learning; it "is a way for them to get better instruction, to get instruction that is more finely tuned (Krashen's phrase, 1981) than it would otherwise be, better adapted to each learner's personal learning needs" (Allwright 1984a: 166). Hence, the finding that negotiated interaction is significantly preferred to non-negotiated interaction supports Allwright's (1984a: 167) claim that "even as things are, learners are potentially getting instruction that is better adjusted and more personal than we might expect, and certainly than we tend actually to plan for as teachers."

To make TL classroom interaction more profitable for learners, some implications of the findings for TL teaching and teacher training are pointed out. By virtue of highlighting the importance of negotiated interaction in the process of TL acquisition, the study has three major implications.

The first implication is that instructing the TL teacher to engage pupils in more negotiated interaction and encourage them to initiate it themselves is highly beneficial for pupils' interlanguage development towards target language norms. Such an implication is based on "the theory that more negotiated interaction would enhance L2 acquisition" (Chaudron 1988: 130). This necessarily implies instructing the TL teacher to create a positive affective environment where pupil initiation of not only 'conjunctive' but also 'disjunctive' negotiation is possible and even appreciated by the teacher.

This pedagogical implication might have consequences not only for the methodology adopted by the TL teacher but also for the syllabus to be taught. For instance, it is beneficial for pupils to be taught those skills enabling them to handle or initiate negotiated interaction themselves (e.g., TL learner communication strategies like 'appeals for assistance', TL learner devices for intake-control (cf. Gaies 1983b), and other interactional negotiation devices). As Allwright (1984a: 168) puts it, "[m]ost learners will probably need training in how to be efficient and effective managers of their own learning." In view of this prospect, the TL teacher might be invited

> to take a cassette machine into the classroom and then study the recording of a lesson or two, [...]. If, for example, the recording suggested that the learners were not as good as they could be at asking for the sorts of help they need, then the teacher could spend a little time, perhaps just a few minutes each lesson for a while, teaching these particular questioning skills, and discussing how they might be used both inside and outside the classroom. Such a modest start could go quite a long way towards helping both teachers and learners develop more awareness of the potential benefits of looking at teaching and learning as the cooperative management of learning (Allwright 1984a: 169).

The second implication for TL teaching and teacher training stems from the finding that there is a significant positive correlation between the frequency of 'referential elicitations' and that of 'conversational negotiation'. Starting from the theory that 'conversational negotiation' promotes TL acquisition and makes classroom interaction more communicative, this finding implies that it is beneficial to train teachers to increase the two-way flow of information in TL classroom interaction by performing more 'referential elicitations'.

Implications for TL Classroom Discourse Analysis

The implications of the study for TL classroom discourse analysis may be captured in three points. Firstly, the study provides further support to the FLIAS system - Boulima's (1990) adapted version of Sinclair & Coulthard's (1975) descriptive system. The FLIAS system has proved to be adequate for structurally and functionally analyzing TL classroom discourse, including all the unpredictable and complicated interactive behaviours involved in negotiated interaction. Secondly, the distinction made between the discourse functions of negotiation genres may give TL classroom discourse analysts further insight into negotiated interaction which, as we have shown, constitutes a considerable part of TL classroom participants' interactive behaviours. Thirdly, the finding that teachers exert the most 'control' over pupils' contributions (by initiating the highest number of negotiated exchanges) in the second grade, provides further empirical support for the finding that teacher talk is adjusted to the proficiency level of the learners (cf. Gaies 1977b, Milk 1985, Schinke-Llano 1983), specifically from a discourse standpoint (Schinke-Llano 1983). Schinke-Llano's (1983) study, which investigated certain discourse characteristics of foreigner talk, namely frequency, type, and length of interaction provided evidence that limited English-proficient students are interacted with differently from non-limited English-proficient students.

Implications for Sociolinguistics

The asymmetrical nature of negotiation work in TL classroom discourse reflects the role and power relationships and the social organization in this context. As revealed by the results, the responsibility for resolving interactional problems mainly lies with the teacher. This certainly indicates teacher power and control in TL classroom discourse. However, as Wrong (1979) points out, the asymmetry of power should not be emphasized to the extent of precluding the possibility of mutual power relations. Power, as Watts (1991: 59) maintains, "is always negotiable and in a constant state of flux." Actually, no matter how asymmetrical power and role relations are, seldom is one so powerful that the other has no bargaining ability whatsoever (Janeway 1980a, 1980b). In the data, this bargaining ability is revealed in the considerable amount of pupil-initiated negotiation and in the preference for 'pupil conversational continuant' over 'teacher conversational continuant', but more importantly in the occurrence of pupil-initiated 'disjunctive negotiations'. These findings may have implications for sociolinguists interested in "discourse where the social structure is one of wide power mismatch for the participants" (Hatch & Long 1980: 16).

Another implication for sociolinguistics lies in the potential information the study may contribute with regard to the discovery and understanding of the tacit interactional and cultural rules at work in the TL classroom. As Garnica (1981: 230) points out,

> [s]ince the rules that group members know and use to make sense of behaviors and situations are tacit and often quite subtle, the technique of studying violations of such rules can potentially contribute information as to the nature of these rules, information that may be difficult to ascertain through other means.

Accordingly, the technique of studying violations of some interactional rules (e.g., 'the turn-taking rule' and 'the complete sentence rule') that seem to be operating in TL classroom discourse, and the technique of studying the sanctions that are issued from the violation of such rules may potentially contribute information about the nature of these rules and about how powerful they are. The finding that 'the turn-taking rule' and 'the complete sentence rule' are complex interactional rules, involving many variables in their operation, reveals that further research is needed to capture the understanding of these rules. On the other hand, the finding that 'comprehension check-', 'complete sentence-', and 'turn-taking-'oriented negotiation are never initiated by the pupil contributes to further the understanding of the mechanisms of certain classroom tacit cultural rules. These rules seem to prescribe that it is improper for the pupil to initiate these negotiations because they are part of the teaching profession.

Suggestions for Further Research

During the interpretation of the findings, we were confronted with relevant issues the study was not designed to systematically investigate. Therefore, these issues are suggested as questions future research might investigate.

Given that the study was not designed to further investigate the hypothesis that advanced EFL learners, in Moroccan secondary schools, are subject to 'fossilization' (a hypothesis made on account of the least frequency of 'medium-oriented negotiation' in advanced classes), the following research question is suggested: (1) Is the decreasing frequency of 'medium-oriented negotiation' in advanced classes due to a decreasing frequency of errors of form or to some other factors?

McHoul's (1978: 188) study on turn-taking in classroom discourse reaches the conclusion that "only teachers can direct speakership in any creative way." Such a conclusion has been criticized by Van Lier (1988) who maintains that

> when a learner's turn is exclusively allocated by the teacher, next speaker will always automatically be prior speaker (i.e., the teacher), so that we can not speak of student-selects-teacher. However, if a student has self-selected, [...], it makes more sense to speak of student-selects-teacher, since the lockstep, as it were, is broken (Van Lier 1988: 137).

In accordance with Van Lier's (1988) argument, the occurrence of pupil-initiated negotiation, in TL classroom discourse, implies that turns are not always allocated by the teacher and that pupils, occasionally, self-select, and as a result may direct speakership in some creative way. On the basis of this consideration, future research may seek to empirically provide an answer to the subsequent question: (2) What effect does pupil-initiated negotiation have on the turn-taking system operating in TL classroom discourse?

Given that 32.63% of the overall violations of 'the complete sentence rule', in the data, has triggered 'complete sentence-oriented negotiation', it is enlightening to investigate whether such negotiation has any import for pupils' TL development. Thus, the following question may be worthy of empirical research: (3) Does 'complete sentence-oriented negotiation' have any positive implications for pupils' TL acquisition, or is it no more than a bad habit that teachers should give up?

There is much enthusiasm, especially in communicative language teaching, about group work activities in the TL classroom. Since our focus in the present study has been on teacher-fronted classrooms, the findings do not offer much insight, however, into how negotiation works in group work; therefore, this is another vital area of research. Researchers might seek to provide an answer to the question: (4) How does negotiated interaction function in group work organization in TL classrooms?

To conclude, it is worth pointing out that the present work has shed light only on certain aspects of negotiated interaction in the TL classroom - namely its discourse functions, frequency, and initiator - as well as on how these aspects relate to the unequal distribution of information and power between the teacher and pupils. Though the findings might indirectly contribute to the understanding of the process of interlanguage development, it appears sound to predict, however, that continued research on negotiated interaction, as a crucial component of TL classroom talk, will yield useful insights into the nature of the process of TL acquisition in the classroom context.

Bibliography

Abunahleh, L., Allen, S., Arthur, B., Beals, S., Butler, M., Drezner, B., Frydenberg,
    1982   G., Galal, M., Gass, S., Hildebrandt, K., Marlos, L., and Ostrander, T.
"The scope and function of language repair in foreigner discourse."
Interlanguage Studies Bulletin 7: 112-20.

Adger, C. T.
    1983   *Communicative Competence in the Culturally Diverse Classroom:
Negotiating Norms for Linguistic Interaction.* Unpublished PhD
dissertation. Georgetown University.

Allwright, R. L.
    1975   "Problems in the study of teachers' treatment of learner error." In
M. K. Burt and H. C. Dulay (eds), *On TESOL '75: New Directions
in Second Language Learning, Teaching and Bilingual Education.*
Washington, D.C.: TESOL.

Allwright, R. L.
    1980   "Turns, topics, and tasks: patterns of participation in language
learning and teaching." In D. Larsen-Freeman (ed), *Discourse
Analysis in Second Language Research.* Rowley, Mass. : Newbury
House.

Allwright, R. L.
    1981   "What do we want teaching materials for?" *ELT Journal* 36: 5-18.

Allwright, R. L.
    1983   "Classroom centered research on language teaching: a brief
historical overview." *TESOL Quarterly* 17: 191-204.

Allwright, R. L.
    1984a   "The importance of interaction in classroom language learning."
Applied Linguistics 5: 156-71.

Allwright, R. L.
    1984b   "Why don't learners learn what teachers teach? - The interaction
hypothesis." In D. M. Singleton and D. G. Little (eds), *Language
Learning in Formal and Informal Contexts.* Dublin: IRAAL.

Allwright, R. L.
　　1988　*Observation in the Language Classroom*. London: Longman
Allwright, R. L. and Bailey, K. M.
　　1991　*Focus on the Classroom: an Introduction to Classroom Research for Language Teachers*. Cambridge: Cambridge University Press.
Annett, J.
　　1969　*Feedback and Human Behavior*. Harmondsworth: Penguin.
Arthur, B., Weiner, R., Culver, M., Lee, Y.J. and Thomas, D.
　　1980　"The register of impersonal discourse to foreigners: verbal adjustments to foreign accent." In D. Larsen-Freeman (ed), *Discourse Analysis in Second Language Acquisition*. Rowley, Mass.: Newbury House.
Aston, G.
　　1986　"Trouble-shooting in interaction with learners: the more the merrier?" *Applied Linguistics* 7: 128-43.
Austin, J. L.
　　1962　*How to Do Things with Words*. Cambridge, Mass.: Harvard University Press.
Bailey, K. M.
　　1980　"An introspective analysis of an individual's language learning experience." In R. C. Scarcella and S. D. Krashen (eds), *Research in Second Language Acquisition*. Rowley, Mass.: Newbury House.
Bailey, K. M.
　　1983　"Competitiveness and anxiety in adult second language learning: looking *at* and *through* the diary studies." In H. W. Seliger and M. H. Long (eds), *Classroom Oriented Research in Second Language Acquisition*. Rowley, Mass.: Newbury House.
Bailey, K. M.
　　1985　"Classroom-centered research on language teaching and learning." In M. Celce-Murcia (ed), *Beyond Basics: Issues and Research in TESOL*. Rowley, Mass.: Newbury House.
Barnes, D.
　　1969　"Language in the secondary classroom." In D. Barnes, J. Britton, and H. Rosen (eds), *Language, the Learner, and the School*. Harmondsworth: Penguin.
Barnes, D.
　　1973　*Language in the Classroom*. London: Open University Press.
Beebe, L. M.
　　1980　"Measuring the use of communication strategies." In R. C. Scarcella and S. D. Krashen (eds), *Research in Second Language Acquisition*. Rowley, Mass.: Newbury House.

Beebe, L. M.
   1981   "Social and situational factors affecting communicative strategy of
           dialect code switching." *International Journal of the Sociology of
           Language* 32: 139-49.
Beebe, L. M. and Zuengler, J.
   1983   "Accommodation theory: an explanation for style shifting in
           second language dialects." In N. Wolfson and E. Judd (eds),
           Sociolinguistics and Language Acquisition. Rowley, Mass.:
           Newbury House.
Beebe, L. M. and Giles, H.
   1984   "Speech-accommodation theories: a discussion in terms of second-
           language acquisition." *International Journal of the Sociology of
           Language* 46: 5-32.
Beebe, L. M. and Takahashi, T.
   1989a   "Sociolinguistic variation in face-threatening speech acts:
           chastisement and disagreement." In M. R. Eisenstein, (ed), *The
           Dynamic Interlanguage: Empirical Studies in Second Language
           Variation*. New York, London: Plenum Press.
Beebe, L. M. and Takahashi, T.
   1989b   ""Do you have a bag?" Social status and patterned variation in
           second language acquisition." In S. Gass, C. Madden, D. Preston
           and L. Selinker (eds). *Variation in Second Language Acquisition*.
           Volume 1: *Discourse and Pragmatics*. Clevedon, Philadelphia:
           Multilingual Matters.
Bellack, A. A., Kliebard, R., Hyman, R., and Smith, F.
   1966   *The Language of the Classroom*. New York: Teachers' College
           Press.
Berko Gleason, J.
   1977   "Talking to children: some notes on feedback." In C. E. Snow and
           C. A. Ferguson (eds), *Talking to Children: Language Input and
           Acquisition*. Cambridge: Cambridge University Press.
Berry, M.
   1981   "Systemic linguistics and discourse analysis: a multi-layered
           approach to exchange structure." In M. Coulthard and M.
           Montgomery (eds), *Studies in Discourse Analysis*. London:
           Routledge and Kegan Paul.
Bialystok, E.
   1978   "A theoretical model of second language learning." *Language
           Learning* 28: 69-83.

Bialystok, E.
    1990   *Communication Strategies in Second Language Acquisition: a Psychological Analysis of Second-Language Use.* Oxford: Basil Blackwell.
Bialystok, E. and Fröhlich, M.
    1980   "Oral Communication Strategies for lexical difficulties." *Interlanguage Studies Bulletin* 5: 3-30.
Bilmes, J.
    1992   "Mishearings." In G. Watson and R. M. Seiler (eds), *Text in Context: Contributions to Ethnomethodology.* Beverly Hills, London, New Delhi: Sage Publications.
Bloomfield, L.
    1933   *Language.* New York: Holt, Rinehart and Winston.
Boulima, J
    1990   *Feedback In EFL Classroom Discourse in Moroccan Secondary Schools: a Developmental Study.* Unpublished D.E.S. thesis. Mohammed V University, Faculty of Letters, Rabat, Morocco.
Bouzzroud, A.
    1989   *An Analysis of Repair in Classroom Discourse.* Unpublished D.E.S. thesis. Mohammed V University, Faculty of Letters, Rabat, Morocco.
Breen, M. P.
    1985   "The social context for language learning - a neglected situation?" *Studies in Second Language Acquisition* 7: 135-58.
Breen, M. P. and Candlin, C. N.
    1980   "The essentials of a communicative curriculum." *Applied Linguistics* 1: 89-112.
Bremer, K., Broeder, P., Roberts, C., Simonot, M. and Vasseur, M. T.
    1988   *Ways of Achieving Understanding: Communicating to Learn in a Second Language.* Final Report, Volume I, ESF project, Strassbourg, London.
Brock, C.
    1986   "The effect of referential questions on ESL classroom discourse." *TESOL Quarterly* 20: 47-59.
Brock, C., Crookes, G., Day, R. R., and Long M. H.
    1986   "The differential effects of corrective feedback in native speaker/ non-native speaker conversation." In R. R. Day (ed), *Talking to learn: Conversation in Second Language Acquisition.* Rowley, Mass.: Newbury House.
Broeder, P.
    1991   *Talking about People: a Multiple Case Study on Adult Language Acquisition.* Amsterdam: Swets and Zeitlinger.

Broeder, P.
1993 "Learning to understand in interethnic communication." *Issues in Applied Linguistics* 4: 57-89.
Brown, B. R.
1977 "Face-saving and face-restoration in negotiation." In D. Druckman (ed), *Negotiations: Social Psychological Perspectives.* Beverly Hills, London, New Delhi: Sage Publications.
Brown, G. and Yule, G.
1983 *Discourse Analysis.* Cambridge: Cambridge University Press.
Brown, H. D.
1987 *Principles of Language Learning and Teaching* (second edition). Englewood Cliffs, NJ: Prentice-Hall, Inc.
Brown, J. D.
1988 *Understanding Research in Second Language Learning: a Teacher's Guide to Statistics and Research Design.*
Brown, J. D.
1992 "Statistics as a foreign language - Part 2: More things to consider in reading statistical language studies." *TESOL Quarterly* 26: 629-64.
Brown, P. and Levinson, S. C.
1978 "Universals in language usage: politeness phenomena." In E. Goody (ed), *Questions and Politeness: Strategies in Social Interaction.* Cambridge: Cambridge University Press.
Brown, R. and Hanlon, C.
1970 "Derivational complexity and order of acquisition in child speech." In J. R. Hayes (ed), *Cognition and the Development of Language.* New York: John Wiley and Sons, Inc.
Brumfit, C. J.
1981 Review of G. Moskowitz: Caring and Sharing in the Foreign Language Class. *ELT Journal* 36: 63-4.
Brumfit, C. J.
1984 *Communicative Methodology in Language Teaching: the Roles of Fluency and Accuracy.* Cambridge: Cambridge University Press.
Brumfit, C. J. and Johnson, K.
1979 *The Communicative Approach to Language Teaching.* Oxford: Oxford University Press.
Brumfit, C. J. and Mitchel, R. (eds)
1990 *Research in the Language Classroom* (ELT Documents 133). Modern English Publications in association with the British Council.
Bruton, A. and Samuda, V.
1980 "Learner and teacher roles in the treatment of oral error in group work." *RELC Journal* 11: 49-63.

Burton, D.
    1981   "Analyzing spoken discourse." In M. Coulthard and M. Montgomery (eds), *Studies in Discourse Analysis*. London: Routledge and Kegan Paul.

Canale, M.
    1983   "From communicative competence to communicative language pedagogy." In J. C. Richards and R. Schmidt (eds), *Language and Communication*. London, New York: Longman.

Canale, M. and Swain, M.
    1980a *Approaches to Communicative Competence*. Singapore: SEAMEO Regional Language Center.

Canale, M. and Swain, M.
    1980b "Theoretical bases of communicative approaches to second language teaching and testing." *Applied Linguistics* 1: 1-47.

Carpenter, C.
    1983   "Foreigner talk in university office-hour appointments." In N. Wolfson and E. Judd, (eds), *Sociolinguistics and Language Acquisition*. Rowley, Mass.: Newbury House.

Carrol, S., Swain, M. and Roberge, Y.
    1992   "The role of feedback in adult second language acquisition: error correction and morphological generalizations." *Applied Psycholinguistics* 13: 173-98.

Cathcart, R. L. and Olsen J. E. W. B.
    1976   "Teachers' and students' preferences for correction of classroom conversation errors." In J. F. Fanselow and R. H. Crymes (eds), *On TESOL '76*. Washington, D. C.: TESOL.

Cazden, C. B.
    1985   "Classroom discourse." In M. C. Wittrock (ed), *Handbook of Research on Teaching*. New York: Macmillan.

Cervantes, R.
    1983   "Say it again Sam: the effect of exact repetition on listening comprehension." ESL 670 term paper, University of Hawaii at Manoa, Honolulu. (mimeo)

Chaudron, C.
    1977   "A descriptive model of discourse in the corrective treatment of learners' errors." *Language learning* 27: 29-46.

Chaudron, C.
    1983   "Foreigner talk in the Classroom - An aid to learning?" In H. W. Seliger and M. H. Long (eds), *Classroom Oriented Research*. Rowley, Mass.: Newbury House.

Chaudron, C.
1985 "Intake: on models and methods for discovering learners' processing of input." *Studies in Second Language Acquisition* 7: 1-14.

Chaudron, C.
1988 *Second Language Classrooms: Research on Teaching and Learning.* Cambridge: Cambridge University Press.

Chesterfield, R., Chesterfield, K. B., Hayes-Latimer, K., and Chávez, R.
1983 "The influence of teachers and peers on second language acquisition in bilingual preschool programs." *TESOL Quarterly* 17: 401-19.

Chun, A. E., Day, R. R., Chenoweth, N. A., and Lupperscu, S.
1982 "Errors, interaction, and correction: a study of native-nonnative conversations." *TESOL Quarterly* 16: 537-47.

Cohen, L. and Manion, L.
1989 *Research Methods in Education* (third edition). London: Routledge.

Cook, V. (ed)
1986 *Experimental Approaches to Second Language Learning.* Oxford: Pergamon.

Cook, G.
1989 *Discourse.* Oxford: Oxford University Press.

Cook, V.
1991 *Second Language Learning and Language Teaching.* London: Edward Arnold.

Corder, S. P.
1967 "The significance of learners' errors." *International Review of Applied Linguistics* 5: 161-70.

Corder, S. P.
1971 "Idiosyncratic dialects and error analysis." *International Review of Applied Linguistics* 9: 147-59.

Corder, S. P.
1977 "Simple codes and the source of the second language learner's initial heuristic hypothesis." *Studies in Second Language Acquisition* 1: 1-10.

Corder, S. P.
1978 "Language learner language." In J. C. Richards (ed), *Understanding Second and foreign Language Learning.* Rowley, Mass.: Newbury House.

Corsaro, W.
1977 "The clarification request as a feature of adult interactive styles with young children." *Language in Society* 6: 183-207.

Corsaro, W.
    1981   "Communication processes in studies of social organization: sociological approaches to discourse analysis." *Text* 1: 5-63.

Coulthard, M.
    1977   *An Introduction to Discourse Analysis.* London: Longman.

Coulthard, M. and Montgomery, M. (eds)
    1981   *Studies in Discourse Analysis.* London: Routledge and Kegan Paul.

Coulthard, M. and Brazil, D.
    1981   "Exchange structure." In M. Coulthard and M. Montgomery (eds), *Studies in Discourse Analysis.* London: Routledge and Kegan Paul.

Coupland, N., Giles, H., Wiemann, J. (eds)
    1991   *"Miscommunication" and Problematic Talk.* Beverly Hills, London, New Delhi: Sage Publications.

Crombie, W.
    1985   *Process and Relation in Discourse and Language Learning.* Oxford: Oxford University Press.

Crookes, G. and Rulon, K. A.
    1985   "Incorporation of corrective feedback in native speaker/non-native speaker conversation." *Technical Report,* N° 3. Honolulu: Center for Second Language Classroom Research, Social Science Research Institute, University of Hawaii at Manoa.

Cross, T.
    1977   "Mothers' speech adjustments: the contribution of selected child listener variables." In C. E. Snow and C. A. Ferguson (eds), *Talking to Children: Language Input and Acquisition.* Cambridge: Cambridge University Press.

Cuff, E. C. and Payne, G. C. F.
    1979   *Perspectives in Sociology and Doing Teaching: the Practical Management of the Classroom.* London: Allen and Unwin.

Cummins, J.
    1984   *Bilingualism and Special Education: Issues in Assessment and Pedagogy.* Clevedon, Philadelphia: Multilingual Matters.

Dahl, D.
    1981   "The role of experience in speech modifications for second language learners." *Mimmesda Papers in Linguistics and Philosophy of Language* 7: 78-93.

Day, R. R.
    1984   "Student participation in the ESL classroom or some imperfections in practice." *Language Learning* 34: 69-102.

Day, R. R.
     1985   "The use of the target language in context and second language
             proficiency" In S. M. Gass and C. G. Madden (eds), *Input in
             Second Language Acquisition*. Rowley, Mass.: Newbury House.
Day, R. R. (ed)
     1986   *Talking to learn: Conversation in Second Language Acquisition*.
             Rowley, Mass.: Newbury House.
Day, R. R., Chenoweth, N. A., Chun, A., and Luppescu, S.
     1984   "Corrective feedback in native-non-native discourse." *Language
             Learning* 34: 19-45.
Deen, J. Y.
     1991   "Comparing interaction in a cooperative learning and teacher-
             centered foreign language classroom." *ITL: Review of Applied
             Linguistics* 93/94: 153-81.
Deen, J. Y.
     1994   "Negotiation of meaning in institutional and informal conversations
             with non-native speakers." In H. Pürschel, E. Bartsch, P. Franklin, U.
             Schmitz, and S. Vandermeeren (eds), *Intercultural Communication.
             Proceedings of the 17th International LAUD Symposium Duisburg
             23-27 March 1992*. Frankfurt am Main: Peter Lang, pp. 159-184.
Deen, J. Y. and Van Hout, R.
     1991   "Clarification sequences in native-non-native interaction." In R. Van
             Hout and E. Huls (eds), *Artikelen van de Eerste Sociolinguïstische
             Conferentie*. Delft: Eburon.
Dickerson, L.
     1992   *Learner Training for Language Learning*. Dublin: Authentic
             Language Learning Resources.
Diez, M. E.
     1986   "Negotiation competence: a conceptualization of the rules of
             negotiation interaction." In D. G. Ellis and W. A. Donohue, (1986).
             Contemporary Issues in Language and Discourse Processes.
             London: Lawrence Erlbaun Associates.
Di Pietro, R. J.
     1987   *Strategic Interaction: Learning Languages through Scenarios*.
             Cambridge: Cambridge University Press.
Dittmar, N. and von Stutterheim, C.
     1985   "On the discourse of immigrant workers: interethnic
             communication and communication strategies." In T. A. Van Dijk
             (ed), *Handbook of Discourse Analysis*. Vol. 4. London: Academic
             Press.

Doughty, C. and Pica, T.
1986 "Information gap tasks: do they facilitate second language acquisition?" *TESOL Quarterly* 20: 305-25.

DuBois, J.
1991 "Transcription design principles for spoken discourse research." *Pragmatics* 1: 71-106.

Duff, P.
1986 "Another look at interlanguage talk: taking task to task." In R. R. Day (ed), *Talking to Learn: Conversation in Second Language Acquisition*. Rowley, Mass.: Newbury House.

Dulay, H. and Burt, M. K.
1974 "A new perspective on the creative construction process in child second language acquisition." *Language Learning* 24: 253-78.

Dulay, H., Burt, M. K., and Krashen S. D.
1982 *Language Two*. Oxford: Oxford University Press.

Duncan, S.
1973 "Toward a grammar for dyadic conversation." *Semiotica* 9: 24-46.

Duranti, A.
1985 "Sociocultural dimensions of discourse." In T. A. Van Dijk (ed), *Handbook of Discourse Analysis*. Vol. 1: *Disciplines of Discourse*. London: Academic Press.

Early, M.
1985 *Input and Interaction in Content Classrooms: Foreigner Talk and Teacher Talk in Classroom Discourse*. Unpublished PhD Dissertation. University of California at Los Angeles.

Edge, J. and Richards, K.
1993 *Teachers Develop Teachers Research: Papers on Classroom Research and Teacher Development*. Oxford: Heinemann.

Edlesky, C.
1981 "Who got the floor?" *Language and Society* 10: 383-421.

Edmondson, W.
1981 *Spoken Discourse: a Model for Analysis*. London: Longman.

Edwards, J. and Lampert, M.
1993 *Talking Data: Transcription and Coding in Discourse Research*. Hillsdale, NJ: Erlbaum.

Ehrlich, S., Avery, P. and Yorio, C.
1989 "Discourse structure and the negotiation of comprehensible input." *Studies in Second Language Acquisition* 11: 397-414.

Eisenstein, M. R. (ed)
1989 *The Dynamic Interlanguage: Empirical Studies in Second Language Variation*. New York, London: Plenum Press.

Ellis, R.
    1980   "Classroom interaction and its relation to second language learning." *RELC Journal* 11: 29-84.

Ellis, R.
    1981   "The role of input in language acquisition: some implications for second language teaching." *Applied Linguistics* 2: 70-82.

Ellis, R.
    1984   *Classroom Second Language Development: a Study of Classroom Interaction and Language Acquisition.* Oxford: Pergamon Press.

Ellis, R.
    1985a   "Teacher-pupil interaction in second language development." In S. Gass and C. Madden (eds), *Input in Second Language Acquisition.* Rowley, Mass. Newbury House.

Ellis, R.
    1985b   *Understanding Second Language Acquisition.* Oxford: Oxford University Press.

Ellis, R. (ed)
    1987   *Second Language Acquisition in Context.* Englewood Cliffs: Prentice-Hall.

Ellis, R.
    1990a   "Researching classroom language learning." In C. J. Brumfit and R. Mitchell (eds), *Research in the Language Classroom.* Modern English Publications and the British Council.

Ellis, R.
    1990b   *Instructed Second Language Acquisition.* Oxford: Basil Blackwell.

Ellis, R.
    1994   *The Study of Second Language Acquisition.* Oxford: Oxford University Press.

Erickson, F.
    1979   "Talking down: some cultural sources of miscommunication in interracial interviews." In A. Wolfgang (ed), *Research in Non-verbal Communication.* New York: Academic Press.

Erickson, F.
    1985   "Qualitative methods in research on teaching." In M. C. Wittrock (ed), *Handbook of Research on Teaching.* New York: Macmillan.

Ervin-Tripp, S.
    1964   "An analysis of the interaction of language, topic, listener." *American Anthropologist* 66: 86-102.

Ervin-Tripp, S.
    1973   *Language Acquisition and Communicative Chance.* Palo Alto: Stanford University Press.

Faerch, C. and Kasper, G.
    1980   "Processes and strategies in foreign language learning and communication." *Interlanguage Studies Bulletin* 5: 47-118.
Faerch, C. and Kasper, G.
    1983a   "Plans and strategies in foreign language communication." In C. Faerch and G. Kasper (eds), *Strategies in Interlanguage Communication*. London: Longman.
Faerch, C. and Kasper, G.
    1983b   "On identifying communication strategies in interlanguage production." In C. Faerch and G. Kasper (eds), *Strategies in Interlanguage Communication*. London: Longman.
Faerch, C. and Kasper, G.
    1985   "Repair in learner-native speaker discourse." In E. Glahn and A. Holmen (eds), *Learner Discourse*. Anglica et Americana 22, Copenhagen: University of Copenhagen.
Faerch, C. and Kasper, G.
    1986   "The role of comprehension in second language learning." *Applied Linguistics* 7: 275-74.
Fanselow, J. F.
    1977a   "Beyond RASHOMON-conceptualizing and describing the teaching act." *TESOL Quarterly* 11: 17-39.
Fanselow, J. F.
    1977b   "The treatment of error in oral work." *Foreign Language Annals* 10: 583-93.
Fanselow, J. F.
    1987   *Breaking Rules: Generating and Exploring Alternatives in Language Teaching*. London, New York: Longman.
Feldman, C. and Westsch, J.
    1976   "Context dependent properties of teacher's speech." *Youth and Society* 7: 227-58.
Ferguson, C. A.
    1971   "Absence of copula and the notion of simplicity: a study of normal speech, baby talk, foreigner talk, and pidgins." In D. Hymes (ed), *Pidginization and Creolization of Languages*. Cambridge: Cambridge University Press.
Ferguson, C. A.
    1975   "Towards a characterization of English foreigner talk." *Anthropological Linguistics* 17: 1-14.
Ferguson, C. A.
    1977   "Simplified registers, broken language, and Gast-arbeiterdentsh." In C. Molongy, H. Zobl, and W. Stoelting (eds), *German in Contact with Other Languages*. Kronberg: Scriptor.

Ferguson, C. A.
  1981   "Foreigner talk as the name of a simplified register." *International Journal of the Sociology of Language* 28: 9-19.
Fillmore, C. J., Kempler, D., and Wong, W. S. Y. (eds)
  1979   *Individual Difference in Language Ability and Language Behaviour*. New York: Academic Press.
Fine, J. (ed)
  1988   *Second Language Discourse: a Textbook of Current Research*. Norwood, NJ: Ablex.
Finocchiaro, M. and Brumfit, C. J.
  1983   *The Functional-Notional Approach: from Theory to Practice*. New York: Oxford University Press.
Fisher, R. and Ury, W.
  1981   *Getting to Yes: Negotiating Agreement without Giving in*. Boston: Houghton Mifflin.
Fisher, S. and Todd, A. D. (eds)
  1986   *Discourse and Institutional Authority: Medicine, Education, and Law*. Norwood, NJ: Ablex.
Flanders, N. A.
  1970   *Analyzing Teaching Behavior*. Reading, Mass.: Addison-Wesley.
Flynn, S.
  1983   "Similarities and differences between first and second language acquisition: setting the parameters of universal grammar." In D. Rogers and J. Slovboda, (eds), *Acquisition of Symbolic Skills*. New York, London: Plenum Press.
Freed, B. F.
  1978   *Foreigner Talk: a Study of Speech Adjustments Made by Native Speakers of English in Conversation with Non-native Speakers*. Unpublished PhD dissertation. University of Pennsylvania.
Freed, B.
  1980   "Talking to foreigners versus talking to children: similarities and differences." In R. C. Scarcella and S. D. Krashen, (ed), *Research in Second Language Acquisition*: Selected Papers of the los Angeles Second Language Acquisition Research Forum. Rowley, Mass.: Newbury House.
Furlong, V. J. and Edwards A. D.
  1983   "language in classroom interaction: theory and data." In M. Stubbs and H. Hiller (eds), *Readings on Language, Schools, and Classrooms*. London: Methuen.
Fujimoto, D., Lubin, J. Sasaki, Y., and Long, M. H.
  1986   "The effect of linguistic and conversational adjustments on the comprehensibility of spoken second language discourse."

Department of ESL, University of Hawaii at Manoa, Honolulu. (mimeo)

Gaies, S. J.
1977a   "The nature of linguistic input in formal second language learning: linguistic and communicative strategies in teachers' classroom language." In H. D. Brown, C. A. Yoris, and R. H. Crymes (eds), *On TESOL '77: Teaching and Learning English as a Second Language: Trends in Research and Practice.* Washington, D. C.: TESOL.

Gaies, S. J.
1977b   *A Comparison of the Classroom Language of ESL Teachers and their Speech among Peers: an Exploratory Syntactic Analysis.* Unpublished PhD dissertation. Indiana University, Bloomington.

Gaies, S. J.
1980   "Learner feedback: a taxonomy of intake control." In J. Fisher, M. Clarke, and J. Schachter (eds), *On TESOL '80: Building Bridges: Research and Practice in Teaching English as a Second Language.* Washington, D. C.: TESOL.

Gaies, S. J.
1981   "Learner feedback and its effects on communication tasks." *Studies in Second Language Acquisition* 4: 46-59.

Gaies, S. J.
1982a   "Native speaker-nonnative speaker interaction among academic peers." *Studies in Second Language Acquisition* 5: 74-82.

Gaies, S. J.
1982b   "Modification of discourse between native and nonnative speaker peers." Paper presented at the 16th Annual TESOL Conference, Honolulu, Hawaii.

Gaies, S. J.
1983a   "The investigation of language classroom processes." *TESOL Quarterly* 17: 205-17.

Gaies, S. J.
1983b   "Learner feedback: an explanatory study of its role in the second language classroom." In H. W. Seliger and M. H. Long (eds), *Classroom Oriented Research in Second Language Acquisition.* Rowley, Mass.: Newbury House.

Gaies, S. J.
1983c   "The investigation of language classroom processes." *TESOL Quarterly* 17: 205-217.

Gardner, R. C.
1985   *Social Psychology and Second Language Learning.* London: Edward Arnold.

Garfinkel, H.
    1967   *Studies in Ethnomethodology*. Englewood Cliffs, NJ: Prentice Hall.
Garnica, O. K.
    1981   "Social dominance and conversational interaction - the Omega child in the classroom." In J. L. Green and C. Wallat (eds), *Ethnography and Language in Educational Settings*. Norwood, NJ: Ablex.
Gaskill, W. H.
    1980   "Correction in native speaker-nonnative speaker conversation." In. D. Larsen-Freeman (ed) *Discourse Analysis in Second Language Research*. Rowley, Mass.: Newbury House.
Gass, S.
    1988   "Integrating research areas: a framework for second language studies." *Applied Linguistics* 9: 198-217.
Gass, S. (ed)
    1989   *Linguistic Perspectives on Second Language Acquisition*. Cambridge: Cambridge University Press.
Gass, S. and Madden, C. (eds)
    1985   *Input in Second Language Acquisition*. Rowley, Mass.: Newbury House.
Gass, S., Madden, C., Preston, D., and Selinker, L.
    1989a   *Variations in Second Language Acquisition: Discourse and Pragmatics*. Clevedon, Philadelphia: Multilingual Matters.
Gass, S., Madden, C., Preston, D., and Selinker, L.
    1989b   *Variation in Second Language Acquisition: Psycholinguistic Issues*. Clevedon, Philadelphia: Multilingual Matters.
Gass, S. and Selinker, L.
    1994   *Second Language Acquisition: an Introductionary Course*. Hillsdale, NJ: Erlbaum.
Gass, S. and Varonis, E. M.
    1984   "The effect of familiarity on the comprehensibility of nonnative speech." *Language Learning* 34: 65-89.
Gass, S. and Varonis, E. M.
    1985a   "Variation in native speaker speech modification to nonnantive speakers." *Studies in Second Language Acquisition* 7: 37-57.
Gass, S. and Varonis, E. M.
    1985b   "Task variation and nonnative/nonnative negotiation of meaning." In S. M. Gass and C. Madden, (eds), *Input in Second Language Acquisition*. Rowley, Mass.: Newbury House.
Gass, S. and Varonis, E. M.
    1986   "Sex differences in nonnative speaker-nonnative speaker interaction." In R. R. Day (ed), *Talking to Learn: Conversation in Second Language Acquisition*. Rowley, Mass.: Newbury House.

Gass, S. and Varonis, E. M.
    1989   "Incorporated repairs in nonnative discourse." In M. R. Eisenstein
            (ed), *The Dynamic Interlanguage: Empirical Studies in Second
            Language Variation*. New York, London: Plenum Press.
Gass, S. and Varonis, E. M.
    1991   "Miscommunication in nonnative speaker discourse." In N.
            Coupland, H. Giles, and J. M. Wiemann (eds), *"Miscommunication"
            and Problematic Talk*. Beverly Hills, London, New Delhi: Sage
            Publications.
Gattegno, C.
    1985   "The learning and teaching of foreign languages." Chapter 13 from
            an unpublished manuscript, *The Science of Education*. Educational
            Solutions, New York.
Gay, W. and Stephenson, B.
    1972   "A new view of reinforcement in learning." *Educational
            Technology* 12: 48-49.
Genesee, F.
    1983   "Bilingual education of majority-language children: the immersion
            experiments in review." *Applied Psycholinguistics* 4: 1-46.
Gibbons, J.
    1995   "The silent period: an examination." *Language Learning* 35: 255-
            67.
Goffman, E.
    1955   "On face work." *Psychiatry* 18: 213-31.
Goffman, E.
    1967   *Interaction Ritual: Essays on Face-to-Face Behavior*. New York:
            Pantheon.
Goffman, E.
    1970   *Strategic Interaction*. Oxford: Basil Blackwell.
Goffman, E.
    1971   *Relations in Public*. Harmondsworth: Penguin.
Goffman, E.
    1974   *Frame Analysis*. New York: Harper and Row.
Goffman, E.
    1981   *Forms of Talk*. Philadelphia: University of Pennsylvania Press.
Goldstein, L.
    1987   "Standard English: the only target for nonnative speakers of
            English?" *TESOL Quarterly* 21: 417-36.
Grice, H. P.
    1975   "Logic and conversation." In P. Cole and J. L. Morgan (eds), *Syntax
            and Semantics, Vol. 3, Speech Acts*. New York: Academic Press.

Griffin, P. and Mehan, H.
    1981   "Sense and ritual in classroom discourse." In F. Coulmas (ed), *Conversational Routine: Explorations in Standardized Communication Situations and Pre-patterned Speech*. The Hague: Mouton.

Gumperz, J.
    1982   *Discourse Strategies*. Cambridge: Cambridge University Press.

Gumperz, J. and Tannen, D.
    1979   "Individual and social differences in language use." In C. J. Fillmore, D. Kemplar, and W. S. Wand (eds), *Individual Differences in Language Ability and Language Behavior*. New York: Academic Press.

Halliday, M. A. K.
    1970   "Language structure and language function." In J. Lyons (ed), *New Horizons in Linguistics*. Harmondsworth: Penguin.

Hamayan, E. V. and Tucker, R. G.
    1980   "Language input in the bilingual classroom and its relationship to second language achievement." *TESOL Quarterly* 14: 453-468.

Harder, P.
    1980   "Discourse as self-expression - on the reduced personality of the second language learner." *Applied Linguistics* 1: 262-70.

Harris, R. and Taylor, T. (eds)
    1991   *Language and Communication*. Oxford: Pergamon.

Hatch, E. (ed)
    1978a   *Second Language Acquisition: a Book of Readings*. Rowley, Mass.: Newbury House.

Hatch, E.
    1978b   "Discourse analysis and second language acquisition." In E. M. Hatch (ed), *Second Language Acquisition: a Book of Readings*. Rowley, Mass,: Newbury House.

Hatch, E.
    1978c   "Discourse analysis, speech acts, and second language acquisition." In W. C. Ritchie (ed), *Second Language Acquisition Research*. New York: Academic Press, Inc.

Hatch, E.
    1983a   *Psycholinguistics: a Second Language Perspective*. Rowley, Mass.: Newbury House.

Hatch, E.
    1983b   "Simplified input and second language acquisition." In R. W. Andersen (ed), *Pidginization and Creolization as Language acquisition*. Rowley, Mass.: Newbury House.

Hatch, E. and Long M. H.
    1980   "Discourse analysis: what's that?" In D. Larsen-Freeman (ed), *Discourse Analysis in Second Language Research*. Rowley, Mass.: Newbury House.

Hatch, E., Shapira, R., and Wagner-Gough, J.
    1978   "Foreigner talk discourse." *ITL: Review of Applied Linguistics* 39/40: 39-60.

Hatch, E. and Farhady, H.
    1982   *Research Design and Statistics for Applied linguistics*. Rowley, Mass.: Newbury House.

Hatch, E., Flashner, V., and Hunt, L.
    1986   "The experience model and language teaching." In R. Day (ed), *Talking to Learn: Conversation in Second Language Acquisition*. Rowley, Mass.: Newbury House.

Hawkins, B.
    1985   "Is an "appropriate response" always so appropriate?" In S. Gass and C. Madden (eds), *Input in Second Language Acquisition*. Rowley, Mass.: Newbury House.

Hawkins, B.
    1988   *Scaffolded Classroom Interaction and its Relation to Second Language Acquisition for Minority School Children*. Unpublished PhD dissertation. University of California, Los Angeles.

Heath, S. B.
    1982   "Questioning at home and school: a comparative study." In G. D. Spindler (ed), *Doing the Ethnography of Schooling: Educational Anthropology in Action*. New York: Holt, Rinehart, and Winston.

Heath, S. B.
    1983   *Ways with Words: Language, Life, and Work in Communities and Classrooms*. Cambridge: Cambridge University Press.

Henderson, K.
    1970   "Reaction to success and failure in complex learning: a post-feedback effect." *Journal of Experimental Psychology* 10: 494-98.

Henzl, V. M.
    1973   "Linguistic register of foreign language instruction." *Language learning* 23: 207-22.

Henzl, V. M.
    1979   "Foreign talk in the classroom." *International Review of Applied Linguistics* 17: 159-67.

Heyde, A. W.
    1977   "The relationship between self-esteem and the oral production of a second language." In H. D. Brown, C. A. Yorio, and R. H. Crymes (eds), *On TESOL '77: Teaching and Learning English as a Second*

Language: Trends in Research and Practice. Washington, D. C.: TESOL.

Holley, F. and King, J.
1971   "Imitation and correction in foreign language learning." *Modern Language Journal* 55: 494-98.

Hymes, D.
1972   "On communicative competence." In J. B. Pride and J. Holmes, (eds), *Sociolinguistics: Selected Readings.* Harmondsworth: Penguin Books.

Hymes, D.
1974   *Foundations in Sociolinguistics.* Philadelphia: University of Pennsylvania Press.

Ishiguro, T.
1986   *Simplification and Elaboration in Foreign Language Teacher Talk and its Source.* Unpublished PhD dissertation, Stanford University, Stanford, Ca.

Janeway, E.
1980a   "Women and the uses of power." In H. Eisenstein and A. Jardine (eds), *The Future of Difference.* Boston: G. K. Hall.

Janeway, E.
1980b   *Powers of the Weak.* New York: Knopf.

Janicki, K.
1986   "Accommodation in native speaker-foreigner interaction." In J. House and S. Blum-Kulka (eds), *Interlingual and Intercultural Communication.* Tübingen: Narr.

Jefferson, G.
1972   "Side sequences." In D. Sudnow (ed), *Studies in Social Interaction.* New York: Free Press.

Jefferson, G.
1973   "A case of precision timing in ordinary conversation: overlapped tag positioned address terms in closing sequences." *Semiotica* 9: 47-96.

Jefferson, G.
1975   "Error correction as an interactional resource." *Language in Society* 2: 181-99.

Jefferson, G.
1979   "A technique for inviting laughter and its subsequent acceptance/declination." In G. Psathas (ed), *Everyday Language: Studies in Ethnomethodology.* New York: Irvington.

Jefferson, G.
1980   "On trouble-premonitory response to inquiry." *Sociological Inquiry* 50: 153-85.

Jefferson, G.
1983 "Notes on some orderlinesses of overlap onset." In G. Jefferson (ed), *Two Explorations of the Organization of Overlapping Talk in Conversation*. Tilburg, Netherlands: Tilburg Papers in Language and Literature. Also in V. D'Urso and P. Leonardi, (eds), *Discourse Analysis and Natural Rhetorics*. Padua: Cleup Editore.

Jefferson, G.
1984 "On the organization of laughter in talk about troubles." In J. M. Atkinson and J. Heritage (eds), *Structures of Social Action: Studies in Conversation Analysis*. Cambridge: Cambridge University Press.

Jefferson, G.
1987 "On exposed and embedded correction." In G. Button and J. R. E. Lee (eds), *Talk and Social Organizations*. Clevedon, Philadelphia: Multilingual Matters.

Jefferson, G. (ed)
1992 *Harvey Sacks: Lectures on Conversation*. Oxford: Basil Blackwell.

Jefferson, G. and Schenkein, J.
1978 "Some sequential negotiations in conversation: unexpanded and expanded versions of projected action sequence." In J. Schenkein (ed), *Studies in the Organization of Conversational Interaction*. New York: Academic Press.

Jefferson, T.
1988 "On the sequential organization of troubles-talk in ordinary conversation." *Social Problems* 35: 418-41.

Johnson, K.
1979 "Communicative approaches and communicative processes." In C. J. Brumfit and K. Johnson (eds), *The Communicative Approach to Language Teaching*. Oxford: Oxford University Press.

Johnson, K. and Morrow, K. (eds)
1981 *Communication in the Classroom*. London: Longman.

Joshi, A. K., Webber, B. L., and Sag, I. A. (eds)
1981 *Elements of Discourse Understanding*. Cambridge: Cambridge University Press.

Kalin, M.
1995 *Coping with Problems in Understanding. Repair Sequences in Conversations between Native and Non-native Speakers*. Unpublished PhD dissertation, University of Jyväskylä, Finland.

Kasper, G.
1989 "Variation in interlanguage speech act realisation." In S. Gass, C. Madden, D. Preston, and L. Selinker (eds), *Variation in Second Language Acquisition*. Volume I, Discourse and Pragmatics. Clevedon, Philadelphia: Multilingual Matters.

Kedar, L. (ed)
1987   *Power Through Discourse*. Norwood: Ablex.
Keenan, E. O.
1976   "The universality of conversational implicature." *Language in Society* 5: 67-80.
Kelch, K.
1985   "Modified input as an aid to comprehension." *Studies in Second Language Acquisition* 7: 81-90.
Kennedy, C. W. and Camden, C. T.
1983   "A new look at interruptions." *Western Journal of Speech Communication* 47: 45-58.
Klein, W.
1986   *Second Language Acquisition*. Cambridge: Cambridge University Press.
Kramarae, C., Schulz, M., and O'Barr, W. (eds)
1984   *Language and Power*. Beverly Hills, London, New Delhi: Sage Publications.
Kramsch, C.
1993   *Context and Culture in Language Teaching*. Oxford: Oxford University Press.
Krashen, S. D.
1977   "Some issues relating to the monitor model." In H. D. Brown, C. A. Yorio, and R. H. Crymes (eds), *On TESOL '77: Teaching and Learning English as a Second Language: Trends in Research and Practice*. Washington D. C.: TESOL.
Krashen, S. D.
1980a   "The theoretical and practical relevance of simple codes in second language acquisition." In R. C. Scarcella and S. D. Krashen (eds), *Research in Second Language Acquisition*. Rowley, Mass.: Newbury House.
Krashen, S. D.
1980b   "The input hypothesis." In J. E. Alatis (ed), *Current Issues in Bilingual Education*. Washington, D.C.: Georgetown University Press.
Krashen, S. D.
1981a   *Second Language Acquisition and Second Language Learning*. Oxford: Pergamon Press.
Krashen, S. D.
1981b   "The 'fundamental pedagogical principle' in second language teaching." *Studia Linguistica* 35: 50-70.

Krashen, S. D.
    1982a   *Principles and Practice in Second Language Acquisition.* New York: Pergamon.

Krashen, S. D.
    1982b   "Accounting for child-adult differences in second language rate and attainment." In S. D. Krashen, R. C. Scarcella, and M. H. Long, (eds), *Child-Adult Differences in Second Language Acquisition.* Rowley, Mass.: Newbury House.

Krashen, S. D.
    1985   *The Input Hypothesis: Issues and Implications.* London: Longman.

Krashen, S. D., Scarcella, R. C., and Long, M. H. (eds)
    1982   *Child-Adult Differences in Second Language Acquisition.* Rowley, Mass: Newbury House.

Krashen, S. D. and Terrel, T.
    1983   *The Natural Approach: Language Acquisition in the Classroom.* New York: Pergamon Press.

Kreckel, M.
    1981   *Communicative Acts and Shared Knowledge in Natural Discourse.* London: Academic Press.

Kumaravadivelu, B.
    1988   "Creation and utilization of learning opportunities." *22nd Annual TESOL Convention*, Chicago, pp. 8-13.

Labov, W.
    1972   "The social stratification of (r) in New York City department stores. In W. Labov, *Sociolinguistic Patterns.* Philadelphia, P.A.: University of Pennsylvania Press.

Labov, W. and Fanshel, D.
    1977   *Therapeutic Discourse: Psychology as Conversation.* New York: Academic Press.

Lakoff, R.
    1974   "What you can do with words: politeness, pragmatics, and performatives." In *Berkeley Studies in Syntax and Semantics I.* Berkeley: Institute of Human Learning, University of California.

Lantolf, J. P. and Labarca, A. (eds)
    1987   *Research in Second Language Learning: Focus on the Classroom.* Norwood, NJ: Ablex.

Lapkin, S., Swain, M., and Cummins, J.
    1983   *Final Report on the Development of French Language Evaluation Units for Saskat-chewan.* Toronto: OISE. (ms).

Larsen-Freeman, D.
    1976   "An explanation for the morpheme acquisition order of second language learners." *language learning* 26: 125-134.

Larsen-Freeman, D.
  1979   "The importance of input in second language acquisition." Paper presented at the winter meeting of the LSA, December, 1979, Los Angeles, CA.
Larsen-Freeman, D. (ed)
  1980   *Discourse Analysis in Second language Research.* Rowley, Mass.: Newbury House.
Larsen-Freeman, D. and Long, M. H.
  1991   *An Introduction to Second Language Acquisition Research.* London: Longman.
Leech, G. N.
  1977   "Language and tact." *LAUT*, Series A, Paper 46. University of Trier.
Leech, G. N.
  1980   *Explorations in Semantics and Pragmatics.* Amsterdam, Philadelphia: John Benjamins.
Leech, G. N.
  1983   *Principles of Pragmatics.* London, New York: Longman.
Leet-Pelligrini, H.
  1980   "Conversation dominance as a function of gender and expertise." In H. Giles, W. P. Robinson, and P. Smith (eds), *Language: Social Psychological Perspectives.* New York: Pergamon.
Levinson, S. C.
  1983   *Pragmatics.* Cambridge: Cambridge University Press.
Littlejohn, A. P.
  1983   "Increasing learner involvement in course management." *TESOL Quarterly* 17: 595-608.
Littlewood, W. T.
  1981   *Communicative Language Teaching.* Cambridge: Cambridge University press.
Littlewood, W. T.
  1992   *Teaching Oral Communication: a Methodological Framework.* Oxford: Basil Blackwell.
Locastro, V.
  1986a   "I agree with you, but... ." Paper presented at JALT '86 Conference, Hamamatsu, Japan, November 1986.
Locastro, V.
  1986b   "The pragmatics of pauses." Paper presented at the second Kyoto Conference on Discourse Analysis, Doshista University, Kyoto, Japan, September 1986.

Long, M. H., Adams, L., Mclean, M., and Castaños, F.
1976 "Doing things with words: verbal interaction in lockstep and small group classroom situations." In J. F. Fanselow and R. Crymes, (eds), *On TESOL '76*. Washington, D. C.: TESOL.

Long, M. H.
1977 "Teacher feedback on learner error: mapping cognitions." In H. D. Brown, C. Yorio, and R. H. Crymes (eds), *On TESOL '77: Teaching and Learning English as a Second Language: Trends in Research and Practice*. Washington, D.C.: TESOL.

Long, M. H.
1980 *Input, Interaction and Second language Acquisition*. Unpublished PhD dissertation. University of California at Los Angeles.

Long, M. H.
1981a "Questions in foreigner talk discourse." *Language Learning* 31: 135-57.

Long, M. H.
1981b "Input, interaction and second language acquisition." In H. Winitz (ed), *Native Language and Foreign Language Acquisition*. Annals of the New York Academy of Sciences Vol. 379. New York: New York Academy of Sciences.

Long, M. H.
1983a "Native speaker/nonnative speaker conversation and the negotiation of comprehensible input." *Applied Linguistics* 4: 126-41.

Long, M. H.
1983b "Native Speaker/nonnative speaker conversation in the second language classroom." In M. A. Clarke and J. Handscombe (eds), *On TESOL '82: Pacific Perspectives on Language Learning and Teaching*. Washington, D. C.: TESOL.

Long, M. H.
1983c "Linguistic and conversational adjustments to non-native speakers." *Studies in Second Language Acquisition* 5: 177-93.

Long, M. H.
1983d "Inside the 'black box': methodological issues in classroom research on language learning." In H. W. Seliger and M. H. Long (eds), *Classroom Oriented Research in Second Language Acquisition*. Rowley, Mass.: Newbury House.

Long, M. H.
1983e "Does second language instruction make a difference?" *TESOL Quarterly* 17: 359-82.

Long, M. H.
    1985   "Input and second language acquisition theory." In S. M. Gass and
             C. G. Madden (eds), *Input in Second Language Acquisition*.
             Rowley, Mass.: Newbury House.

Long, M. H. and Sato, C.
    1983   "Classroom foreigner talk discourse: forms and functions of
             teachers' questions." In H. W. Seliger and M. H. Long (eds),
             Classroom Oriented Research in Second Language Acquisition.
             Rowley, Mass.: Newbury House.

Long, M. H., Brock, C., Crookes, G., Deicke, C., Potter, L., and Zhang, S.
    1984   "The effects of teachers' questioning patterns and wait-time on pupil
             participation in public high school classes in Hawaii for students of
             limited English proficiency." Technical Report. Honolulu: Center
             for Second Language Classroom Research, Social Science Research
             Institute, University of Hawaii at Manoa.

Long, M. H. and Porter, P. A.
    1985   "Group work, interlanguage talk, and second language acquisition."
             TESOL Quarterly 19: 2O7-28.

MacFarlane, J.
    1975   "Focus analysis." In R. L. Allwright (ed), *Working Papers:
             Language Teaching Classroom Research*. Essex: University of
             Essex. Department of Language and Linguistics.

Malinowski, B.
    1935   *Coral Gardens and their Magic*. Volume 2. *The Language of
             Magic and Gardening*. London: Allen and Unwin.

McCurdy, P. L.
    1980   *Talking to Foreigners: the Role of Rapport*. Unpublished PhD
             dissertation. University of California, Berkeley.

McDermott, R. P.
    1977   "Social relations as contexts for learning in school." *Harvard
             Educational Review* 47: 198-213.

McHoul, A. W.
    1978   "The organization of turns at formal talk in the classroom."
             Language in Society 7: 183-213.

McHoul, A. W.
    1990   "The organization of repair in classroom talk." *Language in Society*
             19: 349-77.

McLaughlin, B.
    1987   *Theories of Second Language Learning*. London: Edward Arnold.

Mehan, H.
    1974a   "Accomplishing classroom lessons." In A. V. Cicourel, K. H.
             Jennings, K. C. W. Leiter, R. Mackay, H. Mehan, and D. R. Roth

(eds), *Language Use and School Performance*. New York: Academic press.

Mehan, H.
1974b "The competent student." *Working Papers in Sociolinguistics* 61: 1-34. Austin, Texas.

Mehan, H.
1979 *Learning Lessons: Social Organization in the Classroom.* Cambridge, Mass.: Harvard University Press.

Mehan, H.
1985 "The structure of classroom discourse." In T. A. Van Dijk (ed), *Handbook of Discourse Analysis*, Vol. 3. *Discourse and Dialogue*. London: Academic Press.

Mehan, H. and Griffin, P.
1980 "Socialization: the view from classroom interaction." In D. D. Zimmerman and C. West (eds), *Language and Social Interaction*; Special issue of: *Sociological Inquiry* 50: 357-92.

Meisel, J. M.
1977 "Linguistic simplification: a study of immigrant workers' speech and foreigner talk." In S. P. Corder and E. Roulet (eds), *Actes du 5ème Colloque de Linguistique appliquée de Neuchatel*. Paris: AIMAV/Didier.

Meisel, J. M.
1980 "Linguistic simplification." In S. Felix (ed), *Second Language Development: Trends and Issues*. Tübingen: Gunter Narr Verlag.

Milk, R. D.
1985 "Can foreigners do 'foreigner-talk'? A study of the linguistic input provided by non-native teachers of EFL." Paper presented at the 19th Annual TESOL Convention, New York.

Milroy, L.
1984 "Comprehension and context: successful communication and communicative breakdown." In P. Trudgill (ed), *Applied Sociolinguistics*. London: Academic Press.

Mishler, E. G.
1972 "Implications of teacher strategies for language and cognition: observation in first grade classrooms." In C. B. Cazden, V. P. John, and D. Hymes (eds), *Functions of Language in the Classroom*. New York: Teachers College Press.

Mishler, E. G.
1975 "Studies in dialogue and discourse: an exponential law of successive questioning." *Language in Society* 4: 31-51.

Mitchell, R. and Parkinson, B.
  1979   "A systematic linguistic analysis of strategies of FL teaching in the
         secondary school." Paper presented to the annual meeting of the
         British association for Applied Linguistics, Manchester Polytechnic,
         September 1979.
Morrison, D. M. and Low, G.
  1983   "Monitoring and the second language learner." In J. C. Richards
         and R. W. Schmidts (eds), *Language and Communication*. London:
         Longman.
Morrow, K.
  1981   "Principles of communicative methodology." In K. Johnson and K.
         Morrow (eds), *Communication in the Classroom*. London:
         Longman.
Moskowitz, G.
  1976   "The classroom interaction of outstanding foreign language
         teachers." *Foreign Language Annals* 9: 135-157.
Moskowitz, G.
  1978   *Caring and Sharing in the Foreign Language Class*. Rowley, Mass.:
         Newbury House.
Munby, J.
  1978   *Communicative Syllabus Design*. Cambridge: Cambridge University
         Press.
Naiman, N., Fröhlich, M., Stern, H. H., and Todesco, A.
  1978   *The Good Language Learner*. Toronto: Ontario Institute for Studies
         in Education.
Nation, R. and MacLaughlin, B.
  1986   "Language learning in multilingual subjects: an information
         processing point of view." In V. Cook (ed), *Experimental
         Approaches to Second Language Learning*. Oxford: Pergamon.
Nattinger, J. R.
  1984   "Communicative language teaching: a new metaphor." *TESOL
         Quarterly* 18: 391-407.
Newmeyer, F. J.
  1988   *Linguistics: the Cambridge Survey*, Vol. 4: *Language: the Socio-
         Cultural Context*. Cambridge: Cambridge University Press.
Nofsinger, R. E.
  1991   *Everyday Conversation*. Beverly Hills, London, New Delhi: Sage
         Publications.
Nortier, J. M.
  1990   *Dutch-Moroccan Arabic Code-Switching among Moroccans in the
         Netherlands*. Dordrecht: Foris Publications.

Nystrom, N. J.
  1983   "Teacher-student interaction in bilingual classrooms: four
          approaches to error feedback." In H. W. Seliger and M. H. Long
          (eds), *Classroom Oriented Research in Second Language
          Acquisition*. Rowley, Mass.: Newbury House.
O'Barr, M.
  1982   *Linguistic Evidence: Language, Power, and Strategy in the
          Courtroom*. New York: Academic Press.
Olson, D. and Nickerson, N.
  1978   "Language development through the school years: learning to
          confine interpretation to information in the text." In K. E. Nelson
          (ed), *Children's Language*, 1. New York: Gardener Press.
O'Malley, J. and Chamot, A.
  1989   *Learning Strategies in Second Language Acquisition*. Cambridge:
          Cambridge university Press.
Oreström, B.
  1983   *Turn-taking in English Conversation*. CWK Gleerup, Lund.
Paget. M. A.
  1983   "On the work of talk: studies in misunderstanding." In S. Fisher and
          A. D. Todd (eds), *The Social Organization of Doctor-Patient
          Communication*. Washington, D. C.: Center for Applied Linguistics.
Paribakht, T.
  1985   "Strategic competence and language proficiency." *Applied
          Linguistics* 6: 132-46.
Parret, H. and Verschueren, J. (eds)
  1992   *(On) Searle on Conversation*. Amsterdam, Philadelphia: John
          Benjamins.
Patten, B. V. and Lee, J. F. (eds)
  1990   *Second Language Acquisition/Foreign Language Learning*.
          Clevedon, Philadelphia: Multilingual Matters.
Paul, P.
  1993   *Linguistics for Language Learning*. Melbourne: MacMillan.
Paulston, C. B.
  1974   "Linguistic and communicative competence." *TESOL Quarterly* 8:
          347-67.
Peck, S.
  1985   "Signs of learning: child nonnative speakers in tuturing sessions
          with a child native speaker." Department of English - ESL,
          University of California, Los Angeles. (mimeo)

Perdue, C.
  1984   "Understanding, misunderstanding, and breakdown." In C. Perdue
          (ed) *Second Language Acquisition by Adult Immigrants: a Field
          Manual*. Rowley Mass.: Newbury House.
Peterson, P. L., Wilkinson, L. C., and Hallinan, M. T. (eds)
  1983   *The Social Context of Instruction: Group Organization and Group
          Processes*. Orlando, Fla: Academic Press.
Philips, S. U.
  1974   *The Invisible Culture: Communication in Classroom and
          Community on the Warm Spring Reservation*. Unpublished PhD
          dissertation, Department of Anthropology, University of
          Pennsylvania.
Philips, S. U.
  1987   "On the use of wh-questions in American courtroom discourse: a
          study of the relation between language form and language
          function." In L. Kedar (ed) *Power through Discourse*. Norwood,
          NJ: Ablex.
Pica, T.
  1987   "Second-language acquisition, social interaction, and the
          classroom." *Applied Linguistics* 8: 3-21.
Pica, T.
  1988   "Interlanguage adjustments as an outcome of NS-NNS negotiated
          interaction." *Language Learning* 38: 45-73.
Pica, T.
  1994   "Review article. Research on negotiation: what does it reveal about
          second language learning conditions, processes, and outcomes?"
          Language Learning, 44: 493-527.
Pica, T. and Doughty, C.
  1985   "Input and interaction in the communicative language classroom: a
          comparison of teacher-fronted and group activities." In S. M. Gass
          and C. G. Madden (eds), *Input in Second Language Acquisition*.
          Rowley, Mass.: Newbury House.
Pica, T. and Doughty, C.
  1988   "Variations in classroom interaction as a function of participation
          pattern and task." In J. Fine (ed), *Second Language Discourse*.
          Norwood, NJ: Ablex.
Pica, T. and Long, M. H.
  1986   "The linguistic and conversational performance of experienced and
          inexperienced teachers." In R. R. Day (ed), *Talking to Learn:
          Conversation in Second Language Acquisition*. Rowley, Mass.:
          Newbury House.

312   NEGOTIATED INTERACTION

Pica, T., Doughty, C., and Young, R.
    1986   "Making input comprehensible: do interactional modifications help?" *ITL: Review of Applied linguistics* 72: 1-25.
Pica, T., Holliday, L., Lewis, N., and Morgenthaler, L.
    1989   "Comprehensible output as an outcome of linguistic demands on the learner." *Studies in Second Language Acquisition* 11: 63-90.
Polanyi, L. and Scha, R. J. H.
    1983   "The syntax of discourse." Special issue: formal methods of discourse analysis. *Text* 3: 261-70.
Porter, P. A.
    1983   *Variations in the Conversations of Adult Learners of English as a Function of the Proficiency Level of the Participants.* Unpublished PhD dissertation. Stanford University.
Porter, P. A.
    1986   "How learners talk to each other: input and interaction in task-centered discussions." In R. R. Day (ed), *Talking to Learn: Conversation in Second Language Acquisition.* Rowley, Mass.: Newbury House.
Preston, D. R.
    1989   *Sociolinguistics and Second Language Acquisition.* Oxford: Basil Blackwell.
Pride, J. B.
    1979   "A transactional view of speech functions and code switching." In W. C. McCormack and S. A. Wurm (eds), *Language and Society: Anthropological Issues.* The Hague: Mouton.
Psathas, G. (ed)
    1979   *Everyday Language: Studies in Ethnomethodology.* New York: Irvington.
Psathas, G.
    1992   "The study of extended sequences: the case of the Garden lesson." In G. Watson and R. M. Seiler (eds), *Text in Context.* Beverly Hills, London, New Delhi: Sage Publications.
Ramirez, A. G. and Stromquist, N. P.
    1979   "ESL methodology and student language learning in bilingual elementary schools." *TESOL Quarterly* 13: 145-58.
Rardin, J.
    1977   "The Language teacher as facilitator." *TESOL Quarterly* 11: 383-387.
Richards, J. C.
    1971   "Error analysis and second language strategies." *Language Sciences* 17: 12-22.

Richards, J. C. (ed)
    1978   *Understanding Second and Foreign Language Learning: Issues
            and Approaches*. Rowley, Mass.: Newbury House.
Richards, J. C., Schmidt, R. (eds)
    1983   *Language and Communication*. London, New York: Longman.
Richards J. C., Platt, J., and Webber, H.
    1985   *Longman Dictionary of Applied Linguistics*. London: Longman.
Richards, K. and Skelton, J.
    1989   "Nodes and networks: choosing for real." *Applied Linguistics* 10:
            231-43.
Rietveld, T. and Van Hout, R.
    1993   *Statistical Techniques for the Study of Language and Language
            Behaviour*. Berlin, New York: Mouton de Gruyter.
Ritchie, W. C.
    1978   "The right roof constraint in an adult-acquired language." In W. C.
            Ritchie (ed), *Second Language Acquisition Research: Issues and
            Implications*. New York: Academic Press.
Rivers, W.
    1964   *The Psychologist and the Foreign Language Teacher*. Chicago:
            University of Chicago Press.
Robinson, W. P.
    1985   "Social psychology and discourse." In T. A. Van Dijk (ed),
            Handbook of Discourse Analysis. Vol. 1: *Disciplines of Discourse*.
            London: Academic Press.
Ross, J. R.
    1979   "Sampling, elicitation and interpretation: Orleans and elsewhere." In
            W. C. McCormack and S. A. Wurm (eds), *Language and Society:
            Anthropological Issues*. The Hague: Mouton.
Rounds, P.
    1987   "Characterizing successful classroom discourse for NNS Teaching
            Assistant Training." *TESOL Quarterly* 21: 643-71.
Rulon, K. A. and McCreary, J.
    1986   "Negotiation of content: teacher-fronted and small group
            interaction." In R. R. Day (ed), *Talking to Learn: Conversation in
            Second Language Acquisition*. Rowley, Mass.: Newbury House.
Sachs, J., Bard, B., and Johnson, M.
    1981   "Language learning with restricted input: case studies of two
            hearing children of deaf parents." *Applied Psycholinguistics* 2: 33-
            54.
Sacks, H.
    1966   Unpublished Lectures. University of California at Los Angeles.

Sacks, H.
1972   "An initial investigation of the usability of conversational data for doing sociology." In D. Sudnow (ed), *Studies in Social Interaction*. New York: Free Press.

Sacks, H.
1987   "On the preferences for agreement and contiguity in sequences in conversation." In G. Button and J. R. E. Lee (eds), *Talk and Social Organization*. Clevedon, Philadelphia: Multilingual Matters.

Sacks, H., Schegloff, E. A., and Jefferson, G.
1974   "A simplest systematics for the organization of turn-taking for conversation." *Language* 50: 696-735.

Sato, C.
1986   "Conversation and interlanguage development: rethinking the connection." In R. Day (ed), *Talking to Learn: Conversation in Second Language Acquisition*. Rowley, Mass.: Newbury House.

Savignon, S. J.
1972   *Communicative Competence: an Experiment in Foreign Teaching*. Philadelphia: Center for Curriculum Development.

Saville-Troike, M.
1982   *The Ethnography of Communication*. Oxford: Basil Blackwell.

Saville-Troike, M.
1984   "What really matters in second language learning for academic achievement?" *TESOL Quarterly* 18: 199-219.

Saville-Troike, M.
1987   "Dilingual discourse: the negotiation of meaning without a common code." *Linguistics* 25: 81-106.

Scarcella, R. C.
1983   "Discourse accent in second language performance." In S. Gass and L. Selinker (eds), *Language Transfer in Language Learning*. Rowley, Mass.: Newbury House.

Scarcella, R. C. and Krashen, S. D. (eds)
1980   *Research in Second Language Acquisition*. Rowley, Mass.: Newbury House.

Scarcella, R. C. and Higa, C.
1981   "Input, negotiation and age differences in second language acquisition." *Language Learning* 31: 409-38.

Scarcella, R. C. and Higa, C.
1982   "Input and age differences in second language acquisition." In S. D. Krashen, M. H. Long, and R. C. Scarcella (eds), *Child-Adult Differences in Second Language acquisition*. Rowley, Mass.: Newbury House.

Scarcella, R. C., Andersen, E. S., and Krashen, S. D. (eds)
    1990   *Developing Communicative Competence in a Second Language.*
            Rowley, Mass.: Newbury House.
Schachter, J.
    1974   "An error in error analysis." *Language Learning* 24: 205-214.
Schachter, J.
    1984   "A universal input condition." In W. Rutherford (ed), *Universals
            and Second Language Acquisition.* Amsterdam: John Benjamins.
Schachter, J.
    1986   "Three approaches to the study of input." *Language Learning* 36:
            211-25.
Schachter, J.
    1991   "Corrective feedback in historical perspective." *Second Language
            Research* 7: 89-102.
Schegloff, E. A.
    1968   "Sequencing in conversational openings." *American Anthropologist*
            70: 1075-95.
Schegloff, E. A.
    1972   "Notes on a conversational practice: formulating place." In D.
            Sudnow (ed), *Studies in Social Interaction.* New York: Free Press.
Schegloff, E. A.
    1979   "The relevance of repair to syntax for conversation." In T. Givon
            (ed), *Discourse and Syntax.* New York: Academic Press.
Schegloff, E. A.
    1980   "Preliminaries to preliminaries: can I ask you a question?"
            Sociological Inquiry 50: 104-52.
Schegloff, E. A.
    1982   "Discourse as interactional achievement: some uses of 'uh huh' and
            other things that come between sentences." In D. Tannen (ed),
            *Georgetown University Round-table on Languages and Linguistics
            1981.* Washington: Georgetown University Press.
Schegloff, E. A.
    1984   "On some questions and ambiguities in conversation." In J. M.
            Atkinson and J. Heritage (eds), *Structures of Social Action: Studies
            in Conversation Analysis.* Cambridge: Cambridge University Press.
Schegloff, E. A.
    1986   "The routine as achievement." *Human Studies* 9: 111-52.
Schegloff, E. A.
    1987a   "Some sources of misunderstanding in talk-in-interaction."
            Linguistics 25: 201-18.

Schegloff, E. A.
1987b "Between macro and micro: contexts and other connections." In J. C. Alexander, B. Giesen, R. Munch, and N. J. Smelser (eds), *The Micro-Macro Link*. Berkeley: University of California Press.
Schegloff, E. A.
1987c "Recycled turn beginnings: a precise repair mechanism in conversation's turn-taking organization." In G. Button and J. R. E. Lee (eds), *Talk and Social Organization*. Clevedon, Philadelphia: Multilingual Matters.
Schegloff, E. A. and Sacks, H.
1973 "Opening up closings." In R. Turner (ed), *Ethnomethodology*. London: Penguin.
Schegloff, E. A., Jefferson, G., and Sacks, H.
1977 "The preference for self-correction in the organization of repair in conversation." *Language* 53: 361-82.
Schenkein, J. N.
1978 *Studies in the Organization of Conversational Interaction*. New York: Academic Press.
Schiffrin, D. (ed)
1984 *Georgetown University Round Table on Languages and Linguistics 1984. Meaning, Form and Use in Context: Linguistic Application*. Washington: Georgetown University Press.
Schiffrin, D.
1985a "Multiple constraints on discourse options: a quantitative analysis of casual sequences." *Discourse Processes* 8: 281-303.
Schiffrin, D.
1985b "Everyday argument: the organization of diversity in talk." In T. Van Dijk (ed), *Handbook of Discourse Analysis*, Vol. 3: *Discourse and Dialogue*. London: Academic Press.
Schiffrin, D.
1986 "Turn-initial variation: structure and function in conversation." In D. Sankoff (ed), *Diversity and Diachrony: Current Issues in Linguistic Theory 53*. Amsterdam, Philadelphia: John Benjamins.
Schiffrin, D.
1987 *Discourse Markers*. Cambridge: Cambridge University Press.
Schiffrin, D.
1994 *Approaches to Discourse: Language as Social Interaction*. Oxford: Basil Blackwell.
Schinke-Llano, L.
1983 "Foreigner talk in content classrooms." In H. W. Seliger and M. H. Long (eds), *Classroom Oriented Research in Second Language Acquisition*. Rowley, Mass.: Newbury House.

Schmidt, R. and McCreary, C.
    1977   "Standard and superstandard English: recognition and use of
            prescriptive rules by native and non-native speakers." *TESOL
            Quarterly* 11: 415-29.
Schumann, F. M.
    1980   "Diary of a language learner: a further analysis." In R. C. Scarcella
            and S. D. Krashen (eds), *Research in Second Language
            Acquisition*. Rowley, Mass.: Newbury House.
Schumann, F. M. and Schumann, J. H.
    1977   "Diary of a language learner: an introspective study of second
            language learning." In H. D. Brown, C. Yorio, and R. Crymes (eds),
            *On TESOL '77: Teaching and Learning English as a Second
            Language: Trends in Research and Practice*. Washington, D.C.:
            TESOL.
Schumann, J. H.
    1975   *Second Language Acquisition: the Pidginization Hypothesis*. PhD
            dissertation. Harvard University.
Schwartz, J.
    1980   "The negotiation for meaning: repair in conversations between
            second language learners of English." In D. Larsen-Freeman (ed),
            Discourse Analysis in Second Language Research. Rowley, Mass.:
            Newbury House.
Scollon, R.
    1974   *One Child's Language from One to Two: the Origins of
            Construction*. Unpublished PhD dissertation. University of Hawaii at
            Manoa, Honolulu.
Scollon, R.
    1979   "A real early stage: an unzippered condensation of a dissertation on
            child language." In E. Ochs and B. Schieffelin (eds), *Developmental
            Pragmatics*. New York : Academic Press.
Scollon, R. and Scollon, S.
    1983   "Face in interethnic communication." In J. C. Richards and R.
            Schmidt (eds), *Language and Communication*. London: Longman.
Scotton, C. M.
    1983   "The negotiation of identities in conversation: a theory of
            markedness and code choice." *International Journal of the
            Sociology of Language* 44: 115-36.
Searle, J. R.
    1975   "Indirect speech acts." In P. Cole and J. L. Morgan (eds), *Syntax
            and Semantics*. Volume 3, *Speech Acts*. New York: Academic Press.

Searle, J. R.
    1986   "Introductory essay: notes on conversation." In D. G. Ellis and W. A. Donohue (eds), *Contemporary Issues in Language and Discourse Processes*. Hillsdale, NJ: Lawrence Erlbaum Associates.

Seliger, H. W.
    1977   "Does practice make perfect? A study of interaction patterns and L2 competence." *Language Learning* 27: 263-78.

Seliger, H. W.
    1983   "Learner interaction in the classroom and its effects on language acquisition." In H. W. Seliger and M. H. Long (eds), *Classroom Oriented Research in Second Language Acquisition*. Rowley, Mass.: Newbury House.

Seliger, H. W. and Shohamy, E.
    1989   *Second Language Research Methods*. Oxford: Oxford University Press.

Selinker, L.
    1972   "Interlanguage." *International Review of Applied Linguistics* 10: 201-31.

Selinker, L. and Lamendella, J.
    1979   "The role of extrinsic feedback in interlanguage fossilization - a discussion of 'rule fossilization': a tentative model." *Language Learning* 29: 363-75.

Selinker, L.
    1992   *Rediscovering Interlanguage*. London: Longman.

Selinker, L. and Douglas, D.
    1985   "Wrestling with 'context' in interlanguage theory." *Applied Linguistics* 6: 190-204.

Selinker, L., Swain, M., and Dumas, G.
    1975   "The interlanguage hypothesis extended to children." *Language Learning* 25: 139-52.

Shehadeh, A.
    1991   *Comprehension and Performance in Second Language Acquisition: a Study of Second Language Learner's Production of Modified Comprehensible Output*. Unpublished PhD dissertation, School of English, University of Durham, England.

Shultz, J., Florio, S., and Erickson, F.
    1982   "Where's the floor? Aspects of the cultural organization of social relationships in communication at home and in school." In P. Gilmore and A. Glatthorn (eds), *Ethnography and Education: Children in and out of School*. Philadelphia: University of Pennsylvania Press.

Sinclair, J. McH. and Coulthard, M.
  1975   *Towards an Analysis of Discourse: the English Used by Teachers and Pupils*. Oxford: Oxford University Press.
Sinclair, J. McH. and Brazil, D.
  1982   *Teacher Talk*. Oxford: Oxford University Press.
Skutnabb-Kangas, T. and Cummins, J.
  1988   *Minority Education: from Shame to Struggle*. Clevedon, Philadelphia: Multilingual Matters.
Slobin, D.
  1982   "Universal and particular in the acquisition of language." In E. Wanner and L. Gleitman (eds), *Language Acquisition: State of the Art*. Cambridge: Cambridge University Press.
Smith, F.
  1971   *Understanding Reading*. New York: Holt, Rinehart, and Winston.
Smith, F.
  1978   *Reading without Nonsense*. New York: Teachers' College Press.
Smith, F.
  1982   *Writing and the Writer*. New York: Holt, Rinehart, and Winston.
Smith, L. (ed)
  1987   *Discourse across Cultures: Strategies in World Englishes*. New York: Prentice Hall.
Snow, C. E., Van Eeden, R., and Muysken, P.
  1981   "The interactional origins of foreigner talk." *International Journal of the Sociology of Language* 28: 81-92.
Snow, C. E. and Hoefnagel-Höhle, M.
  1982   "School-age second language learner's access to simplified linguistic input." *Language Learning* 32: 411-30.
Speidel, G. E., Tharp,R. G., and Kobayashi, L.
  1985   "Is there a comprehension problem for children who speak nonstandard English? A study of children with Hawaiian-English backgrounds." *Applied Psycholinguistics* 6: 83-96.
Spolsky, B.
  1989   *Conditions for Second Language Learning*. Oxford: Oxford University Press.
Stern, H. H.
  1983   *Fundamental Concepts of Language Teaching*. Oxford: Oxford University Press.
Stevick, E.
  1976   *Memory, Meaning, and Method*. Rowley, Mass.: Newbury House.
Stevick, E.
  1980   *Teaching Languages: a Way and Ways*. Rowley, Mass.: Newbury House.

Stevick, E.
1981   "The Levertov machine." In R. C. Scarcella and S. D. Krashen (eds), *Research in Second Language Acquisition*. Rowley, Mass.: Newbury House.

Streek, J.
1980   "Speech acts in interaction: a critique of Searle." *Discourse Processes* 3: 133-54.

Strong, M.
1983   "Social styles and the second language acquisition of Spanish-speaking kindergartners." *TESOL Quarterly* 17: 241-258.

Stubbs, M.
1981   "Motivating analysis of exchange structure." In M. Coulthard and M. Montgomery (eds), *Studies in Discourse Analysis*. London: Routledge and Kegan Paul.

Stubbs, M.
1983   *Discourse Analysis: the Sociolinguistic Analysis of Natural Language*. Oxford: Basil Blackwell.

Swain, M.
1981   "Immersion education: applicability for nonvernacular speakers." *Studies in Second Language Acquisition* 4: 1-17.

Swain, M.
1984   "Large-scale communicative language testing: a case study." In S. Savignon and M. Berns (eds), *Initiatives in Communicative Language Teaching*. Reading, Mass.: Addison-Wesley.

Swain, M.
1985   "Communicative competence: some roles of comprehensible input and comprehensible output in its development." In S. Gass and C. Madden, (eds), *Input in Second Language Acquisition*. Rowley, Mass.: Newbury House.

Swain, M. , Lapkin, S., and Andrew, C. M.
1981   "Early French immersion later on." *Journal of Multilingual and Multicultural Development* 2: 1-23.

Swain, M. and Lapkin, S.
1982   *Evaluating Bilingual Education: a Canadien Case Study*. Clevedon, Philadelphia: Multilingual Matters.

Swann, J.
1992   *Girls, Boys, and Language*. Oxford: Basil Blackwell.

Sweet, H.
1899/1964 *The Practical Study of Language*. London: Oxford University Press.

Tannen, D.
   1975   "Communication mix and mix up or how linguistics can ruin a
           marriage." *San Jose State Occasional Papers in Linguistics,* 205-
           211.
Tannen, D.
   1981a   "Indirectness in discourse: ethnicity as conversational style."
           Discourse Processes 4: 221-38.
Tannen, D.
   1981b   "The machine-gun question: an example of conversational style."
           Journal of Pragmatics 5: 383-97.
Tannen, D.
   1982a   *Analyzing Discourse: Text and Talk.* Washington, D.C.: Georgetown
           University Press.
Tannen, D.
   1982b   *Spoken and Written Language: Exploring Orality and Literacy.*
           Norwood, NJ: Ablex.
Tannen, D.
   1983   "When is an overlap not an interruption?" In R. Di Pierto, W.
           Frawley, and A. Wedel (eds), *The First Delaware Symposium on
           Language Studies.* Newark: University of Delaware Press.
Tannen, D.
   1984   *Conversational Style: Analyzing Talk among Friends.* Norwood, NJ:
           Ablex.
Tannen, D.
   1986   *That's Not What I Meant! How Conversational Style Makes or
           Breaks your Relations with Others.* New York: William Morrow.
Tannen, D.
   1987   "Remarks on Discourse and Power." In L. kedar (ed), *Power
           Through Discourse.* Norwood, NJ: Ablex.
Tannen, D. (ed)
   1988   *Linguistics in Context: Connecting Observation and Understanding*
           (Lectures from the 1985 LSA/TESOL and NEH institutes). In the
           series: *Advances in Discourse Processes.* Norwood, NJ: Ablex.
Tannen, D.
   1989   *Talking Voices: Repetition, Dialogue, and Imagery in
           Conversational Discourse.* Cambridge: Cambridge University Press.
Tannen, D. and Wallat, C.
   1983   "Doctor/mother/child communication: linguistic analysis of a
           pediatric interaction." In S. Fisher and A. D. Todd (eds), *The Social
           Organization of Doctor-Patient Communication.* Washington, D. C.:
           The Center for Applied Linguistics.

Tannen, D. and Saville-Troike, M. (eds)
    1985   *Perspectives on Silence*. Norwood, NJ: Ablex.
Tarone, E.
    1977   "Conscious communication strategies in interlanguage." In H. D. Brown, C. A. Yorio, and R. C. Crymes (eds), *On TESOL '77: Teaching and Learning English as a Second Language: Trends in Research and Practice*. Washington, D. C.: TESOL.
Tarone, E.
    1980   "Communication strategies, foreigner talk, and repair in interlanguage." *Language Learning* 30: 417-31.
Tarone, E.
    1981   "Some thoughts on the notion of communication strategy." *TESOL Quarterly* 15: 285-95.
Tarone, E. and Yule, G.
    1989   *Focus on the Language Learner: Approaches to Identifying and Meeting the Needs of Second Language Learners*. Oxford: Oxford University Press.
Taylor, B. P.
    1982   "In search of real reality." *TESOL Quarterly* 16: 29-42.
Taylor, B. P.
    1983   "Teaching ESL: incorporating a communicative, student-centered component." *TESOL Quarterly* 17: 69-88.
Taylor, T.
    1992   *Mutual Misunderstanding*. London: Routledge.
Thomas, J.
    1983a   "Cross-cultural pragmatic failure." *Applied Linguistics* 4: 91-112.
Thomas, J.
    1983b   "The language of unequal encounters: a pragmatic analysis of a police interview." Paper presented at the Hatfield Conference on Discourse analysis, Hatfield Polytechnic, May 1983.
Thomas, J.
    1984   "Cross-cultural discourse as 'unequal encounter': towards a pragmatic analysis." *Applied Linguistics* 5: 226-35.
Thomas, J.
    1995   *Meaning in Interaction: an Introduction to Pragmatics*. Reading, Mass.: Addison-Wesley.
Tracy, K. and Moran, J. P.
    1983   "Conversational relevance in multiple-goal settings." In R. T. Craig and K. Tracy (eds), *Conversational Coherence: Form, Structure, and Strategy*. Beverly Hills, London, New Delhi: Sage Publications.

Treichler, P. A., Frankel, R., M., Kramarae, C., Zoppi, K., and Beckman, H. B.
1984   "Problems and problems: power relations in a medical encounter."
        In C. Kramarae, M. Schulz, and W. O'Barr, (eds), *Language and
        Power*. Beverly Hills, London, New Delhi: Sage Publications.
Van Dam Van Isselt, J.
1991   "Self-correction, the underexplored notion: a discourse approach to
        error and repair." In R. Van Hout and E. Huls (eds), *Artikelen van
        de Eerste Sociolinguistische Conferentie*. Delft: Eburon.
Van Dijk, T. A. (ed)
1985   *Handbook of Discourse Analysis*. Vol. 1: *Disciplines of Discourse*,
        Vol. 2: *Dimensions of Discourse*, Vol. 3: *Discourse and Dialogue*,
        Vol. 4: *Discourse Analysis in Society*. London: Academic Press.
Van Dijk, T. A.
1987   *Discourse and Power*. Unpublished manuscript, University of
        Amsterdam.
Van Dijk, T. A.
1989   "Structures in discourse and structures in power." In J. A. Anderson
        (ed), *Communication Yearbook*, 12. Beverly Hills, London, New
        Delhi: Sage Publications.
Van Els, T., Bongaerts, T., Extra, G., Van Os, C., and Janssen-Van Dieten, A.
1984   *Applied Linguistics and the Learning and Teaching of Foreign
        Languages*. Translated by R. R. Van Oirsouw. London, Maryland:
        Edward Arnold.
Van Lier, L.
1988   *The Classroom and the Language Learner: Ethnography and
        Second Language Classroom Research*. London: Longman.
VanPatten, B.
1987   "On babies and bath water: input in foreign language learning."
        Modern Language Journal 71: 156-64.
VanPatten, B. and Lee, J. F.
1990   *Second Language Acquisition: Foreign Language Learning*.
        Clevedon, Philadelphia: Multilingual Matters.
Varadi, T.
1973   "Strategies of target language learner communication: message
        adjustment." Paper presented at the Sixth Conference of the
        Romanian-English Linguistics Project in Timisoara.
Varadi, T.
1980   "Strategies of target language learner communication: message
        adjustment." *International Review of Applied Linguistics* 18: 59-71.
Varonis, E. M. and Gass, S.
1982   "The comprehensibility of non-native speech." *Studies in Second
        Language Acquisition* 6: 114-36.

Varonis, E. M. and Gass, S.
  1983   "Target language input from non-native speakers." Paper presented
          at the 17th Annual TESOL Convention, Toronto, March 1983.
Varonis, E. M. and Gass, S.
  1985a   "Miscommunication in native/nonnative conversation." *Language in
          Society* 14: 327-43.
Varonis, E. M. and Gass, S.
  1985b   "Nonnative/nonnative conversations: a model for negotiation of
          meaning." *Applied Linguistics* 6: 71-90.
Varonis, E. M. and Gass, S.
  1985c   "Repairs in NNS discourse and the evidence for second language
          development." Paper presented at TESOL Summer Meeting,
          Washington, D. C.
Verschueren, J. (ed)
  1991   *Pragmatics at Issue.* Amsterdam, Philadelphia: John Benjamins.
Vigil, N. and Oller, J.
  1976   " 'Rule fossilization': a tentative model." *Language Learning* 26:
          281-95.
Von Raffler-Engel, W. (ed)
  1989   *Doctor-Patient Interaction.* Amsterdam, Philadelphia: John
          Benjamins.
Wagner-Gough, J. and Hatch, E.
  1975   "The importance of input data in second language acquisition
          studies." *Language Learning* 25: 297-307.
Wajnryb, R.
  1992   *Classroom Observation Tasks: a Resource Book for Language
          Teachers and Trainers.* Cambridge: Cambridge University Press.
Walker, H. and Buckley, N.
  1972   "The effects of reinforcement, punishment, and feedback upon
          academic response rate." *Psychology in the Schools* 9: 186-93.
Ward, C. and Wren, D.
  1982   *Selected Papers in TESOl.* Monterey, California: Monterey Institute
          of International Studies
Wardhaugh, R.
  1975   *Topics in Applied Linguistics.* Rowley, Mass.: Newbury House.
Wardhaugh, R.
  1985   *How Conversation Works.* Oxford: Basil Blackwell.
Wardhaugh, R.
  1987   *Languages in Competition.* Oxford: Basil Blackwell.
Wardhaugh, R.
  1992   *An Introduction to Sociolinguistics.* Oxford: Basil Blackwell.

Watts, R.
1991 *Power in Family Discourse.* Berlin, New York: Mouton de Gruyter.

Whinnom, K.
1971 "Linguistic hybridization and the 'special case' of pidgins and creoles." In D. Hymes (ed), *Pidginization and Creolization of Languages.* Cambridge: Cambridge University Press.

White, L.
1987 "Against comprehensible input: the input hypothesis and the development of second language competence." *Applied Linguistics* 8: 95-110.

Widdowson, H.
1972 "The teaching of English as communication." *English Language Teaching* 27:15-19. Reprinted in Brumfit and Johnson 1979.

Widdowson, H.
1978 *Teaching Language as Communication.* Oxford: Oxford University Press.

Widdowson, H.
1983 *Learning Purpose and Language Use.* Oxford: Oxford University Press

Woken, M. and Swales, J.
1989 "Expertise and authority in native-non-native conversations: the need for a variable account." In S. Gass, C. Madden, D. Preston, and L. Selinker, (eds), *Variation in Second Language Acquisition.* Vol. 1: *Discourse and Pragmatics.* Clevedon, Philadelphia: Multilingual Matters.

Wolfson, N. and Judd, E. (eds)
1983 *Sociolinguistics and Language Acquisition.* Rowley, Mass.: Newbury House.

Wong-Fillmore, L.
1979 "Individual differences in second language acquisition." In C. J. Fillmore, D. Kempler, and W. S. Y. Wong (eds), *Individual Difference in Language Ability and Language Behaviour.* New York: Academic Press.

Wrong, D. H.
1979 *Power: Its Forms, Bases and Uses.* Oxford: Basil Blackwell.

Yngve, V. H.
1970 "On getting a word in edgewise." In *Papers from the Sixth Regional Meeting, Chicago Linguistics Society*: 567-77.

Young, D.
1986 'The relationship between anxiety and foreign language oral proficiency ratings'. *Foreign Language Annals* 19: 439-45.

Young, R.
    1984   "Negotiation of meaning and negotiation of outcome in the reading
              classroom." Paper presented at the tenth World Congress on
              Reading, July 30-Aug. 2, Hong Kong.
Young, R.
    1988a   'Variation and the interlanguage hypothesis'. *Studies in Second
              Language Acquisition* 10: 281-302.
Young, R.
    1988b   'Input and interaction'. *Annual Review of Applied Linguistics* 9:
              122-34.
Young, R.
    1991   *Variation in Interlanguage Morphology.* New York: Peter Lang.
Young, R.
    1993   'Functional constraints on variation in interlanguage morphology'.
              Applied Linguistics 14: 76-97.
Young, R. and Doughty, C.
    1987   "Negotiation in context: a review of research." In J. A. Lantolf and
              A. Labarca (eds), *Research in Second Language Learning: Focus
              on the Classroom.* Norwood, NJ: Ablex.
Yule, G. and MacDonald, D.
    1990   "Resolving referential conflicts in L2 interaction: the effect of
              proficiency and interactive role." *Language Learning* 40: 539-56.
Yule, G. and Tarone, E.
    1991   "The other side of the page: integrating the study of
              communication strategies and negotiated input in SLA." In R.
              Philipson, E. Kellerman, L. Selinker, M. Sharwood Smith, and M.
              Swain (eds), *Foreign/Second Language Pedagogy Research.*
              Clevedon, Philadelphia: Multilingual Matters.
Zahn, C.
    1984   "A re-examination of conversational repair." *Communication
              Monographs* 51: 56-66.
Zamel, V.
    1981   "Cybernetics: a model for feedback in the ESL classroom." *TESOL
              Quarterly* 15: 139-50.
Zuengler, J.
    1987   "Effect of perceived 'expertise' in interactions between native and
              non-native speakers." *Language and Communication* 7: 123-138.
Zuengler, J.
    1989a   "Assessing an interaction-based paradigm: how accommodative
              should we be?" In M. R. Eisenstein (ed), *The Dynamic
              Interlanguage: Empirical Studies in Second Language Variation.*
              New York, London: Plenum Press.

Zuengler, J.
  1989b   "Performance variation in NS-NNS interactions: ethnolinguistic
          difference or discourse domain." In S. Gass, C. Madden, D. Preston,
          and L. Selinker (eds), *Variation in Second Language Acquisition*,
          Vol. 1: *Discourse and Pragmatics*. Clevedon, Philadelphia:
          Multilingual Matters.
Zuengler, J. and Bent, B.
  1991   "Relative knowledge of content domain: an influence on native-
          nonnative conversations." *Applied Linguistics* 12: 397-415.

Author Index

Subject Index

In the PRAGMATICS AND BEYOND NEW SERIES the following titles have been published thus far or are scheduled for publication:

1. WALTER, Bettyruth: *The Jury Summation as Speech Genre: An Ethnographic Study of What it Means to Those who Use it.* Amsterdam/Philadelphia, 1988.
2. BARTON, Ellen: *Nonsentential Constituents: A Theory of Grammatical Structure and Pragmatic Interpretation.* Amsterdam/Philadelphia, 1990.
3. OLEKSY, Wieslaw (ed.): *Contrastive Pragmatics.* Amsterdam/Philadelphia, 1989.
4. RAFFLER-ENGEL, Walburga von (ed.): *Doctor-Patient Interaction.* Amsterdam/ Philadelphia, 1989.
5. THELIN, Nils B. (ed.): *Verbal Aspect in Discourse.* Amsterdam/Philadelphia, 1990.
6. VERSCHUEREN, Jef (ed.): *Selected Papers from the 1987 International Pragmatics Conference. Vol. I: Pragmatics at Issue. Vol. II: Levels of Linguistic Adaptation. Vol. III: The Pragmatics of Intercultural and International Communication* (ed. with Jan Blommaert). Amsterdam/Philadelphia, 1991.
7. LINDENFELD, Jacqueline: *Speech and Sociability at French Urban Market Places.* Amsterdam/Philadelphia, 1990.
8. YOUNG, Lynne: *Language as Behaviour, Language as Code: A Study of Academic English.* Amsterdam/Philadelphia, 1990.
9. LUKE, Kang-Kwong: *Utterance Particles in Cantonese Conversation.* Amsterdam/ Philadelphia, 1990.
10. MURRAY, Denise E.: *Conversation for Action. The computer terminal as medium of communication.* Amsterdam/Philadelphia, 1991.
11. LUONG, Hy V.: *Discursive Practices and Linguistic Meanings. The Vietnamese system of person reference.* Amsterdam/Philadelphia, 1990.
12. ABRAHAM, Werner (ed.): *Discourse Particles. Descriptive and theoretical investigations on the logical, syntactic and pragmatic properties of discourse particles in German.* Amsterdam/Philadelphia, 1991.
13. NUYTS, Jan, A. Machtelt BOLKESTEIN and Co VET (eds): *Layers and Levels of Representation in Language Theory: a functional view.* Amsterdam/Philadelphia, 1990.
14. SCHWARTZ, Ursula: *Young Children's Dyadic Pretend Play.* Amsterdam/Philadelphia, 1991.
15. KOMTER, Martha: *Conflict and Cooperation in Job Interviews.* Amsterdam/Philadelphia, 1991.
16. MANN, William C. and Sandra A. THOMPSON (eds): *Discourse Description: Diverse Linguistic Analyses of a Fund-Raising Text.* Amsterdam/Philadelphia, 1992.
17. PIÉRAUT-LE BONNIEC, Gilberte and Marlene DOLITSKY (eds): *Language Bases ... Discourse Bases.* Amsterdam/Philadelphia, 1991.
18. JOHNSTONE, Barbara: *Repetition in Arabic Discourse. Paradigms, syntagms and the ecology of language.* Amsterdam/Philadelphia, 1991.
19. BAKER, Carolyn D. and Allan LUKE (eds): *Towards a Critical Sociology of Reading Pedagogy. Papers of the XII World Congress on Reading.* Amsterdam/Philadelphia, 1991.
20. NUYTS, Jan: *Aspects of a Cognitive-Pragmatic Theory of Language. On cognition, functionalism, and grammar.* Amsterdam/Philadelphia, 1992.

21. SEARLE, John R. et al.: *(On) Searle on Conversation*. Compiled and introduced by Herman Parret and Jef Verschueren. Amsterdam/Philadelphia, 1992.
22. AUER, Peter and Aldo Di LUZIO (eds): *The Contextualization of Language*. Amsterdam/Philadelphia, 1992.
23. FORTESCUE, Michael, Peter HARDER and Lars KRISTOFFERSEN (eds): *Layered Structure and Reference in a Functional Perspective. Papers from the Functional Grammar Conference, Copenhagen, 1990*. Amsterdam/Philadelphia, 1992.
24. MAYNARD, Senko K.: *Discourse Modality: Subjectivity, Emotion and Voice in the Japanese Language*. Amsterdam/Philadelphia, 1993.
25. COUPER-KUHLEN, Elizabeth: *English Speech Rhythm. Form and function in everyday verbal interaction*. Amsterdam/Philadelphia, 1993.
26. STYGALL, Gail: Trial Language. *A study in differential discourse processing*. Amsterdam/Philadelphia, 1994.
27. SUTER, Hans Jürg: *The Wedding Report: A Prototypical Approach to the Study of Traditional Text Types*. Amsterdam/Philadelphia, 1993.
28. VAN DE WALLE, Lieve: *Pragmatics and Classical Sanskrit*. Amsterdam/Philadelphia, 1993.
29. BARSKY, Robert F.: *Constructing a Productive Other: Discourse theory and the convention refugee hearing*. Amsterdam/Philadelphia, 1994.
30. WORTHAM, Stanton E.F.: *Acting Out Participant Examples in the Classroom*. Amsterdam/Philadelphia, 1994.
31. WILDGEN, Wolfgang: *Process, Image and Meaning. A realistic model of the meanings of sentences and narrative texts*. Amsterdam/Philadelphia, 1994.
32. SHIBATANI, Masayoshi and Sandra A. THOMPSON (eds): *Essays in Semantics and Pragmatics*. Amsterdam/Philadelphia, 1995.
33. GOOSSENS, Louis, Paul PAUWELS, Brygida RUDZKA-OSTYN, Anne-Marie SIMON-VANDENBERGEN and Johan VANPARYS: *By Word of Mouth. Metaphor, metonymy and linguistic action in a cognitive perspective*. Amsterdam/Philadelphia, 1995.
34. BARBE, Katharina: Irony in Context. Amsterdam/Philadelphia, 1995.
35. JUCKER, Andreas H. (ed.): *Historical Pragmatics. Pragmatic developments in the history of English*. Amsterdam/Philadelphia, 1995.
36. CHILTON, Paul, Mikhail V. ILYIN and Jacob MEY: *Political Discourse in Transition in Eastern and Western Europe (1989-1991)*. Amsterdam/Philadelphia, 1998.
37. CARSTON, Robyn and Seiji UCHIDA (eds): *Relevance Theory. Applications and implications*. Amsterdam/Philadelphia, 1998.
38. FRETHEIM, Thorstein and Jeanette K. GUNDEL (eds): *Reference and Referent Accessibility*. Amsterdam/Philadelphia, 1996.
39. HERRING, Susan (ed.): *Computer-Mediated Communication. Linguistic, social, and cross-cultural perspectives*. Amsterdam/Philadelphia, 1996.
40. DIAMOND, Julie: *Status and Power in Verbal Interaction. A study of discourse in a close-knit social network*. Amsterdam/Philadelphia, 1996.
41. VENTOLA, Eija and Anna MAURANEN, (eds): *Academic Writing. Intercultural and textual issues*. Amsterdam/Philadelphia, 1996.
42. WODAK, Ruth and Helga KOTTHOFF (eds): *Communicating Gender in Context*. Amsterdam/Philadelphia, 1997.

43. JANSSEN, Theo A.J.M. and Wim van der WURFF (eds): *Reported Speech. Forms and functions of the verb.* Amsterdam/Philadelphia, 1996.
44. BARGIELA-CHIAPPINI, Francesca and Sandra J. HARRIS: *Managing Language. The discourse of corporate meetings.* Amsterdam/Philadelphia, 1997.
45. PALTRIDGE, Brian: *Genre, Frames and Writing in Research Settings.* Amsterdam/Philadelphia, 1997.
46. GEORGAKOPOULOU, Alexandra: *Narrative Performances. A study of Modern Greek storytelling.* Amsterdam/Philadelphia, 1997.
47. CHESTERMAN, Andrew: *Contrastive Functional Analysis.* Amsterdam/Philadelphia, 1998.
48. KAMIO, Akio: *Territory of Information.* Amsterdam/Philadelphia, 1997.
49. KURZON, Dennis: *Discourse of Silence.* Amsterdam/Philadelphia, 1998.
50. GRENOBLE, Lenore: *Deixis and Information Packaging in Russian Discourse.* Amsterdam/Philadelphia, 1998.
51. BOULIMA, Jamila: *Negotiated Interaction in Target Language Classroom Discourse.* Amsterdam/Philadelphia, 1999.
52. GILLIS, Steven and Annick DE HOUWER (eds): *The Acquisition of Dutch.* Amsterdam/Philadelphia, 1998.
53. MOSEGAARD HANSEN, Maj-Britt: *The Function of Discourse Particles. A study with special reference to spoken standard French.* Amsterdam/Philadelphia, 1998.
54. HYLAND, Ken: *Hedging in Scientific Research Articles.* Amsterdam/Philadelphia, 1998.
55. ALLWOOD, Jens and Peter Gärdenfors (eds): *Cognitive Semantics. Meaning and cognition.* Amsterdam/Philadelphia, 1999.
56. TANAKA, Hiroko: *Language, Culture and Social Interaction. Turn-taking in Japanese and Anglo-American English.* Amsterdam/Philadelphia, n.y.p.
57 JUCKER, Andreas H. and Yael ZIV (eds): *Discourse Markers. Descriptions and theory.* Amsterdam/Philadelphia, 1998.
58. ROUCHOTA, Villy and Andreas H. JUCKER (eds): *Current Issues in Relevance Theory.* Amsterdam/Philadelphia, 1998.
59. KAMIO, Akio and Ken-ichi TAKAMI (eds): *Function and Structure. In honor of Susumu Kuno.* 1999.
60. JACOBS, Geert: *Preformulating the News. An analysis of the metapragmatics of press releases.* 1999.
61. MILLS, Margaret H. (ed.): *Slavic Gender Linguistics.* n.y.p.
62. TZANNE, Angeliki: *Talking at Cross-Purposes. The dynamics of miscommunication.* n.y.p.
63. BUBLITZ, Wolfram, Uta LENK and Eija VENTOLA (eds.): *Coherence in Spoken and Written Discourse. How to create it and how to describe it.Selected papers from the International Workshop on Coherence, Augsburg, 24-27 April 1997.* 1999.
64. SVENNEVIG, Jan: *Getting Acquainted in Conversation. A study of initial interactions.* n.y.p.
65. COOREN, François: *The Organizing Dimension of Communication.* n.y.p.
66. JUCKER, Andreas H., Gerd FRITZ and Franz LEBSANFT (eds.): *Historical Dialogue Analysis.* n.y.p.

67. TAAVITSAINEN, Irma, Gunnel MELCHERS and Paivi PAHTA (eds.): *Dimensions of Writing in Nonstandard English*. n.y.p.
68. ARNOVICK, Leslie: *Diachronic Pragmatics. Seven case studies in English illocutionary development*. n.y.p.
69. NOH, Eun-Ju: *The Semantics and Pragmatics of Metarepresentation in English. A relevance-theoretic account*. n.y.p.
70. SORJONEN, Marja-Leena: *Recipient Activities Particles nii(n) and joo as Responses in Finnish Conversation*. n.y.p.